DISSENTING OPINIONS OF JUSTICE ANTONIN SCALIA

DISSENTING OPINIONS OF JUSTICE ANTONIN SCALIA

Michael H. Hoeflich Caleb Stegall

CO-EDITORS

TALBOT PUBLISHING
Clark, New Jersey

ISBN 978-1-61619-573-1

TALBOT PUBLISHING

AN IMPRINT OF

THE LAWBOOK EXCHANGE, LTD.

33 Terminal Avenue
Clark, New Jersey 07066-1321

Please see our website for a selection of our other publications and fine facsimile reprints of classic works of legal history:
www.lawbookexchange.com

Library of Congress Cataloging-in-Publication Data

Names: Scalia, Antonin, author. | Hoeflich, Michael H., editor. | Stegall, Caleb, 1971- editor, writer of introduction.
Title: Dissenting opinions of Justice Antonin Scalia / Michael H. Hoeflich, Justice Caleb Stegall, co-editors.
Description: Clark, NJ : Talbot Publishing, an imprint of The Lawbook Exchange, Ltd., 2018. | Includes bibliographical references and index.
Identifiers: LCCN 2018003415 | ISBN 9781616195731 (hardcover : alk. paper)
Subjects: LCSH: Dissenting opinions--United States. | Law--United States--Cases. | LCGFT: Court decisions and opinions.
Classification: LCC KF213.S32 H64 2018 | DDC 347.73/26--dc23
LC record available at https://lccn.loc.gov/2018003415

Printed in the United States of America on acid-free paper

Table of Contents

Acknowledgments

Thanks to my research assistants Matthew Beal, KU Law '19 and Shelley Woodard, KU Law '17.

Michael H. Hoeflich

Thanks to my law clerks Sarah Stula & Kurtis Wiard.

Caleb Stegall

Introduction

Caleb Stegall[*]

Why Dissent?

For those of us laboring in the appellate vineyards, this is not a theoretical question. For every appeal decided, every opinion written, I and my colleagues have to decide—can I live not only with this outcome, but this explanation of how it was reached? And if I can't, how will I express my disagreement? A lengthy dissent may sometimes seem like wasted effort in a cause already lost. This reality gave rise to what were colloquially known as "graveyard dissents" on the Burger Court—the practice of silently acquiescing to a decision or opinion one finds objectionable.[1]

Justice William Rehnquist authored perhaps the most famous and humorous graveyard dissent when he dropped this note to Justice Thurgood Marshall: "If this were November rather than June, I would prepare a masterfully crafted dissenting opinion exposing the fallacies of your pre-emption discussion. Since it is June, however, I join."[2] The popularity of this anecdote, and its appearance here, demonstrate that even silent dissents can rise from the grave to haunt a Justice's legacy.

---

[*] Caleb Stegall is an Associate Justice on the Kansas Supreme Court.

[1] Greg Goelzhauser, "Graveyard Dissents on the Burger Court," 40 *J. Sup. Ct. Hist.* 188, 189 (2015).

[2] *Id.* at 192.

There was a time when the very act of dissenting was viewed as a betrayal. In an influential speech delivered in 1898 titled "Evils of Dissenting Opinions," a respected former judge said: "There never should be a dissenting opinion in a case decided by a court of last resort. No judge, lawyer or layman should be permitted to weaken the force of the court's decision, which all must accept as an unappealable finality."[3]

In fact, early in our history, dissents were recognized as the only kind of appeal that could be taken from the decision of the Supreme Court—an appeal over the heads of one's colleagues and "to the people."[4] The sensibility that such appeals were unseemly and unjudicial found regular expression in high places. Chief Justice William Howard Taft wrote, "I don't approve of dissents generally, for I think in many cases where I differ from the majority, it is more important to stand by the Court and give its judgment weight than merely to record my individual dissent."[5]

In this sense, the character of the lonely dissenter as a species of knight errant has a long history. Justice Benjamin Cardozo described the dissenter as "the gladiator making a last stand against the lions."[6] But my favorite quip about the work of appellate judges, though not made specifically about dissents, comes from one of my predecessors on the Kansas Supreme Court, and one of Justice Antonin Scalia's predecessors on the United States Supreme Court—David Brewer. Justice Brewer remarked with his characteristic verve that "every American citizen" would, "according to the peculiar

---

[3] Henry Wollman, "Evils of Dissenting Opinions," 57 *Alb. L. J.* 74, 74 (1898).

[4] *Id.* at 75.

[5] Quoted in Melvin I. Urofsky, *Dissent and the Supreme Court: Its Role the Court's History and the Nation's Constitutional Dialogue*, 3 (2015).

[6] Benjamin N. Cardozo, *Law and Literature* 34 (1931).

construction of his organs of hearing," recognize in the Justices "either the voice of a Daniel or the braying of an ass."[7]

Brewer is right, and his description apt. The dissenter is either Prophet or Fool, and telling the difference is tricky business. But the nature of the dissenter as a "voice of one crying in the wilderness"[8] that may, eventually, be heeded by a wayward and stubborn people has been vindicated in powerful ways. The greatest dissents in history are widely accepted to be those that ultimately prevailed—their appeal to the people so powerful as to finally become law.

For example, Justice Benjamin Curtis's dissent in the *Dred Scott* case, rejecting Chief Justice Roger Taney's reasoning that the Constitution prohibited African American citizenship:

> And when a strict interpretation of the Constitution, according to the fixed rules which govern the interpretation of laws, is abandoned, and the theoretical opinions of individuals are allowed to control its meaning, we have no longer a Constitution; we are under the government of individual men, who for the time being have power to declare what the Constitution is, according to their own views of what it ought to mean.[9]

Likewise, Justice John Marshall Harlan's stirring rejection of the Court's repugnant separate but equal doctrine in *Plessy v. Ferguson*:

> I deny that any legislative body or judicial tribunal may have regard to the race of citizens when the civil rights of those citizens are involved.

---

[7] David J. Brewer, "The Nation's Anchor," 57 *Alb. L. J.* 166, 169 (1898).
[8] John 1:23.
[9] Dred Scott v. Sandford, 60 U.S. 393, 621 (1857) (Curtis, J., dissenting).

. . . .

> But in view of the constitution, in the eye of the law, there is in this country no superior, dominant, ruling class of citizens. There is no caste here. Our constitution is color-blind, and neither knows nor tolerates classes among citizens. In respect of civil rights, all citizens are equal before the law. The humblest is the peer of the most powerful.[10]

Or again, Justice Oliver Wendell Holmes' now canonical dissent in *Lochner*:

> This case is decided upon an economic theory which a large part of the country does not entertain. If it were a question whether I agreed with that theory, I should desire to study it further and long before making up my mind. But I do not conceive that to be my duty, because I strongly believe that my agreement or disagreement has nothing to do with the right of a majority to embody their opinions in law.[11]

In each instance, the dissenter's role as Prophet bore substantial fruit long after the dissent was written. Indeed, picking up on the prophetic nature of classic Supreme Court dissents, Mark Tushnet describes what makes a dissent great in his book, *I Dissent*: "It accurately predicts the future, and perhaps not because it anticipates some social or political change that will make its doctrine seem the right one, but because its vision of democracy and the Constitution and its rhetoric themselves contributed to making its doctrine seem correct."[12]

---

[10] Plessy v. Ferguson, 163 U.S. 537, 554–559 (1896) (Harlan, J., dissenting).

[11] Lochner v. New York, 198 U.S. 45, 75 (1937) (Holmes, J., dissenting).

[12] Mark Tushnet, *I Dissent: Great Opposing Opinions in Landmark Supreme Court Cases* 99 (2008).

Thus, this volume of selected dissents, by one of the masters of the genre, is perhaps best understood as a work of prophecy. The moral and rhetorical force of its vision emerges wholly formed and self-evident for those with ears to hear. Indeed, this volume is representative of a comprehensive appeal—and a warning—addressed directly to the American people. And the people's final judgment has yet to be rendered.

A Snoot Dissents

In 2006, when Justice Scalia first met Bryan Garner (the beginning of a productive literary partnership that would produce two important books about law[13] and lawyering[14]), Scalia had just finished reading David Foster Wallace's essay "Tense Present."[15] "Tense Present" is Wallace's brilliant and idiosyncratic take on language, meaning, and democracy and had already achieved a cult following by the time Scalia read it in 2006—it is also, at least in part, a review of Garner's *A Dictionary of Modern American Usage.*[16]

Justice Scalia praised the essay to Garner and, on review, it is easy to see why.[17] As Wallace describes the struggle over us-

---

[13] Antonin Scalia & Bryan A. Garner, *Reading Law: The Interpretation of Legal Texts* (2012).

[14] Antonin Scalia & Bryan A. Garner, *Making Your Case: The Art of Persuading Judges* (2008). *See* Garner, *Nino and Me: My Unusual Friendship with Justice Antonin Scalia* 18 (2018).

[15] David Foster Wallace, "*Tense Present: Democracy, English, and the Wars over Usage*," *Harper's*, April 2001, at 39.

[16] Bryan A. Garner, *A Dictionary of Modern American Usage* (1998).

[17] The story of Justice Scalia and Garner's first meeting is described by Alex Carp in "Writing with Antonin Scalia, Grammar Nerd," *New Yorker* (July 16, 2012), http://www.newyorker.com/news/news-desk/writing-with-antonin-scalia-grammar-nerd.

age and meaning in America—what he calls the Crisis of Authority—his set piece is the battle he observes between those he dubs the "Snoots" and the "contra-Snoots."[18] The Snoots (and Wallace makes it clear this is his party) are the sticklers for rules.[19] Scalia enjoyed Wallace's essay so much that he appropriated Wallace's term as a gently self-deprecating moniker of affection. In 2007, Scalia made it a point to meet Wallace and took to referring to himself and Wallace as co-Snoots.[20] According to Scalia, "Snoots are those who are nitpickers for the *mot juste*, for using a word precisely the way it should be used, not dulling it by misuse. I am a Snoot."[21]

The Snoot loves language, is fanatical about precise meaning, and understands that syntactical rules *matter*. Wallace again: "We combine a missionary zeal and a ... faith in our beliefs' importance with a curmudgeonly hell-in-a-handbasket despair at the way English is routinely manhandled and corrupted."[22] To a Snoot, listening to most people talk "feels like watching somebody use a Stradivarius to pound nails."[23] Wallace captures with uncanny accuracy how I imagine Scalia felt watching some of his colleagues wield constitutional clauses to solve various problems. The Snoots are "the Few, the Proud, the Appalled."[24]

---

[18] Wallace, *supra* note 14, at 43.

[19] *Id.* at 41.

[20] Jess Bravin, "How David Foster Wallace Prompted a Scalia Book," *Wall St. J.: Wash. Wire* (July 23, 2012, 9:46 AM), https://blogs.wsj.com/washwire/2012/07/23/how-david-foster-wallace-prompted-a-scalia-book/.

[21] Nina Totenberg, "Skip the Legalese and Keep It Short, Justices Say," NPR (June 13, 2011, 12:01 AM), http://www.npr.org/2011/06/13/137036622/skip-the-legalese-and-keep-it-short-justices-say.

[22] Wallace, *supra* note 14, at 41.

[23] *Id.*

[24] *Id.*

But the difference between Snoots and contra-Snoots runs far deeper than a mere sense of style. Wallace makes clear that the very nature of meaning and authority hangs in the balance. It is for this reason that "Tense Present" provides fresh insight into Justice Scalia, the dissenter—an approach I believe Scalia himself would have enjoyed. The dissents collected in this volume are masterpieces of style. But they are far more. They are the work of a man locked in an existential struggle for the possibility of meaning that is objectively knowable—and for the authority of that meaning as the expression of a free and democratic people. For Scalia, this became a struggle for the ongoing existence of law itself.

Wallace, again, helpfully describes what Scalia and the rest of the Snoots are up against. The contra-Snoot school believes that "normative standards" are "nothing but custom and superstition."[25] Wallace finds in Philip Gove's introduction to *Webster's Third New International Dictionary of the English Language* a contra-Snoot manifesto: "1—Language changes constantly; 2—Change is normal; 3—Spoken language is the language; 4—Correctness rests upon usage; 5—All usage is relative."[26] It would be difficult to come up with a more concise and spot-on articulation of the kind of "living" constitutionalism Justice Scalia abhorred, and against which he waged a thirty-year war on the Court.

Gove's five points of relativism helpfully mirror the three maxims of Scalia's school of constitutional interpretation, what came to be known as Originalism: 1) The meaning of the Constitution does not change; 2) that meaning is located exclusively in the text of the Constitution; and 3) the only usage that matters is the original public usage.

---

[25] *Id.* at 43.

[26] *Id.* at 45.

One of Justice Scalia's most entertaining and Snootiest dissents came in the case *PGA Tour, Inc. v. Martin.*[27] Professional golfer Casey Martin had sued the PGA Tour claiming a right, under the Americans with Disabilities Act, to ride a golf cart rather than walk during tournament rounds.[28] The majority of the Court ruled the PGA Tour must accommodate Martin because walking was not part of the "essence" of golf.[29] In other words, the notion that "real" golf requires walking during the round is "nothing but custom and superstition" and must give way to the legitimate purposes of the Americans with Disabilities Act.

To which Scalia responded:

> Nowhere is it writ that PGA TOUR golf must be classic "essential" golf. Why cannot the PGA TOUR, if it wishes, promote a new game, with distinctive rules …? If members of the public do not like the new rules—if they feel that these rules do not truly test the individual's skill at "real golf" … they can withdraw their patronage. But the rules are the rules. They are (as in all games) entirely arbitrary, and there is no basis on which anyone—not even the Supreme Court of the United States—can pronounce one or another of them to be "nonessential" if the rulemaker … deems it to be essential.
>
> If one assumes, however, that the PGA TOUR has some legal obligation to play classic, Platonic golf … then we Justices must confront what is indeed an awesome responsibility. It has been rendered the solemn duty of the Supreme Court of the United States … to decide What Is Golf. I am sure that the Framers of the Constitution, aware of the 1457 edict of King James II of Scotland prohibiting golf because it interfered with the practice of archery, fully expected that sooner or later the paths of golf and govern-

---

[27] PGA Tour, Inc. v. Martin, 532 U.S. 661 (2001).

[28] *Id.* at 669.

[29] *Id.* at 685, 689–690.

> ment, the law and the links, would once again cross, and that the judges of this august Court would some day have to wrestle with that age-old jurisprudential question, for which their years of study in the law have so well prepared them: Is someone riding around a golf course from shot to shot *really* a golfer? The answer, we learn, is yes. The Court ultimately concludes, and it will henceforth be the Law of the Land, that walking is not a "fundamental" aspect of golf.
>
> Either out of humility or out of self-respect (one or the other) the Court should decline to answer this incredibly difficult and incredibly silly question.[30]

I include this lengthy excerpt from an obscure decision in part because it illustrates Justice Scalia at his dissenting best: the understated sarcasm, the easy felicity with history, the common sense appeal to ordinary experience, the jovial spirit of the happy-warrior Snoot, out to save as many Stradivarii from the Philistine nail-pounders as possible. But more significantly, Scalia's discussion of the game of golf provides a powerful metaphor for his understanding of the Constitution.

The rules are the rules. Just as there is no Platonic Golf, accessible in its ontic essence to the wise Justices of the Supreme Court, for Scalia, there is no Platonic Constitution—there is only the text. And when it comes to the Constitution, the attempt to find its "essence" outside the text is not only silly, it is dangerous. When one changes the rules, one ends up with a different game. Here is a key insight into Justice Scalia's jurisprudence. It is why, in Justice Scalia's view, the very nature of our Republic is imperiled by the Court's insistence on questing for the constitutional essence of every legal question.

---

[30] *Id.* at 699–700 (Scalia, J., dissenting).

Structure as Essence

This essentialist error is at the heart of some of the most strident criticisms of Justice Scalia. He has been called "an adversary ... of the just and inclusive society that our Constitution and laws should be interpreted to advance rather than impede";[31] a Justice "devoted ... to making the United States a less fair, less tolerant, and less admirable democracy";[32] and this overwrought obloquy, "Justice Scalia's death has preserved democracy."[33]

But Justice Scalia expressly rejected the notion of the Supreme Court as finder and guardian of Platonic constitutional essences. Indeed, he knew that such a role would prove too great a temptation to mischief. In fact, it is not too much of a stretch to say that for Justice Scalia, the essence of our Republic springs organically *out of the rules* themselves—out of the constitutional structure. This allows us to understand another unique feature of Justice Scalia's mode of constitutional interpretation—he turned early and often to the *structural* elements of the Constitution, seeing in these (rather than in its rights provisions) the firm timbers supporting the weight of House America.

In one of the last major speeches of his life, Justice Scalia said:

---

31 Laurence H. Tribe, "The Scalia Myth," *N.Y. Rev. of Books*: *NYR Daily* (Feb. 27, 2016, 11:01 AM), http://www.nybooks.com/daily/2016/02/27/the-scalia-myth/.

32 Jeffrey Toobin, "Looking Back," *New Yorker* (Feb. 29, 2016), http://www.newyorker.com/magazine/2016/02/29/antonin-scalia-looking-backward.

33 Linda Greenhouse, Opinion, "Pondering the Supreme Court's Future," *N.Y. Times* (Sept. 29, 2016), https://www.nytimes.com/2016/09/29/opinion/pondering-the-supreme-courts-future.html.

> Every tin horn dictator in the world today, every president for life, has a Bill of Rights. … That's not what makes us free; if it did, you would rather live in Zimbabwe. But you wouldn't want to live in most countries in the world that have a Bill of Rights. What has made us free is our Constitution. Think of the word 'constitution;' it means structure.[34]

It was this structure—notably the Constitution's separation of powers—that Scalia was most passionate about defending.

One of the clearest of Justice Scalia's dissents concerning the structure of the Constitution came in the independent counsel case, *Morrison v. Olson.*[35] Scalia's *Morrison* dissent is worth examining at some length, both because it illustrates Scalia's understanding of how structure guards freedom, and because it is an early masterful example of Scalia's power of reasoned argument, moral force, and rhetorical flair.

Succinctly, *Morrison* decided that the independent counsel law by which Congress directed that the Executive Branch must, in certain circumstances, appoint an independent counsel to investigate and potentially prosecute allegations of wrongdoing in the government, did not violate the constitutional separation of powers by allowing the Legislative Branch to impermissibly usurp a function of the Executive Branch.[36]

Justice Scalia would have none of it:

> Without a secure structure of separated powers, our Bill of Rights would be worthless, as are the bills of rights of many

---

[34] Kevin Mooney, "Supreme Court Justice Scalia: Constitution, Not Bill of Rights, Makes Us Free," *Daily Signal* (May 11, 2015), http://dailysignal.com/2015/05/11/supreme-court-justice-scalia-constitution-not-bill-of-rights-makes-us-free/.

[35] Morrison v. Olson, 487 U.S. 654 (1988).

[36] *Id.* at 694–697.

nations of the world that have adopted, or even improved upon, the mere words of ours.

. . . .

That is what this suit is about. Power. The allocation of power among Congress, the President, and the courts in such fashion as to preserve the equilibrium the Constitution sought to establish—so that "a gradual concentration of the several powers in the same department," Federalist No. 51, p. 321 (J. Madison), can effectively be resisted. Frequently an issue of this sort will come before the Court clad, so to speak, in sheep's clothing: the potential of the asserted principle to effect important change in the equilibrium of power is not immediately evident, and must be discerned by a careful and perceptive analysis. But this wolf comes as a wolf.[37]

Scalia gave a characteristically vivid account of the wolf:

Congress has effectively compelled a criminal investigation of a high-level appointee of the President in connection with his actions arising out of a bitter power dispute between the President and the Legislative Branch. Mr. Olson may or may not be guilty of a crime; we do not know. But we do know that the investigation of him has been commenced, [and] not necessarily because the President or his authorized subordinates believe it is in the interest of the United States . ... The decisions regarding the scope of [the] investigation, its duration, and, finally, whether or not prosecution should ensue, are likewise beyond the control of the President and his subordinates.[38]

And then he delivers the devastating blow:

---

[37] *Id.* at 697–699 (Scalia, J., dissenting).

[38] *Id.* at 703.

> If to describe this case is not to decide it, the concept of a government of separate and coordinate powers no longer has meaning.
>
> . . . .
>
> The Court has, nonetheless, replaced the clear constitutional prescription that the executive power belongs to the President with a "balancing test." What are the standards to determine how the balance is to be struck, that is, how much removal of Presidential power is too much? ... Evidently, the governing standard is to be what might be called the unfettered wisdom of a majority of this Court, revealed to an obedient people on a case-by-case basis. This is not only not the government of laws that the Constitution established; it is not a government of laws at all.[39]

Scalia's *Morrison* dissent has achieved classic status because history has proved him right, as even his ideological opponents acknowledge. During the Clinton impeachment proceedings, for example, Senator Harry Reid said from the floor of the Senate: "I invite each of you to look at Justice Scalia's brilliant dissent in the *Morrison* [case] . ... Justice Scalia was visionary . ... [He] could see this coming, and we got just what he said we would get."[40]

Obedience to the Unenforceable

I would be remiss to let the opportunity of this introduction pass without drawing attention to my personal favorite in this collection—Justice Scalia's brief and often overlooked

---

[39] *Id.* at 703–712.

[40] 145 Cong. Rec. S1462-S1637 (daily ed. Feb. 12, 1999) (statement of Sen. Reid).

opinion in the affirmative action case *Grutter v. Bollinger*.[41] It is a favorite not because of its especially brilliant or convincing legal analysis, or even compelling rhetoric. Rather, it contains Justice Scalia's most straightforward confession of an oft-neglected, but I suggest critical, component of his judging: that some lessons, perhaps the most important lessons, can only be taught and perpetuated by life, not by the law. I suggest that at the heart of Justice Scalia's objection to the Court's modern jurisprudence lies his steadfast belief that his colleagues repeatedly confused these two categories.

In *Grutter*, the University of Michigan had sought to provide an "educational benefit" (one ultimately blessed by the *Grutter* majority) of "cross-racial understanding" achieved by "racial discrimination" in admissions.[42] Justice Scalia commented wryly:

> This is not, of course, an "educational benefit" on which students will be graded on their law school transcript (Works and Plays Well with Others: B+) or tested by the bar examiners (Q: Describe in 500 words or less your cross-racial understanding). For it is a lesson of life rather than law—essentially the same lesson taught to (or rather learned by, for it cannot be "taught" in the usual sense) people three feet shorter and 20 years younger than the full-grown adults at the University of Michigan Law School, in institutions ranging from Boy Scout troops to public-school kindergartens.[43]

Here Scalia hints at a view he expressed elsewhere—that the Constitution prevents the Court "from righting every

---

[41] Grutter v. Bollinger, 539 U.S. 306 (2003).

[42] *Id.* at 347 (Scalia, J., dissenting).

[43] *Id.*

wrong."[44] But he does so with deep moral sophistication, reflecting his recognition that too often those who come to the steps of the Supreme Court (and all the other courts in the land) come "dreaming of systems so perfect that no one will need to be good."[45] For Justice Scalia, the power to discern between lessons of life and lessons of the law is the measure of a judge's humility and sense of herself—what she can properly do, and what she cannot.

Scalia's final prophecy may be that, in the end, law cannot bear the weight our society has come to expect it to bear. In this, he echoes another jurist, Lord Fletcher Moulton, who famously described the social middle ground between the realm of absolute law and absolute freedom as "a third large and important domain in which there rules neither Positive Law nor Absolute Freedom. In that domain there is no law which inexorably determines our course of action, and yet we feel that we are not free to choose as we would."[46] This "Obedience to the Unenforceable" is "the obedience of a man to that which he cannot be forced to obey. He is the enforcer of the law upon himself."[47]

To my ears, this sounds very close to the parting advice Justice Scalia is giving to the nation he loved.

---

[44] *Morrison*, 487 U.S. at 710 (Scalia, J., dissenting).

[45] T.S. Eliot, "Choruses from 'The Rock'" (1934), reprinted in *T.S. Eliot: The Complete Poems and Plays 1909–1950*, 96, 106 (Houghton Mifflin Harcourt Publ'g Co. 2014).

[46] Lord Moulton, "Law and Manners," *Atlantic Monthly*, July 1924, at 1, 1, http://www.ruleoflaw.org.au/wp-content/uploads/2012/08/ July-1924-Paper-of-the-Rt.-Hon-Lord-Moulton-Law-and-Manners-The-Atlantic-onthly.pdf.

[47] *Id.*

A Word on Style Qua *Style*

Finally, no introduction to a collection of Scalia dissents would be complete without mentioning his combative style. Though the point stands that for Snoots, there is a real risk of misunderstanding if one attempts to disentangle authorial style from substance (as if style weren't substance!)—it is also true that Scalia's style *qua* style remains one of the most remarkable, and remarked upon, aspects of his corpus.

One simply cannot read Scalia's collection of creative synecdoches, dysphemisms, and outright trash-talk without marveling at the sheer *chutzpah* of the man—"[p]ure applesauce," [48] "jiggery-pokery," [49] "legalistic argle-bargle," [50] "mystical aphorisms of the fortune cookie,"[51] and a barely veiled suggestion that one of his fellow Justices ought to consider (like fans of a hapless college football team) wearing a paper bag on his head.[52] But marvel quickly turns to either raging or cheering depending, of course, on the particular auricular construction of the readers' "organs of hearing"—as I suspect was the author's intent.

Scalia's detractors regularly cited to his objectionable "tone" as his most "concerning" trait. Dean Erwin Chemerinsky tsk-tsked: "there is a ... meanness to his judicial rhetoric"[53] that Chemerinsky frequently blamed for his law students use of

---

[48] King v. Burwell, 135 S. Ct. 2480, 2501 (2015) (Scalia, J., dissenting).

[49] *Id.* at 2500.

[50] U.S. v. Windsor, 133 S. Ct. 2675, 2709 (2013) (Scalia, J., dissenting).

[51] Obergefell v. Hodges, 135 S. Ct. 2584, 2630, n.22 (2015) (Scalia, J., dissenting).

[52] *Id.*

[53] Erwin Chemerinsky, "The Jurisprudence of Justice Scalia: A Critical Appraisal," 22 *U. Haw. L. Rev.* 385, 385 (2000).

"nastiness as a crutch" to compensate for being unable to "win using reason or legal precedent."[54]

Justice Scalia might have wondered, in turn, whether Dean Chemerinsky's concern for civility was but an elaborate put-on disguising some fundamental question begging. Far from being "mean," this supposition merely reflects the stakes of the battle as Scalia understood them (and undoubtedly, as Chemerinsky also understands them). The future of the Republic rides on an outcome that is yet undetermined and very much in doubt.

In my view, Justice Scalia's rhetoric is best understood this way—he was indeed a gladiator, a Daniel, a voice in the wilderness, who thought and cared deeply about this nation, its history, its laws, and above all, its Constitution. His dissents are full-throated because they could not be otherwise. Because, to steal a phrase, Scalia always came as Scalia—he never buried his voice in a graveyard dissent.

---

[54] Erwin Chemerinsky, Opinion, "Justice Scalia: Why He's a Bad Influence," *L.A. Times* (July 14, 2015), http://www.latimes.com/opinion/op-ed/la-oe-0714-chemerinsky-scalia-bad-example-20150714-story.html.

DISSENTING OPINIONS OF JUSTICE ANTONIN SCALIA

1

Constitutional Structure

This wolf comes as a wolf
Morrison v. Olson, 487 U.S. 654 (1988)

No secret repository of rights guaranteeing fairness
BMW of North America, Inc. v. Gore, 517 U.S. 559 (1996)

An unprecedented intrusion upon state sovereignty
Lawyer v. Department of Justice, 521 U.S. 567, (1997)

The very core of liberty
Hamdi v. Rumsfeld, 542 U.S. 507 (2004)

Flabby legal tests invite arbitrary decisions
Tennessee v. Lane, 541 U.S. 509 (2004)

A rule blatantly gerrymandered to the facts of this case
Zivotofsky ex rel. Zivotofsky v. Kerry, 135 S.Ct. 2076 (2015)

There is no subject closer to the core function of the United States Supreme Court than the proper structure of the Union under the Constitution. Particularly important in these dissents is Justice Scalia's vision of the proper division of power both within the federal government and as between the federal government, the States, and the individual citizen. In these cases, Justice Scalia expressed his concern that the majority's decision would diminish the structural checks and balances of our constitutional system by eroding either the principle of Separation of Powers or that of Federalism, thus interfering with the proper allocation of authority under the Constitution.

This wolf comes as a wolf
Morrison v. Olson,
487 U.S. 654 (1988)

Justice Scalia, dissenting.

It is the proud boast of our democracy that we have "a government of laws and not of men." Many Americans are familiar with that phrase; not many know its derivation. It comes from Part the First, Article XXX, of the Massachusetts Constitution of 1780, which reads in full as follows:

> "In the government of this Commonwealth, the legislative department shall never exercise the executive and judicial powers, or either of them: The executive shall never exercise the legislative and judicial powers, or either of them: The judicial shall never exercise the legislative and executive powers, or either of them: to the end it may be a government of laws and not of men."

The Framers of the Federal Constitution similarly viewed the principle of separation of powers as the absolutely central guarantee of a just Government. In No. 47 of *The Federalist*, Madison wrote that "[n]o political truth is certainly of greater intrinsic value, or is stamped with the authority of more enlightened patrons of liberty." *The Federalist* No. 47, p. 301 (C. Rossiter ed. 1961) (hereinafter *Federalist*). Without a secure structure of separated powers, our Bill of Rights would be worthless, as are the bills of rights of many nations of the world that have adopted, or even improved upon, the mere words of ours.

The principle of separation of powers is expressed in our Constitution in the first section of each of the first three Articles. Article I, § 1, provides that "[a]ll legislative Powers herein granted shall be vested in a Congress of the United States, which shall consist of a Senate and House of Representatives." Article III, § 1, provides that "[t]he judicial Power of the United States, shall be vested in one supreme Court, and in such inferior Courts as the Congress may from time to time ordain and establish." And the provision at issue here, Art. II, § 1, cl. 1, provides that "[t]he executive Power shall be vested in a President of the United States of America."

But just as the mere words of a Bill of Rights are not self-effectuating, the Framers recognized "[t]he insufficiency of a mere parchment delineation of the boundaries" to achieve the separation of powers. *Federalist* No. 73, p. 442 (A. Hamilton). "[T]he great security," wrote Madison, "against a gradual concentration of the several powers in the same department consists in giving to those who administer each department the necessary constitutional means and personal motives to resist encroachments of the others. The provision for defense must in this, as in all other cases, be made commensurate to the danger of attack." *Federalist* No. 51, pp. 321–322. Madison continued:

> "But it is not possible to give to each department an equal power of self-defense. In republican government, the legislative authority necessarily predominates. The remedy for this inconveniency is to divide the legislature into different branches; and to render them, by different modes of election and different principles of action, as little connected with each other as the nature of their common functions and their common dependence on the society will admit .... As the weight of the legislative authority requires that it should be thus divided, the weakness of the executive may require, on the other hand, that it should be fortified." *Id.*, at 322–323.

The major "fortification" provided, of course, was the veto power. But in addition to providing fortification, the Founders conspicuously and very consciously declined to sap the Executive's strength in the same way they had weakened the Legislature: by dividing the executive power. Proposals to have multiple executives, or a council of advisers with separate authority were rejected. See 1 M. Farrand, *Records of the Federal Convention of 1787*, pp. 66, 71–74, 88, 91–92 (rev. ed. 1966); 2 *id.*, at 335–337, 533, 537, 542. Thus, while "[a]ll legislative Powers herein granted shall be vested in a Congress of the United States, which shall consist of a Senate *and* House of Representatives," U.S. Const., Art. I, § 1 (emphasis added), "[t]he executive Power shall be vested in *a President of the United States,*" Art. II, § 1, cl. 1 (emphasis added).

That is what this suit is about. Power. The allocation of power among Congress, the President, and the courts in such fashion as to preserve the equilibrium the Constitution sought to establish—so that "a gradual concentration of the several powers in the same department," *Federalist* No. 51, p. 321 (J. Madison), can effectively be resisted. Frequently an issue of this sort will come before the Court clad, so to speak, in sheep's clothing: the potential of the asserted principle to effect important change in the equilibrium of power is not immediately evident, and must be discerned by a careful and perceptive analysis. But this wolf comes as a wolf.

I

The present case began when the Legislative and Executive Branches became "embroiled in a dispute concerning the scope of the congressional investigatory power," *United States v. House of Representatives of United States*, 556 F.Supp. 150, 152 (DC 1983), which—as is often the case with such interbranch conflicts—became quite acrimonious. In the course of oversight hearings into the administration of the Superfund by the Environmental Protection Agency (EPA), two Subcommittees of the House of Representatives requested and then subpoenaed numerous internal EPA documents. The President responded by personally directing the EPA Administrator not to turn over certain of the documents, see Memorandum of November 30, 1982, from President Reagan for the Administrator, Environmental Protection Agency, reprinted in H.R.Rep. No. 99–435, pp. 1166–1167 (1985), and by having the Attorney General notify the congressional Subcommittees of this assertion of executive privilege, see Letters of November 30, 1982, from Attorney General William French Smith to Hon. John D. Dingell and Hon. Elliott H. Levitas, reprinted, *id.*, at 1168–1177. In his decision to assert executive privilege, the President was counseled by appellee Olson, who was then Assistant Attorney General of the Department of Justice for the Office of Legal Counsel, a post that has traditionally had responsibility for providing legal advice to the President (subject to approval of the Attorney General). The House's response was to pass a resolution citing the EPA Administrator, who had possession of the documents, for contempt. Contempt of Congress is a criminal offense. See 2 U.S.C. § 192. The United States Attorney, however, a member of the Executive Branch, initially took no steps to prosecute the contempt citation. Instead, the Executive Branch sought the immediate assistance of the Third Branch by filing a civil action asking the District Court to declare that the EPA Administrator had acted lawfully in withholding the documents under a claim of executive privilege. See *ibid.* The District Court declined (in my view correctly) to get involved in the controversy, and urged the other two branches to try "[c]ompromise and cooperation, rather than confrontation." 556 F.Supp., at 153. After further haggling, the two branches eventually reached an agreement giving the House Subcommittees limited access to the contested documents.

Congress did not, however, leave things there. Certain Members of the House remained angered by the confrontation, particularly by the role played by the Department of Justice. Specifically, the Judiciary Committee remained disturbed by the possibility that the Department had persuaded the President to assert executive privilege despite reservations by the EPA; that the Department had "deliberately and unnecessarily precipitated a constitutional confrontation with Congress"; that the Department had not properly reviewed and selected the documents as to which executive privilege was asserted; that the Department had directed the United States Attorney not to present the contempt certification involving the EPA Administrator to a grand jury for prosecution; that the Department had made the decision to sue the House of Representatives; and that the Department had not adequately advised and represented the President, the EPA, and the EPA Administrator. H.R.Rep. No. 99–435, p. 3 (1985) (describing unresolved "questions" that were the basis of the Judiciary Committee's investigation). Accordingly, staff counsel of the House Judiciary Committee were commissioned (apparently without the knowledge of many of the Committee's members, see *id.*, at 731) to investigate the Justice Department's role in the controversy. That investigation lasted 2½ years, and produced a 3,000-page report issued by the Committee over the vigorous dissent of all but one of its minority-party members. That report, which among other charges questioned the truthfulness of certain statements made by Assistant Attorney General Olson during testimony in front of the Committee during the early stages of its investigation, was sent to the Attorney General along with a formal request that he appoint an independent counsel to investigate Mr. Olson and others.

As a general matter, the Act before us here requires the Attorney General to apply for the appointment of an independent counsel within 90 days after receiving a request to do so, unless he determines within that period that "there are no reasonable grounds to believe that further investigation or prosecution is warranted." 28 U.S.C. § 592(b)(1). As a practical matter, it would be surprising if the Attorney General had any choice (assuming this statute is constitutional) but to seek appointment of an independent counsel to pursue the charges against the principal object of the congressional request, Mr. Olson. Merely the political consequences (to him and the President) of seeming to break the law by refusing to do so would have been substantial. How could it not be, the public would ask, that a 3,000-page indictment drawn by our representatives over 2 ½ years does not even establish "reasonable grounds to believe" that further investigation or prosecution is warranted with respect to at least the principal alleged culprit? But the Act establishes more than just practical compulsion. Although the Court's opinion asserts that the Attorney General had "no duty to comply with the [congressional] request," *ante*, at 2620, that is not entirely accurate. He *had* a duty to comply unless he could conclude that there were "*no reasonable grounds to believe*," not that prosecution was warranted, but merely that "*further investigation*" was warranted, 28 U.S.C. § 592(b)(1) (1982 ed., Supp. V) (emphasis added), after a 90-day investigation in which he was prohibited from using such routine investigative techniques as grand juries, plea bargaining, grants of immunity, or even subpoenas, see § 592(a)(2). The Court also makes much of the fact that "the courts are specifically prevented from reviewing the Attorney General's decision not to seek appointment, § 592(f)." *Ante*, at 2621. Yes, but *Congress* is not prevented from reviewing it. The context of this statute is acrid with the smell of threatened impeachment. Where, as here, a request for appointment of an independent counsel has come from the Judiciary Committee of either House of Congress, the Attorney General must, if he decides not to seek appointment, explain to that Committee why. See also 28 U.S.C. § 595(c) (1982 ed., Supp. V) (independent counsel must report to the House of Representatives information "that may constitute grounds for an impeachment").

Thus, by the application of this statute in the present case, Congress has effectively compelled a criminal investigation of a high-level appointee of the President in connection with his actions arising out of a bitter power dispute between the President and the Legislative Branch. Mr. Olson may or may not be guilty of a crime; we do not know. But we do know that the investigation of him has been commenced, not necessarily because the President or his authorized subordinates believe it is in the interest of the United States, in the sense that it warrants the diversion of resources from other efforts, and is worth the cost in money and in possible damage to other governmental interests; and not even, leaving aside those normally considered factors, because the President or his authorized subordinates necessarily believe that an investigation is likely to unearth a violation worth prosecuting; but only because the Attorney General cannot affirm, as Congress demands, that there are *no reasonable grounds to believe* that further investigation is warranted. The decisions regarding the scope of that further investigation, its duration, and, finally, whether or not prosecution should ensue, are likewise beyond the control of the President and his subordinates.

II

If to describe this case is not to decide it, the concept of a government of separate and coordinate powers no longer has meaning. The Court devotes most of its attention to such relatively technical details as the Appointments Clause and the removal power, addressing briefly and only at the end of its opinion the separation of powers. As my prologue suggests, I think that has it backwards. Our opinions are full of the recognition that it is the principle of separation of powers, and the inseparable corollary that each department's "defense must ... be made commensurate to the danger of attack," *Federalist* No. 51, p. 322 (J. Madison), which gives comprehensible content to the Appointments Clause, and determines the appropriate scope of the removal power. Thus, while I will subsequently discuss why our appointments and removal jurisprudence does not support today's holding, I begin with a consideration of the fountainhead of that jurisprudence, the separation and equilibration of powers.

First, however, I think it well to call to mind an important and unusual premise that underlies our deliberations, a premise not expressly contradicted by the Court's opinion, but in my view not faithfully observed. It is rare in a case dealing, as this one does, with the constitutionality of a statute passed by the Congress of the United States, not to find anywhere in the Court's opinion the usual, almost formulary caution that we owe great deference to Congress' view that what it has done is constitutional, see, *e.g., Rostker v. Goldberg,* 453 U.S. 57, 64, 101 S.Ct. 2646, 2651, 69 L.Ed.2d 478 (1981); *Fullilove v. Klutznick,* 448 U.S. 448, 472, 100 S.Ct. 2758, 2771, 65 L.Ed.2d 902 (1980) (opinion of Burger, C.J.); *Columbia Broadcasting System, Inc. v. Democratic National Committee,* 412 U.S. 94, 102, 93 S.Ct. 2080, 2086, 36 L.Ed.2d 772 (1973); *United States v. National Dairy Products Corp.,* 372 U.S. 29, 32, 83 S.Ct. 594, 597, 9 L.Ed.2d 561 (1963), and that we will decline to apply the statute only if the presumption of constitutionality can be overcome, see *Fullilove, supra,* 448 U.S., at 473, 100 S.Ct., at

2772; *Columbia Broadcasting, supra,* 412 U.S., at 103, 93 S.Ct., at 2087. That caution is not recited by the Court in the present case *because it does not apply.* Where a private citizen challenges action of the Government on grounds unrelated to separation of powers, harmonious functioning of the system demands that we ordinarily give some deference, or a presumption of validity, to the actions of the political branches in what is agreed, between themselves at least, to be within their respective spheres. But where the issue pertains to separation of powers, and the political branches are (as here) in disagreement, neither can be presumed correct. The reason is stated concisely by Madison: "The several departments being perfectly co-ordinate by the terms of their common commission, neither of them, it is evident, can pretend to an exclusive or superior right of settling the boundaries between their respective powers...." *Federalist* No. 49, p. 314. The playing field for the present case, in other words, is a level one. As one of the interested and coordinate parties to the underlying constitutional dispute, Congress, no more than the President, is entitled to the benefit of the doubt.

To repeat, Article II, § 1, cl. 1, of the Constitution provides: "The executive Power shall be vested in a President of the United States."

As I described at the outset of this opinion, this does not mean *some of* the executive power, but *all of* the executive power. It seems to me, therefore, that the decision of the Court of Appeals invalidating the present statute must be upheld on fundamental separation-of-powers principles if the following two questions are answered affirmatively: (1) Is the conduct of a criminal prosecution (and of an investigation to decide whether to prosecute) the exercise of purely executive power? (2) Does the statute deprive the President of the United States of exclusive control over the exercise of that power? Surprising to say, the Court appears to concede an affirmative answer to both questions, but seeks to avoid the inevitable conclusion that since the statute vests some purely executive power in a person who is not the President of the United States it is void.

The Court concedes that "[t]here is no real dispute that the functions performed by the independent counsel are 'executive'," though it qualifies that concession by adding "in the sense that they are law enforcement functions that typically have been undertaken by officials within the Executive Branch." *Ante,* at 2619. The qualifier adds nothing but atmosphere. In what *other* sense can one identify "the executive Power" that is supposed to be vested in the President (unless it includes everything the Executive Branch is given to do) *except* by reference to what has always and everywhere—if conducted by government at all—been conducted never by the legislature, never by the courts, and always by the executive. There is no possible doubt that the independent counsel's functions fit this description. She is vested with the "full power and independent authority to exercise all *investigative and prosecutorial* functions and powers of the Department of Justice [and] the Attorney General." 28 U.S.C. § 594(a) (1982 ed., Supp. V) (emphasis added). Governmental investigation and prosecution of crimes is a quintessentially executive function. See *Heckler v. Chaney,* 470 U.S. 821, 832, 105 S.Ct. 1649, 1656, 84 L.Ed.2d 714 (1985); *Buckley v. Valeo,* 424 U.S. 1, 138, 96 S.Ct. 612, 691, 46 L.Ed.2d 659 (1976); *United States v. Nixon,* 418 U.S. 683, 693, 94 S.Ct. 3090, 3100, 41 L.Ed.2d 1039 (1974).

As for the second question, whether the statute before us deprives the President of exclusive control over that quintessentially executive activity: The Court does not, and could not possibly, assert that it does not. That is indeed the whole object of the statute. Instead, the Court points out that the President, through his Attorney General, has at least *some* control. That concession is alone enough to invalidate the statute, but I cannot refrain from pointing out that the Court greatly exaggerates the extent of that "some" Presidential control. "Most importan[t]" among these controls, the Court asserts, is the Attorney General's "power to remove the counsel for 'good cause.'" *Ante,* at 2621. This is somewhat like referring to shackles as an effective means of locomotion. As we recognized in *Humphrey's Executor v. United States,* 295 U.S. 602, 55 S.Ct. 869, 79 L.Ed. 1611 (1935)—indeed, what *Humphrey's Executor* was all about—limiting removal power to "good cause" is an impediment to, not an effective grant of, Presidential control. We said that limitation was necessary with respect to members of the Federal Trade Commission, which we found to be "an agency of the legislative and judicial departments," and "wholly disconnected from the executive department," *id.,* at 630, 55 S.Ct., at 875, because "it is quite evident that one who holds his office only during the pleasure of another, cannot be depended upon to maintain an attitude of independence against the latter's will." *Id.,* at 629, 55 S.Ct., at 874. What we in *Humphrey's Executor* found to be a means of eliminating Presidential control, the Court today considers the "most importan[t]" means of assuring Presidential control. Congress, of course, operated under no such illusion when it enacted this statute, describing the "good cause" limitation as "protecting the independent counsel's ability to act independently of the President's direct control" since it permits removal only for "misconduct." H.R.Conf.Rep. 100–452, p. 37 (1987).

Moving on to the presumably "less important" controls that the President retains, the Court notes that no independent counsel may be appointed without a specific request from the Attorney General. As I have discussed above, the condition that renders such a request mandatory (inability to find "no reasonable grounds to believe" that further investigation is warranted) is so insubstantial that the Attorney General's discretion is severely confined. And once the referral is made, it is for the Special Division to determine the scope and duration of the investigation. See 28 U.S.C. § 593(b) (1982 ed., Supp. V). And in any event, the limited power over referral is irrelevant to the question whether, *once appointed,* the independent counsel exercises executive power free from the President's control. Finally, the Court points out that the Act directs the independent counsel to abide by general Justice Department policy, except when not "possible." See 28 U.S.C. § 594(f) (1982 ed., Supp. V). The exception alone shows this to be an empty promise. Even without that, however, one would be hard put to come up with many investigative or prosecutorial "policies" (other than those imposed by the Constitution or by Congress through law) that are absolute. Almost all investigative and prosecutorial decisions including the ultimate decision whether, after a technical violation of the law has been found, prosecution is warranted—involve the balancing of innumerable legal and practical considerations. Indeed, even political considerations (in the nonpartisan sense) must be considered, as exemplified by the recent decision of an independent counsel to subpoena the former Ambassador of Canada, producing considerable tension in our relations with that country. See N.Y. Times, May 29, 1987, p. A12, col. 1. Another pre-eminently political decision is whether getting a conviction in a particular case is worth the disclosure of national security information that would be necessary. The Justice Department and our intelligence agencies are often in disagreement on this point, and the Justice Department does not always win. The present Act even goes so far as specifically to take the resolution of that dispute away from the President and give it to the independent counsel. 28 U.S.C. § 594(a)(6). In sum, the balancing of various legal, practical, and political considerations, none of which is absolute, is the very essence of prosecutorial discretion. To take this away is to remove the core of the prosecutorial function, and not merely "some" Presidential control.

As I have said, however, it is ultimately irrelevant *how much* the statute reduces Presidential control. The case is over when the Court acknowledges, as it must, that "[i]t is undeniable that the Act reduces the amount of control or supervision that the Attorney General and, through him, the President exercises over the investigation and prosecution of a certain class of alleged criminal activity." *Ante,* at 2621. It effects a revolution in our constitutional jurisprudence for the Court, once it has determined that (1) purely executive functions are at issue here, and (2) those functions have been given to a person whose actions are not fully within the supervision and control of the President, nonetheless to proceed further to sit in judgment of whether "the President's need to control the exercise of [the independent counsel's] discretion is *so central* to the functioning of the Executive Branch" as to require complete control, *ante,* at 2619 (emphasis added), whether the conferral of his powers upon someone else "*sufficiently* deprives the President of control over the independent counsel to interfere impermissibly with [his] constitutional obligation to ensure the faithful execution of the laws," *ante,* at 2619–2620 (emphasis added), and whether "the Act give[s] the Executive Branch *sufficient* control over the independent counsel to ensure that the President is able to perform his constitutionally assigned duties," *ante,* at 2621 (emphasis added). It is not for us to determine, and we have never presumed to determine, how much of the purely executive powers of government must be within the full control of the President. The Constitution prescribes that they *all* are.

The utter incompatibility of the Court's approach with our constitutional traditions can be made more clear, perhaps, by applying it to the powers of the other two branches. Is it conceivable that if Congress passed a statute depriving itself of less than full and entire control over some insignificant area of legislation, we would inquire whether the matter was "*so central* to the functioning of the Legislative Branch" as really to require complete control, or whether the statute gives Congress "*sufficient* control over the surrogate legislator to ensure that Congress is able to perform its constitutionally assigned duties"? Of course we would have none of that. Once we determined that a purely legislative power was at issue we would require it to be exercised, wholly and entirely, by Congress. Or to bring the point closer to home, consider a statute giving to non-Article III judges just a tiny bit of purely judicial power in a relatively insignificant field, with substantial control, though not total control, in the courts—perhaps "clear error" review, which would be a fair judicial equivalent of the Attorney General's "for cause" removal power here. Is there any doubt that we would not pause to inquire whether the matter was "*so central* to the functioning of the Judicial Branch" as really to require complete control, or whether we retained "*sufficient* control over the matters to be decided that we are able to perform our constitutionally assigned duties"? We would say that our "constitutionally assigned duties" include *complete* control over all exercises of the judicial power—or, as the plurality opinion said in *Northern Pipeline Construction Co. v. Marathon Pipe Line Co.,* 458 U.S. 50, 58–59, 102 S.Ct. 2858, 2865, 73 L.Ed.2d 598 (1982): "The inexorable command of [Article III] is clear and definite: The judicial power of the United States must be exercised by courts having the attributes prescribed in Art. III." We should say here that the President's constitutionally assigned duties include *complete* control over investigation and prosecution of violations of the law, and that the inexorable command of Article II is clear and definite: the executive power must be vested in the President of the United States.

Is it unthinkable that the President should have such exclusive power, even when alleged crimes by him or his close associates are at issue? No more so than that Congress should have the exclusive power of legislation, even when what is at issue is its own exemption from the burdens of certain laws. See Civil Rights Act of 1964, Title VII, 42 U.S.C. § 2000e *et seq.* (prohibiting "employers," not defined to include the United States, from discriminating on the basis of race, color, religion, sex, or national origin). No more so than that this Court should have the exclusive power to pronounce the final decision on justiciable cases and controversies, even those pertaining to the constitutionality of a statute reducing the salaries of the Justices. See *United States v. Will,* 449 U.S. 200, 211–217, 101 S.Ct. 471, 478–482, 66 L.Ed.2d 392 (1980). A system of separate and coordinate powers necessarily involves an acceptance of exclusive power that can theoretically be abused. As we reiterate this very day, "[i]t is a truism that constitutional protections have costs." *Coy v. Iowa,* 487 U.S. 1012, 1020, 108 S.Ct. 2798, ----, 101 L.Ed.2d 857 (1988). While the separation of powers may prevent us from righting every wrong, it does so in order to ensure that we do not lose liberty. The checks against any branch's abuse of its exclusive powers are twofold: First, retaliation by one of the other branch's use of *its* exclusive powers: Congress, for example, can impeach the executive who willfully fails to enforce the laws; the executive can decline to prosecute under unconstitutional statutes, cf. *United States v. Lovett,* 328 U.S. 303, 66 S.Ct. 1073, 90 L.Ed. 1252 (1946); and the courts can dismiss malicious prosecutions. Second, and ultimately, there is the political check that the people will replace those in the political branches (the branches more "dangerous to the political rights of the Constitution,"

Federalist No. 78, p. 465) who are guilty of abuse. Political pressures produced special prosecutors—for Teapot Dome and for Watergate, for example—long before this statute created the independent counsel. See Act of Feb. 8, 1924, ch. 16, 43 Stat. 5–6; 38 Fed.Reg. 30738 (1973).

The Court has, nonetheless, replaced the clear constitutional prescription that the executive power belongs to the President with a "balancing test." What are the standards to determine how the balance is to be struck, that is, how much removal of Presidential power is too much? Many countries of the world get along with an executive that is much weaker than ours—in fact, entirely dependent upon the continued support of the legislature. Once we depart from the text of the Constitution, just where short of that do we stop? The most amazing feature of the Court's opinion is that it does not even purport to give an answer. It simply *announces,* with no analysis, that the ability to control the decision whether to investigate and prosecute the President's closest advisers, and indeed the President himself, is not "so central to the functioning of the Executive Branch" as to be constitutionally required to be within the President's control. Apparently that is so because we say it is so. Having abandoned as the basis for our decision-making the text of Article II that "the executive Power" must be vested in the President, the Court does not even attempt to craft a *substitute* criterion—a "justiciable standard," see, *e.g., Baker v. Carr,* 369 U.S. 186, 210, 82 S.Ct. 691, 706, 7 L.Ed.2d 663 (1962); *Coleman v. Miller,* 307 U.S. 433, 454–455, 59 S.Ct. 972, 982, 83 L.Ed. 1385 (1939), however remote from the Constitution—that today governs, and in the future will govern, the decision of such questions. Evidently, the governing standard is to be what might be called the unfettered wisdom of a majority of this Court, revealed to an obedient people on a case-by-case basis. This is not only not the government of laws that the Constitution established; it is not a government of laws at all.

In my view, moreover, even as an ad hoc, standardless judgment the Court's conclusion must be wrong. Before this statute was passed, the President, in taking action disagreeable to the Congress, or an executive officer giving advice to the President or testifying before Congress concerning one of those many matters on which the two branches are from time to time at odds, could be assured that his acts and motives would be adjudged—insofar as the decision whether to conduct a criminal investigation and to prosecute is concerned—in the Executive Branch, that is, in a forum attuned to the interests and the policies of the Presidency. That was one of the natural advantages the Constitution gave to the Presidency, just as it gave Members of Congress (and their staffs) the advantage of not being prosecutable for anything said or done in their legislative capacities. See U.S. Const., Art. I, § 6, cl. 1; *Gravel v. United States,* 408 U.S. 606, 92 S.Ct. 2614, 33 L.Ed.2d 583 (1972). It is the very object of this legislation to eliminate that assurance of a sympathetic forum. Unless it can honestly be said that there are "no reasonable grounds to believe" that further investigation is warranted, further investigation must ensue; and the conduct of the investigation, and determination of whether to prosecute, will be given to a person neither selected by nor subject to the control of the President—who will in turn assemble a staff by finding out, presumably, who is willing to put aside whatever else they are doing, for an indeterminate period of time, in order to investigate and prosecute the President or a particular named individual in his administration. The prospect is frightening (as I will discuss at some greater length at the conclusion of this opinion) even outside the context of a bitter, interbranch political dispute. Perhaps the boldness of the President himself will not be affected—though I am not even sure of that. (How much easier it is for

Congress, instead of accepting the political damage attendant to the commencement of impeachment proceedings against the President on trivial grounds—or, for that matter, how easy it is for one of the President's political foes outside of Congress—simply to trigger a debilitating criminal investigation of the Chief Executive under this law.) But as for the President's high-level assistants, who typically have no political base of support, it is as utterly unrealistic to think that they will not be intimidated by this prospect, and that their advice to him and their advocacy of his interests before a hostile Congress will not be affected, as it would be to think that the Members of Congress and their staffs would be unaffected by replacing the Speech or Debate Clause with a similar provision. It deeply wounds the President, by substantially reducing the President's ability to protect himself and his staff. That is the whole object of the law, of course, and I cannot imagine why the Court believes it does not succeed.

Besides weakening the Presidency by reducing the zeal of his staff, it must also be obvious that the institution of the independent counsel enfeebles him more directly in his constant confrontations with Congress, by eroding his public support. Nothing is so politically effective as the ability to charge that one's opponent and his associates are not merely wrongheaded, naive, ineffective, but, in all probability, "crooks." And nothing so effectively gives an appearance of validity to such charges as a Justice Department investigation and, even better, prosecution. The present statute provides ample means for that sort of attack, assuring that massive and lengthy investigations will occur, not merely when the Justice Department in the application of its usual standards believes they are called for, but whenever it cannot be said that there are "no reasonable grounds to believe" they are called for. The statute's highly visible procedures assure, moreover, that unlike most investigations these will be widely known and prominently displayed. Thus, in the 10 years since the institution of the independent counsel was established by law, there have been nine highly publicized investigations, a source of constant political damage to two administrations. That they could not remotely be described as merely the application of "normal" investigatory and prosecutory standards is demonstrated by, in addition to the language of the statute ("no reasonable grounds to believe"), the following facts: Congress appropriates approximately $50 million annually for general legal activities, salaries, and expenses of the Criminal Division of the Department of Justice. See 1989 Budget Request of the Department of Justice, Hearings before a Subcommittee of the House Committee on Appropriations, 100th Cong., 2d Sess., pt. 6, pp. 284–285 (1988) (DOJ Budget Request). This money is used to support "[f]ederal appellate activity," "[o]rganized crime prosecution," "[p]ublic integrity" and "[f]raud" matters, "[n]arcotic & dangerous drug prosecution," "[i]nternal security," "[g]eneral litigation and legal advice," "special investigations," "[p]rosecution support," "[o]rganized crime drug enforcement," and "[m]anagement & administration." *Id.*, at 284. By comparison, between May 1986 and August 1987, four independent counsel (not all of whom were operating for that entire period of time) spent almost $5 million (1/10th of the amount annually appropriated to the entire Criminal Division), spending almost $1 million in the month of August 1987 alone. See *Washington Post*, Oct. 21, 1987, p. A21, col. 5. For fiscal year 1989, the Department of Justice has requested $52 million for the entire Criminal Division, DOJ Budget Request 285, and $7 million to support the activities of independent counsel, *id.*, at 25.

In sum, this statute does deprive the President of substantial control over the prosecutory functions performed by the independent counsel, and it does substantially affect the balance of powers. That the Court could possibly conclude otherwise demonstrates both the wisdom of our former constitutional system, in which the degree of reduced control and political impairment were irrelevant, since *all* purely executive power had to be in the President; and the folly of the new system of standardless judicial allocation of powers we adopt today.

III

As I indicated earlier, the basic separation-of-powers principles I have discussed are what give life and content to our jurisprudence concerning the President's power to appoint and remove officers. The same result of unconstitutionality is therefore plainly indicated by our case law in these areas.

Article II, § 2, cl. 2, of the Constitution provides as follows:

> "[The President] shall nominate, and by and with the Advice and Consent of the Senate, shall appoint Ambassadors, other public Ministers and Consuls, Judges of the supreme Court, and all other Officers of the United States, whose Appointments are not herein otherwise provided for, and which shall be established by Law: but the Congress may by Law vest the Appointment of such inferior Officers, as they think proper, in the President alone, in the Courts of Law, or in the Heads of Departments."

Because appellant (who all parties and the Court agree is an officer of the United States, *ante,* at 2608, n. 12) was not appointed by the President with the advice and consent of the Senate, but rather by the Special Division of the United States Court of Appeals, her appointment is constitutional only if (1) she is an "inferior" officer within the meaning of the above Clause, and (2) Congress may vest her appointment in a court of law.

As to the first of these inquiries, the Court does not attempt to "decide exactly" what establishes the line between principal and "inferior" officers, but is confident that, whatever the line may be, appellant "clearly falls on the 'inferior officer' side" of it. *Ante,* at 2608. The Court gives three reasons: *First,* she "is subject to removal by a higher Executive Branch official," namely, the Attorney General. *Ibid. Second,* she is "empowered by the Act to perform only certain, limited duties." *Ante,* at 2608. *Third,* her office is "limited in jurisdiction" and "limited in tenure." *Ibid.*

The first of these lends no support to the view that appellant is an inferior officer. Appellant is removable only for "good cause" or physical or mental incapacity. 28 U.S.C. § 596(a)(1) (1982 ed., Supp. V). By contrast, most (if not all) *principal* officers in the Executive Branch may be removed by the President *at will.* I fail to see how the fact that appellant is more difficult to remove than most principal officers helps to establish that she is an inferior officer. And I do not see how it could possibly make any difference to her superior or inferior status that the President's limited power to remove her must be exercised through the Attorney General. If she were removable at will by the Attorney General, then she would be subordinate to him and thus properly designated as inferior; but the Court essentially admits that she is not subordinate. See *ante,* at 2608. If it were common usage to refer to someone as "inferior" who is subject to removal for cause by another, then one would say that the President is "inferior" to Congress.

The second reason offered by the Court—that appellant performs only certain, limited duties—may be relevant to whether she is an inferior officer, but it mischaracterizes the extent of her powers. As the Court states: "Admittedly, the Act delegates to appellant [the] '*full power and independent authority to exercise all investigative and prosecutorial functions and powers of the Department of Justice.*'" *Ante*, at 2608, quoting 28 U.S.C. § 594(a) (1982 ed., Supp. V) (emphasis added). Moreover, in addition to this general grant of power she is given a broad range of specifically enumerated powers, including a power not even the Attorney General possesses: to "contes[t] in court ... any claim of privilege or attempt to withhold evidence on grounds of national security." § 594(a)(6). Once all of this is "admitted," it seems to me impossible to maintain that appellant's authority is so "limited" as to render her an inferior officer. The Court seeks to brush this away by asserting that the independent counsel's power does not include any authority to "formulate policy for the Government or the Executive Branch." *Ante*, at 2608. But the same could be said for all officers of the Government, with the single exception of the President. All of them only formulate policy within their respective spheres of responsibility—as does the independent counsel, who must comply with the policies of the Department of Justice only to the extent possible. § 594(f).

The final set of reasons given by the Court for why the independent counsel clearly is an inferior officer emphasizes the limited nature of her jurisdiction and tenure. Taking the latter first, I find nothing unusually limited about the independent counsel's tenure. To the contrary, unlike most high-ranking Executive Branch officials, she continues to serve until she (or the Special Division) decides that her work is substantially completed. See §§ 596(b)(1), (b)(2). This particular independent prosecutor has already served more than two years, which is at least as long as many Cabinet officials. As to the scope of her jurisdiction, there can be no doubt that is small (though far from unimportant). But within it she exercises more than the full power of the Attorney General. The Ambassador to Luxembourg is not anything less than a principal officer, simply because Luxembourg is small. And the federal judge who sits in a small district is not for that reason "inferior in rank and authority." If the mere fragmentation of executive responsibilities into small compartments suffices to render the heads of each of those compartments inferior officers, then Congress could deprive the President of the right to appoint his chief law enforcement officer by dividing up the Attorney General's responsibilities among a number of "lesser" functionaries.

More fundamentally, however, it is not clear from the Court's opinion why the factors it discusses—even if applied correctly to the facts of this case—are determinative of the question of inferior officer status. The apparent source of these factors is a statement in *United States v. Germaine,* 99 U.S. (9 Otto) 508, 511 25 L.Ed. 482 (1879) (discussing *United States v. Hartwell,* 6 Wall. 385, 393, 18 L.Ed. 830 (1868)), that "the term [officer] embraces the ideas of tenure, duration, emolument, and duties." See *ante,* at 2608. Besides the fact that this was dictum, it was dictum in a case where the distinguishing characteristics of inferior officers versus superior officers were in no way relevant, but rather only the distinguishing characteristics of an "officer of the United States" (to which the criminal statute at issue applied) as opposed to a mere *employee.* Rather than erect a theory of who is an inferior officer on the foundation of such an irrelevancy, I think it preferable to look to the text of the Constitution and the division of power that it establishes. These demonstrate, I think, that the independent counsel is not an inferior officer because she is not *subordinate* to any officer in the Executive Branch (indeed, not even to the President). Dictionaries in use at the time of the Constitutional Convention gave the word "inferiour" two meanings which it still bears today: (1) "[l]ower in place, ... station, ... rank of life, ... value or excellency," and (2) "[s]ubordinate." S. Johnson, *Dictionary of the English Language* (6th ed. 1785). In a document dealing with the structure (the constitution) of a government, one would naturally expect the word to bear the latter meaning—indeed, in such a context it would be unpardonably careless to use the word *unless* a relationship of subordination was intended. If what was meant was merely "lower in station or rank," one would use instead a term such as "lesser officers." At the only other point in the Constitution at which the word "inferior" appears, it plainly connotes a relationship of subordination. Article III vests the judicial power of the United States in "one supreme Court, and in such *inferior* Courts as the Congress may from time to time ordain and establish." U.S. Const., Art. III, § 1 (emphasis added). In *Federalist* No. 81, Hamilton pauses to describe the "inferior" courts authorized by Article III as inferior in the sense that they are "subordinate" to the Supreme Court. See *id.*, 6 Wall. at 485, n., 490, n.

That "inferior" means "subordinate" is also consistent with what little we know about the evolution of the Appointments Clause. As originally reported to the Committee on Style, the Appointments Clause provided no "exception" from the standard manner of appointment (President with the advice and consent of the Senate) for inferior officers. 2 M. Farrand, *Records of the Federal Convention of 1787*, pp. 498–499, 599 (rev. ed. 1966). On September 15, 1787, the last day of the Convention before the proposed Constitution was signed, in the midst of a host of minor changes that were being considered, Gouverneur Morris moved to add the exceptions clause. *Id.*, at 627. No great debate ensued; the only disagreement was over whether it was necessary at all. *Id.*, at 627–628. Nobody thought that it was a fundamental change, excluding from the President's appointment power and the Senate's confirmation power a category of officers who might function on their own, outside the supervision of those appointed in the more cumbersome fashion. And it is significant that in the very brief discussion Madison mentions (as in apparent contrast to the "inferior officers" covered by the provision) "Superior Officers." *Id.,* at 637. Of course one is not a "superior officer" without some supervisory responsibility, just as, I suggest, one is not an "inferior officer" within the meaning of the provision under discussion unless one is subject to supervision by a "superior officer." It is perfectly obvious, therefore, both from the relative brevity of the discussion this addition received, and from the content of that discussion, that it was intended merely to make clear (what Madison thought already was clear, see *id.,* at 627) that those officers appointed by the President with Senate approval could on their own appoint their subordinates, who would, of course, by chain of command still be under the direct control of the President.

This interpretation is, moreover, consistent with our admittedly sketchy precedent in this area. For example, in *United States v. Eaton,* 169 U.S. 331, 18 S.Ct. 374, 42 L.Ed. 767 (1898), we held that the appointment by an Executive Branch official other than the President of a "vice-consul," charged with the duty of temporarily performing the function of the consul, did not violate the Appointments Clause. In doing so, we repeatedly referred to the "vice-consul" as a "subordinate" officer. *Id.,* at 343, 18 S.Ct., at 879. See also *United States v. Germaine, supra,* 9 Otto at 511 (comparing "inferior" com-missioners and bureau officers to heads of department, describing the former as "mere ... subordinates") (dicta); *United States v. Hartwell, supra,* 6 Wall. at 394 (describing clerk appointed by Assistant Treasurer with approval of Secretary of the Treasury as a "subordinate office [r]") (dicta). More recently, in *United States v. Nixon,* 418 U.S. 683, 94 S.Ct. 3090, 41 L.Ed.2d 1039 (1974), we noted that the Attorney General's appointment of the Watergate Special Prosecutor was made pursuant to the Attorney General's "power to appoint *subordinate officers* to assist him in the discharge of his duties." *Id.,* at 694, 94 S.Ct., at 3100 (emphasis added). The Court's citation of *Nixon* as support for its view that the independent counsel is an inferior officer is simply not supported by a reading of the case. We explicitly stated that the Special Prosecutor was a "subordinate office[r]," *ibid.,* because, in the end, the President or the Attorney General could have removed him at any time, if by no other means than amending or revoking the regulation defining his authority. *Id.,* at 696, 94 S.Ct., at 3101. Nor are any of the other cases cited by the Court in support of its view inconsistent with the natural reading that an inferior officer must at least be subordinate to another officer of the United States. In *Ex parte Siebold,* 100 U.S. (10 Otto) 371, 25 L.Ed. 717 (1880), we upheld the appointment by a court of federal "Judges of Election," who were charged with various duties involving the overseeing of local congressional elections. Contrary to the Court's assertion, see *ante,* at 2609, we did not specifically find that these officials were inferior officers for purposes of the Appointments Clause, probably because no one had contended that they were principal officers. Nor can the case be said to represent even an assumption on our part that they were inferior without being subordinate. The power of assisting in the judging of elections that they were exercising was assuredly not a purely executive power, and if we entertained any assumption it was probably that they, like the marshals who assisted them, see *Siebold,* 100 U.S. (10 Otto), at 380, were subordinate to the courts, see *id.,* 10 Otto at 397. Similarly, in *Go-Bart Importing Co. v. United States,* 282 U.S. 344, 51 S.Ct. 153, 75 L.Ed. 374 (1931), where we held that United States commissioners were inferior officers, we made plain that they were subordinate to the district courts which appointed them: "The commissioner acted not as a court, or as a judge of any court, but as a mere officer of the district court in proceedings of which that court had authority to take control at any time." *Id.*, at 354, 51 S.Ct., at 157.

To be sure, it is not a *sufficient* condition for "inferior" officer status that one be subordinate to a principal officer. Even an officer who is subordinate to a department head can be a principal officer. That is clear from the brief exchange following Gouverneur Morris' suggestion of the addition of the exceptions clause for inferior officers. Madison responded:

> "It does not go far enough if it be necessary at all—*Superior Officers below Heads of Departments* ought in some cases to have the appointment of the lesser offices." 2 M. Farrand, *Records of the Federal Convention of 1787*, p. 627 (rev. ed. 1966) (emphasis added).

But it is surely a *necessary* condition for inferior officer status that the officer be subordinate to another officer.

The independent counsel is not even subordinate to the President. The Court essentially admits as much, noting that "appellant may not be 'subordinate' to the Attorney General (and the President) insofar as she possesses a degree of independent discretion to exercise the powers delegated to her under the Act." *Ante*, at 2608–2609. In fact, there is no doubt about it. As noted earlier, the Act specifically grants her the "*full* power and *independent* authority to exercise *all* investigative and prosecutorial functions of the Department of Justice," 28 U.S.C. § 594(a) (1982 ed., Supp. V), and makes her removable only for "good cause," a limitation specifically intended to ensure that she be *independent* of, not *subordinate* to, the President and the Attorney General. See H.R.Conf.Rep. No. 100–452, p. 37 (1987).

Because appellant is not subordinate to another officer, she is not an "inferior" officer and her appointment other than by the President with the advice and consent of the Senate is unconstitutional.

IV

I will not discuss at any length why the restrictions upon the removal of the independent counsel also violate our established precedent dealing with that specific subject. For most of it, I simply refer the reader to the scholarly opinion of Judge Silberman for the Court of Appeals below. See *In re Sealed Case,* 267 U.S.App.D.C. 178, 838 F.2d 476 (1988). I cannot avoid commenting, however, about the essence of what the Court has done to our removal jurisprudence today.

There is, of course, no provision in the Constitution stating who may remove executive officers, except the provisions for removal by impeachment. Before the present decision it was established, however, (1) that the President's power to remove principal officers who exercise purely executive powers could not be restricted, see *Myers v. United States,* 272 U.S. 52, 127, 47 S.Ct. 21, 28–29, 71 L.Ed. 160 (1926), and (2) that his power to remove inferior officers who exercise purely executive powers, and whose appointment Congress had removed from the usual procedure of Presidential appointment with Senate consent, could be restricted, at least where the appointment had been made by an officer of the Executive Branch, see *ibid.; United States v. Perkins,* 116 U.S. 483, 485, 6 S.Ct. 449, 450, 29 L.Ed. 700 (1886).

The Court could have resolved the removal power issue in this case by simply relying upon its erroneous conclusion that the independent counsel was an inferior officer, and then extending our holding that the removal of inferior officers appointed by the Executive can be restricted, to a new holding that even the removal of inferior officers appointed by the courts can be restricted. That would in my view be a considerable and unjustified extension, giving the Executive full discretion in *neither* the selection *nor* the removal of a purely executive officer.

The course the Court has chosen, however, is even worse.

Since our 1935 decision in *Humphrey's Executor v. United States,* 295 U.S. 602, 55 S.Ct. 869, 79 L.Ed. 1611—which was considered by many at the time the product of an activist, anti-New Deal Court bent on reducing the power of President Franklin Roosevelt—it has been established that the line of permissible restriction upon removal of principal officers lies at the point at which the powers exercised by those officers are no longer purely executive. Thus, removal restrictions have been generally regarded as lawful for so-called "independent regulatory agencies," such as the Federal Trade Commission, see *ibid.;* 15 U.S.C. § 41, the Interstate Commerce Commission, see 49 U.S.C. § 10301(c) (1982 ed., Supp. IV), and the Consumer Product Safety Commission, see 15 U.S.C. § 2053(a), which engage substantially in what has been called the "quasi-legislative activity" of rulemaking, and for members of Article I courts, such as the Court of Military Appeals, see 10 U.S.C. § 867(a)(2), who engage in the "quasi-judicial" function of adjudication. It has often been observed, correctly in my view, that the line between "purely executive" functions and "quasi-legislative" or "quasi-judicial" functions is not a clear one or even a rational one. See *ante,* at 2618–2619; *Bowsher v. Synar,* 478 U.S. 714, 761, n. 3, 106 S.Ct. 3181, 3206, n. 3 (1986) (White, J., dissenting); *FTC v. Ruberoid Co.,* 343 U.S. 470, 487–488, 72 S.Ct. 800, 810, 96 L.Ed. 1081 (1952) (Jackson, J., dissenting). But at least it permitted the identification of certain officers, and certain agencies, whose functions were entirely within the control of the President. Congress had to be aware of that restriction in its legislation. Today, however, *Humphrey's Executor* is swept into the dustbin of repudiated constitutional principles. "[O]ur present considered view," the Court says, "is that the determination of whether the Constitution allows Congress to impose a 'good cause'-type restriction on the President's power to remove an official cannot be made to turn on whether or not that official is classified as 'purely executive.'" *Ante,* at 2617. What *Humphrey's Executor* (and presumably *Myers*) really means, we are now told, is not that there are any "rigid categories of those officials who may or may not be removed at will by the President," but simply that Congress cannot "interefere with the President's exercise of the 'executive power' and his constitutionally appointed duty to 'take care that the laws be faithfully executed,'" *ante,* at 2617–2618.

One can hardly grieve for the shoddy treatment given today to *Humphrey's Executor,* which, after all, accorded the same indignity (with much less justification) to Chief Justice Taft's opinion 10 years earlier in *Myers v. United States,* 272 U.S. 52, 47 S.Ct. 21, 71 L.Ed. 160 (1926)—gutting, in six quick pages devoid of textual or historical precedent for the novel principle it set forth, a carefully researched and reasoned 70-page opinion. It is in fact comforting to witness the reality that he who lives by the *ipse dixit* dies by the *ipse dixit.* But one must grieve for the Constitution. *Humphrey's Executor* at least had the decency formally to observe the constitutional principle that the President had to be the repository of *all* executive power, see 295 U.S., at 627–628, 55 S.Ct., at 874, which, as *Myers* carefully explained, necessarily means that he must be able to discharge those who do not perform executive functions according to his liking. As we noted in *Bowsher,* once an officer is appointed "'it is only the authority that can remove him, and not the authority that appointed him, that he must fear and, in the performance of his functions, obey.'" 478 U.S., at 726, 106 S.Ct., at 3188, quoting *Synar v. United States,* 626 F.Supp. 1374, 1401 (DC 1986) (Scalia, Johnson, and Gasch, JJ.). By contrast, "our present considered view" is simply that *any* executive officer's removal can be restricted, so long as the President remains "able to accomplish his constitutional role." *Ante,* at 2618. There are now no lines. If the removal of a prosecutor, the virtual embodiment of the power to "take care that the laws be faithfully executed," can be restricted, what officer's removal cannot? This is an open invitation for Congress to experiment. What about a special Assistant Secretary of State, with responsibility for one very narrow area of foreign policy, who would not only have to be confirmed by the Senate but could also be removed only pursuant to certain carefully designed restrictions? Could this possibly render the President "[un]able to accomplish his constitutional role"? Or a special Assistant Secretary of Defense for Procurement? The possibilities are endless, and the Court does not understand what the separation of powers, what "[a]mbition ... counteract [ing] ambition," *Federalist* No. 51, p. 322 (Madison), is all about, if it does not expect Congress to try them. As far as I can discern from the Court's opinion, it is now open season upon the President's removal power for all executive officers, with not even the superficially principled restriction of *Humphrey's Executor* as cover. The Court essentially says to the President: "Trust us. We will make sure that you are able to accomplish your constitutional role." I think the Constitution gives the President—and the people—more protection than that.

V

The purpose of the separation and equilibration of powers in general, and of the unitary Executive in particular, was not merely to assure effective government but to preserve individual freedom. Those who hold or have held offices covered by the Ethics in Government Act are entitled to that protection as much as the rest of us, and I conclude my discussion by considering the effect of the Act upon the fairness of the process they receive.

Only someone who has worked in the field of law enforcement can fully appreciate the vast power and the immense discretion that are placed in the hands of a prosecutor with respect to the objects of his investigation. Justice Robert Jackson, when he was Attorney General under President Franklin Roosevelt, described it in a memorable speech to United States Attorneys, as follows:

> "There is a most important reason why the prosecutor should have, as nearly as possible, a detached and impartial view of all groups in his community. Law enforcement is not automatic. It isn't blind. One of the greatest difficulties of the position of prosecutor is that he must pick his cases, because no prosecutor can even investigate all of the cases in which he receives complaints. If the Department of Justice were to make even a pretense of reaching every probable violation of federal law, ten times its present staff will be inadequate. We know that no local police force can strictly enforce the traffic laws, or it would arrest half the driving population on any given morning. What every prosecutor is practically required to do is to select the cases for prosecution and to select those in which the offense is the most flagrant, the public harm the greatest, and the proof the most certain.
>
> "If the prosecutor is obliged to choose his case, it follows that he can choose his defendants. Therein is the most dangerous power of the prosecutor: that he will pick people that he thinks he should get, rather than cases that need to be prosecuted. With the law books filled with a great assortment of crimes, a prosecutor stands a fair chance of finding at least a technical violation of some act on the part of almost anyone. In such a case, it is not a question of discovering the commission of a crime and then looking for the man who has committed it, it is a question of picking the man and then searching the law books, or putting investigators to work, to pin some offense on him. It is in this realm—in which the prosecutor picks some person whom he dislikes or desires to embarrass, or selects some group of

> unpopular persons and then looks for an offense, that the greatest danger of abuse of prosecuting power lies. It is here that law enforcement becomes personal, and the real crime becomes that of being unpopular with the predominant or governing group, being attached to the wrong political views, or being personally obnoxious to or in the way of the prosecutor himself." R. Jackson, *The Federal Prosecutor, Address Delivered at the Second Annual Conference of United States Attorneys*, April 1, 1940.

Under our system of government, the primary check against prosecutorial abuse is a political one. The prosecutors who exercise this awesome discretion are selected and can be removed by a President, whom the people have trusted enough to elect. Moreover, when crimes are not investigated and prosecuted fairly, nonselectively, with a reasonable sense of proportion, the President pays the cost in political damage to his administration. If federal prosecutors "pick people that [they] thin[k] [they] should get, rather than cases that need to be prosecuted," if they amass many more resources against a particular prominent individual, or against a particular class of political protesters, or against members of a particular political party, than the gravity of the alleged offenses or the record of successful prosecutions seems to warrant, the unfairness will come home to roost in the Oval Office. I leave it to the reader to recall the examples of this in recent years. That result, of course, was precisely what the Founders had in mind when they provided that all executive powers would be exercised by a *single* Chief Executive. As Hamilton put it, "[t]he ingredients which constitute safety in the republican sense are a due dependence on the people, and a due responsibility." *Federalist* No. 70, p. 424. The President is directly dependent on the people, and since there is only *one* President, *he* is responsible. The people know whom to blame, whereas "one of the weightiest objections to a plurality in the executive ... is that it tends to conceal faults and destroy responsibility." *Id.*, at 427.

That is the system of justice the rest of us are entitled to, but what of that select class consisting of present or former high-level Executive Branch officials? If an allegation is made against them of any violation of any federal criminal law (except Class B or C misdemeanors or infractions) the Attorney General must give it his attention. That in itself is not objectionable. But if, after a 90–day investigation without the benefit of normal investigatory tools, the Attorney General is unable to say that there are "no reasonable grounds to believe" that further investigation is warranted, a process is set in motion that is *not* in the full control of persons "dependent on the people," and whose flaws cannot be blamed on the President. An independent counsel is selected, and the scope of his or her authority prescribed, by a panel of judges. What if they are politically partisan, as judges have been known to be, and select a prosecutor antagonistic to the administration, or even to the particular individual who has been selected for this special treatment? There is no remedy for that, not even a political one. Judges, after all, have life tenure, and appointing a surefire enthusiastic prosecutor could hardly be considered an impeachable offense. So if there is anything wrong with the selection, there is effectively no one to blame. The independent counsel thus selected proceeds to assemble a staff. As I observed earlier, in the nature of things this has to be done by finding lawyers who are willing to lay aside their current careers for an indeterminate amount of time, to take on a job that has no prospect of permanence and little prospect for promotion. One thing is certain, however: it involves investigating and perhaps prosecuting a particular individual. Can one imagine a less equitable manner of fulfilling the executive responsibility to investigate and prosecute? What would be the reaction if, in an area not covered by this statute, the Justice Department posted a public notice inviting applicants to assist in an investigation and possible prosecution of a certain prominent person? Does this not invite what Justice Jackson described as "picking the man and then searching the law books, or putting investigators to work, to pin some offense on him"? To be sure, the investigation must relate to the area of criminal offense specified by the life-tenured judges. But that has often been (and nothing prevents it from being) very broad—and should the independent counsel or his or her staff come up with something beyond that scope, nothing prevents him or her from asking the judges to expand his or her authority or, if that does not work, referring it to the Attorney General, whereupon the whole process would recommence and, if there was "reasonable basis to believe" that further investigation was warranted, that new offense would be referred to the Special Division, which would in all likelihood assign it to the same independent counsel. It seems to me not conducive to fairness. But even if it were entirely evident that unfairness was in fact the result—the judges hostile to the administration, the independent counsel an old foe of the President, the staff refugees from the recently defeated administration—*there would be no one accountable to the public to whom the blame could be assigned.*

I do not mean to suggest that anything of this sort (other than the inevitable self-selection of the prosecutory staff) occurred in the present case. I know and have the highest regard for the judges on the Special Division, and the independent counsel herself is a woman of accomplishment, impartiality, and integrity. But the fairness of a process must be adjudged on the basis of what it permits to happen, not what it produced in a particular case. It is true, of course, that a similar list of horribles could be attributed to an ordinary Justice Department prosecution—a vindictive prosecutor, an antagonistic staff, etc. But the difference is the difference that the Founders envisioned when they established a single Chief Executive accountable to the people: the blame can be assigned to someone who can be punished.

The above described possibilities of irresponsible conduct must, as I say, be considered in judging the constitutional acceptability of this process. But they will rarely occur, and in the average case the threat to fairness is quite different. As described in the brief filed on behalf of three ex-Attorneys General from each of the last three administrations:

> "The problem is less spectacular but much more worrisome. It is that the institutional environment of the Independent Counsel—specifically, her isolation from the Executive Branch and the internal checks and balances it supplies—is designed to heighten, not to check, all of the occupational hazards of the dedicated prosecutor; the danger of too narrow a focus, of the loss of perspective, of preoccupation with the pursuit of one alleged suspect to the exclusion of other interests." Brief for Edward H. Levi, Griffin B. Bell, and William French Smith as *Amici Curiae* 11.

It is, in other words, an additional advantage of the unitary Executive that it can achieve a more uniform application of the law. Perhaps that is not always achieved, but the mechanism to achieve it is there. The mini-Executive that is the independent counsel, however, operating in an area where so little is law and so much is discretion, is intentionally cut off from the unifying influence of the Justice Department, and from the perspective that multiple responsibilities provide. What would normally be regarded as a technical violation (there are no rules defining such things), may in his or her small world assume the proportions of an indictable offense. What would normally be regarded as an investigation that has reached the level of pursuing such picayune matters that it should be concluded, may to him or her be an investigation that ought to go on for another year. How frightening it must be to have your own independent counsel and staff appointed, with nothing else to do but to investigate you until investigation is no longer worthwhile—with whether it is worthwhile not depending upon what such judgments usually hinge on, competing responsibilities. And to have that counsel and staff decide, with no basis for comparison, whether what you have done is bad enough, willful enough, and provable enough, to warrant an indictment. How admirable the constitutional system that provides the means to avoid such a distortion. And how unfortunate the judicial decision that has permitted it.

3

The notion that every violation of law should be prosecuted, including—indeed, *especially*—every violation by those in high places, is an attractive one, and it would be risky to argue in an election campaign that that is not an absolutely overriding value. *Fiat justitia, ruat coelum.* Let justice be done, though the heavens may fall. The reality is, however, that it is not an absolutely overriding value, and it was with the hope that we would be able to acknowledge and apply such realities that the Constitution spared us, by life tenure, the necessity of election campaigns. I cannot imagine that there are not many thoughtful men and women in Congress who realize that the benefits of this legislation are far outweighed by its harmful effect upon our system of government, and even upon the nature of justice received by those men and women who agree to serve in the Executive Branch. But it is difficult to vote not to enact, and even more difficult to vote to repeal, a statute called, appropriately enough, the Ethics in Government Act. If Congress is controlled by the party other than the one to which the President belongs, it has little incentive to repeal it; if it is controlled by the same party, it dare not. By its shortsighted action today, I fear the Court has permanently encumbered the Republic with an institution that will do it great harm.

Worse than what it has done, however, is the manner in which it has done it. A government of laws means a government of rules. Today's decision on the basic issue of fragmentation of executive power is ungoverned by rule, and hence ungoverned by law. It extends into the very heart of our most significant constitutional function the "totality of the circumstances" mode of analysis that this Court has in recent years become fond of. Taking all things into account, we conclude that the power taken away from the President here is not really *too* much. The next time executive power is assigned to someone other than the President we may conclude, taking all things into account, that it *is* too much. That opinion, like this one, will not be confined by any rule. We will describe, as we have today (though I hope more accurately) the effects of the provision in question, and will authoritatively announce: "The President's need to control the exercise of the [subject officer's] discretion *is* so central to the functioning of the Executive Branch as to require complete control." This is not analysis; it is ad hoc judgment. And it fails to explain why it is not true that—as the text of the Constitution seems to require, as the Founders seemed to expect, and as our past cases have uniformly assumed—all purely executive power must be under the control of the President.

The ad hoc approach to constitutional adjudication has real attraction, even apart from its work-saving potential. It is guaranteed to produce a result, in every case, that will make a majority of the Court happy with the law. The law is, by definition, precisely what the majority thinks, taking all things into account, it *ought* to be. I prefer to rely upon the judgment of the wise men who constructed our system, and of the people who approved it, and of two centuries of history that have shown it to be sound. Like it or not, that judgment says, quite plainly, that "[t]he executive Power shall be vested in a President of the United States."

No secret repository of rights guaranteeing fairness

BMW of North America, Inc. v. Gore,
517 U.S. 559 (1996)

Justice SCALIA, with whom Justice THOMAS joins, dissenting.

Today we see the latest manifestation of this Court's recent and increasingly insistent "concern about punitive damages that 'run wild.'" *Pacific Mut. Life Ins. Co. v. Haslip,* 499 U.S. 1, 18, 111 S.Ct. 1032, 1043, 113 L.Ed.2d 1 (1991). Since the Constitution does not make that concern any of our business, the Court's activities in this area are an unjustified incursion into the province of state governments.

In earlier cases that were the prelude to this decision, I set forth my view that a state trial procedure that commits the decision whether to impose punitive damages, and the amount, to the discretion of the jury, subject to some judicial review for "reasonableness," furnishes a defendant with all the process that is "due." See *TXO Production Corp. v. Alliance Resources Corp.,* 509 U.S. 443, 470, 113 S.Ct. 2711, 2726, 125 L.Ed.2d 366 (1993) (SCALIA, J., concurring in judgment); *Haslip, supra,* at 25–28, 111 S.Ct., at 1046–1049 (SCALIA, J., concurring in judgment); cf. *Honda Motor Co. v. Oberg,* 512 U.S. 415, 435–436, 114 S.Ct. 2331, 2342, 129 L.Ed.2d 336 (1994) (SCALIA, J., concurring). I do not regard the Fourteenth Amendment's Due Process Clause as a secret repository of substantive guarantees against *599 "unfairness"—neither the unfairness of an excessive civil compensatory award, nor the unfairness of an "unreasonable" punitive award. What the Fourteenth Amendment's procedural guarantee assures is an opportunity to contest the reasonableness of a damages judgment in state court; but there is no federal guarantee a damages award actually *be* reasonable. See *TXO, supra,* at 471, 113 S.Ct., at 2727 (Scalia, J., concurring in judgment).

This view, which adheres to the text of the Due *Process* Clause, has not prevailed in our punitive damages cases. See *TPXO,* 509 U.S., at 453–462, 113 S.Ct., at 2718–2723 (plurality opinion); *id.,* at 478–481, 113 S.Ct., at 2730–2732 (O'Connor, J., dissenting); *Haslip, supra,* at 18, 111 S.Ct., at 1043. When, however, a constitutional doctrine adopted by the Court is not only mistaken but also insusceptible of principled application, I do not feel bound to give it *stare decisis* effect—indeed, I do not feel justified in doing so. See, *e.g., Witte v. United States,* 515 U.S. 389, 406, 115 S.Ct. 2199, 2209, 132 L.Ed.2d 351 (1995) (Scalia, J., concurring in judgment); *Walton v. Arizona,* 497 U.S. 639, 673, 110 S.Ct. 3047, 3067–3068, 111 L.Ed.2d 511 (1990) (Scalia, J., concurring in judgment in part and dissenting in part). Our punitive damages jurisprudence compels such a response. The Constitution provides no warrant for federalizing yet another aspect of our Nation's legal culture (no matter how much in need of correction it may be), and the application of the Court's new rule of constitutional law is constrained by no principle other than the Justices' subjective assessment of the "reasonableness" of the award in relation to the conduct for which it was assessed.

Because today's judgment represents the first instance of this Court's invalidation of a state-court punitive assessment as simply unreasonably large, I think it a proper occasion to discuss these points at some length.

I

The most significant aspects of today's decision—the identification of a "substantive due process" right against a "grossly excessive" award, and the concomitant assumption of ultimate authority to decide anew a matter of "reasonableness" resolved in lower court proceedings—are of course not new. *Haslip* and *TXO* revived the notion, moribund since its appearance in the first years of this century, that the measure of civil punishment poses a question of constitutional dimension to be answered by this Court. Neither of those cases, however, nor any of the precedents upon which they relied, actually took the step of declaring a punitive award unconstitutional simply because it was "too big."

At the time of adoption of the Fourteenth Amendment, it was well understood that punitive damages represent the assessment by the jury, as the voice of the community, of the measure of punishment the defendant deserved. See, *e.g.*, *Barry v. Edmunds,* 116 U.S. 550, 565, 6 S.Ct. 501, 509, 29 L.Ed. 729 (1886); *Missouri Pacific R. Co. v. Humes,* 115 U.S. 512, 521, 6 S.Ct. 110, 113, 29 L.Ed. 463 (1885); *Day v. Woodworth,* 13 How. 363, 371, 14 L.Ed. 181 (1852). See generally *Haslip, supra,* at 25–27, 111 S.Ct., at 1047–1048 (Scalia, J., concurring in judgment). Today's decision, though dressed up as a legal opinion, is really no more than a disagreement with the community's sense of indignation or outrage expressed in the punitive award of the Alabama jury, as reduced by the State Supreme Court. It reflects not merely, as the concurrence candidly acknowledges, "a judgment about a matter of degree," *ante,* at 1609; but a judgment about the appropriate degree of indignation or outrage, which is hardly an analytical determination.

There is no precedential warrant for giving our judgment priority over the judgment of state courts and juries on this matter. The only support for the Court's position is to be found in a handful of errant federal cases, bunched within a few years of one other, which invented the notion that an unfairly severe civil sanction amounts to a violation of constitutional liberties. These were the decisions upon which the *TXO* plurality relied in pronouncing that the Due Process Clause "imposes substantive limits 'beyond which penalties may not go,'" 509 U.S., at 454, 113 S.Ct., at 2718 (quoting *Seaboard Air Line R. Co. v. Seegers,* 207 U.S. 73, 78, 28 S.Ct. 28, 30, 52 L.Ed. 108 (1907)); see also 509 U.S., at 478–481, 113 S.Ct., at 2730–2732 (O'Connor, J., dissenting); *Haslip, supra,* 499 U.S., at 18, 111 S.Ct., at 1043. Although they are our precedents, they are themselves too shallowly rooted to justify the Court's recent undertaking. The only case relied upon in which the Court actually invalidated a civil sanction does not even support constitutional review for excessiveness, since it really concerned the validity, as a matter of *procedural* due process, of state legislation that imposed a significant penalty on a common carrier which lacked the means of determining the legality of its actions before the penalty was imposed. See *Southwestern Telegraph & Telephone Co. v. Danaher,* 238 U.S. 482, 489–491, 35 S.Ct. 886, 887–888, 59 L.Ed. 1419 (1915). The *amount* of the penalty was not a subject of independent scrutiny. As for the remaining cases, while the opinions do consider arguments that statutory penalties can, by reason of their excessiveness, violate due process, not a single one of these judgments invalidates a damages award. See *Seaboard, supra,* at 78–79, 28 S.Ct., at 30; *Waters-Pierce Oil Co. v. Texas (No. 1),* 212 U.S. 86, 111–112, 29 S.Ct. 220, 227, 53 L.Ed. 417 (1909); *Standard Oil Co. of Ind. v. Missouri,* 224 U.S. 270, 286, 290, 32 S.Ct. 406, 411, 412, 56 L.Ed. 760 (1912); *St. Louis, I.M. & S.R. Co. v. Williams,* 251 U.S. 63, 66–67, 40 S.Ct. 71, 73, 64 L.Ed. 139 (1919).

More importantly, this latter group of cases—which again are the *sole* precedential foundation put forward for the rule of constitutional law espoused by today's Court—simply fabricated the "substantive due process" right at issue. *Seaboard* assigned no precedent to its bald assertion that the Constitution imposes "limits beyond which penalties may not go," 207 U.S., at 78, 28 S.Ct., at 30. *Waters-Pierce* cited only *Coffey v. County of Harlan,* 204 U.S. 659, 27 S.Ct. 305, 51 L.Ed. 666 (1907), a case which inquired into the constitutionality of state *procedure, id.,* at 662–663, 27 S.Ct., at 305–306. *Standard Oil* simply cited *Waters-Pierce,* and *St. Louis, I.M. & S. R. Co.* offered in addition to these cases only *Collins v. Johnston,* 237 U.S. 502, 35 S.Ct. 649, 59 L.Ed. 1071 (1915), which said nothing to support the notion of a "substantive due process" right against excessive civil penalties, but to the contrary asserted that the prescribing and imposing of criminal punishment were "functions peculiarly belonging to the several States," *id.,* at 509–510, 35 S.Ct., at 652–653. Thus, the only authority for the Court's position is simply not authoritative. These cases fall far short of what is needed to supplant this country's longstanding practice regarding exemplary awards, see, *e.g., Haslip,* 499 U.S., at 15–18, 111 S.Ct., at 1041–1043; *id.,* at 25–28, 111 S.Ct., at 1047–1048 (Scalia, J., concurring in judgment).

II

One might understand the Court's eagerness to enter this field, rather than leave it with the state legislatures, if it had something useful to say. In fact, however, its opinion provides virtually no guidance to legislatures, and to state and federal courts, as to what a "constitutionally proper" level of punitive damages might be.

We are instructed at the outset of Part II of the Court's opinion—the beginner of its substantive analysis—that "the federal excessiveness inquiry ... begins with an identification of the state interests that a punitive award is designed to serve." *Ante,* at 1595. On first reading this, one is faced with the prospect that federal punitive damages law (the new field created by today's decision) will be beset by the sort of "interest analysis" that has laid waste the formerly comprehensible field of conflict of laws. The thought that each assessment of punitive damages, as to each offense, must be examined to determine the precise "state interests" pursued, is most unsettling. Moreover, if those "interests" are the most fundamental determinant of an award, one would think that due process would require the assessing jury to be *instructed* about them.

It appears, however (and I certainly hope), that all this is a false alarm. As Part II of the Court's opinion unfolds, it turns out to be directed, not to the question "How much punishment is too much?" but rather to the question "Which acts can be punished?" "Alabama does not have the power," the Court says, "to punish BMW for conduct that was lawful where it occurred and that had no impact on Alabama or its residents." *Ante,* at 1597. That may be true, though only in the narrow sense that a person cannot be *held liable to be punished* on the basis of a lawful act. But if a person has been held subject to punishment because he committed an *un*lawful act, the *degree* of his punishment assuredly *can* be increased on the basis of any other conduct of his that displays his wickedness, unlawful or not. Criminal sentences can be computed, we have said, on the basis of "information concerning every aspect of a defendant's life," *Williams v. New York,* 337 U.S. 241, 250–252, 69 S.Ct. 1079, 1085, 93 L.Ed. 1337 (1949). The Court at one point seems to acknowledge this, observing that, although a sentencing court "[cannot] properly *punish* lawful conduct," it may in assessing the penalty "consider ... lawful conduct that bears on the defendant's character." *Ante,* at 1598, n. 19. That concession is quite incompatible, however, with the later assertion that, since "neither the jury nor the trial court was presented with evidence that any of BMW's out-of-state conduct was unlawful," the Alabama Supreme Court "therefore properly eschewed reliance on BMW's out-of-state conduct, ... and based its remitted award solely on conduct that occurred within Alabama." *Ante*, at 1598. Why could the Supreme Court of Alabama not consider lawful (but disreputable) conduct, both inside and outside Alabama, for the purpose of assessing just how bad an actor BMW was?

The Court follows up its statement that "Alabama does not have the power ... to punish BMW for conduct that was lawful where it occurred" with the statement: "Nor may Alabama impose sanctions on BMW in order to deter conduct that is lawful in other jurisdictions." *Ante*, at 1597–1598. The Court provides us no citation of authority to support this proposition—other than the barely analogous cases cited earlier in the opinion, see *ante*, at 1596–1597—and I know of none.

These significant issues pronounced upon by the Court are not remotely presented for resolution in the present case. There is no basis for believing that Alabama has sought to control conduct elsewhere. The statutes at issue merely permit civil juries to treat conduct such as petitioner's as fraud, and authorize an award of appropriate punitive damages in the event the fraud is found to be "gross, oppressive, or malicious," Ala.Code § 6–11–20(b)(1) (1993). To be sure, respondent did invite the jury to consider out-of-state conduct in its calculation of damages, but any increase in the jury's initial award based on that consideration is not a component of the remitted judgment before us. As the Court several times recognizes, in computing the amount of the remitted award the Alabama Supreme Court—whether it was constitutionally required to or not—"expressly disclaimed any reliance on acts that occurred in other jurisdictions." *Ante*, at 1595 (internal quotation marks omitted); see also *ante*, at 1598. Thus, the only question presented by this case is whether that award, limited to petitioner's Alabama conduct and viewed in light of the factors identified as properly informing the inquiry, is excessive. The

Court's sweeping (and largely unsupported) statements regarding the relationship of punitive awards to lawful or unlawful out-of-state conduct are the purest dicta.

III

In Part III of its opinion, the Court identifies "[t]hree guideposts" that lead it to the conclusion that the award in this case is excessive: degree of reprehensibility, ratio between punitive award and plaintiff's actual harm, and legislative sanctions provided for comparable misconduct. *Ante,* at 1598–1604. The legal significance of these "guideposts" is nowhere explored, but their necessary effect is to establish federal standards governing the hitherto exclusively state law of damages. Apparently (though it is by no means clear) all three federal "guideposts" can be overridden if "necessary to deter future misconduct," *ante,* at 1603–1604—a loophole that will encourage state reviewing courts to uphold awards as necessary for the "adequat[e] protect[ion]" of state consumers, *ibid.* By effectively requiring state reviewing courts to concoct rationalizations—whether within the "guideposts" or through the loophole—to justify the intuitive punitive reactions of state juries, the Court accords neither category of institution the respect it deserves.

Of course it will not be easy for the States to comply with this new federal law of damages, no matter how willing they are to do so. In truth, the "guideposts" mark a road to nowhere; they provide no real guidance at all. As to "degree of reprehensibility" of the defendant's conduct, we learn that " 'nonviolent crimes are less serious than crimes marked by violence or the threat of violence,'" *ante,* at 1599 (quoting *Solem v. Helm,* 463 U.S. 277, 292–293, 103 S.Ct. 3001, 3011, 77 L.Ed.2d 637 (1983)), and that " 'trickery and deceit'" are "more reprehensible than negligence," *ante,* at 1599. As to the ratio of punitive to compensatory damages, we are told that a "'general concer[n] of reasonableness ... enter[s] into the constitutional calculus,'" *ante,* at 1602 (quoting *TXO,* 509 U.S., at 458, 113 S.Ct., at 2720)—though even "a breathtaking 500 to 1" will not necessarily do anything more than "'raise a suspicious judicial eyebrow,'" *ante,* at 1603 (quoting *TXO, supra,* at 481, 113 S.Ct., at 2732 (O'Connor, J., dissenting), an opinion which, when confronted with that "breathtaking" ratio, approved it). And as to legislative sanctions provided for comparable misconduct, they should be accorded " 'substantial deference,'" *ante,* at 1603 (quoting *Browning-Ferris Industries of Vt., Inc. v. Kelco Disposal, Inc.,* 492 U.S. 257, 301, 109 S.Ct. 2909, 2934, 106 L.Ed.2d 219 (1989) (O'Connor, J., concurring in part and dissenting in part)). One expects the Court to conclude: "To thine own self be true."

These crisscrossing platitudes yield no real answers in no real cases. And it must be noted that the Court nowhere says that these three "guideposts" are the *only* guideposts; indeed, it makes very clear that they are not—explaining away the earlier opinions that do not really follow these "guideposts" on the basis of *additional* factors, thereby "reiterat[ing] our rejection of a categorical approach." *Ante,* at 1602. In other words, even these utter platitudes, if they should ever happen to produce an answer, may be overridden by other unnamed considerations. The Court has constructed a framework that does not genuinely constrain, that does not inform state legislatures and lower courts—that does nothing at all except confer an artificial air of doctrinal analysis upon its essentially ad hoc determination that this particular award of punitive damages was not "fair."

The Court distinguishes today's result from *Haslip* and *TXO* partly on the ground that "the record in this case discloses no deliberate false statements, acts of affirmative misconduct, or concealment of evidence of improper motive, such as were present in *Haslip* and *TXO.*" *Ante,* at 1601. This seemingly rejects the findings necessarily made by the jury—that petitioner had committed a fraud that was "gross, oppressive, or malicious," Ala.Code § 6–11–20(b)(1) (1993). Perhaps that rejection is intentional; the Court does not say.

The relationship between judicial application of the new "guideposts" and jury findings poses a real problem for the Court, since as a matter of logic there is no more justification for ignoring the jury's determination as to *how* reprehensible petitioner's conduct was (*i.e.,* how much it deserves to be punished), than there is for ignoring its determination that it was reprehensible *at all* (*i.e.,* that the wrong was willful and punitive damages are therefore recoverable). That the issue has been framed in terms of a constitutional right against unreasonably *excessive* awards should not obscure the fact that the logical and necessary consequence of the Court's approach is the recognition of a constitutional right against unreasonably *imposed* awards as well. The elevation of "fairness" in punishment to a principle of "substantive due process" means that every punitive award unreasonably imposed is unconstitutional; such an award is by definition excessive, since it attaches a penalty to conduct undeserving of punishment. Indeed, if the Court is correct, it must be that every claim that a state jury's award of *compensatory* damages is "unreasonable" (because not supported by the evidence) amounts to an assertion of constitutional injury. See *TXO, supra,* at 471, 113 S.Ct., at 2727 (Scalia, J. concurring in judgment). And the same would be true for determinations of liability. By today's logic, *every* dispute as to evidentiary sufficiency in a state civil suit poses a question of constitutional moment, subject to review in this Court. That is a stupefying proposition.

For the foregoing reasons, I respectfully dissent.

An unprecedented intrusion upon state sovereignty
Lawyer v. Department of Justice, 521 U.S. 567 (1997)

Justice Scalia, with whom Justice O'Connor, Justice Kennedy, and Justice Thomas join, dissenting.

The Court today affirms a Federal District Court's redrawing of Florida Senate District 21, despite the fact that the District Court never determined that District 21 was unconstitutional, and never gave the State an opportunity to do its own redrawing of the district to remedy whatever unconstitutional features it contained. In my view, the District Court's actions represent an unprecedented intrusion upon state sovereignty.

I

The District Court held that it could exercise its authority under the Fourteenth Amendment to "compel the nullification and re-establishment of state legislative boundaries" without finding a violation of the Fourteenth Amendment, so long as "the case presents a sufficient evidentiary and legal basis to warrant the *bona fide* intervention of a federal court into matters typically reserved to a state." 920 F.Supp. 1248, 1251–1252 (M.D.Fla.1996). Although acknowledging that the "'[d]efendants and defendant-intervenors deny these assertions [of unconstitutionality],'" *id.*, at 1252–1253, n. 3 (quoting Settlement Agreement), the District Court determined that the claim that District 21 was unconstitutional was "fairly litigable," *id.*, at 1253, n. 3, and found this enough to justify its reapportionment order.

The only authority cited by the District Court for the proposition that a court can mandate a remedy without finding liability is Justice O'Connor's concurring opinion in *Wygant v. Jackson Bd. of Ed.*, 476 U.S. 267, 284, 106 S.Ct. 1842, 1852, 90 L.Ed.2d 260 (1986). But that opinion has no bearing on the present case. It dealt with the question whether a school board could, consistent with the Constitution, implement an affirmative-action program without first making contemporaneous findings that such a program is justified by specific instances of past discrimination. *Id.*, at 289-291, 106 S.Ct., at 1854–1856. Quite obviously, whether a State may take *voluntary* action without first determining that it has violated the law has nothing to do with whether a federal court may *impose* a remedy without first determining that the State has violated the law.

The Court evidently believes that an adjudication of unconstitutionality of District 21 was unnecessary here because the State entered into a consent agreement accepting judicial imposition of Plan 386. For this proposition it relies upon *Firefighters v. Cleveland,* 478 U.S. 501, 106 S.Ct. 3063, 92 L.Ed.2d 405 (1986), which said that "it is the parties' agreement that serves as the source of the [District Court's] authority to enter ... judgment...." *Id.*, at 522, 106 S.Ct., at 3075. However, that passage from *Firefighters* is of no help to the Court-even putting aside the fact that the "agreement" there at issue, unlike the one here, was an agreement to remedy unlawful conduct (a "pattern of racial discrimination") that *had been adjudged, id.*, at 506, 511–512, 106 S.Ct., at 3067, 3069-3070. *Firefighters* was a Title VII action by minority firefighters, alleging that the city discriminated against them in promotions. A union representing the majority of the city's firefighters intervened as a party-plaintiff and objected to the settlement, contending, among other things, that its consent was required in order for the District Court to enter a consent decree. We disagreed. The minority firefighters and the city, we said, could have reached an out-of-court agreement to resolve their dispute. See *id.*, at 522–523, and n. 13, 106 S.Ct., at 3075–3076, and n. 13. "[T]he choice of an enforcement scheme-whether to rely on contractual remedies or to have an agreement entered as a consent decree-is itself made voluntarily by the parties." *Id.*, at 523, 106 S.Ct., at 3076.

In today's case, by contrast, neither the appellant nor the other original plaintiffs (now appellees) could have concluded a binding out-of-court "redistricting agreement" with representatives of the Florida Legislature, or with the state attorney general-and the Court does not contend otherwise. The Florida Constitution, Art. III, § 16, requires the legislature to draw districts "by joint resolution," and provides no authority for the attorney general to do so. Any "redistricting agreement" entered into by these officials with individual voters would obviously be null and void. And a court decree that does not purport to be in remediation of an adjudged violation of law cannot make it binding. See *Firefighters, supra,* at 522–523, 106 S.Ct., at 3075–3076. See also, *e.g., Perkins v. Chicago Heights,* 47 F.3d 212, 216 (C.A.7 1995).

These principles would suffice to invalidate an unauthorized private agreement as the basis for a federal judicial decree in even the ordinary case, but they should apply even more rigorously to an agreement purportedly supporting a federal judicial decree of state reapportionment, which we have described as an "unwelcome obligation," *Connor v. Finch,* 431 U.S. 407, 415, 97 S.Ct. 1828, 1834, 52 L.Ed.2d 465 (1977), that should be undertaken by a district court only as a last resort, see, *e.g., White v. Weiser,* 412 U.S. 783, 93 S.Ct. 2348, 37 L.Ed.2d 335 (1973). Indeed, even if it were possible for the Florida Legislature to authorize two of its members to negotiate an apportionment agreement that could be the basis for a federal court decree, one would think that the special solicitude we have shown for preservation of the States' apportionment authority would cause the court to demand clearer credentials on the part of those who purport to speak for the legislature. The District Court asserted that "Florida's House and Senate ... manifested ... the authority to consent," 920 F.Supp., at 1251, but it points to no resolution conferring such authority upon the individual legislators before the court; and as to the Senate, at least, there is some evidence no such authority exists. The record contains a letter from State Senator Howard C. Forman to the District Court reading in part as follows:

> "This letter is intended to communicate to you in the strongest possible terms that the Florida Senate has not agreed to any proposed settlement. As a constitutionally established collegial body, the Florida Senate can agree to nothing without open debate and action by the entire body. As a duly elected Member of the Florida Senate, I have never waived my constitutional duty and responsibility to participate in all Senate matters. And, under no circumstances does any individual Senator, or group of individual Senators, have the right to agree to anything in my name....
>
> "Therefore, I challenge any representation that the Florida Senate has agreed to any proposed settlement in this case." Record 152.

But in fact all these inquiries into authorization to enter private agreements are supererogatory. Even an *authorized* private agreement cannot serve as the basis for a federal apportionment decree. We have said explicitly, and in unmistakable terms, that "[f]ederal courts are *barred* from intervening in state apportionment in the absence of a *violation* of federal law." *Voinovich v. Quilter*, 507 U.S. 146, 156, 113 S.Ct. 1149, 1156, 122 L.Ed.2d 500 (1993) (emphasis added). As Chief

Judge Tjoflat's concurrence below correctly stated, "to enter the judgment in question, the court must find that District 21 is unconstitutional." 920 F.Supp., at 1256–1257. I would adhere to that principle.

Finally, I find no merit in the Court's apparent suggestion, *ante,* at 2193, that appellant has no standing to complain of this defect. A judicial decree entered without jurisdiction has mooted his suit. Surely that is enough to sustain his appeal.

II

The District Court's failure to find the pre-existing District 21 unconstitutional is alone enough to require reversal of the judgment. But the District Court committed a second error, in failing to give the Florida Legislature the opportunity to redraw the district before imposing a court-ordered solution. We have repeatedly emphasized that federal interference with state districting "represents a serious intrusion on the most vital of local functions," *Miller v. Johnson,* 515 U.S. 900, 915, 115 S.Ct. 2475, 2488, 132 L.Ed.2d 762 (1995), and that "reapportionment[, which] is primarily the duty and responsibility of the State," *Chapman v. Meier,* 420 U.S. 1, 27, 95 S.Ct. 751, 766, 42 L.Ed.2d 766 (1975), "'is primarily a matter for legislative consideration and determination,'" *Connor v. Finch, supra,* at 414, 97 S.Ct., at 1833 (quoting *Reynolds v. Sims,* 377 U.S. 533, 586, 84 S.Ct. 1362, 1394, 12 L.Ed.2d 506 (1964)). "'[J]udicial relief becomes appropriate,'" we have said, "'only when a legislature fails to reapportion according to federal constitutional requisites in a timely fashion after having had an adequate opportunity to do so.'" *White v. Weiser, supra,* at 794–795, 93 S.Ct., at 2354 (quoting *Reynolds, supra,* at 586, 84 S.Ct., at 1394). See also *Growe v. Emison,* 507 U.S. 25, 33-34, 113 S.Ct. 1075, 1080-1081, 122 L.Ed.2d 388 (1993); *Upham v. Seamon,*

456 U.S. 37, 41–42, 102 S.Ct. 1518, 1521–1522, 71 L.Ed.2d 725 (1982) (*per curiam*); *McDaniel v. Sanchez,* 452 U.S. 130, 142, 101 S.Ct. 2224, 2232, 68 L.Ed.2d 724 (1981); *Wise v. Lipscomb,* 437 U.S. 535, 540, 98 S.Ct. 2493, 2497, 57 L.Ed.2d 411 (1978) (opinion of White, J.). The District Court's failure to give Florida a reasonable opportunity to craft its own solution after a judicial finding that the current districting was unconstitutional—or even (since here such a finding was never made) after the judicial finding that a constitutional claim is "fairly litigable"—was most assuredly error.

The District Court repeatedly referred to Plan 386 as a "legislative solution," 920 F.Supp., at 1255, and the concurrence described it as a "plan that the Florida legislature has proposed," *id.,* at 1257. But judicial characterization does not overcome reality. The fact that the Speaker of Florida's House of Representatives and the President of Florida's Senate participated in the negotiations and consented to the settlement does not magically convert Plan 386 into a Florida law. The "opportunity to apportion" that our case law requires the state legislature to be afforded is an opportunity to apportion through normal legislative processes, not through courthouse negotiations attended by one member of each House, followed by a court decree.

Appellees contend that the District Court actually offered the legislature the opportunity to redistrict, but that the legislature declined. This contention is based upon the fact that the representatives of the Florida Legislature informed the District Court, prior to any proceedings on the merits, that the legislature would likely not *sua sponte* redraw the districts in response to *Miller v. Johnson, supra,* and on the status reports filed by the Florida Senate, see *ante,* at 2193, n. 5. But the requisite opportunity that our cases describe is an opportunity to redraw districts after the extant districts have been ruled unconstitutional-not after a Supreme Court case has been announced which may or may not ultimately lead to a ruling that the extant districts are unconstitutional. See, *e.g., Growe, supra,* at 34, 113 S.Ct., at 1081; *McDaniel, supra,* at 142, 101 S.Ct., at 2232; *Reynolds, supra,* at 585-586, 84 S.Ct., at 1393–1394. The State is under no obligation to redistrict unless and until a determination has been made that there has been a violation of federal law.

* * *

Because the District Court lacked the authority to mandate redistricting without first having found a constitutional violation; and because the District Court failed to give the State an opportunity to redistrict on its own after notice of the constitutional violation (or even after notice of the court's intention to proceed with its own plan), I would reverse the judgment of the District Court and remand for further proceedings. Given my conclusion on appellant's first two challenges to the District Court's judgment, I have no occasion to consider the constitutionality of the court-drawn district, Plan 386.

I respectfully dissent.

The very core of liberty
Hamdi v. Rumsfeld,
542 U.S. 507 (2004)

Justice Scalia, with whom Justice Stevens joins, dissenting.

Petitioner Yaser Hamdi, a presumed American citizen, has been imprisoned without charge or hearing in the Norfolk and Charleston Naval Brigs for more than two years, on the allegation that he is an enemy combatant who bore arms against his country for the Taliban. His father claims to the contrary, that he is an inexperienced aid worker caught in the wrong place at the wrong time. This case brings into conflict the competing demands of national security and our citizens' constitutional right to personal liberty. Although I share the plurality's evident unease as it seeks to reconcile the two, I do not agree with its resolution.

Where the Government accuses a citizen of waging war against it, our constitutional tradition has been to prosecute him in federal court for treason or some other crime. Where the exigencies of war prevent that, the Constitution's Suspension Clause, Art. I, § 9, cl. 2, allows Congress to relax the usual protections temporarily. Absent suspension, however, the Executive's assertion of military exigency has not been thought sufficient to permit detention without charge. No one contends that the congressional Authorization for Use of Military Force, on which the Government relies to justify its actions here, is an implementation of the Suspension Clause. Accordingly, I would reverse the judgment below.

I

The very core of liberty secured by our Anglo-Saxon system of separated powers has been freedom from indefinite imprisonment at the will of the Executive. Blackstone stated this principle clearly:

> "Of great importance to the public is the preservation of this personal liberty: for if once it were left in the power of any, the highest, magistrate to imprison arbitrarily whomever he or his officers thought proper ... there would soon be an end of all other rights and immunities. ... To bereave a man of life, or by violence to confiscate his estate, without accusation or trial, would be so gross and notorious an act of despotism, as must at once convey the alarm of tyranny throughout the whole kingdom. But confinement of the person, by secretly hurrying him to gaol, where his sufferings are unknown or forgotten; is a less public, a less striking, and therefore a more dangerous engine of arbitrary government. ...
>
> "To make imprisonment lawful, it must either be, by process from the courts of judicature, or by warrant from some legal officer, having authority to commit to prison; which warrant must be in writing, under the hand and seal of the magistrate, and express the causes of the commitment, in order to be examined into (if necessary) upon a *habeas corpus*. If there be no cause expressed, the gaoler is not bound to detain the prisoner. For the law judges in this respect, ... that it is unreasonable to send a prisoner, and not to signify withal the crimes alleged against him." 1 W. Blackstone, *Commentaries on the Laws of England* 131–133 (1765) (hereinafter *Blackstone*).

These words were well known to the Founders. Hamilton quoted from this very passage in *The Federalist* No. 84, p. 444 (G. Carey & J. McClellan eds. 2001). The two ideas central to Blackstone's understanding—due process as the right secured, and habeas corpus as the instrument by which due process could be insisted upon by a citizen illegally imprisoned found expression in the Constitution's Due Process and Suspension

Clauses. See Amdt. 5; Art. I, § 9, cl. 2.

The gist of the Due Process Clause, as understood at the founding and since, was to force the Government to follow those common-law procedures traditionally deemed necessary before depriving a person of life, liberty, or property. When a citizen was deprived of liberty because of alleged criminal conduct, those procedures typically required committal by a magistrate followed by indictment and trial. See, *e.g.*, 2 & 3 Philip & Mary, ch. 10 (1555); 3 J. Story, *Commentaries on the Constitution of the United States* § 1783, p. 661 (1833) (hereinafter *Story*) (equating "due process of law" with "due presentment or indictment, and being brought in to answer thereto by due process of the common law"). The Due Process Clause "in effect affirms the right of trial according to the process and proceedings of the common law." *Ibid.* See also T. Cooley, *General Principles of Constitutional Law* 224 (1880) ("When life and liberty are in question, there must in every instance be judicial proceedings; and that requirement implies an accusation, a hearing before an impartial tribunal, with proper jurisdiction, and a conviction and judgment before the punishment can be inflicted" (internal quotation marks omitted)).

To be sure, certain types of permissible *non* criminal detention—that is, those not dependent upon the contention that the citizen had committed a criminal act—did not require the protections of criminal procedure. However, these fell into a limited number of well-recognized exceptions—civil commitment of the mentally ill, for example, and temporary detention in quarantine of the infectious. See *Opinion on the Writ of Habeas Corpus*, Wilm. 77, 88–92, 97 Eng. Rep. 29, 36–37 (H.L.1758) (Wilmot, J.). It is unthinkable that the Executive could render otherwise criminal grounds for detention noncriminal merely by disclaiming an intent to prosecute, or by asserting that it was incapacitating dangerous offenders rather than punishing wrongdoing. Cf. *Kansas v. Hendricks,* 521 U.S. 346, 358, 117 S.Ct. 2072, 138 L.Ed.2d 501 (1997) ("A finding of dangerousness, standing alone, is ordinarily not a sufficient ground upon which to justify indefinite involuntary commitment").

These due process rights have historically been vindicated by the writ of habeas corpus. In England before the founding, the writ developed into a tool for challenging executive confinement. It was not always effective. For example, in *Darnel's Case,* 3 How. St. Tr. 1 (K.B.1627), King Charles I detained without charge several individuals for failing to assist England's war against France and Spain. The prisoners sought writs of habeas corpus, arguing that without specific charges, "imprisonment shall not continue on for a time, but for ever; and the subjects of this kingdom may be restrained of their liberties perpetually." *Id.,* at 8. The Attorney General replied that the Crown's interest in protecting the realm justified imprisonment in "a matter of state ... not ripe nor timely" for the ordinary process of accusation and trial. *Id.,* at 37. The court denied relief, producing widespread outrage, and Parliament responded with the Petition of Right, accepted by the King in 1628, which expressly prohibited imprisonment without formal charges, see 3 Car. 1, ch. 1, §§ 5, 10.

The struggle between subject and Crown continued, and culminated in the Habeas Corpus Act of 1679, 31 Car. 2, ch. 2, described by Blackstone as a "second *magna carta,* and stable bulwark of our liberties." 1 *Blackstone* 133. The Act governed all persons "committed or detained ... for any crime." § 3. In cases other than felony or treason plainly expressed in the warrant of commitment, the Act required release upon appropriate sureties (unless the commitment was for a nonbailable offense). *Ibid.* Where the commitment was for felony or high treason, the Act did not require immediate release, but instead required the Crown to commence criminal proceedings within a specified time. § 7. If the prisoner was not "indicted some Time in the next Term," the judge was "required ... to set at Liberty the Prisoner upon Bail" unless the King was unable to produce his witnesses. *Ibid.* Able or no, if the prisoner was not brought to trial by the *next* succeeding term, the Act provided that "he shall be discharged from his Imprisonment." *Ibid.* English courts sat four terms per year, see 3 *Blackstone* 275–277, so the practical effect of this provision was that imprisonment without indictment or trial for felony or high treason under § 7 would not exceed approximately three to six months.

The writ of habeas corpus was preserved in the Constitution—the only common-law writ to be explicitly mentioned. See Art. I, § 9, cl. 2. Hamilton lauded "the establishment of the writ of *habeas corpus*" in his Federalist defense as a means to protect against "the practice of arbitrary imprisonments ... in all ages, [one of] the favourite and most formidable instruments of tyranny." *The Federalist* No. 84, at 444. Indeed, availability of the writ under the new Constitution (along with the requirement of trial by jury in criminal cases, see Art. III, § 2, cl. 3) was his basis for arguing that additional, explicit procedural protections were unnecessary. See *The Federalist* No. 83, at 433.

II

The allegations here, of course, are no ordinary accusations of criminal activity. Yaser Esam Hamdi has been imprisoned because the Government believes he participated in the waging of war against the United States. The relevant question, then, is whether there is a different, special procedure for imprisonment of a citizen accused of wrongdoing *by aiding the enemy in wartime.*

A

Justice O'Connor, writing for a plurality of this Court, asserts that captured enemy combatants (other than those suspected of war crimes) have traditionally been detained until the cessation of hostilities and then released. *Ante,* at 2640. That is probably an accurate description of wartime practice with respect to enemy *aliens.* The tradition with respect to American citizens, however, has been quite different. Citizens aiding the enemy have been treated as traitors subject to the criminal process.

As early as 1350, England's Statute of Treasons made it a crime to "levy War against our Lord the King in his Realm, or be adherent to the King's Enemies in his Realm, giving to them Aid and Comfort, in the Realm, or elsewhere." 25 Edw. 3, Stat. 5, c. 2. In his 1762 *Discourse on High Treason*, Sir Michael Foster explained:

> "With regard to Natural-born Subjects there can be no Doubt. They owe Allegiance to the Crown at all Times and in all Places.
>
> .....
>
> "The joining with Rebels in an Act of Rebellion, or with Enemies in Acts of Hostility, will make a Man a Traitor: in the one Case within the Clause of Levying War, in the other within that of Adhering to the King's enemies.
>
> .....
>
> "States in Actual Hostility with Us, though no War be solemnly Declared, are Enemies within the meaning of the Act. And therefore in an Indictment on the Clause of Adhering to the King's Enemies, it is sufficient to Aver that the Prince or State Adhered to *is an Enemy,* without shewing any War Proclaimed .... And if the Subject of a Foreign Prince in Amity with Us, invadeth the Kingdom without Commission from his Sovereign, He is an Enemy. And a Subject of *Eng-*

> *land* adhering to Him is a Traitor within this Clause of the Act." *A Report of Some Proceedings on the Commission ... for the Trial of the Rebels in the Year 1746 in the County of Surry, and of Other Crown Cases*, Introduction, § 1, p. 183; Ch. 2, § 8, p. 216; § 12, p. 219.

Subjects accused of levying war against the King were routinely prosecuted for treason. *E.g., Harding's Case,* 2 Ventris 315, 86 Eng. Rep. 461 (K.B.1690); *Trial of Parkyns,* 13 How. St. Tr. 63 (K.B.1696); *Trial of Vaughan,* 13 How. St. Tr. 485 (K.B.1696); *Trial of Downie,* 24 How. St. Tr. 1 (1794). The Founders inherited the understanding that a citizen's levying war against the Government was to be punished criminally. The Constitution provides: "Treason against the United States, shall consist only in levying War against them, or in adhering to their Enemies, giving them Aid and Comfort"; and establishes a heightened proof requirement (two witnesses) in order to "convic[t]" of that offense. Art. III, § 3, cl. 1.

In more recent times, too, citizens have been charged and tried in Article III courts for acts of war against the United States, even when their noncitizen co-conspirators were not. For example, two American citizens alleged to have participated during World War I in a spying conspiracy on behalf of Germany were tried in federal court. See *United States v. Fricke,* 259 F. 673 (S.D.N.Y.1919); *United States v. Robinson,* 259 F. 685 (S.D.N.Y.1919). A German member of the same conspiracy was subjected to military process. See *United States ex rel. Wessels v. McDonald,* 265 F. 754 (E.D.N.Y.1920). During World War II, the famous German saboteurs of *Ex parte Quirin,* 317 U.S. 1, 63 S.Ct. 2, 87 L.Ed. 3 (1942), received military process, but the citizens who associated with them (with the exception of one citizen-saboteur, discussed below) were punished under the criminal process. See *Haupt v. United States,* 330 U.S. 631, 67 S.Ct. 874, 91 L.Ed. 1145 (1947); L. Fisher, Nazi

Saboteurs on Trial 80–84 (2003); see also *Cramer v. United States,* 325 U.S. 1, 65 S.Ct. 918, 89 L.Ed. 1441 (1945).

The modern treason statute is 18 U.S.C. § 2381; it basically tracks the language of the constitutional provision. Other provisions of Title 18 criminalize various acts of warmaking and adherence to the enemy. See, *e.g.*, § 32 (destruction of aircraft or aircraft facilities), § 2332a (use of weapons of mass destruction), § 2332b (acts of terrorism transcending national boundaries), § 2339A (providing material support to terrorists), § 2339B (providing material support to certain terrorist organizations), § 2382 (misprision of treason), § 2383 (rebellion or insurrection), § 2384 (seditious conspiracy), § 2390 (enlistment to serve in armed hostility against the United States). See also 31 CFR § 595.204 (2003) (prohibiting the "making or receiving of any contribution of funds, goods, or services" to terrorists); 50 U.S.C. § 1705(b) (criminalizing violations of 31 CFR § 595.204). The only citizen other than Hamdi known to be imprisoned in connection with military hostilities in Afghanistan against the United States *was* subjected to criminal process and convicted upon a guilty plea. See *United States v. Lindh,* 212 F.Supp.2d 541 (E.D.Va.2002) (denying motions for dismissal); Seelye, N.Y. Times, Oct. 5, 2002, p. A1, col. 5.

B

There are times when military exigency renders resort to the traditional criminal process impracticable. English law accommodated such exigencies by allowing legislative suspension of the writ of habeas corpus for brief periods. Blackstone explained:

> "And yet sometimes, when the state is in real danger, even this [*i.e.*, executive detention] may be a necessary measure.

> But the happiness of our constitution is, that it is not left to the executive power to determine when the danger of the state is so great, as to render this measure expedient. For the parliament only, or legislative power, whenever it sees proper, can authorize the crown, by suspending the *habeas corpus* act for a short and limited time, to imprison suspected persons without giving any reason for so doing .... In like manner this experiment ought only to be tried in cases of extreme emergency; and in these the nation parts with it[s] libertyfor a while, in order to preserve it for ever." 1 *Blackstone* 132.

Where the Executive has not pursued the usual course of charge, committal, and conviction, it has historically secured the Legislature's explicit approval of a suspension. In England, Parliament on numerous occasions passed temporary suspensions in times of threatened invasion or rebellion. *E.g.*, 1 W. & M., c. 7 (1688) (threatened return of James II); 7 & 8 Will. 3, c. 11 (1696) (same); 17 Geo. 2, c. 6 (1744) (threatened French invasion); 19 Geo. 2, c. 1 (1746) (threatened rebellion in Scotland); 17 Geo. 3, c. 9 (1777) (the American Revolution). Not long after Massachusetts had adopted a clause in its constitution explicitly providing for habeas corpus, see Mass. Const. pt. 2, ch. 6, art. VII (1780), reprinted in 3 *Federal and State Constitutions, Colonial Charters and Other Organic Laws* 1888, 1910 (F. Thorpe ed.1909), it suspended the writ in order to deal with Shay's Rebellion, see Act for Suspending the Privilege of the Writ of Habeas Corpus, ch. 10, 1786 Mass. Acts p. 510.

Our Federal Constitution contains a provision explicitly permitting suspension, but limiting the situations in which it may be invoked: "The Privilege of the Writ of Habeas Corpus shall not be suspended, unless when in Cases of Rebellion or Invasion the public Safety may require it." Art. I, § 9, cl. 2. Although this provision does not state that suspension must be effected by, or authorized by, a legislative act, it has been so understood, consistent with English practice and the Clause's placement in Article I. See *Ex parte Bollman,* 4 Cranch 75, 101, 2 L.Ed. 554 (1807); *Ex parte Merryman,* 17 F. Cas. 144, 151–152 (C.D.Md. 1861) (Taney, C. J., rejecting Lincoln's unauthorized suspension); 3 *Story* § 1336, at 208–209.

The Suspension Clause was by design a safety valve, the Constitution's only "express provision for exercise of extraordinary authority because of a crisis," *Youngstown Sheet & Tube Co. v. Sawyer,* 343 U.S. 579, 650, 72 S.Ct. 863, 96 L.Ed. 1153 (1952) (Jackson, J., concurring). Very early in the Nation's history, President Jefferson unsuccessfully sought a suspension of habeas corpus to deal with Aaron Burr's conspiracy to overthrow the Government. See 16 Annals of Congress 402–425 (1807). During the Civil War, Congress passed its first Act authorizing executive suspension of the writ of habeas corpus, see Act of Mar. 3, 1863, 12 Stat. 755, to the relief of those many who thought President Lincoln's unauthorized proclamations of suspension (*e.g.,* Proclamation No. 1, 13 Stat. 730) unconstitutional. Later Presidential proclamations of suspension relied upon the congressional authorization, *e.g.,* Proclamation No. 7, 13 Stat. 734. During Reconstruction, Congress passed the Ku Klux Klan Act, which included a provision authorizing suspension of the writ, invoked by President Grant in quelling a rebellion in nine South Carolina counties. See Act of Apr. 20, 1871, ch. 22, § 4, 17 Stat. 14; A Proclamation [of Oct. 17, 1871], 7 *Compilation of the Messages and Papers of the Presidents* 136–138 (J. Richardson ed. 1899) (hereinafter *Messages and Papers*); *id.,* at 138–139.

Two later Acts of Congress provided broad suspension authority to governors of U.S. possessions. The Philippine Civil Government Act of 1902 provided that the Governor of the Philippines could suspend the writ in case of rebellion, insurrection, or invasion. Act of July 1, 1902, ch. 1369, § 5, 32 Stat. 692. In 1905 the writ was suspended for nine months by proclamation of the Governor. See *Fisher v. Baker,* 203 U.S. 174, 179–181, 27 S.Ct. 135, 51 L.Ed. 142 (1906). The Hawaiian Organic Act of 1900 likewise provided that the Governor of Hawaii could suspend the writ in case of rebellion or invasion (or threat thereof). Ch. 339, § 67, 31 Stat. 153.

III

Of course the extensive historical evidence of criminal convictions and habeas suspensions does not *necessarily* refute the Government's position in this case. When the writ is suspended, the Government is entirely free from judicial oversight. It does not claim such total liberation here, but argues that it need only produce what it calls "some evidence" to satisfy a habeas court that a detained individual is an enemy combatant. See Brief for Respondents 34. Even if suspension of the writ on the one hand, and committal for criminal charges on the other hand, have been the only *traditional* means of dealing with citizens who levied war against their own country, it is theoretically possible that the Constitution does not *require* a choice between these alternatives.

I believe, however, that substantial evidence does refute that possibility. First, the text of the 1679 Habeas Corpus Act makes clear that indefinite imprisonment on reasonable suspicion is not an available option of treatment for those accused of aiding the enemy, absent a suspension of the writ. In the United States, this Act was read as "enforc[ing] the common law," *Ex parte Watkins,* 3 Pet. 193, 202, 7 L.Ed. 650 (1830), and shaped the early understanding of the scope of the writ. As noted above, see *supra,* at 2662, § 7 of the Act specifically addressed those committed for high treason, and provided a remedy if they were not *indicted and tried* by the second succeeding court term. That remedy was *not* a bobtailed judicial inquiry into whether there were reasonable grounds to believe the prisoner had taken up arms against the King. Rather, if the prisoner was not indicted and tried within the prescribed time, "he shall be discharged from his Imprisonment." 31 Car. 2, c. 2, § 7. The Act does not contain any exception for wartime. That omission is conspicuous, since § 7 explicitly addresses the offense of "High Treason," which often involved offenses of a military nature. See cases cited *supra,* at 2663.

Writings from the founding generation also suggest that, without exception, the only constitutional alternatives are to charge the crime or suspend the writ. In 1788, Thomas Jefferson wrote to James Madison questioning the need for a Suspension Clause in cases of rebellion in the proposed Constitution. His letter illustrates the constraints under which the Founders understood themselves to operate:

> "Why suspend the Hab. corp. in insurrections and rebellions? The parties who may be arrested may be charged instantly with a well defined crime. Of course the judge will remand them. If the publick safety requires that the government should have a man imprisoned on less probable testimony in those than in other emergencies; let him be taken and tried, retaken and retried, while the necessity continues, only giving him redress against the government for damages." 13 *Papers of Thomas Jefferson* 442 (July 31, 1788) (J. Boyd ed.1956).

A similar view was reflected in the 1807 House debates over suspension during the armed uprising that came to be known as Burr's conspiracy:

> "With regard to those persons who may be implicated in the conspiracy, if the writ of habeas corpus be not suspended, what will be the consequence? When apprehended, they will

> be brought before a court of justice, who will decide whether there is any evidence that will justify their commitment for farther prosecution. From the communication of the Executive, it appeared there was sufficient evidence to authorize their commitment. Several months would elapse before their final trial, which would give time to collect evidence, and if this shall be sufficient, they will not fail to receive the punishment merited by their crimes, and inflicted by the laws of their country." 16 *Annals of Congress*, at 405 (remarks of Rep. Burwell).

The absence of military authority to imprison citizens indefinitely in wartime—whether or not a probability of treason had been established by means less than jury trial—was confirmed by three cases decided during and immediately after the War of 1812. In the first, *In re Stacy,* 10 Johns. (N.Y.1813), a citizen was taken into military custody on suspicion that he was "carrying provisions and giving information to the enemy." *Id.,* at *330 (emphasis deleted). Stacy petitioned for a writ of habeas corpus, and, after the defendant custodian attempted to avoid complying, Chief Justice Kent ordered attachment against him. Kent noted that the military was "without any color of authority in any military tribunal to try a citizen for that crime" and that it was "holding him in the closest confinement, and contemning the civil authority of the state." *Id.,* at *333–*334.

Two other cases, later cited with approval by this Court in *Ex parte Milligan,* 4 Wall. 2, 128–129, 18 L.Ed. 281 (1866), upheld verdicts for false imprisonment against military officers. In *Smith v. Shaw,* 12 Johns. (N.Y.1815), the court affirmed an award of damages for detention of a citizen on suspicion that he was, among other things, "an enemy's spy in time of war." *Id.,* at *265. The court held that "[n]one of the offences charged against *Shaw* were cognizable by a court-martial, except that which related to his being a spy; and if he was an *American* citizen, he could not be charged with such an offence. He might be amenable to the civil authority for treason; but could not be punished, under martial law, as a spy." *Ibid.* "If the defendant was justifiable in doing what he did, every citizen of the *United States* would, in time of war, be equally exposed to a like exercise of military power and authority." *Id.*, at *266. Finally, in *M'Connell v. Hampton,* 12 Johns. (N.Y.1815), a jury awarded $9,000 for false imprisonment after a military officer confined a citizen on charges of treason; the judges on appeal did not question the verdict but found the damages excessive, in part because "it does not appear that [the defendant] ... knew [the plaintiff] was a citizen." *Id.*, at *238 (Spencer, J.). See generally Wuerth, "The President's Power to Detain 'Enemy Combatants': Modern Lessons from Mr. Madison's Forgotten War," 98 *Nw. U.L.Rev.* 1567 (2004).

President Lincoln, when he purported to suspend habeas corpus without congressional authorization during the Civil War, apparently did not doubt that suspension was required if the prisoner was to be held without criminal trial. In his famous message to Congress on July 4, 1861, he argued only that he could suspend the writ, not that even without suspension, his imprisonment of citizens without criminal trial was permitted. See Special Session Message, 6 *Messages and Papers* 20–31.

Further evidence comes from this Court's decision in *Ex parte Milligan, supra.* There, the Court issued the writ to an American citizen who had been tried by military commission for offenses that included conspiring to overthrow the Government, seize munitions, and liberate prisoners of war. *Id.*, at 6–7. The Court rejected in no uncertain terms the Government's assertion that military jurisdiction was proper "under the 'laws and usages of war,'" *id.*, at 121:

> "It can serve no useful purpose to inquire what those laws and usages are, whence they originated, where found, and

> on whom they operate; they can never be applied to citizens in states which have upheld the authority of the government, and where the courts are open and their process unobstructed," *ibid.*

Milligan is not exactly this case, of course, since the petitioner was threatened with death, not merely imprisonment. But the reasoning and conclusion of *Milligan* logically cover the present case. The Government justifies imprisonment of Hamdi on principles of the law of war and admits that, absent the war, it would have no such authority. But if the law of war cannot be applied to citizens where courts are open, then Hamdi's imprisonment without criminal trial is no less unlawful than Milligan's trial by military tribunal.

Milligan responded to the argument, repeated by the Government in this case, that it is dangerous to leave suspected traitors at large in time of war:

> "If it was dangerous, in the distracted condition of affairs, to leave Milligan unrestrained of his liberty, because he 'conspired against the government, afforded aid and comfort to rebels, and incited the people to insurrection,' the *law* said arrest him, confine him closely, render him powerless to do further mischief; and then present his case to the grand jury of the district, with proofs of his guilt, and, if indicted, try him according to the course of the common law. If this had been done, the Constitution would have been vindicated, the law of 1863 enforced, and the securities for personal liberty preserved and defended." *Id.*, at 122.

Thus, criminal process was viewed as the primary means—and the only means absent congressional action suspending the writ—not only to punish traitors, but to incapacitate them.

The proposition that the Executive lacks indefinite wartime detention authority over citizens is consistent with the

Founders' general mistrust of military power permanently at the Executive's disposal. In the Founders' view, the "blessings of liberty" were threatened by "those military establishments which must gradually poison its very fountain." *The Federalist* No. 45, p. 238 (J. Madison). No fewer than 10 issues of the *Federalist* were devoted in whole or part to allaying fears of oppression from the proposed Constitution's authorization of standing armies in peacetime. Many safeguards in the Constitution reflect these concerns. Congress's authority "[t]o raise and support Armies" was hedged with the proviso that "no Appropriation of Money to that Use shall be for a longer Term than two Years." U.S. Const., Art. I, § 8, cl. 12. Except for the actual command of military forces, all authorization for their maintenance and all explicit authorization for their use is placed in the control of Congress under Article I, rather than the President under Article II. As Hamilton explained, the President's military authority would be "much inferior" to that of the British King:

> "It would amount to nothing more than the supreme command and direction of the military and naval forces, as first general and admiral of the confederacy: while that of the British king extends to the *declaring* of war, and to the *raising* and *regulating* of fleets and armies; all which, by the constitution under consideration, would appertain to the legislature." *The Federalist* No. 69, p. 357.

A view of the Constitution that gives the Executive authority to use military force rather than the force of law against citizens on American soil flies in the face of the mistrust that engendered these provisions.

IV

The Government argues that our more recent jurisprudence ratifies its indefinite imprisonment of a citizen within the territorial jurisdiction of federal courts. It places primary reliance upon *Ex parte Quirin,* 317 U.S. 1, 63 S.Ct. 2, 87 L.Ed. 3 (1942), a World War II case upholding the trial by military commission of eight German saboteurs, one of whom, Herbert Haupt, was a U.S. citizen. The case was not this Court's finest hour. The Court upheld the commission and denied relief in a brief *per curiam* issued the day after oral argument concluded, see *id.,* at 18–19, 63 S.Ct. 2, unnumbered note; a week later the Government carried out the commission's death sentence upon six saboteurs, including Haupt. The Court eventually explained its reasoning in a written opinion issued several months later.

Only three paragraphs of the Court's lengthy opinion dealt with the particular circumstances of Haupt's case. See *id.,* at 37–38, 45–46, 63 S.Ct. 2. The Government argued that Haupt, like the other petitioners, could be tried by military commission under the laws of war. In agreeing with that contention, *Quirin* purported to interpret the language of *Milligan* quoted above (the law of war "can never be applied to citizens in states which have upheld the authority of the government, and where the courts are open and their process unobstructed") in the following manner:

> "Elsewhere in its opinion ... the Court was at pains to point out that Milligan, a citizen twenty years resident in Indiana, who had never been a resident of any of the states in rebellion, was not an enemy belligerent either entitled to the status of a prisoner of war or subject to the penalties imposed upon unlawful belligerents. We construe the Court's statement as to the inapplicability of the law of war to Milli-

> gan's case as having particular reference to the facts before it. From them the Court concluded that Milligan, not being a part of or associated with the armed forces of the enemy, was a non-belligerent, not subject to the law of war ...." 317 U.S., at 45, 63 S.Ct. 2.

In my view this seeks to revise *Milligan* rather than describe it. *Milligan* had involved (among other issues) two separate questions: (1) whether the military trial of Milligan was justified by the laws of war, and if not (2) whether the President's suspension of the writ, pursuant to congressional authorization, prevented the issuance of habeas corpus. The Court's categorical language about the law of war's inapplicability to citizens where the courts are open (with no exception mentioned for citizens who were prisoners of war) was contained in its discussion of the first point. See 4 Wall., at 121. The factors pertaining to whether Milligan could reasonably be considered a belligerent and prisoner of war, while mentioned earlier in the opinion, see *id.*, at 118, were made relevant and brought to bear in the Court's later discussion, see *id.*, at 131, of whether Milligan came within the statutory provision that effectively made an exception to Congress's authorized suspension of the writ for (as the Court described it) "all parties, not prisoners of war, resident in their respective jurisdictions, ... who were citizens of states in which the administration of the laws in the Federal tribunals was unimpaired," *id.*, at 116. *Milligan* thus understood was in accord with the traditional law of habeas corpus I have described: Though treason often occurred in wartime, there was, absent provision for special treatment in a congressional suspension of the writ, no exception to the right to trial by jury for citizens who could be called "belligerents" or "prisoners of war."

But even if *Quirin* gave a correct description of *Milligan,* or made an irrevocable revision of it, *Quirin* would still not justify denial of the writ here. In *Quirin* it was uncontested that the petitioners were members of enemy forces. They were "*admitted* enemy invaders," 317 U.S., at 47, 63 S.Ct. 2 (emphasis added), and it was "undisputed" that they had landed in the United States in service of German forces, *id.*, at 20, 63 S.Ct. 2. The specific holding of the Court was only that, "upon the *conceded* facts," the petitioners were "plainly within [the] boundaries" of military jurisdiction, *id.*, at 46, 63 S.Ct. 2 (emphasis added). But where those jurisdictional facts are *not* conceded where the petitioner insists that he is *not* a belligerent—*Quirin* left the pre-existing law in place: Absent suspension of the writ, a citizen held where the courts are open is entitled either to criminal trial or to a judicial decree requiring his release.

V

It follows from what I have said that Hamdi is entitled to a habeas decree requiring his release unless (1) criminal proceedings are promptly brought, or (2) Congress has suspended the writ of habeas corpus. A suspension of the writ could, of course, lay down conditions for continued detention, similar to those that today's opinion prescribes under the Due Process Clause. Cf. Act of Mar. 3, 1863, 12 Stat. 755. But there is a world of difference between the people's representatives' determining the need for that suspension (and prescribing the conditions for it), and this Court's doing so.

The plurality finds justification for Hamdi's imprisonment in the Authorization for Use of Military Force, 115 Stat. 224, which provides:

> "That the President is authorized to use all necessary and appropriate force against those nations, organizations, or persons he determines planned, authorized, committed, or

> aided the terrorist attacks that occurred on September 11, 2001, or harbored such organizations or persons, in order to prevent any future acts of international terrorism against the United States by such nations, organizations or persons." § 2(a).

This is not remotely a congressional suspension of the writ, and no one claims that it is. Contrary to the plurality's view, I do not think this statute even authorizes detention of a citizen with the clarity necessary to satisfy the interpretive canon that statutes should be construed so as to avoid grave constitutional concerns, see *Edward J. DeBartolo Corp. v. Florida Gulf Coast Building & Constr. Trades Council,* 485 U.S. 568, 575, 108 S.Ct. 1392, 99 L.Ed.2d 645 (1988); with the clarity necessary to comport with cases such as *Ex parte Endo,* 323 U.S. 283, 300, 65 S.Ct. 208, 89 L.Ed. 243 (1944), and *Duncan v. Kahanamoku,* 327 U.S. 304, 314–316, 324, 66 S.Ct. 606, 90 L.Ed. 688 (1946); or with the clarity necessary to overcome the statutory prescription that "[n]o citizen shall be imprisoned or otherwise detained by the United States except pursuant to an Act of Congress," 18 U.S.C. § 4001(a). But even if it did, I would not permit it to overcome Hamdi's entitlement to habeas corpus relief. The Suspension Clause of the Constitution, which carefully circumscribes the conditions under which the writ can be withheld, would be a sham if it could be evaded by congressional prescription of requirements *other than the common-law requirement of committal for criminal prosecution* that render the writ, though available, unavailing. If the Suspension Clause does not guarantee the citizen that he will either be tried or released, unless the conditions for suspending the writ exist and the grave action of suspending the writ has been taken; if it merely guarantees the citizen that he will not be detained unless Congress by ordinary legislation says he can be detained; it guarantees him very little indeed.

It should not be thought, however, that the plurality's evisceration of the Suspension Clause augments, principally, the power of Congress. As usual, the major effect of its constitutional improvisation is to increase the power of the Court. Having found a congressional authorization for detention of citizens where none clearly exists; and having discarded the categorical procedural protection of the Suspension Clause; the plurality then proceeds, under the guise of the Due Process Clause, to prescribe what procedural protections *it* thinks appropriate. It "weigh[s] the private interest ... against the Government's asserted interest," *ante,* at 2646 (internal quotation marks omitted), and—just as though writing a new Constitution—comes up with an unheard-of system in which the citizen rather than the Government bears the burden of proof, testimony is by hearsay rather than live witnesses, and the presiding officer may well be a "neutral" military officer rather than judge and jury. See *ante,* at 2648–2649. It claims authority to engage in this sort of "judicious balancing" from *Mathews v. Eldridge,* 424 U.S. 319, 96 S.Ct. 893, 47 L.Ed.2d 18 (1976), a case involving ... *the withdrawal of disability benefits!* Whatever the merits of this technique when newly recognized property rights are at issue (and even there they are questionable), it has no place where the Constitution and the common law already supply an answer.

Having distorted the Suspension Clause, the plurality finishes up by transmogrifying the Great Writ—disposing of the present habeas petition by remanding for the District Court to "engag[e] in a factfinding process that is both prudent and incremental," *ante,* at 2652. "In the absence of [the Executive's prior provision of procedures that satisfy due process], ... a court that receives a petition for a writ of habeas corpus from an alleged enemy combatant must itself ensure that the minimum requirements of due process are achieved." *Ante,* at

2651–2652. This judicial remediation of executive default is unheard of. The role of habeas corpus is to determine the legality of executive detention, not to supply the omitted process necessary to make it legal. See *Preiser v. Rodriguez,* 411 U.S. 475, 484, 93 S.Ct. 1827, 36 L.Ed.2d 439 (1973) ("[T]he essence of habeas corpus is an attack by a person in custody upon the legality of that custody, and ... the traditional function of the writ is to secure release from illegal custody"); 1 *Blackstone* 132–133. It is not the habeas court's function to make illegal detention legal by supplying a process that the Government could have provided, but chose not to. If Hamdi is being imprisoned in violation of the Constitution (because without due process of law), then his habeas petition should be granted; the Executive may then hand him over to the criminal authorities, whose detention for the purpose of prosecution will be lawful, or else must release him.

There is a certain harmony of approach in the plurality's making up for Congress's failure to invoke the Suspension Clause and its making up for the Executive's failure to apply what it says are needed procedures—an approach that reflects what might be called a Mr. Fix-it Mentality. The plurality seems to view it as its mission to Make Everything Come Out Right, rather than merely to decree the consequences, as far as individual rights are concerned, of the other two branches' actions and omissions. Has the Legislature failed to suspend the writ in the current dire emergency? Well, we will remedy that failure by prescribing the reasonable conditions that a suspension should have included. And has the Executive failed to live up to those reasonable conditions? Well, we will ourselves make that failure good, so that this dangerous fellow (if he is dangerous) need not be set free. The problem with this approach is not only that it steps out of the courts' modest and limited role in a democratic society; but that by repeatedly doing what it thinks the political branches ought to do it encourages their lassitude and saps the vitality of government by the people.

VI

Several limitations give my views in this matter a relatively narrow compass. They apply only to citizens, accused of being enemy combatants, who are detained within the territorial jurisdiction of a federal court. This is not likely to be a numerous group; currently we know of only two, Hamdi and Jose Padilla. Where the citizen is captured outside and held outside the United States, the constitutional requirements may be different. Cf. *Johnson v. Eisentrager,* 339 U.S. 763, 769–771, 70 S.Ct. 936, 94 L.Ed. 1255 (1950); *Reid v. Covert,* 354 U.S. 1, 74–75, 77 S.Ct. 1222, 1 L.Ed.2d 1148 (1957) (Harlan, J., concurring in result); *Rasul v. Bush, post,* 542 U.S. 466, 502–504, 124 S.Ct. 2686, 2708–2709, 159 L.Ed.2d 548, 2004 WL 1432134 (2004) (Scalia, J., dissenting). Moreover, even within the United States, the accused citizen-enemy combatant may lawfully be detained once prosecution is in progress or in contemplation. See, *e.g., County of Riverside v. McLaughlin,* 500 U.S. 44, 111 S.Ct. 1661, 114 L.Ed.2d 49 (1991) (brief detention pending judicial determination after warrantless arrest); *United States v. Salerno,* 481 U.S. 739, 107 S.Ct. 2095, 95 L.Ed.2d 697 (1987) (pretrial detention under the Bail Reform Act). The Government has been notably successful in securing conviction, and hence long-term custody or execution, of those who have waged war against the state.

I frankly do not know whether these tools are sufficient to meet the Government's security needs, including the need to obtain intelligence through interrogation. It is far beyond my competence, or the Court's competence, to determine that. But it is not beyond Congress's. If the situation demands it, the Executive can ask Congress to authorize suspension of the writ—which can be made subject to whatever conditions Congress deems appropriate, including even the procedural novelties invented by the plurality today. To be sure, suspension is limited by the Constitution to cases of rebellion or invasion. But whether the attacks of September 11, 2001, constitute an "invasion," and whether those attacks still justify suspension several years later, are questions for Congress rather than this Court. See 3 *Story* § 1336, at 208–209. If civil rights are to be curtailed during wartime, it must be done openly and democratically, as the Constitution requires, rather than by silent erosion through an opinion of this Court.

* * *

The Founders well understood the difficult tradeoff between safety and freedom. "Safety from external danger," Hamilton declared,

> "is the most powerful director of national conduct. Even the ardent love of liberty will, after a time, give way to its dictates. The violent destruction of life and property incident to war; the continual effort and alarm attendant on a state of continual danger, will compel nations the most attached to liberty, to resort for repose and security to institutions which have a tendency to destroy their civil and political rights. To be more safe, they, at length, become willing to run the risk of being less free." *The Federalist* No. 8, p. 33. The Founders warned us about the risk, and equipped us with a Constitution designed to deal with it.

Many think it not only inevitable but entirely proper that liberty give way to security in times of national crisis—that, at the extremes of military exigency, *inter arma silent leges.*

Whatever the general merits of the view that war silences law or modulates its voice, that view has no place in the interpretation and application of a Constitution designed precisely to confront war and, in a manner that accords with democratic principles, to accommodate it. Because the Court has proceeded to meet the current emergency in a manner the Constitution does not envision, I respectfully dissent.

Flabby legal tests invite arbitrary decisions
Tennessee v. Lane,
541 U.S. 509 (2004)

Justice Scalia, dissenting.

Section 5 of the Fourteenth Amendment provides that Congress "shall have power to enforce, by appropriate legislation, the provisions" of that Amendment—including, of course, the Amendment's Equal Protection and Due Process Clauses. In *Katzenbach v. Morgan,* 384 U.S. 641, 86 S.Ct. 1717, 16 L.Ed.2d 828 (1966), we decided that Congress could, under this provision, forbid English literacy tests for Puerto Rican voters in New York State who met certain educational criteria. Though those tests were not themselves in violation of the Fourteenth Amendment, we held that § 5 authorizes prophylactic legislation—that is, "legislation that proscribes facially constitutional conduct," *Nevada Dept. of Human Resources v. Hibbs,* 538 U.S. 721, 728, 123 S.Ct. 1972, 155 L.Ed.2d 953 (2003), when Congress determines such proscription is desirable "'to make the amendments fully effective,'" *Morgan, supra,* at 648, 86 S.Ct. 1717 (quoting *Ex parte Virginia,* 100 U.S. 339, 345, 25 L.Ed. 676 (1880)). We said that "the measure of what constitutes 'appropriate legislation' under § 5 of the Fourteenth Amendment" is the flexible "necessary and proper" standard of *M'Culloch v. Maryland,* 4 Wheat. 316, 342, 421, 4 L.Ed. 579 (1819). *Morgan,* 384 U.S., at 651, 86 S.Ct. 1717. We described § 5 as "a positive grant of legislative power authorizing Congress to exercise its discretion in determining whether and what legislation is needed to secure the guarantees of the Fourteenth Amendment." *Ibid.*

The *Morgan* opinion followed close upon our decision in *South Carolina v. Katzenbach,* 383 U.S. 301, 86 S.Ct. 803, 15

L.Ed.2d 769 (1966), which had upheld prophylactic application of the similarly worded "enforce" provision of the Fifteenth Amendment (§ 2) to challenged provisions of the Voting Rights Act of 1965. But the Fourteenth Amendment, unlike the Fifteenth, is not limited to denial of the franchise and not limited to the denial of other rights on the basis of race. In *City of Boerne v. Flores,* 521 U.S. 507, 117 S.Ct. 2157, 138 L.Ed.2d 624 (1997), we confronted Congress's inevitable expansion of the Fourteenth Amendment, as interpreted in *Morgan,* beyond the field of racial discrimination. There Congress had sought, in the Religious Freedom Restoration Act of 1993, 107 Stat. 1488, 42 U.S.C. § 2000bb *et seq.,* to impose upon the States an interpretation of the First Amendment's Free Exercise Clause that this Court had explicitly rejected. To avoid placing in congressional hands effective power to rewrite the Bill of Rights through the medium of § 5, we formulated the "congruence and proportionality" test for determining what legislation is "appropriate." When Congress enacts prophylactic legislation, we said, there must be "proportionality or congruence between the means adopted and the legitimate end to be achieved." 521 U.S., at 533, 117 S.Ct. 2157.

I joined the Court's opinion in *Boerne* with some misgiving. I have generally rejected tests based on such malleable standards as "proportionality," because they have a way of turning into vehicles for the implementation of individual judges' policy preferences. See, *e.g., Ewing v. California,* 538 U.S. 11, 31–32, 123 S.Ct. 1179, 155 L.Ed.2d 108 (2003) (Scalia, J., concurring in judgment) (declining to apply a "proportionality" test to the Eighth Amendment's ban on cruel and unusual punishment); *Stenberg v. Carhart,* 530 U.S. 914, 954–956, 120 S.Ct. 2597, 147 L.Ed.2d 743 (2000) (Scalia, J., dissenting) (declining to apply the "undue burden" standard of *Planned Parenthood of Southeastern Pa. v. Casey,* 505 U.S. 833, 112 S.Ct. 2791, 120 L.Ed.2d 674

(1992)); *BMW of North America, Inc. v. Gore,* 517 U.S. 559, 599, 116 S.Ct. 1589, 134 L.Ed.2d 809 (1996) (Scalia, J., dissenting) (declining to apply a "reasonableness" test to punitive damages under the Due Process Clause). Even so, I signed on to the "congruence and proportionality" test in *Boerne,* and adhered to it in later cases: *Florida Prepaid Postsecondary Ed. Expense Bd. v. College Savings Bank,* 527 U.S. 627, 119 S.Ct. 2199, 144 L.Ed.2d 575 (1999), where we held that the provisions of the Patent and Plant Variety Protection Remedy Clarification Act, 35 U.S.C. §§ 271(h), 296(a), were "'so out of proportion to a supposed remedial or preventive object that [they] cannot be understood as responsive to, or designed to prevent, unconstitutional behavior,'" 527 U.S., at 646, 119 S.Ct. 2199 (quoting *Boerne, supra,* at 532, 117 S.Ct. 2157); *Kimel v. Florida Bd. of Regents,* 528 U.S. 62, 120 S.Ct. 631, 145 L.Ed.2d 522 (2000), where we held that the Age Discrimination in Employment Act of 1967, 81 Stat. 602, as amended, 29 U.S.C. § 621 *et seq.* (1994 ed. and Supp. III), imposed on state and local governments requirements "disproportionate to any unconstitutional conduct that conceivably could be targeted by the Act," 528 U.S., at 83, 120 S.Ct. 631; *United States v. Morrison,* 529 U.S. 598, 120 S.Ct. 1740, 146 L.Ed.2d 658 (2000), where we held that a provision of the Violence Against Women Act of 1994, 42 U.S.C. § 13981, lacked congruence and proportionality because it was "not aimed at proscribing discrimination by officials which the Fourteenth Amendment might not itself proscribe," 529 U.S., at 626, 120 S.Ct. 1740; and *Board of Trustees of Univ. of Ala. v. Garrett,* 531 U.S. 356, 121 S.Ct. 955, 148 L.Ed.2d 866 (2001), where we said that Title I of the Americans with Disabilities Act of 1990(ADA), 104 Stat. 330, 42 U.S.C. §§ 12111–12117, raised "the same sort of concerns as to congruence and proportionality as were found in *City of Boerne,*" 531 U.S., at 372, 121 S.Ct. 955.

But these cases were soon followed by *Nevada Dept. of*

Human Resources v. Hibbs, in which the Court held that the Family and Medical Leave Act of 1993, 107 Stat. 9, 29 U.S.C. § 2612 *et seq.*, which required States to provide their employees up to 12 work weeks of unpaid leave (for various purposes) annually, was "congruent and proportional to its remedial object [of preventing sex discrimination], and can be understood as responsive to, or designed to prevent, unconstitutional behavior." 538 U.S., at 740, 123 S.Ct. 1972 (internal quotation marks omitted). I joined Justice Kennedy's dissent, which established (conclusively, I thought) that Congress had identified no unconstitutional state action to which the statute could conceivably be a proportional response. And now we have today's decision, holding that Title II of the ADA is congruent and proportional to the remediation of constitutional violations, in the face of what seems to me a compelling demonstration of the opposite by the Chief Justice's dissent. I yield to the lessons of experience. The "congruence and proportionality" standard, like all such flabby tests, is a standing invitation to judicial arbitrariness and policy-driven decisionmaking. Worse still, it casts this Court in the role of Congress's taskmaster. Under it, the courts (and ultimately this Court) must regularly check Congress's homework to make sure that it has identified sufficient constitutional violations to make its remedy congruent and proportional. As a general matter, we are ill advised to adopt or adhere to constitutional rules that bring us into constant conflict with a coequal branch of Government. And when conflict is unavoidable, we should not come to do battle with the United States Congress armed only with a test ("congruence and proportionality") that has no demonstrable basis in the text of the Constitution and cannot objectively be shown to have been met or failed. As I wrote for the Court in an earlier case, "low walls and vague distinctions will not be judicially defensible in the heat of interbranch conflict." *Plaut v. Spendthrift Farm, Inc.*, 514 U.S. 211, 239, 115 S.Ct. 1447, 131 L.Ed.2d 328 (1995).

I would replace "congruence and proportionality" with another test—one that provides a clear, enforceable limitation supported by the text of § 5. Section 5 grants Congress the power "to *enforce*, by appropriate legislation," the other provisions of the Fourteenth Amendment. U.S. Const., Amdt. 14 (emphasis added). *Morgan* notwithstanding, one does not, within any normal meaning of the term, "enforce" a prohibition by issuing a still broader prohibition directed to the same end. One does not, for example, "enforce" a 55-mile-per-hour speed limit by imposing a 45-mile-per-hour speed limit—even though that is indeed directed to the same end of automotive safety and will undoubtedly result in many fewer violations of the 55-mile-per-hour limit. And one does not "enforce" the right of access to the courts at issue in this case, see *ante*, at 1993, by requiring that disabled persons be provided access to *all* of the "services, programs, or activities" furnished or conducted by the State, 42 U.S.C. § 12132. That is simply not what the power to enforce means—or ever meant. The 1860 edition of Noah Webster's *American Dictionary of the English Language*, current when the Fourteenth Amendment was adopted, defined "enforce" as: "To put in execution; to cause to take effect; as, to *enforce* the laws." *Id.*, at 396. See also J. Worcester, *Dictionary of the English Language* 484 (1860) ("To put in force; to cause to be applied or executed; as, 'To *enforce* a law'"). Nothing in § 5 allows Congress to go *beyond* the provisions of the Fourteenth Amendment to proscribe, prevent, or "remedy" conduct that does not *itself* violate any provision of the Fourteenth Amendment. So-called "prophylactic legislation" is reinforcement rather than enforcement.

Morgan asserted that this commonsense interpretation "would confine the legislative power ... to the insignificant role of abrogating only those state laws that the judicial branch was prepared to adjudge unconstitutional, or of merely informing the judgment of the judiciary by particularizing the 'majestic generalities' of § 1 of the Amendment." 384 U.S., at 648–649, 86 S.Ct. 1717. That is not so. One must remember "that in 1866 the lower federal courts had no general jurisdiction of cases alleging a deprivation of rights secured by the Constitution." R. Berger, *Government By Judiciary* 247 (2d ed.1997). If, just after the Fourteenth Amendment was ratified, a State had enacted a law imposing racially discriminatory literacy tests (different questions for different races) a citizen prejudiced by such a test would have had no means of asserting his constitutional right to be free of it. Section 5 authorizes Congress to create a cause of action through which the citizen may vindicate his Fourteenth Amendment rights. One of the first pieces of legislation passed under Congress's § 5 power was the Ku Klux Klan Act of April 20, 1871, 17 Stat. 13, entitled "*An Act to enforce the Provisions of the Fourteenth Amendment to the Constitution of the United States, and for other Purposes.*" Section 1 of that Act, later codified as Rev. Stat. § 1979, 42 U.S.C. § 1983, authorized a cause of action against "any person who, under color of any law, statute, ordinance, regulation, custom, or usage of any State, shall subject, or cause to be subjected, any person within the jurisdiction of the United States to the deprivation of any rights, privileges, or immunities secured by the Constitution of the United States." 17 Stat. 13. Section 5 would also authorize measures that do not restrict the States' substantive scope of action but impose requirements directly related to the *facilitation* of "enforcement"—for example, reporting requirements that would enable violations of the Fourteenth Amendment to be identified. But what § 5 does *not* authorize is so-called "prophylactic" measures, prohibiting primary conduct that is itself not forbidden by the Fourteenth Amendment.

The major impediment to the approach I have suggested is *stare decisis.* A lot of water has gone under the bridge since *Morgan,* and many important and well-accepted measures, such as the Voting Rights Act, assume the validity of *Morgan* and *South Carolina.* As Prof. Archibald Cox put it in his Supreme Court Foreword: "The etymological meaning of section 5 may favor the narrower reading. Literally, 'to enforce' means to compel performance of the obligations imposed; but the linguistic argument lost much of its force once the *South Carolina* and *Morgan* cases decided that the power to enforce embraces any measure appropriate to effectuating the performance of the state's constitutional duty." Foreword: "Constitutional Adjudication and the Promotion of Human Rights," 80 *Harv. L.Rev.* 91, 110–111 (1966).

However, *South Carolina* and *Morgan,* all of our later cases except *Hibbs* that give an expansive meaning to "enforce" in § 5 of the Fourteenth Amendment, and all of our earlier cases that even suggest such an expansive meaning in dicta, involved congressional measures that were directed exclusively against, or were used in the particular case to remedy, *racial discrimination.* See *Oregon v. Mitchell,* 400 U.S. 112, 91 S.Ct. 260, 27 L.Ed.2d 272 (1970) (see discussion *infra*); *Ex parte Virginia,* 100 U.S. 339, 25 L.Ed. 676 (1880) (dictum in a case involving a statute that imposed criminal penalties for officials' racial discrimination in jury selection); *Strauder v. West Virginia,* 100 U.S. 303, 311–312, 25 L.Ed. 664 (1880) (dictum in a case involving a statute that permitted removal to federal court of a black man's claim that his jury had been selected in a racially discriminatory manner); *Virginia v. Rives,* 100 U.S. 313, 318, 25 L.Ed. 667 (1880) (dictum in a racial discrimination case involving the same statute). See also *City of Rome v. United States,* 446 U.S. 156, 173–178, 100 S.Ct. 1548, 64 L.Ed.2d 119 (1980) (upholding as valid legislation under § 2 of the Fifteenth

Amendment the most sweeping provisions of the Voting Rights Act of 1965); *Jones v. Alfred H. Mayer Co.*, 392 U.S. 409, 439–441, 88 S.Ct. 2186, 20 L.Ed.2d 1189 (1968) (upholding a law, 42 U.S.C. § 1982, banning public or private racial discrimination in the sale and rental of property as appropriate legislation under § 2 of the Thirteenth Amendment).

Giving § 5 more expansive scope with regard to measures directed against racial discrimination by the States accords to practices that are distinctively violative of the principal purpose of the Fourteenth Amendment a priority of attention that this Court envisioned from the beginning, and that has repeatedly been reflected in our opinions. In the *Slaughter-House Cases,* 16 Wall. 36, 81, 21 L.Ed. 394 (1873), the Court's first confrontation with the Fourteenth Amendment, we said the following with respect to the Equal Protection Clause:

> "We doubt very much whether any action of a State not directed by way of discrimination against the negroes as a class, or on account of their race, will ever be held to come within the purview of this provision. It is so clearly a provision for that race and that emergency, that a strong case would be necessary for its application to any other."

Racial discrimination was the practice at issue in the early cases (cited in *Morgan*) that gave such an expansive description of the effects of § 5. See 384 U.S., at 648, 86 S.Ct. 1717 (citing *Ex parte Virginia*); 384 U.S., at 651, 86 S.Ct. 1717 (citing *Strauder v. West Virginia* and *Virginia v. Rives*). In those early days, bear in mind, the guarantee of equal protection had not been extended beyond race to sex, age, and the many other categories it now covers. Also still to be developed were the incorporation doctrine (which holds that the Fourteenth Amendment incorporates and applies against the States the Bill of Rights, see *Duncan v. Louisiana,* 391 U.S. 145, 147–148,

88 S.Ct. 1444, 20 L.Ed.2d 491 (1968)) and the doctrine of so-called "substantive due process" (which holds that the Fourteenth Amendment's Due Process Clause protects unenumerated liberties, see generally *Lawrence v. Texas,* 539 U.S. 558, 123 S.Ct. 2472, 156 L.Ed.2d 508 (2003); *Planned Parenthood of Southeastern Pa. v. Casey,* 505 U.S. 833, 112 S.Ct. 2791, 120 L.Ed.2d 674 (1992)). Thus, the Fourteenth Amendment did not include the many guarantees that it now provides. In such a seemingly limited context, it did not appear to be a massive expansion of congressional power to interpret § 5 broadly. Broad interpretation was particularly appropriate with regard to racial discrimination, since that was the principal evil against which the Equal Protection Clause was directed, and the principal constitutional prohibition that some of the States stubbornly ignored. The former is still true, and the latter remained true at least as late as *Morgan.*

When congressional regulation has not been targeted at racial discrimination, we have given narrower scope to § 5. In *Oregon v. Mitchell,* 400 U.S. 112, 91 S.Ct. 260, 27 L.Ed.2d 272 (1970), the Court upheld, under § 2 of the Fifteenth Amendment, that provision of the Voting Rights Act Amendments of 1970, 84 Stat. 314, which barred literacy tests and similar voter-eligibility requirements—classic tools of the racial discrimination in voting that the Fifteenth Amendment forbids; but found to be *beyond* the § 5 power of the Fourteenth Amendment the provision that lowered the voting age from 21 to 18 in state elections. See 400 U.S., at 124–130, 91 S.Ct. 260 (opinion of Black, J.); *id.,* at 153–154, 91 S.Ct. 260 (Harlan, J., concurring in part and dissenting in part); *id.,* at 293–296, 91 S.Ct. 260 (Stewart, J., joined by Burger, C. J., and Blackmun, J., concurring in part and dissenting in part). A third provision, which forbade States from disqualifying voters by reason of residency requirements, was also upheld—but only a minority of the Justices believed that § 5 was adequate authority. Justice Black's opinion in that case described exactly the line I am drawing here, suggesting that Congress's enforcement power is broadest when directed "to the goal of eliminating discrimination on account of race." *Id.,* at 130, 91 S.Ct. 260. And of course the *results* reached in *Boerne, Florida Prepaid, Kimel, Morrison,* and *Garrett* are consistent with the narrower compass afforded congressional regulation that does not protect against or prevent racial discrimination.

Thus, principally for reasons of *stare decisis,* I shall henceforth apply the permissive *McCulloch* standard to congressional measures designed to remedy racial discrimination by the States. I would not, however, abandon the requirement that Congress may impose prophylactic § 5 legislation only upon those particular States in which there has been an identified history of relevant constitutional violations. See *Hibbs,* 538 U.S., at 741–743, 123 S.Ct. 1972 (Scalia, J., dissenting); *Morrison,* 529 U.S., at 626–627, 120 S.Ct. 1740; *Morgan,* 384 U.S., at 666–667, 669, 670–671, 86 S.Ct. 1717 (Harlan, J., dissenting). I would also adhere to the requirement that the prophylactic remedy predicated upon such state violations must be directed against the States or state actors rather than the public at large. See *Morrison, supra,* at 625–626, 120 S.Ct. 1740. And I would not, of course, permit any congressional measures that violate other provisions of the Constitution. When those requirements have been met, however, I shall leave it to Congress, under constraints no tighter than those of the Necessary and Proper Clause, to decide what measures are appropriate under § 5 to prevent or remedy racial discrimination by the States.

I shall also not subject to "congruence and proportionality" analysis congressional action under § 5 that is *not* directed to racial discrimination. Rather, I shall give full effect to that action when it consists of "enforcement" of the provisions of the Fourteenth Amendment, within the broad but not unlimited meaning of that term I have described above. When it goes beyond enforcement to prophylaxis, however, I shall consider it ultra vires. The present legislation is plainly of the latter sort.

* * *

Requiring access for disabled persons to all public buildings cannot remotely be considered a means of "enforcing" the Fourteenth Amendment. The considerations of long accepted practice and of policy that sanctioned such distortion of language where state racial discrimination is at issue do not apply in this field of social policy far removed from the principal object of the Civil War Amendments. "The seductive plausibility of single steps in a chain of evolutionary development of a legal rule is often not perceived until a third, fourth, or fifth 'logical' extension occurs. Each step, when taken, appeared a reasonable step in relation to that which preceded it, although the aggregate or end result is one that would never have been seriously considered in the first instance. This kind of gestative propensity calls for the 'line drawing' familiar in the judicial, as in the legislative process: 'thus far but not beyond.'" *United States v. 12 200-ft. Reels of Super 8MM. Film,* 413 U.S. 123, 127, 93 S.Ct. 2665, 37 L.Ed.2d 500 (1973) (Burger, C. J., for the Court) (footnote omitted). It is past time to draw a line limiting the uncontrolled spread of a well-intentioned textual distortion.

For these reasons, I respectfully dissent from the judgment of the Court.

A rule blatantly gerrymandered to the facts of this case

Zivotofsky ex rel. Zivotofsky v. Kerry, 135 S.Ct. 2076 (2015)

Justice Scalia, with whom the Chief Justice and Justice Alito join, dissenting.

Before this country declared independence, the law of England entrusted the King with the exclusive care of his kingdom's foreign affairs. The royal prerogative included the "sole power of sending ambassadors to foreign states, and receiving them at home," the sole authority to "make treaties, leagues, and alliances with foreign states and princes," "the sole prerogative of making war and peace," and the "sole power of raising and regulating fleets and armies." 1 W. *Blackstone, Commentaries* *253, *257, *262. The People of the United States had other ideas when they organized our Government. They considered a sound structure of balanced powers essential to the preservation of just government, and international relations formed no exception to that principle.

The People therefore adopted a Constitution that divides responsibility for the Nation's foreign concerns between the legislative and executive departments. The Constitution gave the President the "executive Power," authority to send and responsibility to receive ambassadors, power to make treaties, and command of the Army and Navy—though they qualified some of these powers by requiring consent of the Senate. Art. II, §§ 1–3. At the same time, they gave Congress powers over war, foreign commerce, naturalization, and more. Art. I, § 8. "Fully eleven of the powers that Article I, § 8 grants Congress deal in some way with foreign affairs." L. Tribe, *American Constitutional Law*, § 5–18, p. 965.

This case arises out of a dispute between the Executive and Legislative Branches about whether the United States should treat Jerusalem as a part of Israel. The Constitution contemplates that the political branches will make policy about the territorial claims of foreign nations the same way they make policy about other international matters: The President will exercise his powers on the basis of his views, Congress its powers on the basis of its views. That is just what has happened here.

I

The political branches of our Government agree on the real-world fact that Israel controls the city of Jerusalem. See Jerusalem Embassy Act of 1995, 109 Stat. 398; Brief for Respondent 3. They disagree, however, about how official documents should record the birthplace of an American citizen born in Jerusalem. The Executive does not accept any state's claim to sovereignty over Jerusalem, and it maintains that the birthplace designation "Israel" would clash with this stance of neutrality. But the National Legislature has enacted a statute that provides: "For purposes of the registration of birth, certification of nationality, or issuance of a passport of a United States citizen born in the city of Jerusalem, the Secretary [of State] shall, upon the request of the citizen or the citizen's legal guardian, record the place of birth as Israel." Foreign Relations Authorization Act, Fiscal Year 2003, § 214(d), 116 Stat. 1366. Menachem Zivotofsky's parents seek enforcement of this statutory right in the issuance of their son's passport and consular report of birth abroad. They regard their son's birthplace as a part of Israel and insist as "a matter of conscience" that his Israeli nativity "not be erased" from his identity documents. App. 26.

Before turning to Presidential power under Article II, I think it well to establish the statute's basis in congressional power under Article I. Congress's power to "establish an uniform Rule of Naturalization," Art. I, § 8, cl. 4, enables it to grant American citizenship to someone born abroad. *United States v. Wong Kim Ark,* 169 U.S. 649, 702–703, 18 S.Ct. 456, 42 L.Ed. 890 (1898). The naturalization power also enables Congress to furnish the people it makes citizens with papers verifying their citizenship—say a consular report of birth abroad (which certifies citizenship of an American born outside the United States) or a passport (which certifies citizenship for purposes of international travel). As the Necessary and Proper Clause confirms, every congressional power "carries with it all those incidental powers which are necessary to its complete and effectual execution." *Cohens v. Virginia,* 6 Wheat. 264, 429, 5 L.Ed. 257 (1821). Even on a miserly understanding of Congress's incidental authority, Congress may make grants of citizenship "effectual" by providing for the issuance of certificates authenticating them.

One would think that if Congress may grant Zivotofsky a passport and a birth report, it may also require these papers to record his birthplace as "Israel." The birthplace specification promotes the document's citizenship-authenticating function by identifying the bearer, distinguishing people with similar names but different birthplaces from each other, helping authorities uncover identity fraud, and facilitating retrieval of the Government's citizenship records. See App. 70. To be sure, recording Zivotofsky's birthplace as "Jerusalem" rather than "Israel" would fulfill these objectives, but when faced with alternative ways to carry its powers into execution, Congress has the "discretion" to choose the one it deems "most beneficial to the people." *McCulloch v. Maryland,* 4 Wheat. 316, 421, 4 L.Ed. 579 (1819). It thus has the right to decide that recording birthplaces as "Israel" makes for better foreign policy. Or that regardless of international politics, a passport or birth report should respect its bearer's conscientious belief that Jerusalem belongs to Israel.

No doubt congressional discretion in executing legislative powers has its limits; Congress's chosen approach must be not only "necessary" to carrying its powers into execution, but also "proper." Congress thus may not transcend boundaries upon legislative authority stated or implied elsewhere in the Constitution. But as we shall see, § 214(d) does not transgress any such restriction.

II

The Court frames this case as a debate about recognition. Recognition is a sovereign's official acceptance of a status under international law. A sovereign might recognize a foreign entity as a state, a regime as the other state's government, a place as part of the other state's territory, rebel forces in the other state as a belligerent power, and so on. 2 M. Whiteman, *Digest of International Law* § 1 (1963) (hereinafter *Whiteman*). President Truman recognized Israel as a state in 1948, but Presidents have consistently declined to recognize Jerusalem as a part of Israel's (or any other state's) sovereign territory.

The Court holds that the Constitution makes the President alone responsible for recognition and that § 214(d) invades this exclusive power. I agree that the Constitution *empowers* the President to extend recognition on behalf of the United States, but I find it a much harder question whether it makes that power exclusive. The Court tells us that "the weight of historical evidence" supports exclusive executive authority over "the formal determination of recognition." *Ante*, at 2091. But even with its attention confined to formal recognition, the Court is forced to admit that "history is not all on one side." *Ibid.* To take a stark example, Congress legislated in 1934 to grant independence to the Philippines, which were then an

American colony. 48 Stat. 456. In the course of doing so, Congress directed the President to "recognize the independence of the Philippine Islands as a separate and self-governing nation" and to "acknowledge the authority and control over the same of the government instituted by the people thereof." § 10, *id.*, at 463. Constitutional? And if Congress may control recognition when exercising its power "to dispose of ... the Territory or other Property belonging to the United States," Art. IV, § 3, cl. 2, why not when exercising other enumerated powers? Neither text nor history nor precedent yields a clear answer to these questions. Fortunately, I have no need to confront these matters today—nor does the Court—because § 214(d) plainly does not concern recognition.

Recognition is more than an announcement of a policy. Like the ratification of an international agreement or the termination of a treaty, it is a formal legal act with effects under international law. It signifies acceptance of an international status, and it makes a commitment to continued acceptance of that status and respect for any attendant rights. See, *e.g.*, Convention on the Rights and Duties of States, Art. 6, Dec. 26, 1933, 49 Stat. 3100, T.S. No. 881. "Its legal effect is to create an estoppel. By granting recognition, [states] debar themselves from challenging in future whatever they have previously acknowledged." 1 G. Schwarzenberger, *International Law* 127 (3d ed. 1957). In order to extend recognition, a state must perform an act that unequivocally manifests that intention. *Whiteman* § 3. That act can consist of an express conferral of recognition, or one of a handful of acts that by international custom imply recognition—chiefly, entering into a bilateral treaty, and sending or receiving an ambassador. *Ibid.*

To know all this is to realize at once that § 214(d) has nothing to do with recognition. Section 214(d) does not require the Secretary to make a formal declaration about Israel's sovereignty over Jerusalem. And nobody suggests that international custom infers acceptance of sovereignty from the birthplace designation on a passport or birth report, as it does from bilateral treaties or exchanges of ambassadors. Recognition would preclude the United States (as a matter of international law) from later contesting Israeli sovereignty over Jerusalem. But making a notation in a passport or birth report does not encumber the Republic with any international obligations. It leaves the Nation free (so far as international law is concerned) to change its mind in the future. That would be true even if the statute required *all* passports to list "Israel." But in fact it requires only those passports to list "Israel" for which the citizen (or his guardian) *requests* "Israel"; all the rest, under the Secretary's policy, list "Jerusalem." It is utterly impossible for this deference to private requests to constitute an act that unequivocally manifests an intention to grant recognition.

Section 214(d) performs a more prosaic function than extending recognition. Just as foreign countries care about what our Government has to say about their borders, so too American citizens often care about what our Government has to say about their identities. Cf. *Bowen v. Roy,* 476 U.S. 693, 106 S.Ct. 2147, 90 L.Ed.2d 735 (1986). The State Department does not grant or deny recognition in order to accommodate these individuals, but it does make exceptions to its rules about how it records birthplaces. Although normal protocol requires specifying the bearer's country of birth in his passport, Dept. of State, 7 *Foreign Affairs Manual* (FAM) § 1300, App. D, § 1330(a) (2014), the State Department will, if the bearer protests, specify the city of birth instead—so that an Irish nationalist may have his birthplace recorded as "Belfast" rather than "United Kingdom," *id.,* § 1380(a). And although normal protocol requires specifying the country with *present* sovereignty over the bearer's place of birth, *id.,* § 1330(b), a special exception allows a bearer born before 1948 in what was then Palestine to have his birthplace listed as "Palestine," *id.*, § 1360(g). Section 214(d) requires the State Department to make a further accommodation. Even though the Department normally refuses to specify a country that lacks recognized sovereignty over the bearer's birthplace, it must suspend that policy upon the request of an American citizen born in Jerusalem. Granting a request to specify "Israel" rather than "Jerusalem" does not recognize Israel's sovereignty over Jerusalem, just as granting a request to specify "Belfast" rather than "United Kingdom" does not derecognize the United Kingdom's sovereignty over Northern Ireland.

The best indication that § 214(d) does not concern recognition comes from the State Department's policies concerning Taiwan. According to the Solicitor General, the United States "acknowledges the Chinese position" that Taiwan is a part of China, but "does not take a position" of its own on that issue. Brief for Respondent 51–52. Even so, the State Department has for a long time recorded the birthplace of a citizen born in Taiwan as "China." It indeed *insisted* on doing so until Congress passed a law (on which § 214(d) was modeled) giving citizens the option to have their birthplaces recorded as "Taiwan." See § 132, 108 Stat. 395, as amended by § 1(r), 108 Stat. 4302. The Solicitor General explains that the designation "China" "involves a geographic description, not an assertion that Taiwan is ... part of sovereign China." Brief for Respondent 51–52. Quite so. Section 214(d) likewise calls for nothing beyond a "geographic description"; it does not require the Executive even to assert, never mind formally recognize, that Jerusalem is a part of sovereign Israel. Since birthplace specifications in citizenship documents are matters within Congress's control, Congress may treat Jerusalem as a part of Israel when regulating the recording of birthplaces, even if the President does not do so when extending recognition. Section 214(d), by the way, expressly directs the Secretary to "record the place of birth as Israel" "[*f*]*or purposes of* the registration of birth, certification of nationality, or issuance of a passport." (Emphasis added.) And the law bears the caption, "Record of Place of Birth as Israel *for Passport Purposes*." (Emphasis added.) Finding recognition in this provision is rather like finding admission to the Union in a provision that treats American Samoa as a State for purposes of a federal highway safety program, 23 U.S.C. § 401.

III

The Court complains that § 214(d) requires the Secretary of State to issue official documents implying that Jerusalem is a part of Israel; that it appears in a section of the statute bearing the title "United States Policy with Respect to Jerusalem as the Capital of Israel"; and that foreign "observers interpreted [it] as altering United States policy regarding Jerusalem." *Ante,* at 2115. But these features do not show that § 214(d) recognizes Israel's sovereignty over Jerusalem. They show only that the law displays symbolic support for Israel's territorial claim. That symbolism may have tremendous significance as a matter of international diplomacy, but it makes no difference as a matter of constitutional law.

Even if the Constitution gives the President sole power to extend recognition, it does not give him sole power to make all decisions relating to foreign disputes over sovereignty. To the contrary, a fair reading of Article I allows Congress to decide for itself how its laws should handle these controversies. Read naturally, power to "regulate Commerce with foreign Nations," § 8, cl. 3, includes power to regulate imports from Gibraltar as British goods or as Spanish goods. Read naturally, power to "regulate the Value ... of foreign Coin," § 8, cl. 5, includes power to honor (or not) currency issued by Taiwan. And so on for the other enumerated powers. These are not airy hypotheticals. A trade statute from 1800, for example, provided that "the whole of the island of Hispaniola"—whose status was then in controversy—"shall for purposes of [the] act be considered as a dependency of the French Republic." § 7, 2 Stat. 10. In 1938, Congress allowed admission of the Vatican City's public records in federal courts, decades before the United States extended formal recognition. ch. 682, 52 Stat. 1163; *Whiteman* § 68. The Taiwan Relations Act of 1979 grants Taiwan capacity to sue and be sued, even though the United States does not recognize it as a state. 22 U.S.C. § 3303(b)(7). Section 214(d) continues in the same tradition.

The Constitution likewise does not give the President exclusive power to determine which claims to statehood and territory "are legitimate in the eyes of the United States," *ante*, at 2086. Congress may express its own views about these matters by declaring war, restricting trade, denying foreign aid, and much else besides. To take just one example, in 1991, Congress responded to Iraq's invasion of Kuwait by enacting a resolution authorizing use of military force. 105 Stat. 3. No doubt the resolution reflected Congress's views about the legitimacy of Iraq's territorial claim. The preamble referred to Iraq's "illegal occupation" and stated that "the international community has demanded ... that Kuwait's independence and legitimate government be restored." *Ibid.* These statements are far more categorical than the caption "United States Policy with Respect to Jerusalem as the Capital of Israel." Does it follow that the authorization of the use of military force invaded the President's exclusive powers? Or that it would have done so had the President recognized Iraqi sovereignty over Kuwait?

History does not even support an exclusive Presidential power to make what the Court calls "formal statements" about "the legitimacy of a state or government and its territorial bounds," *ante,* at 2096. For a long time, the Houses of Congress have made formal statements announcing their own positions on these issues, again without provoking constitutional objections. A recent resolution expressed the House of Representatives' "strong support for the legitimate, democratically-elected Government of Lebanon" and condemned an "illegitimate" and "unjustifiable" insurrection by "the terrorist group Hizballah." H. Res. 1194, 110th Cong, 2d Sess., 1, 4 (2008). An earlier enactment declared "the sense of the Congress that ... Tibet ... is an occupied country under the established principles of international law" and that "Tibet's true representatives are the Dalai Lama and the Tibetan Government in exile." § 355, 105 Stat. 713 (1991). After Texas won independence from Mexico, the Senate resolved that "the State of Texas having established and maintained an independent Government, ... it is expedient and proper ... that the independent political existence of the said State be acknowledged by the Government of the United States." Cong. Globe, 24th Cong., 2d Sess., 83 (1837); see *id.,* at 270.

In the final analysis, the Constitution may well deny Congress power to recognize—the power to make an international commitment accepting a foreign entity as a state, a regime as its government, a place as a part of its territory, and so on. But whatever else § 214(d) may do, it plainly does not make (or require the President to make) a commitment accepting Israel's sovereignty over Jerusalem.

IV

The Court does not try to argue that § 214(d) extends recognition; nor does it try to argue that the President holds the exclusive power to make all nonrecognition decisions relating to the status of Jerusalem. As just shown, these arguments would be impossible to make with a straight face.

The Court instead announces a rule that is blatantly gerrymandered to the facts of this case. It concludes that, in addition to the exclusive power to make the "formal recognition determination," the President holds an ancillary exclusive power "to control ... formal statements by the Executive Branch acknowledging the legitimacy of a state or government and its territorial bounds." *Ante,* at 2096. It follows, the Court explains, that Congress may not "requir[e] the President to contradict an earlier recognition determination in an official document issued by the Executive Branch." *Ibid.* So requiring imports from Jerusalem to be taxed like goods from Israel is fine, but requiring Customs to issue an official invoice to that effect is not? Nonsense.

Recognition is a type of legal act, not a type of statement. It is a leap worthy of the Mad Hatter to go from exclusive authority over making legal commitments about sovereignty to exclusive authority over making statements or issuing documents about national borders. The Court may as well jump from power over issuing declaratory judgments to a monopoly on writing law-review articles.

No consistent or coherent theory supports the Court's decision. At times, the Court seems concerned with the possibility of congressional interference with the President's ability to extend or withhold legal recognition. The Court concedes, as it must, that the notation required by § 214(d) "would not itself constitute a formal act of recognition." *Ante,* at 2095. It still frets, however, that Congress *could* try to regulate the President's "statements" in a way that "override[s] the President's recognition determination." *Ibid.* But "[t]he circumstance, that ... [a] power may be abused, is no answer. All powers may be abused." 2 J. Story, *Commentaries on the Constitution of the United States* § 921, p. 386 (1833). What matters is whether *this* law interferes with the President's ability to withhold recognition. It would be comical to claim that it does. The Court identifies no reason to believe that the United States—or indeed any other country—uses the place-of-birth field in passports and birth reports as a forum for performing the act of recognition. That is why nobody thinks the United States withdraws recognition from Canada when it accommodates a Quebec nationalist's request to have his birthplace recorded as "Montreal."

To the extent doubts linger about whether the United States recognizes Israel's sovereignty over Jerusalem, § 214(d) leaves the President free to dispel them by issuing a disclaimer of intent to recognize. A disclaimer always suffices to prevent an act from effecting recognition. Restatement (Second) of Foreign Relations Law of the United States § 104(1) (1962). Recall that an earlier law grants citizens born in Taiwan the right to have their birthplaces recorded as "Taiwan." The State Department has complied with the law, but states in its Foreign Affairs Manual: "The United States does not officially recognize Taiwan as a 'state' or 'country,' although passport issuing officers may enter 'Taiwan' as a place of birth." 7 FAM § 1300, App. D, § 1340(d)(6). Nothing stops a similar disclaimer here.

At other times, the Court seems concerned with Congress's failure to give effect to a recognition decision that the President has already made. The Court protests, for instance, that § 214(d) "directly contradicts" the President's refusal to recognize Israel's sovereignty over Jerusalem. *Ante,* at 2095. But even if the Constitution empowers the President alone to extend recognition, it nowhere obliges Congress to align its laws with the President's recognition decisions. Because the President and Congress are "perfectly co-ordinate by the terms of their common commission," *The Federalist* No. 49, p. 314

(C. Rossiter ed. 1961) (Madison), the President's use of the recognition power does not constrain Congress's use of its legislative powers.

Congress has legislated without regard to recognition for a long time and in a range of settings. For example, responding in 1817 and 1818 to revolutions in Latin America, Congress amended federal neutrality laws—which originally prohibited private military action for or against *recognized* states—to prohibit private hostilities against *unrecognized* states too. ch. 58, 3 Stat. 370; ch. 88, 3 Stat. 447; see *The Three Friends,* 166 U.S. 1, 52–59, 17 S.Ct. 495, 41 L.Ed. 897 (1897). Legislation from 90 years ago provided for the revision of national immigration quotas upon one country's surrender of territory to another, even if "the transfer ... has not been recognized by the United States." § 12(c), 43 Stat. 161 (1924). Federal law today prohibits murdering a foreign government's officials, 18 U.S.C. § 1116, counterfeiting a foreign government's bonds, § 478, and using American vessels to smuggle goods in violation of a foreign government's laws, § 546—all "irrespective of recognition by the United States," §§ 11, 1116. Just as Congress may legislate independently of recognition in all of those areas, so too may it legislate independently of recognition when regulating the recording of birthplaces.

The Court elsewhere objects that § 214(d) interferes with the autonomy and unity of the Executive Branch, setting the branch against itself. The Court suggests, for instance, that the law prevents the President from maintaining his neutrality about Jerusalem in "his and his agent's statements." *Ante,* at 2095. That is of no constitutional significance. As just shown, Congress has power to legislate without regard to recognition, and where Congress has the power to legislate, the President has a duty to "take Care" that its legislation "be faithfully executed," Art. II, § 3. It is likewise "the duty of the secretary of state to conform to the law"; where Congress imposes a responsibility on him, "he is so far the officer of the law; is amenable to the laws for his conduct; and cannot at his discretion sport away the vested rights of others." *Marbury v. Madison,* 1 Cranch 137, 158, 166, 2 L.Ed. 60 (1803). The Executive's involvement in carrying out this law does not affect its constitutionality; the Executive carries out every law.

The Court's error could be made more apparent by applying its reasoning to the President's power "to make Treaties," Art. II, § 2, cl. 2. There is no question that Congress may, if it wishes, pass laws that openly flout treaties made by the President. *Head Money Cases,* 112 U.S. 580, 597, 5 S.Ct. 247, 28 L.Ed. 798 (1884). Would anyone have dreamt that the President may refuse to carry out such laws—or, to bring the point closer to home, refuse to execute federal courts' judgments under such laws—so that the Executive may "speak with one voice" about the country's international obligations? To ask is to answer. Today's holding puts the implied power to recognize territorial claims (which the Court infers from the power to recognize states, which it infers from the responsibility to receive ambassadors) on a higher footing than the express power to make treaties. And this, even though the *Federalist* describes the making of treaties as a "delicate and important prerogative," but the reception of ambassadors as "more a matter of dignity than of authority," "a circumstance which will be without consequence in the administration of the government." *The Federalist* No. 69, p. 420 (Hamilton).

In the end, the Court's decision does not rest on text or history or precedent. It instead comes down to "functional considerations"—principally the Court's perception that the Nation "must speak with one voice" about the status of Jerusalem. *Ante,* at 2086 (ellipsis and internal quotation marks omitted). The vices of this mode of analysis go beyond mere lack of footing in the Constitution. Functionalism of the sort the Court practices today will *systematically* favor the unitary President over the plural Congress in disputes involving foreign affairs. It is possible that this approach will make for more effective foreign policy, perhaps as effective as that of a monarchy. It is certain that, in the long run, it will erode the structure of separated powers that the People established for the protection of their liberty.

V

Justice Thomas's concurrence deems § 214(d) constitutional to the extent it regulates birth reports, but unconstitutional to the extent it regulates passports. *Ante,* at 2101–2102 (opinion concurring in judgment in part and dissenting in part). The concurrence finds no congressional power that would extend to the issuance or contents of passports. Including the power to regulate foreign commerce—even though passports facilitate the transportation of passengers, "a part of our commerce with foreign nations," *Henderson v. Mayor of New York,* 92 U.S. 259, 270, 23 L.Ed. 543 (1876). Including the power over naturalization—even though passports issued to citizens, like birth reports, "have the same force and effect as proof of United States citizenship as certificates of naturalization," 22 U.S.C. § 2705. Including the power to enforce the Fourteenth Amendment's guarantee that "[a]ll persons born or naturalized in the United States ... are citizens of the United States"—even though a passport provides evidence of citizenship and so helps enforce this guarantee abroad. Including the power to exclude persons from the territory of the United States, see Art. I, § 9, cl. 1—even though passports are the principal means of identifying citizens entitled to entry. Including the powers under which Congress has restricted the ability of various people to leave the country (fugitives from justice, for example, see 18 U.S.C. § 1073)—even though passports are the principal means of controlling exit. Including the power to "make all needful Rules and Regulations respecting the Territory or other Property belonging to the United States," Art. IV, § 3, cl. 2—even though "[a] passport remains at all times the property of the United States," 7 FAM § 1317 (2013). The concurrence's stingy interpretation of the enumerated powers forgets that the Constitution does not "partake of the prolixity of a legal code," that "only its great outlines [are] marked, its important objects designated, and the minor ingredients which compose those objects [left to] be deduced from the nature of the objects themselves." *McCulloch,* 4 Wheat., at 407. It forgets, in other words, "that it is a *constitution* we are expounding." *Ibid.*

Defending Presidential primacy over passports, the concurrence says that the royal prerogative in England included the power to issue and control travel documents akin to the modern passport. *Ante,* at 2085 – 2086. Perhaps so, but that power was assuredly not exclusive. The Aliens Act 1793, for example, enacted almost contemporaneously with our Constitution, required an alien traveling within England to obtain "a passport from [a] mayor or ... [a] justice of [the] peace," "in which passport shall be expressed the name and rank, occupation or description, of such alien." 33 Geo. III, ch. 4, § 8, in 39 Eng. Stat. at Large 12. The Aliens Act 1798 prohibited aliens from leaving the country without "a passport ... first obtained from one of his Majesty's principal secretaries of state," and instructed customs officers to mark, sign, and date passports before allowing their bearers to depart. 38 Geo. III, ch. 50, § 8, in 41 Eng. Stat. at Large 684. These and similar laws discredit any claim that, in the "Anglo-American legal tradition," travel documents have "consistently been issued *and controlled* by the body exercising executive power," *ante,* at 2101 (emphasis added).

Returning to this side of the Atlantic, the concurrence says that passports have a "historical pedigree uniquely associated with the President." *Ante,* at 2111. This statement overlooks the reality that, until Congress restricted the issuance of passports to the State Department in 1856, "passports were also issued by governors, mayors, and even ... notaries public." Assn. of the Bar of the City of New York, Special Committee to Study Passport Procedures, Freedom to Travel 6 (1958). To be sure, early Presidents granted passports without express congressional authorization. *Ante,* at 2086–2087. But this point establishes Presidential authority over passports in the face of congressional *silence,* not Presidential authority in the face of congressional *opposition.* Early in the Republic's history, Congress made it a crime for a consul to "grant a passport or other paper certifying that any alien, knowing him or her to be such, is a citizen of the United States." § 8, 2 Stat. 205 (1803). Closer to the Civil War, Congress expressly authorized the granting of passports, regulated passport fees, and prohibited the issuance of passports to foreign citizens. § 23, 11 Stat. 60–61 (1856). Since then, Congress has made laws about eligibility to receive passports, the duration for which passports remain valid, and even the type of paper used to manufacture passports. 22 U.S.C. §§ 212, 217a; § 617(b), 102 Stat. 1755. (The concurrence makes no attempt to explain how these laws were supported by congressional powers other than those it rejects in the present case.) This Court has held that the President may not curtail a citizen's travel by withholding a passport, *except on grounds approved by Congress. Kent v. Dulles,* 357 U.S. 116, 129, 78 S.Ct. 1113, 2 L.Ed.2d 1204 (1958). History and precedent thus refute any suggestion that the Constitution disables Congress from regulating the President's issuance and formulation of passports.

The concurrence adds that a passport "contains [a] communication directed at a foreign power." *Ante,* at 2111. The "communication" in question is a message that traditionally appears in each passport (though no statute, to my knowledge, expressly requires its inclusion): "The Secretary of State of the United States of America hereby requests all whom it may concern to permit the citizen/national of the United States named herein to pass without delay or hindrance and in case of need to give all lawful aid and protection." App. 22. I leave it to the reader to judge whether a request to "all whom it may concern" qualifies as a "communication directed at a foreign power." Even if it does, its presence does not affect § 214(d)'s constitutionality. Requesting protection is only a "subordinate" function of a passport. *Kent, supra,* at 129, 78 S.Ct. 1113. This subordinate function has never been thought to invalidate other laws regulating the contents of passports; why then would it invalidate this one?

That brings me, in analytic crescendo, to the concurrence's suggestion that *even if* Congress's enumerated powers otherwise encompass § 214(d), and *even if* the President's power to regulate the contents of passports is not exclusive, the law might *still* violate the Constitution, because it "conflict[s]" with the President's passport policy. *Ante,* at 2093. It turns the Constitution upside-down to suggest that in areas of shared authority, it is the executive policy that preempts the law, rather than the other way around. Congress *may* make laws necessary and proper for carrying into execution the President's powers, Art. I, § 8, cl. 18, but the President *must* "take Care" that Congress's legislation "be faithfully executed," Art. II, § 3. And Acts of Congress made in pursuance of the Constitution are the "supreme Law of the Land"; acts of the President (apart from treaties) are not. Art. VI, cl. 2. That is why Chief Justice Marshall was right to think that a law prohibiting the seizure of foreign ships trumped a military order requiring it. *Little v. Barreme,* 2 Cranch 170, 178–179, 2 L.Ed. 243 (1804). It is why Justice Jackson was right to think that a President who "takes measures incompatible with the expressed or implied will of Congress" may "rely only upon his own constitutional powers *minus any constitutional powers of Congress over the matter.*" *Youngstown Sheet & Tube Co. v. Sawyer,* 343 U.S. 579, 637, 72 S.Ct. 863, 96 L.Ed. 1153 (1952) (concurring opinion) (emphasis added). And it is why Justice THOMAS is wrong to think that even if § 214(d) operates in a field of shared authority the President might still prevail.

Whereas the Court's analysis threatens congressional power over foreign affairs with gradual erosion, the concurrence's approach shatters it in one stroke. The combination of (a) the concurrence's assertion of broad, unenumerated "residual powers" in the President, see *ante,* at 2081–2085; (b) its parsimonious interpretation of Congress's enumerated powers, see *ante,* at 2087–2090; and (c) its even more parsimonious interpretation of Congress's authority to enact laws "necessary and proper for carrying into Execution" the President's executive powers, see *ante,* at 2089–2091; produces (d) a presidency more reminiscent of George III than George Washington.

* * *

International disputes about statehood and territory are neither rare nor obscure. Leading foreign debates during the 19th century concerned how the United States should respond to revolutions in Latin America, Texas, Mexico, Hawaii, Cuba. During the 20th century, attitudes toward Communist governments in Russia and China became conspicuous subjects of agitation. Disagreements about Taiwan, Kashmir, and Crimea remain prominent today. A President empowered to decide all questions relating to these matters, immune from laws embodying congressional disagreement with his position, would have uncontrolled mastery of a vast share of the Nation's foreign affairs.

That is not the chief magistrate under which the American People agreed to live when they adopted the national charter. They believed that "[t]he accumulation of all powers, legislative, executive, and judiciary, in the same hands, ... may justly be pronounced the very definition of tyranny." *The Federalist* No. 47, p. 301 (Madison). For this reason, they did not entrust either the President or Congress with sole power to adopt uncontradictable policies about *any* subject—foreign-sovereignty disputes included. They instead gave each political department its own powers, and with that the freedom to contradict the other's policies. Under the Constitution they approved, Congress may require Zivotofsky's passport and birth report to record his birthplace as Israel, even if that requirement clashes with the President's preference for neutrality about the status of Jerusalem.

I dissent.

2

The Judicial Power

Committing substantive-due-process atrocities
City of Chicago v. Morales, 527 U.S. 41 (1999)

An immense and frightening antidemocratic power
Dickerson v. United States, 530 U.S. 428 (2000)

A curious constitution only a judge could love
Rogers v. Tennessee, 532 U.S. 451 (2001)

Judges gone wild
Brown v. Plata, 563 U.S. 493 (2011)

The United States Supreme Court is not only a court of final appeal, it is also the highest Court in the federal judiciary and, as such, the Justices must regulate all aspects of the federal court system including access to the courts and the proper allocation of power among the judiciary, the Executive, and Congress. The cases in this chapter present a series of questions to the Court that touch on basic issues of fairness and due process, including the "vagueness" doctrine and retroactivity of laws. They also touch upon the extent to which Congress can exercise its powers on the Courts and vice versa. Justice Scalia's dissents reflect his textualist approach to the Constitution, his strong belief in the rights of states versus expansive Congressional legislation, and his strict approach to Constitutional interpretation.

Committing substantive-due-process atrocities
City of Chicago v. Morales,
527 U.S. 41 (1999)

Justice Scalia, dissenting.

The citizens of Chicago were once free to drive about the city at whatever speed they wished. At some point Chicagoans (or perhaps Illinoisans) decided this would not do, and imposed prophylactic speed limits designed to assure safe operation by the average (or perhaps even subaverage) driver with the average (or perhaps even subaverage) vehicle. This infringed upon the "freedom" of all citizens, but was not unconstitutional.

Similarly, the citizens of Chicago were once free to stand around and gawk at the scene of an accident. At some point Chicagoans discovered that this obstructed traffic and caused more accidents. They did not make the practice unlawful, but they did authorize police officers to order the crowd to disperse, and imposed penalties for refusal to obey such an order. Again, this prophylactic measure infringed upon the "freedom" of all citizens, but was not unconstitutional.

Until the ordinance that is before us today was adopted, the citizens of Chicago were free to stand about in public places with no apparent purpose—to engage, that is, in conduct that appeared to be loitering. In recent years, however, the city has been afflicted with criminal street gangs. As reflected in the record before us, these gangs congregated in public places to deal in drugs, and to terrorize the neighborhoods by demonstrating control over their "turf." Many residents of the inner city felt that they were prisoners in their own homes. Once again, Chicagoans decided that to eliminate the problem it was worth restricting some of the freedom that they once enjoyed. The means they took was similar to the second, and more mild, example given above rather than the first: Loitering was not made unlawful, but when a group of people occupied a public place without an apparent purpose and in the company of a known gang member, police officers were authorized to order them to disperse, and the failure to obey such an order was made unlawful. See Chicago Municipal Code § 8-4-015 (1992). The minor limitation upon the free state of nature that this prophylactic arrangement imposed upon all Chicagoans seemed to them (and it seems to me) a small price to pay for liberation of their streets.

The majority today invalidates this perfectly reasonable measure by ignoring our rules governing facial challenges, by elevating loitering to a constitutionally guaranteed right, and by discerning vagueness where, according to our usual standards, none exists.

I

Respondents' consolidated appeal presents a facial challenge to the Chicago ordinance on vagueness grounds. When a facial challenge is successful, the law in question is declared to be unenforceable in *all* its applications, and not just in its particular application to the party in suit. To tell the truth, it is highly questionable whether federal courts have any business making such a declaration. The rationale for our power to review federal legislation for constitutionality, expressed in *Marbury v. Madison,* 1 Cranch 137, 2 L.Ed. 60 (1803), was that we *had* to do so in order to decide the case before us. But that rationale only extends so far as to require us to determine that the statute is unconstitutional as applied to *this* party, in the circumstances of *this* case.

That limitation was fully grasped by Tocqueville, in his famous chapter on the power of the judiciary in American society:

> "The second characteristic of judicial power is, that it pronounces on special cases, and not upon general principles. If a judge, in deciding a particular point, destroys a general principle by passing a judgment which tends to reject all the inferences from that principle, and consequently to annul it, he remains within the ordinary limits of his functions. But if he directly attacks a general principle without having a particular case in view, he leaves the circle in which all nations have agreed to confine his authority; he assumes a more important, and perhaps a more useful influence, than that of the magistrate; but he ceases to represent the judicial power.
>
> .....

"Whenever a law which the judge holds to be unconstitutional is invoked in a tribunal of the United States, he may refuse to admit it as a rule .... But as soon as a judge has refused to apply any given law in a case, that law immediately loses a portion of its moral force. Those to whom it is prejudicial learn that means exist of overcoming its authority; and similar suits are multiplied, until it becomes powerless. ... The political power which the Americans have intrusted to their courts of justice is therefore immense; but the evils of this power are considerably diminished by the impossibility of attacking the laws except through the courts of justice. ... [W]hen a judge contests a law in an obscure debate on some particular case, the importance of his attack is concealed from public notice; his decision bears upon the interest of an individual, and the law is slighted only incidentally. Moreover, although it is censured, it is not abolished; its moral force may be diminished, but its authority is not taken away; and its final destruction can be accomplished only by the reiterated attacks of judicial functionaries." *Democracy in America* 73, 75–76 (R. Heffner ed.1956).

As Justice Sutherland described our system in his opinion for a unanimous Court in *Massachusetts v. Mellon,* 262 U.S.

447, 488, 43 S.Ct. 597, 67 L.Ed. 1078 (1923):

> "We have no power *per se* to review and annul acts of Congress on the ground that they are unconstitutional. That question may be considered only when the justification for some direct injury suffered or threatened, presenting a justiciable issue, is made to rest upon such an act. Then the power exercised is that of ascertaining and declaring the law applicable to the controversy. It amounts to little more than the negative power to disregard an unconstitutional enactment, which otherwise would stand in the way of the enforcement of a legal right.... If a case for preventive relief be presented the court enjoins, in effect, not the execution of the statute, but the acts of the official, the statute notwithstanding."

And as Justice Brennan described our system in his opinion for a unanimous Court in *United States v. Raines,* 362 U.S. 17, 20–22, 80 S.Ct. 519, 4 L.Ed.2d 524 (1960):

> "The very foundation of the power of the federal courts to declare Acts of Congress unconstitutional lies in the power and duty of those courts to decide cases and controversies before them.... This Court, as is the case with all federal courts, 'has no jurisdiction to pronounce any statute, either of a State or of the United States, void, because irreconcilable with the Constitution, except as it is called upon to adjudge the legal rights of litigants in actual controversies. In the exercise of that jurisdiction, it is bound by two rules, to which it has rigidly adhered, one, never to anticipate a question of constitutional law in advance of the necessity of deciding it; the other never to formulate a rule of constitutional law broader than is required by the precise facts to which it is to be applied.' ... Kindred to these rules is the rule that one to whom application of a statute is constitutional will not be heard to attack the statute on the ground that

> impliedly it might also be taken as applying to other persons or other situations in which its application might be unconstitutional.... The delicate power of pronouncing an Act of Congress unconstitutional is not to be exercised with reference to hypothetical cases thus imagined."

It seems to me fundamentally incompatible with this system for the Court not to be content to find that a statute is unconstitutional as applied to the person before it, but to go further and pronounce that the statute is unconstitutional in *all* applications. Its reasoning may well suggest as much, but to pronounce a *holding* on that point seems to me no more than an advisory opinion—which a federal court should never issue at all, see *Hayburn's Case,* 2 Dall. 408, 1 L.Ed. 436 (1792), and *especially* should not issue with regard to a constitutional question, as to which we seek to avoid even *non* advisory opinions, see, *e.g.,* *Ashwander v. TVA,* 297 U.S. 288, 347, 56 S.Ct. 466, 80 L.Ed. 688 (1936) (Brandeis, J., concurring). I think it quite improper, in short, to ask the constitutional claimant before us: Do you just want us to say that this statute cannot constitutionally be applied to you in this case, or do you want to go for broke and try to get the statute pronounced void in all its applications?

I must acknowledge, however, that for some of the present century we have done just this. But until recently, at least, we have—except in free-speech cases subject to the doctrine of overbreadth, see, *e.g., New York v. Ferber,* 458 U.S. 747, 769–773, 102 S.Ct. 3348, 73 L.Ed.2d 1113 (1982)—*required* the facial challenge to *be* a go-for-broke proposition. That is to say, before declaring a statute to be void in all its applications (something we should not be doing in the first place), we have at least imposed upon the litigant the eminently reasonable requirement that he establish that the statute was *unconstitutional* in all its applications. (I say that is an eminently reasonable requirement, not only because we should not be holding a statute void in all its applications unless it is unconstitutional in all its applications, but also because *unless* it is unconstitutional in all its applications we do not even know, without conducting an as-applied analysis, whether it is void with regard to the very litigant *before* us—whose case, after all, was the occasion for undertaking this inquiry in the first place.)

As we said in *United States v. Salerno,* 481 U.S. 739, 745, 107 S.Ct. 2095, 95 L.Ed.2d 697 (1987):

> "A facial challenge to a legislative Act is, of course, the most difficult challenge to mount successfully, since the *challenger must establish that no set of circumstances exists under which the Act would be valid.* The fact that [a legislative Act] might operate unconstitutionally under some conceivable set of circumstances is insufficient to render it wholly invalid, since we have not recognized an 'overbreadth' doctrine outside the limited context of the First Amendment." (Emphasis added.)

This proposition did not originate with *Salerno,* but had been expressed in a line of prior opinions. See, *e.g., Members of City Council of Los Angeles v. Taxpayers for Vincent,* 466 U.S. 789, 796, 104 S.Ct. 2118, 80 L.Ed.2d 772 (1984) (opinion for the Court by Stevens, J.) (statute not implicating First Amendment rights is invalid on its face if "it is unconstitutional in every conceivable application"); *Schall v. Martin,* 467 U.S. 253, 269, n. 18, 104 S.Ct. 2403, 81 L.Ed.2d 207 (1984); *Hoffman Estates v. Flipside, Hoffman Estates, Inc.,* 455 U.S. 489, 494–495, 497, 102 S.Ct. 1186, 71 L.Ed.2d 362 (1982); *United States v. National Dairy Products Corp.,* 372 U.S. 29, 31–32, 83 S.Ct. 594, 9 L.Ed.2d 561 (1963); *Raines,* 362 U.S., at 21, 80 S.Ct. 519. And the proposition has been reaffirmed in many cases and opinions since. See, *e.g., Anderson v. Edwards,* 514 U.S. 143,

155–156, n. 6, 115 S.Ct. 1291, 131 L.Ed.2d 178 (1995) (unanimous Court); *Babbitt v. Sweet Home Chapter, Communities for Great Ore.,* 515 U.S. 687, 699, 115 S.Ct. 2407, 132 L.Ed.2d 597 (1995) (opinion for the Court by Stevens, J.) (facial challenge asserts that a challenged statute or regulation is invalid "in every circum-stance"); *Reno v. Flores,* 507 U.S. 292, 301, 113 S.Ct. 1439, 123 L.Ed.2d 1 (1993); *Rust v. Sullivan,* 500 U.S. 173, 183, 111 S.Ct. 1759, 114 L.Ed.2d 233 (1991); *Ohio v. Akron Center for Reproductive Health,* 497 U.S. 502, 514, 110 S.Ct. 2972, 111 L.Ed.2d 405 (1990) (opinion of Kennedy, J.); *Webster v. Reproductive Health Servs.,* 492 U.S. 490, 523–524, 109 S.Ct. 3040, 106 L.Ed.2d 410 (1989) (O'Connor, J., concurring in part and concurring in judgment); *New York State Club Assn., Inc. v. City of New York,* 487 U.S. 1, 11–12, 108 S.Ct. 2225, 101 L.Ed.2d 1 (1988). Unsurprisingly, given the clarity of our general jurisprudence on this point, the Federal Courts of Appeals *all* apply the *Salerno* standard in adjudicating facial challenges.

I am aware, of course, that in some recent facial-challenge cases the Court has, without any attempt at explanation, created entirely irrational exceptions to the "unconstitutional in every conceivable application" rule, when the statutes at issue concerned hot-button social issues on which "informed opinion" was zealously united. See *Romer v. Evans,* 517 U.S. 620, 643, 116 S.Ct. 1620, 134 L.Ed.2d 855 (1996) (Scalia, J., dissenting) (homosexual rights); *Planned Parenthood of Southeastern Pa. v. Casey,* 505 U.S. 833, 895, 112 S.Ct. 2791, 120 L.Ed.2d 674 (1992) (abortion rights). But the present case does not even lend itself to such a "political correctness" exception—which, though illogical, is at least predictable. It is not *à la mode* to favor gang members and associated loiterers over the beleaguered law-abiding residents of the inner city.

When our normal criteria for facial challenges are applied, it is clear that the Justices in the majority have transposed the burden of proof. Instead of requiring respondents, who are challenging the ordinance, to show that it is invalid in all its applications, they have required petitioner to show that it is valid in all its applications. Both the plurality opinion and the concurrences display a lively imagination, creating hypothetical situations in which the law's application would (in their view) be ambiguous. But that creative role has been usurped from petitioner, who can defeat respondents' facial challenge by conjuring up *a single valid application* of the law. My contribution would go something like this: Tony, a member of the Jets criminal street gang, is standing alongside and chatting with fellow gang members while staking out their turf at Promontory Point on the South Side of Chicago; the group is flashing gang signs and displaying their distinctive tattoos to passersby. Officer Krupke, applying the ordinance at issue here, orders the group to disperse. After some speculative discussion (probably irrelevant here) over whether the Jets are depraved because they are deprived, Tony and the other gang members break off further conversation with the statement—not entirely coherent, but evidently intended to be rude—"Gee, Officer Krupke, krup you." A tense standoff ensues until Officer Krupke arrests the group for failing to obey his dispersal order. Even assuming (as the Justices in the majority do, but I do not) that a law requiring obedience to a dispersal order is impermissibly vague unless it is clear to the objects of the order, before its issuance, that their conduct justifies it, I find it hard to believe that the Jets would not have known they had it coming. That should settle the matter of respondents' facial challenge to the ordinance's vagueness.

Of course respondents would still be able to claim that the ordinance was vague as applied to them. But the ultimate demonstration of the inappropriateness of the Court's holding of *facial* invalidity is the fact that it is doubtful whether some of these respondents could even sustain an *as-applied* challenge on the basis of the majority's own criteria. For instance, respondent Jose Renteria—who admitted that he was a member of the Satan Disciples gang—was observed by the arresting officer loitering on a street corner with other gang members. The officer issued a dispersal order, but when she returned to the same corner 15 to 20 minutes later, Renteria was still there with his friends, whereupon he was arrested. In another example, respondent Daniel Washington and several others—who admitted they were members of the Vice Lords gang—were observed by the arresting officer loitering in the street, yelling at passing vehicles, stopping traffic, and preventing pedestrians from using the sidewalks. The arresting officer issued a dispersal order, issued *another* dispersal order later when the group did not move, and finally arrested the group when they were found loitering in the same place still later. Finally, respondent Gregorio Gutierrez—who had previously admitted to the arresting officer his membership in the Latin Kings gang—was observed loitering with two other men. The officer issued a dispersal order, drove around the block, and arrested the men after finding them in the same place upon his return. See Brief for Petitioner 7, n. 5; Brief for United States as *Amicus Curiae* 16, n. 11. Even on the majority's assumption that to avoid vagueness it must be clear to the object of the dispersal order *ex ante* that his conduct is covered by the ordinance, it seems most improbable that any of these as-applied challenges would be sustained. Much less is it possible to say that the ordinance is invalid in *all* its applications.

II

The plurality's explanation for its departure from the usual rule governing facial challenges is seemingly contained in the following statement: "[This] is a criminal law that contains no *mens rea* requirement ... *and* infringes on constitutionally protected rights .... When vagueness permeates the text of *such* a law, it is subject to facial attack." *Ante,* at 1858 (emphasis added). The proposition is set forth with such assurance that one might suppose that it repeats some well-accepted formula in our jurisprudence: (Criminal law without *mens rea* requirement) + (infringement of constitutionally protected right) + (vagueness) = (entitlement to facial invalidation). There is no such formula; the plurality has made it up for this case, as the absence of any citation demonstrates.

But no matter. None of the three factors that the plurality relies upon exists anyway. I turn first to the support for the proposition that there is a constitutionally protected right to loiter—or, as the plurality more favorably describes it, for a person to "remain in a public place of his choice." *Ibid.* The plurality thinks much of this Fundamental Freedom to Loiter, which it contrasts with such lesser, constitutionally *un* protected, activities as doing (ugh!) *business*: "This is not an ordinance that simply regulates business behavior and contains a scienter requirement.... It is a criminal law that contains no *mens rea* requirement ... and infringes on constitutionally protected rights." *Ibid.* (internal quotation marks omitted). (Poor Alexander Hamilton, who has seen his "commercial republic" devolve, in the eyes of the plurality, at least, into an "indolent republic," see *The Federalist* No. 6, p. 56; No. 11, pp. 84–91 (C. Rossiter ed.1961).)

Of course every activity, even scratching one's head, can be called a "constitutional right" if one means by that term nothing more than the fact that the activity is covered (as all are) by the Equal Protection Clause, so that those who engage in it cannot be singled out without "rational basis." See *FCC v. Beach Communications, Inc.,* 508 U.S. 307, 313, 113 S.Ct. 2096,

124 L.Ed.2d 211 (1993). But using the term in that sense utterly impoverishes our constitutional discourse. We would then need a *new* term for those activities—such as political speech or religious worship—that cannot be forbidden even *with* rational basis.

The plurality tosses around the term "constitutional right" in this renegade sense, because there is not the slightest evidence for the existence of a genuine constitutional right to loiter. Justice Thomas recounts the vast historical tradition of criminalizing the activity. *Post,* at 1881–1883 (dissenting opinion). It is simply not maintainable that the right to loiter would have been regarded as an essential attribute of liberty at the time of the framing or at the time of adoption of the Fourteenth Amendment. For the plurality, however, the historical practices of our people are nothing more than a speed bump on the road to the "right" result. Its opinion blithely proclaims: "Neither this history nor the scholarly compendia in Justice Thomas' dissent, [*ibid.*], persuades us that the right to engage in loitering that is entirely harmless in both purpose and effect is not a part of the liberty protected by the Due Process Clause." *Ante,* at 1858, n. 20. The entire practice of using the Due Process Clause to add judicially favored rights to the limitations upon democracy set forth in the Bill of Rights (usually under the rubric of so-called "substantive due process") is in my view judicial usurpation. But we have, recently at least, sought to limit the damage by tethering the courts' "right-making" power to an objective criterion. In *Washington v. Glucksberg,* 521 U.S. 702, 720–721, 117 S.Ct. 2258, 138 L.Ed.2d 772 (1997), we explained our "established method" of substantive due process analysis: carefully and narrowly describing the asserted right, and then examining whether that right is manifested in "[o]ur Nation's history, legal traditions, and practices." See also *Collins v. Harker Heights,* 503 U.S. 115,

125–126, 112 S.Ct. 1061, 117 L.Ed.2d 261 (1992); *Michael H. v. Gerald D.*, 491 U.S. 110, 122–123, 109 S.Ct. 2333, 105 L.Ed.2d 91 (1989); *Moore v. East Cleveland,* 431 U.S. 494, 502–503, 97 S.Ct. 1932, 52 L.Ed.2d 531 (1977). The plurality opinion not only ignores this necessary limitation, but it leaps far beyond any substantive-due-process atrocity we have ever committed, by actually placing the burden of proof upon the defendant to establish that loitering is *not* a "fundamental liberty." It never does marshal any support *for* the proposition that loitering *is* a constitutional right, contenting itself with a (transparently inadequate) explanation of why the historical record of laws banning loitering does not positively *contradict* that proposition, and the (transparently erroneous) assertion that the city of Chicago appears to have conceded the point. It is enough for the Members of the plurality that "history ... [fails to] persuad[e] us that the right to engage in loitering that is entirely harmless in both purpose and effect is *not* a part of the liberty protected by the Due Process Clause," *ante,* at 1858, n. 20 (emphasis added); they apparently think it quite unnecessary for anything to persuade them that it *is.*

It would be unfair, however, to criticize the plurality's failed attempt to establish that loitering is a constitutionally protected right while saying nothing of the concurrences. The plurality at least makes an attempt. The concurrences, on the other hand, make no pretense at attaching their broad "vagueness invalidates" rule to a liberty interest. As far as appears from Justice O'Connor's and Justice Breyer's opinions, *no* police officer may issue *any* order, affecting *any* insignificant sort of citizen conduct (except, perhaps, an order addressed to the unprotected class of "gang members") unless the standards for the issuance of that order are precise. No modern urban society—and probably none since London got big enough to have sewers—could function under such a rule. There are innumerable reasons why it may be important for a constable to tell a pedestrian to "move on"—and even if it were possible to list in an ordinance all of the reasons that are known, many are simply unpredictable. Hence the (entirely reasonable) Rule of the city of New York which reads: "No person shall fail, neglect or refuse to comply with the lawful direction or command of any Police Officer, Urban Park Ranger, Parks Enforcement Patrol Officer or other [Parks and Recreation] Department employee, indicated verbally, by gesture or otherwise." 56 RCNY § 1-03(c)(1) (1996). It is one thing to uphold an "as-applied" challenge when a pedestrian disobeys such an order that is unreasonable—or even when a pedestrian asserting some true "liberty" interest (holding a political rally, for instance) disobeys such an order that is reasonable *but unexplained.* But to say that such a general ordinance permitting "lawful orders" is void *in all its applications* demands more than a safe and orderly society can reasonably deliver.

Justice Kennedy apparently recognizes this, since he acknowledges that "some police commands will subject a citizen to prosecution for disobeying whether or not the citizen knows why the order is given," including, for example, an order "tell[ing] a pedestrian not to enter a building" when the reason is "to avoid impeding a rescue team." *Ante,* at 1865 (opinion concurring in part and concurring in judgment). But his only explanation of why the present interference with the "right to loiter" does not fall within that permitted scope of action is as follows: "The predicate of an order to disperse is not, in my view, sufficient to eliminate doubts regarding the adequacy of notice under this ordinance." *Ibid.* I have not the slightest idea what this means. But I *do* understand that the followup explanatory sentence, showing how this principle invalidates the present ordinance, applies equally to the rescue-team example that Justice Kennedy thinks is constitutional—as is demonstrated by substituting for references to the facts of the present case (shown in italics) references to his rescue-team hypothetical (shown in brackets): "A citizen, while engaging in a wide array of innocent conduct, is not likely to know when he may be subject to a *dispersal order* [order not to enter a building] based on the officer's own knowledge of *the identity or affiliations of other persons with whom the citizen is congregating* [what is going on in the building]; nor may the citizen be able to assess what an officer might conceive to be *the citizen's lack of an apparent purpose* [the impeding of a rescue team]." *Ibid.*

III

I turn next to that element of the plurality's facial-challenge formula which consists of the proposition that this criminal ordinance contains no *mens rea* requirement. The first step in analyzing this proposition is to determine what the *actus reus,* to which that *mens rea* is supposed to be attached, consists of. The majority believes that loitering forms part of (indeed, the essence of) the offense, and must be proved if conviction is to be obtained. See *ante,* at 1854, 1856, 1857–1858, 1859–1860, 1861, 1862 (plurality and majority opinions); *ante,* at 1863–1864 (O'Connor, J., concurring in part and concurring in judgment); *ante,* at 1865 (Kennedy, J., concurring in part and concurring in judgment); *ante,* at 1866–1867 (Breyer, J., concurring in part and concurring in judgment). That is not what the ordinance provides. The only part of the ordinance that refers to loitering is the portion that addresses, not the punishable conduct of the defendant, but what the police officer must observe before he can issue an order to disperse; and what he must observe is carefully defined in terms of what the defendant *appears* to be doing, not in terms of what the defendant is *actually* doing. The ordinance does not require that the defendant have been loitering (*i.e.*, have been remaining in one place with no purpose), but rather that the police officer have observed him remaining in one place without any *apparent* purpose. Someone who in fact *has* a genuine purpose for remaining where he is (waiting for a friend, for example, or waiting to hold up a bank) *can* be ordered to move on (assuming the other conditions of the ordinance are met), so long as his remaining has no *apparent* purpose. It is likely, to be sure, that the ordinance will come down most heavily upon those who are *actually* loitering (those who *really* have no purpose in remaining where they are); but that activity is not a condition for issuance of the dispersal order.

The *only* act of a defendant that is made punishable by the ordinance—or, indeed, that is even mentioned by the ordinance—is his failure to "promptly obey" an order to disperse. The question, then, is whether that *actus reus* must be accompanied by any wrongful intent—and of course it must. As the Court itself describes the requirement, "a person must *disobey* the officer's order." *Ante*, at 1854 (emphasis added). No one thinks a defendant could be successfully prosecuted under the ordinance if he did not hear the order to disperse, or if he suffered a paralysis that rendered his compliance impossible. The willful failure to obey a police order is wrongful intent enough.

IV

Finally, I address the last of the three factors in the plurality's facial-challenge formula: the proposition that the ordinance is vague. It is not. Even under the ersatz overbreadth standard applied in *Kolender v. Lawson*, 461 U.S. 352, 358, n. 8, 103 S.Ct. 1855, 75 L.Ed.2d 903 (1983), which allows facial challenges if a law reaches "a substantial amount of constitutionally protected conduct," respondents' claim fails because the ordinance would not be vague in most or even a substantial number of applications. A law is unconstitutionally vague if its lack of definitive standards either (1) fails to apprise persons of ordinary intelligence of the prohibited conduct, or (2) encourages arbitrary and discriminatory enforcement. See, *e.g.*, *Grayned v. City of Rockford,* 408 U.S. 104, 108, 92 S.Ct. 2294, 33 L.Ed.2d 222 (1972).

The plurality relies primarily upon the first of these aspects. Since, it reasons, "the loitering is the conduct that the ordinance is designed to prohibit," and "an officer may issue an order only after prohibited conduct has already occurred," *ante,* at 1860, the order to disperse cannot itself serve "to apprise persons of ordinary intelligence of the prohibited conduct." What counts for purposes of vagueness analysis, however, is not what the ordinance is "designed to prohibit," but what it actually subjects to criminal penalty. As discussed earlier, that consists of nothing but the refusal to obey a dispersal order, as to which there is no doubt of adequate notice of the prohibited conduct. The plurality's suggestion that even the dispersal order *itself* is unconstitutionally vague, because it does not specify *how far to disperse(!),* see *ante,* at 1860, scarcely requires a response. If it were true, it would render unconstitutional for vagueness many of the Presidential proclamations issued under that provision of the United States Code which requires the President, before using the militia or the Armed Forces for law enforcement, to issue a proclamation ordering the insurgents to disperse. See 10 U.S.C. § 334. President Eisenhower's proclamation relating to the obstruction of court-ordered enrollment of black students in public schools at Little Rock, Arkansas, read as follows: "I ... command all persons engaged in such obstruction of justice to cease and desist therefrom, and to disperse forthwith." Presidential Proclamation No. 3204, 3 CFR 132 (1954–1958 Comp.). See also Presidential Proclamation No. 3645, 3 CFR 103 (1964–1965 Comp.) (ordering those obstructing the civil rights march from Selma to Montgomery, Alabama, to "disperse ... forthwith"). See also *Boos v. Barry,* 485 U.S. 312, 331, 108 S.Ct. 1157, 99 L.Ed.2d 333 (1988) (rejecting overbreadth/vagueness challenge to a law allowing police officers to order congregations near foreign embassies to disperse); *Cox v. Louisiana,* 379 U.S. 536, 551, 85 S.Ct. 453, 13 L.Ed.2d 471 (1965) (rejecting vagueness challenge to the dispersal-order prong of a breach-of-the-peace statute and describing that prong as "narrow and specific").

For its determination of unconstitutional vagueness, the Court relies secondarily—and Justice O'Connor's and Justice Breyer's concurrences exclusively—upon the second aspect of that doctrine, which requires sufficient specificity to prevent arbitrary and discriminatory law enforcement. See *ante,* at 1861 (majority opinion); *ante,* at 1863 (O'Connor, J., concurring in part and concurring in judgment); *ante,* at 1866, 1867 (Breyer, J., concurring in part and concurring in judgment). In discussing whether Chicago's ordinance meets that requirement, the Justices in the majority hide behind an artificial construct of judicial restraint. They point to the Supreme Court of Illinois' statement that the "apparent purpose" standard "provides absolute discretion to police officers to decide what activities constitute loitering," 177 Ill.2d 440, 457, 227 Ill.Dec. 130, 140, 687 N.E.2d 53, 63 (1997), and protest that it would be wrong to construe the language of the ordinance more narrowly than did the State's highest court. *Ante,* at 1861, 1862 (majority opinion); *ante,* at 1864–1865 (O'Connor, J., concurring in part and concurring in judgment). The "absolute discretion" statement, however, is nothing more than the Illinois Supreme Court's *characterization* of what the language achieved—after that court refused (as I do) to read in any limitations that the words do not fairly contain. It is not a construction of the language (to which we are bound) but a legal conclusion (to which we most assuredly are not bound).

The criteria for issuance of a dispersal order under the Chicago ordinance could hardly be clearer. First, the law requires police officers to "reasonably believ[e]" that one of the group to which the order is issued is a "criminal street gang member." This resembles a probable-cause standard, and the Chicago Police Department's General Order 92-4 (1992)—promulgated to govern enforcement of the ordinance—makes the probable-cause requirement explicit. Under the Order, officers must have probable cause to believe that an individual is a member of a criminal street gang, to be substantiated by the officer's "experience and knowledge of the alleged offenders" and by "specific, documented and reliable information" such as reliable witness testimony or an individual's admission of gang membership or display of distinctive colors, tattoos, signs, or other markings worn by members of particular criminal street gangs. App. to Pet. for Cert. 67a–69a, 71a–72a.

Second, the ordinance requires that the group be "remain[ing] in any one place with no apparent purpose." Justice O'Connor's assertion that this applies to "any person standing in a public place," *ante,* at 1864, is a distortion. The ordinance does not apply to "standing," but to "remain [ing]"—a term which in this context obviously means "[to] endure or persist," see *American Heritage Dictionary* 1525 (1992). There may be some ambiguity at the margin, but "remain[ing] in one place" requires more than a temporary stop, and is clear in most of its applications, including all of those represented by the facts surrounding respondents' arrests described *supra,* at 1872–1873.

As for the phrase "with no apparent purpose": Justice O'Connor again distorts this adjectival phrase, by separating it from the word that it modifies. "[A]ny person standing on the street," her concurrence says, "has a general 'purpose'—even if it is simply to stand," and thus "the ordinance permits police officers to choose which purposes are *permissible.*" *Ante,* at 1863. But Chicago police officers enforcing the ordinance are not looking for people with no apparent purpose (who are regrettably in oversupply); they are looking for people who "remain in any one place with no apparent purpose"—that is, who remain there without any apparent reason *for remaining there.* That is not difficult to perceive.

The Court's attempt to demonstrate the vagueness of the ordinance produces the following peculiar statement: "The 'no apparent purpose' standard for making [the decision to issue an order to disperse] is inherently subjective because its application depends on whether some purpose is 'apparent' to the officer on the scene." *Ante,* at 1862. In the Court's view, a person's lack of any purpose in staying in one location is presumably an *objective* factor, and what the ordinance requires as a condition of an order to disperse—the absence of any *apparent* purpose—is a *subjective* factor. This side of the looking glass, just the opposite is true.

Elsewhere, of course, the Court acknowledges the clear, objective commands of the ordinance, and indeed relies upon them to paint it as unfair:

> "In any public place in the city of Chicago, persons who stand or sit in the company of a gang member may be ordered to disperse unless their purpose is apparent. The mandatory language in the enactment directs the police to issue an order without first making any inquiry about their possible purposes. It matters not whether the reason that a gang member and his father, for example, might loiter near Wrigley Field is to rob an unsuspecting fan or just to get a glimpse of Sammy Sosa leaving the ballpark; in either event, if their purpose is not apparent to a nearby police officer, she may—indeed, she 'shall'—order them to disperse." *Ante,* at 1861.

Quite so. And the fact that this clear instruction to the officers "reach [es] a substantial amount of innocent conduct," *ibid.*, would be invalidating if that conduct were constitutionally protected against abridgment, such as speech or the practice of religion. Remaining in one place is *not* so protected, and so (as already discussed) it is up to the citizens of Chicago—not us—to decide whether the tradeoff is worth it.

Justice Breyer's concurrence tries to perform the impossible feat of affirming our unquestioned rule that a criminal statute that is so vague as to give constitutionally inadequate notice to *some* violators may nonetheless be enforced against those whose conduct is clearly covered, see *ante,* at 1866, citing *Parker v. Levy,* 417 U.S. 733, 94 S.Ct. 2547, 41 L.Ed.2d 439 (1974), while at the same time asserting that a statute which "delegates too much discretion to a police officer" is invalid in *all* its applications, even where the officer uses his discretion "wisely," *ante,* at 1866. But the vagueness that causes notice to be inadequate is the very same vagueness that causes "too much discretion" to be lodged in the enforcing officer. Put another way: A law that gives the policeman clear guidance in all cases gives the public clear guidance in all cases as well. Thus, what Justice Breyer gives with one hand, he takes away with the other. In his view, vague statutes that nonetheless give adequate notice to *some* violators are not unenforceable against those violators because of inadequate notice, but *are* unenforceable against them "because the policeman enjoys too much discretion in *every* case," *ibid.* This is simply contrary to our case law, including *Parker v. Levy, supra.*

V

The plurality points out that Chicago already has several laws that reach the intimidating and unlawful gang-related conduct the ordinance was directed at. See *ante,* at 1857, n. 17. The problem, of course, well recognized by Chicago's city council, is that the gang members cease their intimidating and unlawful behavior under the watchful eye of police officers, but return to it as soon as the police drive away. The only solution, the council concluded, was to clear the streets of congregations of gangs, their drug customers, and their associates.

Justice O'Connor's concurrence proffers the same empty solace of existing laws useless for the purpose at hand, see *ante,* at 1864, but seeks to be helpful by suggesting some measures *similar* to this ordinance that *would* be constitutional. It says that Chicago could, for example, enact a law that "directly prohibit[s] the presence of a large collection of obviously brazen, insistent, and lawless gang members and hangers-on on the public ways, that intimidates residents." *Ibid.* (internal quotation marks omitted). (If the majority considers the present ordinance too vague, it would be fun to see what it makes of "a large collection of obviously brazen, insistent, and lawless gang members.") This prescription of the concurrence is largely a quotation from the plurality—which itself answers the concurrence's suggestion that such a law would be helpful by pointing out that the city already "has several laws that serve this purpose." *Ante,* at 1857, n. 17 (plurality opinion) (citing extant laws against "intimidation," "streetgang criminal drug conspiracy," and "mob action"). The problem, again, is that the intimidation and lawlessness do not occur when the police are in sight.

Justice O'Connor's concurrence also proffers another cure: "If the ordinance applied only to persons reasonably believed to be gang members, this requirement might have cured the ordinance's vagueness because it would have directed the manner in which the order was issued by specifying to whom the order could be issued." *Ante,* at 1864 (the Court agrees that this might be a cure, see *ante,* at 1862). But the ordinance already specifies to whom the order can be issued: persons remaining in one place with no apparent purpose in the company of a gang member. And if "remain[ing] in one place with no apparent purpose" is so vague as to give the police unbridled discretion in controlling the conduct of nongang members, it surpasses understanding how it ceases to be so vague when applied to gang members *alone.* Surely gang members cannot be decreed to be outlaws, subject to the merest whim of the police as the rest of us are not.

* * *

The fact is that the present ordinance is entirely clear in its application, cannot be violated except with full knowledge and intent, and vests no more discretion in the police than innumerable other measures authorizing police orders to preserve the public peace and safety. As suggested by their tortured analyses, and by their suggested solutions that bear no relation to the identified constitutional problem, the majority's real quarrel with the Chicago ordinance is simply that it permits (or indeed requires) too much harmless conduct by innocent citizens to be proscribed. As Justice O'Connor's concurrence says with disapprobation, "the ordinance applies to hundreds of thousands of persons who are *not* gang members, standing on any sidewalk or in any park, coffee shop, bar, or other location open to the public." *Ante,* at 1864 (internal quotation marks omitted).

But in our democratic system, how much harmless conduct to proscribe is not a judgment to be made by the courts. So long as constitutionally guaranteed rights are not affected, and so long as the proscription has a rational basis, *all sorts* of perfectly harmless activity by millions of perfectly innocent people can be forbidden—riding a motorcycle without a safety helmet, for example, starting a campfire in a national forest, or selling a safe and effective drug not yet approved by the Food and Drug Administration. All of these acts are entirely innocent and harmless in themselves, but because of the *risk* of harm that they entail, the freedom to engage in them has been abridged. The citizens of Chicago have decided that depriving themselves of the freedom to "hang out" with a gang member is necessary to eliminate pervasive gang crime and intimidation—and that the elimination of the one is worth the deprivation of the other. This Court has no business second-guessing either the degree of necessity or the fairness of the trade.

I dissent from the judgment of the Court.

An immense and frightening antidemocratic power

Dickerson v. United States, 530 U.S. 428 (2000)

Justice Scalia, with whom Justice Thomas joins, dissenting.

Those to whom judicial decisions are an unconnected series of judgments that produce either favored or disfavored results will doubtless greet today's decision as a paragon of moderation, since it declines to overrule *Miranda v. Arizona,* 384 U.S. 436, 86 S.Ct. 1602, 16 L.Ed.2d 694 (1966). Those who understand the judicial process will appreciate that today's decision is not a reaffirmation of *Miranda,* but a radical revision of the most significant element of *Miranda* (as of all cases): the rationale that gives it a permanent place in our jurisprudence.

Marbury v. Madison, 1 Cranch 137, 2 L.Ed. 60 (1803), held that an Act of Congress will not be enforced by the courts if what it prescribes violates the Constitution of the United States. That was the basis on which *Miranda* was decided. One will search today's opinion in vain, however, for a statement (surely simple enough to make) that what 18 U.S.C. § 3501 prescribes—the use at trial of a voluntary confession, even when a *Miranda* warning or its equivalent has failed to be given—violates the Constitution. The reason the statement does not appear is not only (and perhaps not so much) that it would be absurd, inasmuch as § 3501 excludes from trial precisely what the Constitution excludes from trial, viz., compelled confessions; but also that Justices whose votes are needed to compose today's majority are on record as believing that a violation of *Miranda* is *not* a violation of the Constitution. See *Davis v. United States,* 512 U.S. 452, 457–458, 114 S.Ct. 2350,

129 L.Ed.2d 362 (1994) (opinion of the Court, in which Kennedy, J., joined); *Duckworth v. Eagan,* 492 U.S. 195, 203, 109 S.Ct. 2875, 106 L.Ed.2d 166 (1989) (opinion of the Court, in which Kennedy, J., joined); *Oregon v. Elstad,* 470 U.S. 298, 105 S.Ct. 1285, 84 L.Ed.2d 222 (1985) (opinion of the Court by O'Connor, J.); *New York v. Quarles,* 467 U.S. 649, 104 S.Ct. 2626, 81 L.Ed.2d 550 (1984) (opinion of the Court by Rehnquist, J.). And so, to justify today's agreed-upon result, the Court must adopt a significant *new,* if not entirely comprehensible, principle of constitutional law. As the Court chooses to describe that principle, statutes of Congress can be disregarded, not only when what they prescribe violates the Constitution, but when what they prescribe contradicts a decision of this Court that "announced a constitutional rule," *ante,* at 2333. As I shall discuss in some detail, the only thing that can possibly mean in the context of this case is that this Court has the power, not merely to apply the Constitution but to expand it, imposing what it regards as useful "prophylactic" restrictions upon Congress and the States. That is an immense and frightening antidemocratic power, and it does not exist.

It takes only a small step to bring today's opinion out of the realm of power-judging and into the mainstream of legal reasoning: The Court need only go beyond its carefully couched iterations that "*Miranda* is a constitutional decision," *ante,* at 2333, that "*Miranda* is constitutionally based," *ante,* at 2334, that *Miranda* has "constitutional underpinnings," *ante,* at 2334, n. 5, and come out and say quite clearly: "We reaffirm today that custodial interrogation that is not preceded by *Miranda* warnings or their equivalent violates the Constitution of the United States." It cannot say that, because a majority of the Court does not believe it. The Court therefore acts in plain violation of the Constitution when it denies effect to this Act of Congress.

I

Early in this Nation's history, this Court established the sound proposition that constitutional government in a system of separated powers requires judges to regard as inoperative any legislative Act, even of Congress itself, that is "repugnant to the Constitution."

> "So if a law be in opposition to the constitution; if both the law and the constitution apply to a particular case, so that the court must either decide that case conformably to the law, disregarding the constitution; or conformably to the constitution, disregarding the law; the court must determine which of these conflicting rules governs the case." *Marbury, supra,* at 178.

The power we recognized in *Marbury* will thus permit us, indeed require us, to "disregar[d]" § 3501, a duly enacted statute governing the admissibility of evidence in the federal courts, only if it "be in opposition to the constitution"—here, assertedly, the dictates of the Fifth Amendment.

It was once possible to characterize the so-called *Miranda* rule as resting (however implausibly) upon the proposition that what the statute here before us permits—the admission at trial of un-*Mirandized* confessions—violates the Constitution. That is the fairest reading of the *Miranda* case itself. The Court began by announcing that the Fifth Amendment privilege against self-incrimination applied in the context of extrajudicial custodial interrogation, see 384 U.S., at 460–467, 86 S.Ct. 1602—itself a doubtful proposition as a matter both of history and precedent, see *id.,* 510–511, 86 S.Ct. 1602 (Harlan, J., dissenting) (characterizing the Court's conclusion that the Fifth Amendment privilege, rather than the Due Process Clause, governed station house confessions as a "*trompe l'oeil* "). Having extended the privilege into the confines of the station house, the Court liberally sprinkled throughout its sprawling 60-page opinion suggestions that, because of the compulsion inherent in custodial interrogation, the privilege was violated by any statement thus obtained that did not conform to the rules set forth in *Miranda*, or some functional equivalent. See *id.*, at 458, 86 S.Ct. 1602 ("Unless adequate protective devices are employed to dispel the compulsion *inherent* in custodial surroundings, *no* statement obtained from the defendant can truly be the product of his free choice" (emphases added)); *id.*, at 461, 86 S.Ct. 1602 ("An individual swept from familiar surroundings into police custody, surrounded by antagonistic forces, and subjected to the techniques of persuasion described above cannot be otherwise than under compulsion to speak"); *id.*, at 467, 86 S.Ct. 1602 ("We have concluded that without proper safeguards the process of in-custody interrogation ... contains inherently compelling pressures which work to undermine the individual's will to resist and to compel him to speak where he would not otherwise do so freely"); *id.*, at 457, n. 26, 86 S.Ct. 1602 (noting the "absurdity of denying that a confession obtained under these circumstances is compelled").

The dissenters, for their part, also understood *Miranda's* holding to be based on the "premise ... that pressure on the suspect must be eliminated though it be only the subtle influence of the atmosphere and surroundings." *Id.*, at 512, 86 S.Ct. 1602 (Harlan, J., dissenting). See also *id.*, at 535, 86 S.Ct. 1602 (White, J., dissenting) ("[I]t has never been suggested, until today, that such questioning was so coercive and accused persons so lacking in hardihood that the very first response to the very first question following the commencement of custody must be conclusively presumed to be the product of an overborne will"). And at least one case decided shortly after *Miranda* explicitly confirmed the view. See *Orozco v. Texas*, 394 U.S. 324, 326, 89 S.Ct. 1095, 22 L.Ed.2d 311 (1969) ("[T]he use of these admissions obtained in the absence of the required warnings was a flat violation of the Self-Incrimination Clause of the Fifth Amendment as construed in *Miranda* ").

So understood, *Miranda* was objectionable for innumerable reasons, not least the fact that cases spanning more than 70 years had rejected its core premise that, absent the warnings and an effective waiver of the right to remain silent and of the (thitherto unknown) right to have an attorney present, a statement obtained pursuant to custodial interrogation was necessarily the product of compulsion. See *Crooker v. California,* 357 U.S. 433, 78 S.Ct. 1287, 2 L.Ed.2d 1448 (1958) (confession not involuntary despite denial of access to counsel); *Cicenia v. La Gay,* 357 U.S. 504, 78 S.Ct. 1297, 2 L.Ed.2d 1523 (1958) (same); *Powers v. United States,* 223 U.S. 303, 32 S.Ct. 281, 56 L.Ed. 448 (1912) (lack of warnings and counsel did not render statement before United States Commissioner involuntary); *Wilson v. United States,* 162 U.S. 613, 16 S.Ct. 895, 40 L.Ed. 1090 (1896) (same). Moreover, history and precedent aside, the decision in *Miranda,* if read as an explication of what the Constitution *requires,* is preposterous. There is, for example, simply no basis in reason for concluding that a response to the very first question asked, by a suspect who already *knows* all of the rights described in the *Miranda* warning, is anything other than a volitional act. See *Miranda, supra,* at 533–534, 86 S.Ct. 1602 (White, J., dissenting). And even if one assumes that the elimination of compulsion absolutely requires informing even the most knowledgeable suspect of his right to remain silent, it cannot conceivably require the right to have *counsel* present. There is a world of difference, which the Court recognized under the traditional voluntariness test but ignored in *Miranda,* between compelling a suspect to incriminate himself and preventing him from foolishly doing so of his own accord. Only the latter (which is *not* required by the Constitution) could explain the Court's inclusion of a right to counsel and the requirement that it, too, be knowingly and intelligently waived. Counsel's presence is not required to tell the suspect that he *need* not speak; the interrogators can do that. The only good reason for having counsel there is that he can be counted on to advise the suspect that he *should* not speak. See *Watts v. Indiana,* 338 U.S. 49, 59, 69 S.Ct. 1347, 93 L.Ed. 1801 (1949) (Jackson, J., concurring in result in part and dissenting in part) ("[A]ny lawyer worth his salt will tell the suspect in no uncertain terms to make no statement to police under any circumstances").

Preventing foolish (rather than compelled) confessions is likewise the only conceivable basis for the rules (suggested in *Miranda,* see 384 U.S., at 444–445, 473–474, 86 S.Ct. 1602), that courts must exclude any confession elicited by questioning conducted, without interruption, after the suspect has indicated a desire to stand on his right to remain silent, see *Michigan v. Mosley,* 423 U.S. 96, 105–106, 96 S.Ct. 321, 46 L.Ed.2d 313 (1975), or initiated by police after the suspect has expressed a desire to have counsel present, see *Edwards v. Arizona,* 451 U.S. 477, 484–485, 101 S.Ct. 1880, 68 L.Ed.2d 378 (1981). Nonthreatening attempts to persuade the suspect to reconsider that initial decision are not, without more, enough to render a change of heart the product of anything other than the suspect's free will. Thus, what is most remarkable about the *Miranda* decision—and what made it unacceptable as a matter of straightforward constitutional interpretation in the *Marbury* tradition—is its palpable hostility toward the act of confession *per se,* rather than toward what the Constitution abhors, *compelled* confession. See *United States v. Washington,* 431 U.S. 181, 187, 97 S.Ct. 1814, 52 L.Ed.2d 238 (1977) ("[F]ar from being prohibited by the Constitution, admissions of guilt by wrongdoers, if not coerced, are inherently desirable"). The

Constitution is not, unlike the *Miranda* majority, offended by a criminal's commendable qualm of conscience or fortunate fit of stupidity. Cf. *Minnick v. Mississippi,* 498 U.S. 146, 166–167, 111 S.Ct. 486, 112 L.Ed.2d 489 (1990) (Scalia, J., dissenting).

For these reasons, and others more than adequately developed in the *Miranda* dissents and in the subsequent works of the decision's many critics, any conclusion that a violation of the *Miranda* rules *necessarily* amounts to a violation of the privilege against compelled self-incrimination can claim no support in history, precedent, or common sense, and as a result would at least presumptively be worth reconsidering even at this late date. But that is unnecessary, since the Court has (thankfully) long since abandoned the notion that failure to comply with *Miranda's* rules is itself a violation of the Constitution.

II

As the Court today acknowledges, since *Miranda* we have explicitly, and repeatedly, interpreted that decision as having announced, not the circumstances in which custodial interrogation runs afoul of the Fifth or Fourteenth Amendment, but rather only "prophylactic" rules that go beyond the right against compelled self-incrimination. Of course the seeds of this "prophylactic" interpretation of *Miranda* were present in the decision itself. See *Miranda,* 384 U.S., at 439, 86 S.Ct. 1602 (discussing the "necessity for procedures which assure that the [suspect] is accorded his privilege"); *id.,* at 447, 86 S.Ct. 1602 ("[u]nless a proper limitation upon custodial interrogation is achieved—such as these decisions will advance—there can be no assurance that practices of this nature will be eradicated"); *id.,* at 457, 86 S.Ct. 1602 ("[i]n these cases, we might not find the defendants' statements to have been involuntary in traditional terms"); *ibid.* (noting "concern for adequate safeguards to protect precious Fifth Amendment rights" and the "potentiality for compulsion" in Ernesto Miranda's interrogation). In subsequent cases, the seeds have sprouted and borne fruit: The Court has squarely concluded that it is possible—indeed not uncommon—for the police to violate *Miranda* without also violating the Constitution.

Michigan v. Tucker, 417 U.S. 433, 94 S.Ct. 2357, 41 L.Ed.2d 182 (1974), an opinion for the Court written by then-Justice Rehnquist, rejected the true-to-*Marbury,* failure-to-warn-as-constitutional-violation interpretation of *Miranda.* It held that exclusion of the "fruits" of a *Miranda* violation—the statement of a witness whose identity the defendant had revealed while in custody—was not required. The opinion explained that the question whether the "police conduct complained of directly infringed upon respondent's right against compulsory self-incrimination" was a "separate question" from "whether it instead violated only the prophylactic rules developed to protect that right." 417 U.S., at 439, 86 S.Ct. 1602. The "procedural safeguards" adopted in *Miranda,* the Court said, "were not themselves rights protected by the Constitution but were instead measures to insure that the right against compulsory self-incrimination was protected," and to "provide practical reinforcement for the right," 417 U.S., at 444, 86 S.Ct. 1602. Comparing the particular facts of the custodial interrogation with the "historical circumstances underlying the privilege," *ibid.,* the Court concluded, unequivocally, that the defendant's statement could not be termed "involuntary as that term has been defined in the decisions of this Court," *id.,* at 445, 86 S.Ct. 1602, and thus that there had been no constitutional violation, notwithstanding the clear violation of the "procedural rules later established in *Miranda,*" *ibid.* Lest there be any confusion on the point, the Court reiterated that the "police conduct at issue here did not abridge respondent's constitutional privilege against compulsory self-incrimination, but departed only from the prophylactic standards later laid down by this Court in *Miranda* to safeguard that privilege." *Id.*, at 446, 86 S.Ct. 1602. It is clear from our cases, of course, that if the statement in *Tucker had* been obtained in violation of the Fifth Amendment, the statement and its fruits would have been excluded. See *Nix v. Williams,* 467 U.S. 431, 442, 104 S.Ct. 2501, 81 L.Ed.2d 377 (1984).

The next year, in *Oregon v. Hass,* 420 U.S. 714, 95 S.Ct. 1215, 43 L.Ed.2d 570 (1975), the Court held that a defendant's statement taken in violation of *Miranda* that was nonetheless *voluntary* could be used at trial for impeachment purposes. This holding turned upon the recognition that violation of *Miranda* is not unconstitutional compulsion, since statements obtained in actual violation of the privilege against compelled self-incrimination, "as opposed to ... taken in violation of *Miranda,*" quite simply "may not be put to any testimonial use whatever against [the defendant] in a criminal trial," including as impeachment evidence. *New Jersey v. Portash,* 440 U.S. 450, 459, 99 S.Ct. 1292, 59 L.Ed.2d 501 (1979). See also *Mincey v. Arizona,* 437 U.S. 385, 397–398, 98 S.Ct. 2408, 57 L.Ed.2d 290 (1978) (holding that while statements obtained in violation of *Miranda* may be used for impeachment if otherwise trustworthy, the Constitution prohibits "*any* criminal trial use against a defendant of his *involuntary* statement").

Nearly a decade later, in *New York v. Quarles,* 467 U.S. 649, 104 S.Ct. 2626, 81 L.Ed.2d 550 (1984), the Court relied upon the fact that "[t]he prophylactic *Miranda* warnings ... are 'not themselves rights protected by the Constitution,'" *id.,* at 654, 104 S.Ct. 2626 (quoting *Tucker, supra,* at 444, 94 S.Ct. 2357), to create a "public safety" exception. In that case, police apprehended, after a chase in a grocery store, a rape suspect known to be carrying a gun. After handcuffing and searching him (and finding no gun)—but before reading him his *Miranda* warnings—the police demanded to know where the gun was. The defendant nodded in the direction of some empty cartons and responded that "the gun is over there." The Court held that both the unwarned statement—"the gun is over there"—and the recovered weapon were admissible in the prosecution's case in chief under a "public safety exception" to the "prophylactic rules enunciated in *Miranda*." 467 U.S., at 653, 104 S.Ct. 2626. It explicitly acknowledged that if the *Miranda* warnings were an imperative of the Fifth Amendment itself, such an exigency exception would be impossible, since the Fifth Amendment's bar on compelled self-incrimination is absolute, and its " 'strictures, unlike the Fourth's are not removed by showing reasonableness,'" 467 U.S., at 653, n. 3, 104 S.Ct. 2626. (For the latter reason, the Court found it necessary to note that respondent did not "claim that [his] statements were actually compelled by police conduct which overcame his will to resist," *id.*, at 654, 104 S.Ct. 2626.)

The next year, the Court again declined to apply the "fruit of the poisonous tree" doctrine to a *Miranda* violation, this time allowing the admission of a suspect's properly warned statement even though it had been preceded (and, arguably, induced) by an earlier inculpatory statement taken in violation of *Miranda*. *Oregon v. Elstad,* 470 U.S. 298, 105 S.Ct. 1285, 84 L.Ed.2d 222 (1985). As in *Tucker,* the Court distinguished the case from those holding that a confession obtained as a result of an unconstitutional search is inadmissible, on the ground that the violation of *Miranda* does not involve an "actual infringement of the suspect's constitutional rights," 470 U.S., at 308, 105 S.Ct. 1285. *Miranda,* the Court explained, "sweeps more broadly than the Fifth Amendment itself," and "*Miranda*'s preventive medicine provides a remedy even to the defendant who has suffered no identifiable constitutional harm." 470 U.S., at 306–307, 105 S.Ct. 1285. "[E]rrors [that] are made by law enforcement officers in administering the prophylactic *Miranda* procedures ... should not breed the same irremediable consequences as police infringement of the Fifth Amendment itself." *Id.*, at 308–309, 105 S.Ct. 1285.

In light of these cases, and our statements to the same effect in others, see, *e.g., Davis v. United States,* 512 U.S., at 457–458, 114 S.Ct. 2350; *Withrow v. Williams,* 507 U.S. 680, 690–691, 113 S.Ct. 1745, 123 L.Ed.2d 407 (1993); *Eagan,* 492 U.S., at 203, 109 S.Ct. 2875, it is simply no longer possible for the Court to conclude, even if it wanted to, that a violation of *Miranda's* rules is a violation of the Constitution. But as I explained at the outset, that is what is required before the Court may disregard a law of Congress governing the admissibility of evidence in federal court. The Court today insists that the *decision* in *Miranda* is a "constitutional" one, *ante,* at 2329–2330, 2333; that it has "constitutional underpinnings," *ante,* at 2334, n. 5; a "constitutional basis" and a "constitutional origin," *ante,* at 2333, n. 3; that it was "constitutionally based," *ante,* at 2334; and that it announced a "constitutional rule," *ante,* at 2332–2333, 2334, 2335, 2336. It is fine to play these word games; but what makes a decision "constitutional" in the only sense relevant here—in the sense that renders it impervious to supersession by congressional legislation such as § 3501—is the determination that the Constitution *requires* the result that the decision announces and the statute ignores. By disregarding congressional action that concededly does not violate the Constitution, the Court flagrantly offends fundamental principles of separation of powers, and arrogates to itself prerogatives reserved to the representatives of the people.

The Court seeks to avoid this conclusion in two ways: First, by misdescribing these post-*Miranda* cases as mere dicta. The Court concedes only "that there is language in some of our opinions that supports the view" that *Miranda's* protections are not "constitutionally required." *Ante,* at 2333. It is not a matter of *language;* it is a matter of *holdings.* The proposition that failure to comply with *Miranda*'s rules does not establish a constitutional violation was central to the *holdings* of *Tucker, Hass, Quarles,* and *Elstad.*

The second way the Court seeks to avoid the impact of these cases is simply to disclaim responsibility for reasoned decisionmaking. It says:

> "These decisions illustrate the principle—not that *Miranda* is not a constitutional rule—but that no constitutional rule is immutable. No court laying down a general rule can possibly foresee the various circumstances in which counsel will seek to apply it, and the sort of modifications represented by these cases are as much a normal part of constitutional law as the original decision." *Ante,* at 2335.

The issue, however, is not whether court rules are "mutable"; they assuredly are. It is not whether, in the light of "various circumstances," they can be "modifi[ed]"; they assuredly can. The issue is whether, *as mutated and modified,* they must *make sense.* The requirement that they do so is the only thing that prevents this Court from being some sort of nine-headed Caesar, giving thumbs-up or thumbs-down to whatever outcome, case by case, suits or offends its collective fancy. And if confessions procured in violation of *Miranda* are confessions "compelled" in violation of the Constitution, the post-*Miranda* decisions I have discussed do not make sense. The only reasoned basis for their outcome was that a violation of *Miranda* is *not* a violation of the Constitution. If, for example, as the Court acknowledges was the holding of *Elstad,* "the traditional 'fruits' doctrine developed in Fourth Amendment cases" (that the fruits of evidence obtained unconstitutionally must be excluded from trial) does *not* apply to the fruits of *Miranda* violations, *ante,* at 2334–2335; and if the reason for the difference is *not* that *Miranda* violations are not constitutional violations (which is plainly and flatly what *Elstad* said); then the Court must come up with some *other* explanation for the difference. (That will take quite a bit of doing, by the way, since it is *not* clear on the face of the Fourth Amendment that evidence obtained in violation of that guarantee must be excluded from trial, whereas it *is* clear on the face of the Fifth Amendment that unconstitutionally compelled confessions cannot be used.) To say simply that "unreasonable searches under the Fourth Amendment are different from unwarned interrogation under the Fifth Amendment," *ante,* at 2335, is true but supremely unhelpful.

Finally, the Court asserts that *Miranda* must be a "constitutional decision" announcing a "constitutional rule," and thus immune to congressional modification, because we have since its inception applied it to the States. If this argument is meant as an invocation of *stare decisis,* it fails because, though it is true that our cases applying *Miranda* against the States must be reconsidered if *Miranda* is not required by the Constitution, it is likewise true that our cases (discussed above) based on the principle that *Miranda* is *not* required by the Constitution will have to be reconsidered if it *is.* So the *stare decisis* argument is a wash. If, on the other hand, the argument is meant as an appeal to logic rather than *stare decisis,* it is a classic example of begging the question: Congress's attempt to set aside *Miranda,* since it represents an assertion that violation of *Miranda* is not a violation of the Constitution, *also* represents an assertion that the Court has no power to impose *Miranda* on the States. To answer this assertion—not by showing why violation of *Mi-*

randa is a violation of the Constitution—but by asserting that *Miranda* does apply against the States, is to assume precisely the point at issue. In my view, our continued application of the *Miranda* code to the States despite our consistent statements that running afoul of its dictates does not necessarily—or even usually—result in an actual constitutional violation, represents not the source of *Miranda*'s salvation but rather evidence of its ultimate illegitimacy. See generally J. Grano, *Confessions, Truth, and the Law* (1993) 173–198; Grano, "Prophylactic Rules in Criminal Procedure: A Question of Article III Legitimacy," 80 *Nw. U.L.Rev.* 100 (1985). As Justice Stevens has elsewhere explained: "This Court's power to require state courts to exclude probative self-incriminatory statements rests entirely on the premise that the use of such evidence violates the Federal Constitution.... If the Court does not accept that premise, it must regard the holding in the *Miranda* case itself, as well as all of the federal jurisprudence that has evolved from that decision, as nothing more than an illegitimate exercise of raw judicial power." *Elstad,* 470 U.S., at 370, 105 S.Ct. 1285 (dissenting opinion). Quite so.

III

There was available to the Court a means of reconciling the established proposition that a violation of *Miranda* does not itself offend the Fifth Amendment with the Court's assertion of a right to ignore the present statute. That means of reconciliation was argued strenuously by both petitioner and the United States, who were evidently more concerned than the Court is with maintaining the coherence of our jurisprudence. It is not mentioned in the Court's opinion because, I assume, a majority of the Justices intent on reversing believes that incoherence is the lesser evil. They may be right.

Petitioner and the United States contend that there is nothing at all exceptional, much less unconstitutional, about the Court's adopting prophylactic rules to buttress constitutional rights, and enforcing them against Congress and the States. Indeed, the United States argues that "[p]rophylactic rules are now and have been for many years a feature of this Court's constitutional adjudication." Brief for United States 47. That statement is not wholly inaccurate, if by "many years" one means since the mid–1960's. However, in their zeal to validate what is in my view a lawless practice, the United States and petitioner greatly overstate the frequency with which we have engaged in it. For instance, petitioner cites several cases in which the Court quite simply exercised its traditional judicial power to define the scope of constitutional protections and, relatedly, the circumstances in which they are violated. See *Loretto v. Teleprompter Manhattan CATV Corp.*, 458 U.S. 419, 436–437, 102 S.Ct. 3164, 73 L.Ed.2d 868 (1982) (holding that a permanent physical occupation constitutes a *per se* taking); *Maine v. Moulton,* 474 U.S. 159, 176, 106 S.Ct. 477, 88 L.Ed.2d 481 (1985) (holding that the Sixth Amendment right to the assistance of counsel is *actually* "violated when the State obtains incriminating statements by knowingly circumventing the accused's right to have counsel present in a confrontation between the accused and a state agent").

Similarly unsupportive of the supposed practice is *Bruton v. United States,* 391 U.S. 123, 88 S.Ct. 1620, 20 L.Ed.2d 476 (1968), where we concluded that the Confrontation Clause of the Sixth Amendment forbids the admission of a nontestifying codefendant's facially incriminating confession in a joint trial, even where the jury has been given a limiting instruction. That decision was based, not upon the theory that this was desirable protection "beyond" what the Confrontation Clause technically required; but rather upon the self-evident proposition that the inability to cross-examine an available witness whose damaging out-of-court testimony is introduced violates the Confrontation Clause, combined with the conclusion that in these circumstances a mere jury instruction can never be relied upon to prevent the testimony from being damaging, see *Richardson v. Marsh,* 481 U.S. 200, 207–208, 107 S.Ct. 1702, 95 L.Ed.2d 176 (1987) .

The United States also relies on our cases involving the question whether a State's procedure for appointed counsel's withdrawal of representation on appeal satisfies the State's constitutional obligation to "'affor[d] adequate and effective appellate review to indigent defendants.'" *Smith v. Robbins,* 528 U.S. 259, 276, 120 S.Ct. 746, 145 L.Ed.2d 756 (2000) (quoting *Griffin v. Illinois,* 351 U.S. 12, 20, 76 S.Ct. 585, 100 L.Ed. 891 (1956)). In *Anders v. California,* 386 U.S. 738, 87 S.Ct. 1396, 18 L.Ed.2d 493 (1967), we concluded that California's procedure governing withdrawal fell short of the constitutional minimum, and we outlined a procedure that *would* meet that standard. But as we made clear earlier this Term in *Smith,* which upheld a procedure *different* from the one *Anders* suggested, the benchmark of constitutionality is the constitutional requirement of adequate representation, and not some excrescence upon that requirement decreed, for safety's sake, by this Court.

In a footnote, the United States directs our attention to certain overprotective First Amendment rules that we have adopted to ensure "breathing space" for expression. See *Gertz v. Robert Welch, Inc.,* 418 U.S. 323, 340, 342, 94 S.Ct. 2997, 41 L.Ed.2d 789 (1974) (recognizing that in *New York Times Co. v. Sullivan,* 376 U.S. 254, 84 S.Ct. 710, 11 L.Ed.2d 686 (1964), we "extended a measure of strategic protection to defamatory falsehood" of public officials); *Freedman v. Maryland,* 380 U.S. 51, 58, 85 S.Ct. 734, 13 L.Ed.2d 649 (1965) (setting forth "procedural safeguards designed to obviate the dangers of a censorship system" with respect to motion picture obscenity). In these cases, and others involving the First Amendment, the Court has acknowledged that in order to guarantee that protected speech is not "chilled" and thus forgone, it is in some instances necessary to incorporate in our substantive rules a "measure of strategic protection." But that is because the Court has viewed the importation of "chill" as *itself* a violation of the First Amendment—not because the Court thought it could go beyond what the First Amendment *demanded* in order to provide some prophylaxis.

Petitioner and the United States are right on target, however, in characterizing the Court's actions in a case decided within a few years of *Miranda, North Carolina v. Pearce,* 395 U.S. 711, 89 S.Ct. 2072, 23 L.Ed.2d 656 (1969). There, the Court concluded that due process would be offended were a judge vindictively to resentence with added severity a defendant who had successfully appealed his original conviction. Rather than simply announce that vindictive sentencing violates the Due Process Clause, the Court went on to hold that "[i]n order to assure the absence of such a [vindictive] motivation, ... the reasons for [imposing the increased sentence] must affirmatively appear" and must "be based upon objective information concerning identifiable conduct on the part of the defendant occurring after the time of the original sentencing proceeding." *Id.,* at 726, 89 S.Ct. 2072. The Court later explicitly acknowledged *Pearce*'s prophylactic character, see *Michigan v. Payne,* 412 U.S. 47, 53, 93 S.Ct. 1966, 36 L.Ed.2d 736 (1973). It is true, therefore, that the case exhibits the same fundamental flaw as does *Miranda* when deprived (as it has been) of its original (implausible) pretension to announcement of what the Constitution itself required. That is, although the Due Process Clause may well prohibit punishment based on judicial vindictiveness, the Constitution by no means vests in the courts "any general power to prescribe particular devices 'in order to assure the absence of such a motivation,'" 395 U.S., at 741, 89 S.Ct. 2072 (Black, J., dissenting). Justice Black surely had the right idea when he derided the Court's requirement as "pure legislation if there ever was legislation," *ibid.*, although in truth *Pearce*'s rule pales as a legislative achievement when compared to the detailed code promulgated in *Miranda*.

The foregoing demonstrates that, petitioner's and the United States' suggestions to the contrary notwithstanding, what the Court did in *Miranda* (assuming, as later cases hold, that *Miranda* went beyond what the Constitution actually requires) is in fact extraordinary. That the Court has, on rare and recent occasion, repeated the mistake does not transform error into truth, but illustrates the potential for future mischief that the error entails. Where the Constitution has wished to lodge in one of the branches of the Federal Government some limited power to supplement its guarantees, it has said so. See Amdt. 14, § 5 ("The Congress shall have power to enforce, by appropriate legislation, the provisions of this article"). The power with which the Court would endow itself under a "prophylactic" justification for *Miranda* goes far beyond what it has permitted Congress to do under authority of that text. Whereas we have insisted that congressional action under § 5 of the Fourteenth Amendment must be "congruent" with, and "proportional" to, a *constitutional violation,* see *City of Boerne v. Flores,* 521 U.S. 507, 520, 117 S.Ct. 2157, 138 L.Ed.2d 624 (1997), the *Miranda* nontextual power to embellish confers authority to prescribe preventive measures against not only constitutionally prohibited compelled confessions, but also (as discussed earlier) foolhardy ones.

I applaud, therefore, the refusal of the Justices in the majority to enunciate this boundless doctrine of judicial empowerment as a means of rendering today's decision rational. In nonetheless joining the Court's judgment, however, they overlook two truisms: that actions speak louder than silence, and that (in judge-made law at least) logic will out. Since there is in fact no other principle that can reconcile today's judgment with the post-*Miranda* cases that the Court refuses to abandon, what today's decision will stand for, whether the Justices can bring themselves to say it or not, is the power of the Supreme Court to write a prophylactic, extraconstitutional Constitution, binding on Congress and the States.

IV

Thus, while I agree with the Court that § 3501 cannot be upheld without also concluding that *Miranda* represents an illegitimate exercise of our authority to review state-court judgments, I do not share the Court's hesitation in reaching that conclusion. For while the Court is also correct that the doctrine of *stare decisis* demands some "special justification" for a departure from longstanding precedent—even precedent of the constitutional variety—that criterion is more than met here. To repeat Justice Stevens' cogent observation, it is "[o]bviou[s]" that "the Court's power to reverse Miranda's conviction rested *entirely* on the determination that a violation of the Federal Constitution had occurred." *Elstad,* 470 U.S., at 367, n. 9, 105 S.Ct. 1285 (dissenting opinion) (emphasis added). Despite the Court's Orwellian assertion to the contrary, it is undeniable that later cases (discussed above) have "undermined [*Miranda*'s] doctrinal underpinnings," *ante,* at 2336, denying constitutional violation and thus stripping the holding of its only constitutionally legitimate support. *Miranda*'s critics and supporters alike have long made this point. See Office of Legal Policy, U.S. Dept. of Justice, Report to Attorney General on Law of Pre-Trial Interrogation 97 (Feb. 12, 1986) ("The current Court has repudiated the premises on which *Miranda* was based, but has drawn back from recognizing the full implications of its decisions"); *id.*, at 78 ("*Michigan v. Tucker* accordingly repudiated the doctrinal basis of the *Miranda* decision"); Sonenshein, "*Miranda* and the Burger Court: Trends and Countertrends," 13 *Loyola U. Chi. L.J.* 405, 407–408 (1982) ("Although the Burger Court has not overruled *Miranda,* the Court has consistently undermined the rationales, assumptions, and values which gave *Miranda* life"); *id.*, at 425–426 ("Seemingly, the Court [in *Michigan v. Tucker*] utterly destroyed both *Miranda's* rationale and its holding"); Stone, The Miranda Doctrine in the Burger Court, 1977 S.Ct. Rev. 99, 118 ("Mr. Justice Rehnquist's conclusion that there is a violation of the Self-Incrimination Clause only if a confession is involuntary ... is an outright rejection of the core premises of *Miranda* ").

The Court cites *Patterson v. McLean Credit Union,* 491 U.S. 164, 173, 109 S.Ct. 2363, 105 L.Ed.2d 132 (1989), as accurately reflecting our standard for overruling, see *ante,* at 2336—which I am pleased to accept, even though *Patterson* was speaking of overruling statutory cases and the standard for constitutional decisions is somewhat more lenient. What is set forth there reads as though it was written precisely with the current status of *Miranda* in mind:

> "In cases where statutory precedents have been overruled, the primary reason for the Court's shift in position has been the intervening development of the law, through either the growth of judicial doctrine or further action taken by Congress. Where such changes have removed or weakened the conceptual underpinnings from the prior decision, ... or where the later law has rendered the decision irreconcilable with competing legal doctrines or policies, ... the Court has not hesitated to overrule an earlier decision." 491 U.S., at 173, 109 S.Ct. 2363.

Neither am I persuaded by the argument for retaining *Miranda* that touts its supposed workability as compared with the totality-of-the-circumstances test it purported to replace. *Miranda's* proponents cite *ad nauseam* the fact that the Court was called upon to make difficult and subtle distinctions in applying the "voluntariness" test in some 30-odd due process "coerced confessions" cases in the 30 years between *Brown v. Mississippi,* 297 U.S. 278, 56 S.Ct. 461, 80 L.Ed. 682 (1936), and *Miranda.* It is not immediately apparent, however, that the judicial burden has been eased by the "bright-line" rules adopted in *Miranda.* In fact, in the 34 years since *Miranda* was decided, this Court has been called upon to decide nearly *60* cases involving a host of *Miranda* issues, most of them predicted with remarkable prescience by Justice White in his *Miranda* dissent. 384 U.S., at 545, 86 S.Ct. 1602.

Moreover, it is not clear why the Court thinks that the "totality-of-the-circumstances test ... is more difficult than *Miranda* for law enforcement officers to conform to, and for courts to apply in a consistent manner." *Ante,* at 2336. Indeed, I find myself persuaded by Justice O'Connor's rejection of this same argument in her opinion in *Williams,* 507 U.S., at 711–712, 113 S.Ct. 1745 (O'Connor, J., joined by Rehnquist, C. J., concurring in part and dissenting in part):

> "*Miranda,* for all its alleged brightness, is not without its difficulties; and voluntariness is not without its strengths....
>
> "... *Miranda* creates as many close questions as it resolves. The task of determining whether a defendant is in 'custody' has proved to be 'a slippery one.' And the supposedly 'bright' lines that separate interrogation from spontaneous declaration, the exercise of a right from waiver, and the adequate warning from the inadequate, likewise have turned out to be rather dim and ill defined....
>
> "The totality-of-the-circumstances approach, on the

> other hand, permits each fact to be taken into account without resort to formal and dispositive labels. By dispensing with the difficulty of producing a yes-or-no answer to questions that are often better answered in shades and degrees, *the voluntariness inquiry often can make judicial decisionmaking easier rather than more onerous.*" (Emphasis added; citations omitted.)

But even were I to agree that the old totality-of-the-circumstances test was more cumbersome, it is simply not true that *Miranda* has banished it from the law and replaced it with a new test. Under the current regime, which the Court today retains in its entirety, courts are frequently called upon to undertake *both* inquiries. That is because, as explained earlier, voluntariness remains the *constitutional* standard, and as such continues to govern the admissibility for impeachment purposes of statements taken in violation of *Miranda,* the admissibility of the "fruits" of such statements, and the admissibility of statements challenged as unconstitutionally obtained *despite* the interrogator's compliance with *Miranda,* see, *e.g., Colorado v. Connelly,* 479 U.S. 157, 107 S.Ct. 515, 93 L.Ed.2d 473 (1986).

Finally, I am not convinced by petitioner's argument that *Miranda* should be preserved because the decision occupies a special place in the "public's consciousness." Brief for Petitioner 44. As far as I am aware, the public is not under the illusion that we are infallible. I see little harm in admitting that we made a mistake in taking away from the people the ability to decide for themselves what protections (beyond those required by the Constitution) are reasonably affordable in the criminal investigatory process. And I see much to be gained by reaffirming for the people the wonderful reality that they govern themselves—which means that "[t]he powers not delegated to the United States by the Constitution" that the people adopted, "nor prohibited ... to the States" by that Constitution, "are reserved to the States respectively, or to the people," U.S. Const., Amdt. 10.

* * *

Today's judgment converts *Miranda* from a milestone of judicial overreaching into the very Cheops' Pyramid (or perhaps the Sphinx would be a better analogue) of judicial arrogance. In imposing its Court-made code upon the States, the original opinion at least *asserted* that it was demanded by the Constitution. Today's decision does not pretend that it is—and yet *still* asserts the right to impose it against the will of the people's representatives in Congress. Far from believing that *stare decisis* compels this result, I believe we cannot allow to remain on the books even a celebrated decision—*especially* a celebrated decision—that has come to stand for the proposition that the Supreme Court has power to impose extraconstitutional constraints upon Congress and the States. This is not the system that was established by the Framers, or that would be established by any sane supporter of government by the people.

I dissent from today's decision, and, until § 3501 is repealed, will continue to apply it in all cases where there has been a sustainable finding that the defendant's confession was voluntary.

A curious constitution only a judge could love
Rogers v. Tennessee,
532 U.S. 451 (2001)

Justice Scalia, with whom Justice Stevens and Justice Thomas join, and with whom Justice Breyer joins as to Part II, dissenting.

The Court today approves the conviction of a man for a murder that was not murder (but only manslaughter) when the offense was committed. It thus violates a principle-encapsulated in the maxim *nulla poena sine lege*-which "dates from the ancient Greeks" and has been described as one of the most "widely held value-judgment[s] in the entire history of human thought." J. Hall, *General Principles of Criminal Law* 59 (2d ed.1960). Today's opinion produces, moreover, a curious constitution that only a judge could love. One in which (by virtue of the *Ex Post Facto* Clause) the elected representatives of all the people cannot retroactively make murder what was not murder when the act was committed; but in which unelected judges can do precisely that. One in which the predictability of parliamentary lawmaking cannot validate the retroactive creation of crimes, but the predictability of judicial lawmaking can do so. I do not believe this is the system that the Framers envisioned-or, for that matter, that any reasonable person would imagine.

I

A

To begin with, let us be clear that the law here was altered after the fact. Petitioner, whatever else he was guilty of, was innocent of murder under the law as it stood at the time of the stabbing, because the victim did not die until after a year and a day had passed. The requisite condition subsequent of the murder victim's death within a year and a day is no different from the requisite condition subsequent of the rape victim's raising a "hue and cry" which we held could not retroactively be eliminated in *Carmell v. Texas,* 529 U.S. 513, 120 S.Ct. 1620, 146 L.Ed.2d 577 (2000) . Here, as there, it operates to bar conviction. Indeed, if the present condition differs at all from the one involved in *Carmell* it is in the fact that it does not merely pertain to the "quantum of evidence" necessary to corroborate a charge, *id.,* at 530, 120 S.Ct. 1620, but is an actual *element* of the crime-a "substantive principle of law," 992 S.W.2d 393, 399 (Tenn.1999), the failure to establish which "entirely precludes a murder prosecution," *id.,* at 400, 992 S.W.2d 393. Though the Court spends some time questioning whether the year-and-a-day rule was ever truly established in Tennessee, see *ante,* at 1701–1703, the Supreme Court of Tennessee said it was, see 992 S.W.2d, at 396, 400, and this reasonable reading of state law by the State's highest court is binding upon us.

Petitioner's claim is that his conviction violated the Due Process Clause of the Fourteenth Amendment, insofar as that Clause contains the principle applied against the legislature by the *Ex Post Facto* Clause of Article I. We first discussed the relationship between these two Clauses in *Bouie v. City of Columbia,* 378 U.S. 347, 84 S.Ct. 1697, 12 L.Ed.2d 894 (1964). There, we considered Justice Chase to have spoken for the Court in *Calder v. Bull,* 3 Dall. 386, 390, 1 L.Ed. 648 (1798), when he defined an *ex post facto* law as, *inter alia,* one that "aggravates a crime, or makes it greater than it was, when committed." 378 U.S., at 353, 84 S.Ct. 1697 (emphasis deleted). We concluded that, "[i]f a state legislature is barred by the *Ex Post Facto* Clause from passing such a law, it must follow that a State Supreme Court is barred by the Due Process Clause from achieving precisely the same result by judicial construction." *Id.*, at 353–354, 84 S.Ct. 1697. The Court seeks to avoid the obvious import of this language by characterizing it as mere dicta. See *ante,* at 1698–1699. Only a concept of dictum that includes the very reasoning of the opinion could support this characterization. The *ratio decidendi* of *Bouie* was that the principle applied to the legislature though the *Ex Post Facto* Clause was contained in the Due Process Clause insofar as judicial action is concerned. I cannot understand why the Court derives such comfort from the fact that later opinions applying *Bouie* have referred to the Due Process Clause rather than the *Ex Post Facto* Clause, see *ante,* at 1699; that is entirely in accord with the rationale of the case, which I follow and which the Court discards.

The Court attempts to cabin *Bouie* by reading it to prohibit only " 'unexpected and indefensible'" judicial law revision, and to permit retroactive judicial changes so long as the defendant has had "fair warning" that the changes might occur. *Ante,* at 1700. This reading seems plausible because *Bouie* does indeed use those quoted terms; but they have been wrenched entirely out of context. The "fair warning" to which *Bouie* and subsequent cases referred was not "fair warning that the law might be changed," but fair warning *of what constituted the crime at the time of the offense.* And *Bouie* did not express disapproval of "unexpected and indefensible changes in the law" (and thus implicitly approve "expected or defensible changes"). It expressed disapproval of "*judicial construction* of a criminal statute" that is "unexpected and indefensible *by reference to the law which had been expressed prior to the conduct in issue.*" 378 U.S., at 354, 84 S.Ct. 1697 (emphasis added; internal quotation marks omitted). It thus implicitly approved only a judicial construction that was an expected or defensible application of prior cases interpreting the statute. Extending this principle from statutory crimes to common-law crimes would result in the approval of retroactive holdings that accord with prior cases expounding the common law, and the disapproval of retroactive holdings that clearly depart from prior cases expounding the common law. According to *Bouie,* not just "unexpected and indefensible" retroactive changes in the common law of crimes are bad, but *all* retroactive changes.

Bouie rested squarely upon "[t]he fundamental principle that 'the required criminal law must have existed when the conduct in issue occurred,'" *ibid.* (*Nulla poena sine lege.*) Proceeding from that principle, *Bouie* said that "a State Supreme Court is barred by the Due Process Clause from achieving precisely the same result [prohibited by the *Ex Post Facto* Clause] by judicial construction." *Id.,* at 353–354, 84 S.Ct. 1697. There is no doubt that "fair warning" of the legislature's intent to change the law does not insulate retroactive *legislative* criminalization. Such a statute violates the *Ex Post Facto* Clause, no matter that, at the time the offense was committed, the bill enacting the change was pending and assured of passage-or indeed, had already been passed but not yet signed by the President whose administration had proposed it. It follows from the analysis of *Bouie* that "fair warning" of impending change cannot insulate retroactive *judicial* criminalization either.

Nor is there any reason in the nature of things why it should. According to the Court, the exception is necessary because prohibiting retroactive judicial criminalization would "place an unworkable and unacceptable restraint on normal judicial processes," would be "incompatible with the resolution of uncertainty that marks any evolving legal system," and would "unduly impair the incremental and reasoned development of precedent that is the foundation of the common law system." *Ante,* at 1700. That assessment ignores the crucial difference between simply applying a law to a new set of circumstances and changing the law that has previously been applied to the very circumstances before the court. Many criminal cases present some factual nuance that arguably distinguishes them from cases that have come before; a court applying the penal statute to the new fact pattern does not purport to *change* the law. That, however, is not the action before us here, but rather, a square, head-on *overruling* of prior law-or, more accurately, something even more extreme than that: a judicial opinion acknowledging that under prior law, for reasons that used to be valid, the accused could not be convicted, but decreeing that, because of changed circumstances, "we hereby abolish the common law rule," 992 S.W.2d, at 401, and upholding the conviction by applying the new rule to conduct that occurred before the change in law was announced. Even in civil cases, and even in modern times, such retroactive revision of a concededly valid legal rule is extremely rare. With regard to criminal cases, I have no hesitation in affirming that it was unheard of at the time the original Due Process Clause was adopted. As I discuss in detail in the following section, proceeding in that fashion would have been regarded as contrary to the judicial traditions embraced within the concept of due process of law.

B

The Court's opinion considers the judgment at issue here "a routine exercise of common law decisionmaking," whereby the Tennessee court "brought the law into conformity with reason and common sense," by "laying to rest an archaic and outdated rule." *Ante,* at 1703. This is an accurate enough description of what modern "common law decisionmaking" consists of-but it is not an accurate description of the theoretical model of common-law decisionmaking accepted by those who adopted the Due Process Clause. At the time of the framing, common-law jurists believed (in the words of Sir Francis Bacon) that the judge's "office is *jus dicere,* and not *jus dare;* to interpret law, and not to make law, or give law." Bacon, "Essays, Civil and Moral," in 3 *Harvard Classics* 130 (C. Eliot ed.1909) (1625). Or as described by Blackstone, whose *Commentaries* were widely read and "accepted [by the framing generation] as the most satisfactory exposition of the common law of England," see *Schick v. United States,* 195 U.S. 65, 69, 24 S.Ct. 826, 49 L.Ed. 99 (1904), "judicial decisions are the principal and most authoritative *evidence,* that can be given, of the existence of such a custom as shall form a part of the common law," 1 W. Blackstone, *Commentaries* *69 (hereinafter *Blackstone*) (emphasis added).

Blackstone acknowledged that the courts' exposition of what the law was could change. *Stare decisis,* he said, "admits of exception, where the former determination is most evidently contrary to reason...." *Ibid.* But "in such cases the subsequent judges do not pretend to make a new law, but to vindicate the old one from misrepresentation." *Id.,* at *70. To fit within this category of bad law, a law must be "manifestly absurd or unjust." It would not suffice, he said, that "the particular reason [for the law] can at this distance of time [not be] precisely assigned." "[F]or though [its] reason be not obvious at first view, yet we owe such a deference to former times as not to suppose they acted wholly without consideration." *Ibid.* By way of example, Blackstone pointed to the seemingly unreasonable rule that one cannot inherit the estate of one's half brother. Though he accepted that the feudal reason behind the law was no longer obvious, he wrote "yet it is not *in [a common law judge's] power* to alter it." *Id.,* at *70–*71 (emphasis added). Moreover, "the unreasonableness of a custom in modern circumstances will not affect its validity if the Court is satisfied of a reasonable origin." Allen 140–141. "A custom once reasonable and tolerable, if after it become grievous, and not answerable to the reason, whereupon it was grounded, yet is to be ... taken away by act of parliament." 2 E. Coke, *Institutes of the Laws of England* (hereinafter *Institutes*); see also *id.*, at *97 ("No law, or custome of England can be taken away, abrogated, or adnulled, but by authority of parliament"); Of Oaths before an Ecclesiastical Judge Ex Officio, 12 Co. Rep. *26, *29 (1655) ("[T]he law and custom of England is the inheritance of the subject, which he cannot be deprived of without his assent in Parliament").

There are, of course, stray statements and doctrines found in the historical record that-read out of context-could be thought to support the modern-day proposition that the common law was always meant to evolve. Take, for instance, Lord Coke's statement in the *Institutes* that "the reason of the law ceasing, the law itself ceases." This maxim is often cited by modern devotees of a turbulently changing common law-often in its Latin form *(cessante ratione legis, cessat ipse lex)* to create the impression of great venerability. In its original context, however, it had nothing to do with the power of common-law courts to change the law. At the point at which it appears in the Institutes, Coke was discussing the exception granted abbots and mayors from the obligation of military service to the King which attached to land ownership. Such service would be impracticable for a man of the cloth or a mayor. But, said Coke, "if they convey over the lands to any naturall man and his heires," the immunity "by the conveyance over ceaseth." 1 *Institutes* *70. In other words, the service which attached to the land would apply to any subsequent owner not cloaked in a similar immunity. It was in describing this change that Coke employed the Latin maxim *cessante ratione legis, cessat ipse lex.* It had to do, not with a changing of the common-law rule, but with a change of circumstances that rendered the common-law rule no longer applicable to the case.

The same is true of the similar quotation from Coke: "[*R*]*atio legis est anima legis, et mutata legis ratione, mutatur et lex*"-reason is the soul of the law; the reason of the law being changed, the law is also changed. This is taken from Coke's report of *Milborn's Case,* 7 Co. Rep. 6b, 7a (1587), a suit involving a town's responsibility for a murder committed within its precincts. The common-law rule had been that a town could be amerced for failure to apprehend a murderer who committed his crime on its streets during the day, but not a murderer who struck after nightfall, when its citizens were presumably asleep. Parliament, however, enacted a statute requiring towns to close their gates at night, and the court reasoned that thereafter a town that left its gates open could be amerced for the nocturnal homicide as well, since the town's violation of the Act was negligence that facilitated the escape. This perhaps partakes more of a new right of action implied from legislation than of any common-law rule. But to the extent it involved the common law, it assuredly did not *change* the prior rule: A town not in violation of the statute would continue to be immune. *Milborn's Case* simply held that the rule would not be extended to towns that wrongfully failed to close their gates-which involves no overruling, but nothing more than normal, case-by-case common-law adjudication.

It is true that framing-era judges in this country considered themselves authorized to reject English common-law precedent they found "barbarous" and "ignorant," see 1 Z. Swift, *A System of the Laws of the State of Connecticut* 46 (1795) (hereinafter *Swift*); N. Chipman, "A Dissertation on the Act Adopting the Common and Statute Laws of England," in *Reports and Dissertations* 117, 128 (1793) (hereinafter *Chipman*). That, however, was not an assertion of *judges'* power to *change* the common law. For, as Blackstone wrote, the common law was a law for England, and did not automatically transfer to the American Colonies; rather, it had to be adopted. See 1 *Blackstone* *107–*108 (observing that "the common law of England, as such, has no allowance or authority" in "[o]ur American plantations"); see also 1 *Swift* 46 ("The English common law is not in itself binding in this state"); *id.*, at 44–45 ("The English common law has never been considered to be more obligatory here, than the Roman law has been in England"). In short, the colonial courts felt themselves perfectly free to pick and choose which parts of the English common law they would adopt. As stated by *Chipman* 128: "If no reason can be assigned, in support of rules, or precedents, *not already adopted in practice,* to adopt such rules, is certainly contrary to the principles of our government." (Emphasis added.) This discretion not to adopt would not presuppose, or even support, the power of colonial courts subsequently to change the accumulated colonial common law. The absence of belief in *that* power is demonstrated by the following passage from 1 Horwitz 5: "Massachusetts Chief Justice Hutchison could declare in 1767 that 'laws should be established, else Judges and Juries must go according to their Reason, that is, their Will.' It was also imperative 'that *the Judge* should never be the *Legislator:* Because, then the Will of the Judge would be the Law: and this tends to a State of Slavery.'" Or, as Judge Swift put it, courts "ought never to be allowed to depart from the well known boundaries of express law, into the wide fields of discretion." 2 *Swift* 366.

Nor is the framing era's acceptance of common-law crimes support for the proposition that the Framers accepted an evolving common law. The acknowledgment of a new crime, not thitherto rejected by judicial decision, was not a *changing* of the common law, but an *application* of it. At the time of the framing, common-law crimes were considered unobjectionable, for "'a law founded on the law of nature may be retrospective, because it always existed,'" 1 Horwitz 7, quoting *Blackwell v. Wilkinson,* Jefferson's Rep. 73, 77 (Va.1768) (argument of then-Attorney General John Randolph). Of course, the notion of a common-law crime is utterly anathema today, which leads one to wonder why that is so. The obvious answer is that we now agree with the perceptive chief justice of Connecticut, who wrote in 1796 that common-law crimes "partak[e] of the odious nature of an ex post facto law." 2 *Swift* 365–366. But, as Horwitz makes clear, a widespread sharing of Swift's "preoccupation with the unfairness of administering a system of judge-made criminal law was a distinctly *post-revolutionary* phenomenon, reflecting a profound change in sensibility. For the inarticulate premise that lay behind Swift's warnings against the danger of judicial discretion was *a growing perception that judges no longer merely discovered law; they also made it.*" 1 Horwitz 14–15 (emphases added). In other words, the connection between *ex post facto* lawmaking and common-law judging would not have become widely apparent *until* common-law judging *became* lawmaking, not (as it had been) law declaring. This did not happen, see *id.,* at 1–4, until the 19th century, *after* the framing.

What occurred in the present case, then, is precisely what Blackstone said—and the Framers believed—would not suffice. The Tennessee Supreme Court made no pretense that the year-and-a-day rule was "bad" law from the outset; rather, it asserted, the need for the rule, as a means of assuring causality of the death, had disappeared with time. Blackstone—and the Framers who were formed by Blackstone-would clearly have regarded that *change* in law as a matter for the legislature, beyond the *power* of the court. It may well be that some common-law decisions of the era in fact changed the law while purporting not to. But that is beside the point. What is important here is that it was an undoubted point of principle, at the time the Due Process Clause was adopted, that courts could not "change" the law. That explains why the Constitution restricted only the legislature from enacting *ex post facto* laws. Under accepted norms of judicial process, an *ex post facto* law (in the sense of a judicial holding, not that a prior decision was erroneous, but that the prior valid law is hereby retroactively *changed*) was simply not an option for the courts. This attitude subsisted, I may note, well beyond the founding era, and beyond the time when due process guarantees were extended against the States by the Fourteenth Amendment. In an 1886 admiralty case, for example, this Court said the following: "The rights of persons in this particular under the maritime law of this country are not different from those under the common law, and as it is the duty of courts to declare the law, not to make it, we cannot change this rule." *The Harrisburg,* 119 U.S. 199, 213-214, 7 S.Ct. 140, 30 L.Ed. 358 (1886), overruled by *Moragne v. States Marine Lines, Inc.,* 398 U.S. 375, 90 S.Ct. 1772, 26 L.Ed.2d 339 (1970).

It is not a matter, therefore, of "[e]xtending the [*Ex Post Facto*] Clause to courts through the rubric of due process," and thereby "circumvent [ing] the clear constitutional text," *ante,* at 1699. It is simply a matter of determining what due judicial process consists of-and it does not consist of retroactive creation of crimes. The *Ex Post Facto* Clause is relevant only because it demonstrates beyond doubt that, however much the acknowledged and accepted role of common-law courts could evolve (as it has) in other respects, retroactive revision of the criminal law was regarded as so fundamentally unfair that an alteration of the judicial role which permits *that* will be a denial of due process. Madison wrote that "*ex-post-facto* laws ... are contrary to the first principles of the social compact, and to every principle of social legislation." *The Federalist* No. 44, p. 282 (C. Rossiter ed.1961). I find it impossible to believe, as the

Court does, that this strong sentiment attached only to retroactive laws passed by the legislature, and would not apply equally (or indeed with even greater force) to a court's production of the same result through disregard of the traditional limits upon judicial power. Insofar as the "first principles of the social compact" are concerned, what possible difference does it make that "[a] court's opportunity for discrimination" by retroactively changing a law "is more limited than a legislature's, in that it can only act in construing existing law in actual litigation"? *Ante,* at 1699 (internal quotation marks and citation omitted). The injustice to the individuals affected is no less.

II

Even if I agreed with the Court that the Due Process Clause is violated only when there is lack of "fair warning" of the impending retroactive change, I would not find such fair warning here. It is not clear to me, in fact, what the Court believes the fair warning consisted of. Was it the mere fact that "[t]he year and a day rule is widely viewed as an outdated relic of the common law"? *Ante,* at 1701. So are many of the elements of common-law crimes, such as "breaking the close" as an element of burglary, or "asportation" as an element of larceny. See W. LaFave & A. Scott, *Criminal Law* 631–633, 708–710 (1972). Are all of these "outdated relics" subject to retroactive judicial rescission? Or perhaps the fair warning consisted of the fact that "the year and a day rule has been legislatively or judicially abolished in the vast majority of jurisdictions recently to have addressed the issue." *Ante,* at 1701. But why not count in petitioner's favor (as giving him no reason to expect a change in law) those even more numerous jurisdictions that have chosen *not* "recently to have addressed the issue"? And why not also count in petitioner's favor (rather than *against* him) those jurisdictions that have abolished the rule *legislatively,* and those jurisdictions that have abolished it through *prospective* rather than *retroactive* judicial rulings (together, a large majority of the abolitions, see 992 S.W.2d, at 397, n. 4, 402 (listing statutes and cases))? That is to say, even if it was predictable that the rule would be changed, it was *not* predictable that it would be changed *retroactively,* rather than in the *prospective* manner to which legislatures are restricted by the *Ex Post Facto* Clause, or in the *prospective* manner that most other courts have employed.

In any event, as the Court itself acknowledges, "[d]ue process ... does not require a person to apprise himself of the common law of all 50 States in order to guarantee that his actions will not subject him to punishment in light of a developing trend in the law that has not yet made its way to his State." *Ante,* at 1701. The Court tries to counter this self-evident point with the statement that "[a]t the same time, however, the fact that a vast number of jurisdictions have abolished a rule that has so clearly outlived its purpose is surely relevant to whether the abolition of the rule in a particular case can be said to be unexpected and indefensible by reference to the law as it then existed," *ibid.* This retort rests upon the fallacy that I discussed earlier: that "expected or defensible" "abolition" of prior law was approved by *Bouie.* It was not-and according such conclusive effect to the "defensibility" (by which I presume the Court means the "reasonableness") of the change in law will validate the retroactive creation of many new crimes.

Finally, the Court seeks to establish fair warning by discussing at great length, *ante,* at 1701–1703, how unclear it was that the year-and-a-day rule was ever the law in Tennessee. As I have already observed, the Supreme Court of Tennessee is the authoritative expositor of Tennessee law, and has said categorically that the year-and-a-day rule was the law. Does the Court mean to establish the principle that fair warning of impending change exists-or perhaps fair warning can be dispensed with-when the prior law is not crystal clear? Yet another boon for retroactively created crimes.

I reiterate that the only "fair warning" discussed in our precedents, and the only "fair warning" relevant to the issue before us here, is fair warning *of what the law is*. That warning, unlike the new one that today's opinion invents, goes well beyond merely "safeguarding defendants against *unjustified* and *unpredictable* breaks with prior law," *ante*, at 1700 (emphasis added). It safeguards them against *changes in the law after the fact*. But even accepting the Court's novel substitute, the opinion's conclusion that this watered-down standard has been met seems to me to proceed on the principle that a large number of almost-valid arguments makes a solid case. As far as I can tell, petitioner had nothing that could fairly be called a "warning" that the Supreme Court of Tennessee would retroactively eliminate one of the elements of the crime of murder.

* * *

To decide this case, we need only conclude that due process prevents a court from (1) acknowledging the validity, when they were rendered, of prior decisions establishing a particular element of a crime; (2) changing the prior law so as to eliminate that element; and (3) applying that change to conduct that occurred under the prior regime. A court would remain free to apply common-law criminal rules to new fact patterns, see *ante*, at 1700, so long as that application is consistent with a fair reading of prior cases. It would remain free to conclude that a prior decision or series of decisions establishing a particular element of a crime was in error, and to apply that conclusion retroactively (so long as the "fair notice" requirement of *Bouie* is satisfied). It would even remain free, insofar as the *ex post facto* element of the Due Process Clause is concerned, to "reevaluat[e] and refin[e]" the elements of common-law crimes to its heart's content, so long as it does so prospectively. (The majority of state courts that have abolished the year-and-a-day rule have done so in this fashion.) And, of course (as Blackstone and the Framers envisioned), legislatures would be free to eliminate outmoded elements of common-law crimes for the future *by law*. But what a court cannot do, consistent with due process, is what the Tennessee Supreme Court did here: avowedly *change* (to the defendant's disadvantage) the criminal law governing past acts.

For these reasons, I would reverse the judgment of the Supreme Court of Tennessee.

Judges gone wild
Brown v. Plata,
563 U.S. 493 (2011)

Justice Scalia, with whom Justice Thomas joins, dissenting.

Today the Court affirms what is perhaps the most radical injunction issued by a court in our Nation's history: an order requiring California to release the staggering number of 46,000 convicted criminals.

There comes before us, now and then, a case whose proper outcome is so clearly indicated by tradition and common sense, that its decision ought to shape the law, rather than vice versa. One would think that, before allowing the decree of a federal district court to release 46,000 convicted felons, this Court would bend every effort to read the law in such a way as to avoid that outrageous result. Today, quite to the contrary, the Court disregards stringently drawn provisions of the governing statute, and traditional constitutional limitations upon the power of a federal judge, in order to uphold the absurd.

The proceedings that led to this result were a judicial travesty. I dissent because the institutional reform the District Court has undertaken violates the terms of the governing statute, ignores bedrock limitations on the power of Article III judges, and takes federal courts wildly beyond their institutional capacity.

I

A

The Prison Litigation Reform Act (PLRA) states that "[p]rospective relief in any civil action with respect to prison conditions shall extend no further than necessary to correct the violation of the Federal right of a particular plaintiff or plaintiffs"; that such relief must be "narrowly drawn, [and] exten[d] no further than necessary to correct the violation of the Federal right"; and that it must be "the least intrusive means necessary to correct the violation of the Federal right." 18 U.S.C. § 3626(a)(1)(A). In deciding whether these multiple limitations have been complied with, it is necessary to identify with precision what is the "violation of the Federal right of a particular plaintiff or plaintiffs" that has been alleged. What has been alleged here, and what the injunction issued by the court is tailored (narrowly or not) to remedy is the running of a prison system with inadequate medical facilities. That may result in the denial of needed medical treatment to "a particular [prisoner] or [prisoners]," thereby violating (according to our cases) his or their Eighth Amendment rights. But the mere existence of the inadequate system does not subject to cruel and unusual punishment the entire prison population in need of medical care, including those who receive it.

The Court acknowledges that the plaintiffs "do not base their case on deficiencies in care provided on any one occasion"; rather, "[p]laintiffs rely on systemwide deficiencies in the provision of medical and mental health care that, taken as a whole, subject sick and mentally ill prisoners in California to 'substantial risk of serious harm' and cause the delivery of care in the prisons to fall below the evolving standards of decency that mark the progress of a maturing society." *Ante,* at 1925, n. 3. But our judge-empowering "evolving standards of decency" jurisprudence (with which, by the way, I heartily disagree, see, *e.g., Roper v. Simmons,* 543 U.S. 551, 615–616, 125 S.Ct. 1183, 161 L.Ed.2d 1 (2005) (Scalia, J., dissenting)) does not prescribe (or at least has not until today prescribed) rules for the "decent" running of schools, prisons, and other government institutions. It forbids "indecent" treatment of individuals—in the context of this case, the *denial of medical care* to those who need it. And the persons who have a constitutional claim for denial of medical care are those who are denied medical care—not all who face a "substantial risk" (whatever that is) of being denied medical care.

The *Coleman* litigation involves "the class of seriously mentally ill persons in California prisons," *ante,* at 1926, and the *Plata* litigation involves "the class of state prisoners with serious medical conditions," *ante,* at 1926. The plaintiffs do not appear to claim—and it would absurd to suggest—that every single one of those prisoners has personally experienced "torture or a lingering death," *ante,* at 1928 (internal quotation marks omitted), as a consequence of that bad medical system. Indeed, it is inconceivable that anything more than a small proportion of prisoners in the plaintiff classes have personally received sufficiently atrocious treatment that their Eighth Amendment right was violated —which, as the Court recognizes, is why the plaintiffs do not premise their claim on "deficiencies in care provided on any one occasion." *Ante,* at 1925, n. 3. Rather, the plaintiffs' claim is that they are all part of a medical system so defective that some number of prisoners will inevitably be injured by incompetent medical care, and that this number is sufficiently high so as to render the system, as a whole, unconstitutional.

But what procedural principle justifies certifying a class of plaintiffs so they may assert a claim of systemic unconstitutionality? I can think of two possibilities, both of which are untenable. The first is that although some or most plaintiffs in the class do not *individually* have viable Eighth Amendment claims, the class as a whole has collectively suffered an Eighth Amendment violation. That theory is contrary to the bedrock rule that the sole purpose of classwide adjudication is to aggregate claims that are individually viable. "A class action, no less than traditional joinder (of which it is a species), merely enables a federal court to adjudicate claims of multiple parties at once, instead of in separate suits. And like traditional joinder, it leaves the parties' legal rights and duties intact and the rules of decision unchanged." *Shady Grove Orthopedic Associates, P.A. v. Allstate Ins. Co.*, 559 U.S. 393, ----, 130 S.Ct. 1431, 1443, 176 L.Ed.2d 311 (2010) (plurality opinion).

The second possibility is that every member of the plaintiff class *has* suffered an Eighth Amendment violation merely by virtue of being a patient in a poorly-run prison system, and the purpose of the class is merely to aggregate all those individually viable claims. This theory has the virtue of being consistent with procedural principles, but at the cost of a gross substantive departure from our case law. Under this theory, each and every prisoner who happens to be a patient in a system that has systemic weaknesses—such as "hir[ing] any doctor who had a license, a pulse and a pair of shoes," *ante*, at 1927 (internal quotation marks omitted)—has suffered cruel or unusual punishment, even if that person cannot make an individualized showing of mistreatment. Such a theory of the Eighth Amendment is preposterous. And we have said as much in the past: "If ... a healthy inmate who had suffered no deprivation of needed medical treatment were able to claim violation of his constitutional right to medical care ... simply on the ground that the prison medical facilities were inadequate, the essential distinction between judge and executive would have disappeared: it would have become the function of the courts to assure adequate medical care in prisons." *Lewis v. Casey*, 518 U.S. 343, 350, 116 S.Ct. 2174, 135 L.Ed.2d 606 (1996).

Whether procedurally wrong or substantively wrong, the notion that the plaintiff class can allege an Eighth Amendment violation based on "systemwide deficiencies" is assuredly wrong. It follows that the remedy decreed here is also contrary to law, since the theory of systemic unconstitutionality is central to the plaintiffs' case. The PLRA requires plaintiffs to establish that the systemwide injunction entered by the District Court was "narrowly drawn" and "extends no further than necessary" to correct "the violation of the Federal right of a particular plaintiff or plaintiffs." If (as is the case) the only viable constitutional claims consist of individual instances of mistreatment, then a remedy reforming the system as a whole goes far beyond what the statute allows.

It is also worth noting the peculiarity that the vast majority of inmates most generously rewarded by the re-lease order—the 46,000 whose incarceration will be ended—do not form part of any aggrieved class even under the Court's expansive notion of constitutional violation. Most of them will not be prisoners with medical conditions or severe mental illness; and many will undoubtedly be fine physical specimens who have developed intimidating muscles pumping iron in the prison gym.

B

Even if I accepted the implausible premise that the plaintiffs have established a systemwide violation of the Eighth Amendment, I would dissent from the Court's endorsement of a decrowding order. That order is an example of what has become known as a "structural injunction." As I have previously explained, structural injunctions are radically different from the injunctions traditionally issued by courts of equity, and presumably part of "the judicial Power" conferred on federal courts by Article III:

> "The mandatory injunctions issued upon termination of litigation usually required 'a single simple act.' H. McClintock, *Principles of Equity* § 15, pp. 32–33 (2d ed.1948). Indeed, there was a 'historical prejudice of the court of chancery

> against rendering decrees which called for more than a single affirmative act.' *Id.*, § 61, at 160. And where specific performance of contracts was sought, it was the categorical rule that no decree would issue that required ongoing supervision.... Compliance with these 'single act' mandates could, in addition to being simple, be quick; and once it was achieved the contemnor's relationship with the court came to an end, at least insofar as the subject of the order was concerned. Once the document was turned over or the land conveyed, the litigant's obligation to the court, and the court's coercive power over the litigant, ceased .... The court did not engage in any ongoing supervision of the litigant's conduct, nor did its order continue to regulate its behavior." *Mine Workers v. Bagwell,* 512 U.S. 821, 841–842, 114 S.Ct. 2552, 129 L.Ed.2d 642 (1994) (Scalia, J., concurring).

Structural injunctions depart from that historical practice, turning judges into long-term administrators of complex social institutions such as schools, prisons, and police departments. Indeed, they require judges to play a role essentially indistinguishable from the role ordinarily played by executive officials. Today's decision not only affirms the structural injunction but vastly expands its use, by holding that an entire system is unconstitutional because it *may produce* constitutional violations.

The drawbacks of structural injunctions have been described at great length elsewhere. See, *e.g., Lewis, supra,* at 385–393, 116 S.Ct. 2174 (1996) (Thomas, J., concurring); *Missouri v. Jenkins,* 515 U.S. 70, 124–133, 115 S.Ct. 2038, 132 L.Ed.2d 63 (1995) (Thomas, J., concurring); Horowitz, "Decreeing Organizational Change: Judicial Supervision of Public Institutions," 1983 *Duke L.J.* 1265. This case illustrates one of their most pernicious aspects: that they force judges to engage in a form of factfinding-as-policymaking that is outside the traditional judicial role. The factfinding judges traditionally engage in involves the determination of past or present facts based (except for a limited set of materials of which courts may take "judicial notice") exclusively upon a closed trial record. That is one reason why a district judge's factual findings are entitled to plain-error review: because having viewed the trial first hand he is in a better position to evaluate the evidence than a judge reviewing a cold record. In a very limited category of cases, judges have also traditionally been called upon to make some predictive judgments: which custody will best serve the interests of the child, for example, or whether a particular one-shot injunction will remedy the plaintiff's grievance. When a judge manages a structural injunction, however, he will inevitably be required to make very broad empirical predictions necessarily based in large part upon policy views—the sort of predictions regularly made by legislators and executive officials, but inappropriate for the Third Branch.

This feature of structural injunctions is superbly illustrated by the District Court's proceeding concerning the decrowding order's effect on public safety. The PLRA requires that, before granting " [p]rospective relief in [a] civil action with respect to prison conditions," a court must "give substantial weight to any adverse impact on public safety or the operation of a criminal justice system caused by the relief." 18 U.S.C. § 3626(a)(1)(A). Here, the District Court discharged that requirement by making the "factual finding" that "the state has available methods by which it could readily reduce the prison population to 137.5% design capacity or less without an adverse impact on public safety or the operation of the criminal justice system." Juris. Statement App., O.T.2009, No. 09-416, p. 253a. It found the evidence "clear" that prison overcrowding would "perpetuate a criminogenic prison system that itself threatens public safety," *id.,* at 186a, and volunteered its opinion that "[t]he population could be reduced even further with the reform of California's antiquated sentencing policies and other related changes to the laws." *Id.*, at 253a. It "reject[ed] the testimony that inmates released early from prison would commit additional new crimes," *id.*, at 200a, finding that "shortening the length of stay through earned credits would give inmates incentives to participate in programming designed to lower recidivism," *id.*, at 204a, and that "slowing the flow of technical parole violators to prison, thereby substantially reducing the churning of parolees, would by itself improve both the prison and parole systems, and public safety." *Id.*, at 209a. It found that "the diversion of offenders to community correctional programs has significant beneficial effects on public safety," *id.*, at 214a, and that "additional rehabilitative programming would result in a significant population reduction while improving public safety," *id.*, at 216a.

The District Court cast these predictions (and the Court today accepts them) as "factual findings," made in reliance on the procession of expert witnesses that testified at trial. Because these "findings" have support in the record, it is difficult to reverse them under a plain-error standard of review. *Ante*, at 38. And given that the District Court devoted nearly 10 days of trial and 70 pages of its opinion to this issue, it is difficult to dispute that the District Court has discharged its statutory obligation to give "substantial weight to any adverse impact on public safety."

But the idea that the three District Judges in this case relied solely on the credibility of the testifying expert witnesses is fanciful. *Of course* they were relying largely on their own beliefs about penology and recidivism. And *of course* different district judges, of different policy views, would have "found" that rehabilitation would not work and that releasing prisoners would increase the crime rate. I am not saying that the District Judges rendered their factual findings in bad faith. I am saying that it is impossible for judges to make "factual findings" without inserting their own policy judgments, when the factual findings *are* policy judgments. What occurred here is no more judicial factfinding in the ordinary sense than would be the factual findings that deficit spending will not lower the unemployment rate, or that the continued occupation of Iraq will decrease the risk of terrorism. Yet, because they have been branded "factual findings" entitled to deferential review, the policy preferences of three District Judges now govern the operation of California's penal system.

It is important to recognize that the dressing-up of policy judgments as factual findings is not an error peculiar to this case. It is an unavoidable concomitant of institutional-reform litigation. When a district court issues an injunction, it must make a factual assessment of the anticipated consequences of the injunction. And when the injunction undertakes to restructure a social institution, assessing the factual consequences of the injunction is necessarily the sort of predictive judgment that our system of government allocates to other government officials.

But structural injunctions do not simply invite judges to indulge policy preferences. They invite judges to indulge *incompetent* policy preferences. Three years of law school and familiarity with pertinent Supreme Court precedents give no insight whatsoever into the management of social institutions. Thus, in the proceeding below the District Court determined that constitutionally adequate medical services could be provided if the prison population was 137.5% of design capacity. This was an empirical finding it was utterly unqualified to make. Admittedly, the court did not generate that number entirely on its own; it heard the numbers 130% and 145% bandied about by various witnesses and decided to split the difference. But the ability of judges to spit back or even average-out numbers spoon-fed to them by expert witnesses does not render them competent decisionmakers in areas in which they are otherwise unqualified.

The District Court also relied heavily on the views of the Receiver and Special Master, and those reports play a starring role in the Court's opinion today. The Court notes that "the Receiver and the Special Master filed reports stating that overcrowding posed a significant barrier to their efforts" and deems those reports "persuasive evidence that, absent a reduction in overcrowding, any remedy might prove unattainable and would at the very least require vast expenditures of resources by the State." *Ante*, at 1939. The use of these reports is even less consonant with the traditional judicial role than the District Court's reliance on the expert testimony at trial. The latter, even when, as here, it is largely the expression of policy judgments, is at least subject to cross-examination. Relying on the un-cross-examined findings of an investigator, sent into the field to prepare a factual report and give suggestions on how to improve the prison system, bears no resemblance to ordinary judicial decisionmaking. It is true that the PLRA contemplates the appointment of Special Masters (although not Receivers), but Special Masters are authorized only to "conduct hearings and prepare proposed findings of fact" and "assist in the development of remedial plans," 18 U.S.C. § 3626(f)(6). This does not authorize them to make factual findings (unconnected to hearings) that are given seemingly wholesale deference. Neither the Receiver nor the Special Master was selected by California to run its prisons, and the fact that they may be experts in the field of prison reform does not justify the judicial imposition of their perspectives on the state.

C

My general concerns associated with judges' running social institutions are magnified when they run prison systems, and doubly magnified when they force prison officials to release convicted criminals. As we have previously recognized:

> "[C]ourts are ill equipped to deal with the increasingly urgent problems of prison administration and reform.... [T]he problems of prisons in America are complex and intractable, and, more to the point, they are not readily susceptible of resolution by decree.... Running a prison is an inordinately difficult undertaking that requires expertise, planning, and the commitment of resources, all of which are peculiarly within the province of the legislative and executive branches of government. Prison is, moreover, a task that has been committed to the responsibility of those branches, and separation of powers concerns counsel a policy of judicial restraint. Where a state penal system is involved, federal courts have ... additional reason to accord deference to the appropriate prison authorities." *Turner v. Safley,* 482 U.S. 78, 84–85, 107 S.Ct. 2254, 96 L.Ed.2d 64 (1987) (internal quotation marks omitted).

These principles apply doubly to a prisoner-release order. As the author of today's opinion explained earlier this Term, granting a writ of habeas corpus " 'disturbs the State's significant interest in repose for concluded litigation, denies society the right to punish some admitted offenders, and intrudes on state sovereignty to a degree matched by few exercises of federal judicial authority.'" *Harrington v. Richter,* 562 U.S. ––––, ––––, 131 S.Ct. 770, 787, 178 L.Ed.2d 624 (2011) (quoting *Harris v. Reed,* 489 U.S. 255, 282, 109 S.Ct. 1038, 103 L.Ed.2d 308 (1989) (Kennedy, J., dissenting)). Recognizing that habeas relief must be granted sparingly, we have reversed the Ninth Circuit's erroneous grant of habeas relief to individual California prisoners four times this Term alone. *Cullen v. Pinholster,* 563 U.S. ––––, 131 S.Ct. 1388, 179 L.Ed.2d 557 (2011); *Felkner v. Jackson,* 562 U.S. ––––, 131 S.Ct. 1305, 179 L.Ed.2d 374

(2011) *(per curiam); Swarthout v. Cooke,* 562 U.S. ----, 131 S.Ct. 859, 178 L.Ed.2d 732 (2011) *(per curiam); Harrington, supra.* And yet here, the Court affirms an order granting the functional equivalent of 46,000 writs of habeas corpus, based on its paean to courts' "substantial flexibility when making these judgments." *Ante,* at 1944. It seems that the Court's respect for state sovereignty has vanished in the case where it most matters.

II

The Court's opinion includes a bizarre coda noting that "[t]he State may wish to move for modification of the three-judge court's order to extend the deadline for the required reduction to five years." *Ante,* at 1947. The District Court, it says, "may grant such a request provided that the State satisfies necessary and appropriate preconditions designed to ensure the measures are taken to implement the plan without undue delay"; and it gives vague suggestions of what these preconditions "may include," such as "interim benchmarks." *Ante,* at 1947. It also invites the District Court to "consider whether it is appropriate to order the State to begin without delay to develop a system to identify prisoners who are unlikely to reoffend," and informs the State that it "should devise systems to select those prisoners least likely to jeopardize public safety." *Ibid.* (What a good idea!)

The legal effect of this passage is unclear—I suspect intentionally so. If it is nothing but a polite remainder to the State and to the District Court that the injunction is subject to modification, then it is entirely unnecessary. As both the State and the District Court are undoubtedly aware, a party is *always* entitled to move to modify an equitable decree, and the PLRA contains an express provision authorizing District Courts to modify or terminate prison injunctions. See 18 U.S.C. § 3626(b).

I suspect, however, that this passage is a warning shot across the bow, telling the District Court that it had *better* modify the injunction if the State requests what we invite it to request. Such a warning, if successful, would achieve the benefit of a marginal reduction in the inevitable murders, robberies, and rapes to be committed by the released inmates. But it would achieve that at the expense of intellectual bankruptcy, as the Court's "warning" is entirely alien to ordinary principles of appellate review of injunctions. When a party moves for modification of an injunction, the district court is entitled to rule on that motion first, subject to review for abuse of discretion if it declines to modify the order. *Horne v. Flores,* 557 U.S. 433, ––––, ––––, 129 S.Ct. 2579, 2593–2599, 174 L.Ed.2d 406 (2009). Moreover, when a district court enters a new decree with new benchmarks, the selection of those benchmarks is also reviewed under a deferential, abuse-of-discretion standard of review—a point the Court appears to recognize. *Ante,* at 1945. Appellate courts are not supposed to "affirm" injunctions while preemptively noting that the State "may" request, and the District Court "may" grant, a request to extend the State's deadline to release prisoners by three years based on some suggestions on what appropriate preconditions for such a modification "may" include.

Of course what is really happening here is that the Court, overcome by common sense, disapproves of the results reached by the District Court, but cannot remedy them (it thinks) by applying ordinary standards of appellate review. It has therefore selected a solution unknown in our legal system: A deliberately ambiguous set of suggestions on how to modify the injunction, just deferential enough so that it can say with a straight face that it is "affirming," just stern enough to put the District Court on notice that it will likely get reversed if it does not follow them. In doing this, the Court has aggrandized itself, grasping authority that appellate courts are not supposed to have, and using it to enact a compromise solution with no legal basis other than the Court's say-so. That we are driven to engage in these extralegal activities should be a sign that the entire project of permitting district courts to run prison systems is misbegotten.

But perhaps I am being too unkind. The Court, or at least a majority of the Court's majority, must be aware that the judges of the District Court are likely to call its bluff, since they know full well it cannot possibly be an abuse of discretion to refuse to accept the State's proposed modifications in an injunction that has just been approved (*affirmed*) in its present form. An injunction, after all, does not have to be perfect; only good enough for government work, which the Court today says this *is*. So perhaps the coda is nothing more than a ceremonial washing of the hands—making it clear for all to see, that if the terrible things sure to happen as a consequence of this outrageous order do happen, they will be none of this Court's responsibility. After all, did we not want, and indeed even suggest, something better?

III

In view of the incoherence of the Eighth Amendment claim at the core of this case, the nonjudicial features of institutional reform litigation that this case exemplifies, and the unique concerns associated with mass prisoner releases, I do not believe this Court can affirm this injunction. I will state my approach briefly: In my view, a court may not order a prisoner's release unless it determines that the prisoner is suffering from a violation of his constitutional rights, and that his release, and no other relief, will remedy that violation. Thus, if the court determines that a particular prisoner is being denied constitutionally required medical treatment, and the release of that prisoner (and no other remedy) would enable him to obtain medical treatment, then the court can order his release; but a court may not order the release of prisoners who have suffered no violations of their constitutional rights, merely to make it less likely that that will happen to them in the future.

This view follows from the PLRA's text that I discussed at the outset, 18 U.S.C. § 3626(a)(1)(A). "[N]arrowly drawn" means that the relief applies only to the "particular [prisoner] or [prisoners]" whose constitutional rights are violated; "extends no further than necessary" means that prisoners whose rights are not violated will not obtain relief; and "least intrusive means necessary to correct the violation of the Federal right" means that no other relief is available.

I acknowledge that this reading of the PLRA would severely limit the circumstances under which a court could issue structural injunctions to remedy allegedly unconstitutional prison conditions, although it would not eliminate them entirely. If, for instance, a class representing all prisoners in a particular institution alleged that the temperature in their cells was so cold as to violate the Eighth Amendment, or that they were deprived of all exercise time, a court could enter a prisonwide injunction ordering that the temperature be raised or exercise time be provided. Still, my approach may invite the objection that the PLRA appears to contemplate structural injunctions in general and mass prisoner-release orders in particular. The statute requires courts to "give substantial weight to any adverse impact on public safety or the operation of a criminal justice system caused by the relief" and authorizes them to appoint Special Masters, § 3626(a)(1)(A), (f), provisions that seem to presuppose the possibility of a structural remedy. It also sets forth criteria under which courts may issue orders that have "the purpose or effect of reducing or limiting the prisoner population," § 3626(g)(4).

I do not believe that objection carries the day. In addition to imposing numerous limitations on the ability of district courts to order injunctive relief with respect to prison conditions, the PLRA states that "[n]othing in this section shall be construed to ... repeal or detract from otherwise applicable limitations on the remedial powers of the courts." § 3626(a)(1)(C). The PLRA is therefore best understood as an attempt to constrain the discretion of courts issuing structural injunctions—not as a mandate for their use. For the reasons I have outlined, structural injunctions, especially prisoner-release orders, raise grave separation-of-powers concerns and veer significantly from the historical role and institutional capability of courts. It is appropriate to construe the PLRA so as to constrain courts from entering injunctive relief that would exceed that role and capability.

* * *

The District Court's order that California release 46,000 prisoners extends "further than necessary to correct the violation of the Federal right of a particular plaintiff or plaintiffs" who have been denied needed medical care. 18 U.S.C. § 3626(a)(1)(A). It is accordingly forbidden by the PLRA—besides defying all sound conception of the proper role of judges.

3

Statutory Interpretation

Textual enactment through textual construction
Houston v. Lack, 487 U.S. 266 (1988)

Statutes are not weapons to be wielded by well-intentioned judges
Chisom v. Roemer, 501 U.S. 380 (1991)

The rules are the rules
PGA Tour, Inc. v. Martin, 532 U.S. 661 (2001)

Statutory Interpretation 101: begin with the text
Zuni Public School Dist. No. 89 v. Department of Educ., 550 U.S. 81 (2007)

When words no longer have meaning
King v. Burwell, 135 S.Ct. 2480 (2015)

Justice Scalia was a wordsmith and a jurist of incomparable talent. One of the subjects on which he wrote most often both in his opinions and in books and articles he authored was the proper way for a court to interpret statutes, including the United States Constitution, and prior case decisions. He was a champion of using historical sources, particularly contemporary or near contemporary texts, to interpret the meaning of statutes. He was highly critical of the notion of legislative history and, in the constitutional arena, of the idea of a "living constitution." He was, above all, a textualist, who believed that texts carried meaning independent of the wishes of their readers. In this position, he often clashed with his brethren on the Court, many of whom found his approach constraining and illiberal. The cases in this section show how, in dissent, Justice Scalia applied his textual virtuosity to complex texts and criticized the majority's readings.

Textual enactment through textual construction

Houston v. Lack,
487 U.S. 266 (1988)

Justice Scalia, with whom the Chief Justice, Justice O'Connor, and Justice Kennedy join, dissenting.

Today's decision obliterates the line between textual construction and textual enactment. It would be within the realm of normal judicial creativity (though in my view wrong) to interpret the phrase "filed with the clerk" to mean "mailed to the clerk," or even "mailed to the clerk or given to a person bearing an obligation to mail to the clerk." But interpreting it to mean "delivered to the clerk or, if you are a prisoner, delivered to your warden" is no more acceptable than any of an infinite number of variants, such as: "delivered to the clerk or, if you are out of the country, delivered to a United States consul"; or "delivered to the clerk or, if you are a soldier on active duty in a war zone, delivered to your commanding officer"; or "delivered to the clerk or, if you are held hostage in a foreign country, meant to be delivered to the clerk." Like these other examples, the Court's rule makes a good deal of sense. I dissent only because it is not the rule that we have promulgated through congressionally prescribed procedures.

I

This case requires us to construe one statutory provision and two provisions of the Federal Rules of Appellate Procedure. The former is 28 U.S.C. § 2107, which sets a statutory, juridsictional deadline for the filing of notices of appeal in civil actions such as this habeas proceeding. It provides:

> "[N]o appeal shall bring any judgment, order or decree in an action, suit, or proceeding of a civil nature before a court of appeals for review unless notice of appeal is *filed,* within thirty days after the entry of such judgment, order or decree" (emphasis added).

Although the statute itself does not define when a notice of appeal has been "filed" or designate with whom it must be filed, the Federal Rules of Appellate Procedure fill in these details. Federal Rule of Appellate Procedure 3(a) provides:

> "An appeal permitted by law as of right from a district court to a court of appeals shall be taken by *filing a notice of appeal with the clerk of the district court* within the time allowed by Rule 4" (emphasis added).

This is supplemented by Federal Rule of Appellate Procedure 4(a)(1), which provides:

> "In a civil case in which an appeal is permitted by law as of right from a district court to a court of appeals the notice of appeal required by Rule 3 shall be *filed with the clerk of the district court* within 30 days after the date of entry of the judgment or order appealed from..." (emphasis added).

It is clear, then, that there was a notice of appeal effective to give the Court of Appeals jurisdiction in this case if, and only if, it was "filed with the clerk of the district court" within the 30-day period.

The Court observes that "filed with the clerk" could mean many different things, including merely "mailed to the clerk." *Ante,* slip op., at 2383–2384. That is unquestionable. But it is the practice in construing such a phrase to pick a single meaning, and not to impart first one, and then another, as the judicially perceived equities of individual cases might require.

Some statutory terms, such as "restraint of trade," *Business Electronics Corp. v. Sharp Electronics Corp.*, 485 U.S. 717, 731–733, 108 S.Ct. 1515, ---- - ----, 99 L.Ed.2d 808 (1988), invite judicial judgment from case to case; but a provision establishing a deadline upon which litigants are supposed to rely is not of that sort. That is why we adopted the proviso in Rule 28.2 of our own Rules, which the Court unexpectedly invokes in support of its position. Rule 28.2 reads:

> "To be timely filed, a document must be received by the Clerk within the time specified for filing, *except that* any document shall be deemed timely filed if it has been deposited in a United States post office or mailbox, with first-class postage prepaid, and properly addressed to the Clerk of this Court, within the time allowed for filing, and if there is filed with the Clerk a notarized statement by a member of the Bar of this Court, setting forth the details of the mailing, and stating that to his knowledge the mailing took place on a particular date within the permitted time." (Emphasis added.)

Since "received by the Clerk" must, in the context of such a rule, reasonably be understood to have a unitary meaning, which would of course normally be actual receipt, we felt constrained to *specify* an exception in which mailing would suffice. It would have been as inappropriate (though no less possible) there as in the present case to create the exception through interpretation-reasoning that the Post Office can be deemed the agent of the addressee, *Household Fire & Carriage Accident Ins. Co. v. Grant*, 4 Ex.D. 216 (1879) ("[P]ost office [is] the agent of both parties"), and hence it is theoretically possible to consider the document "received by" the Clerk when it is mailed, and the policy considerations usually militating in favor of a rule of actual receipt are well enough satisfied by an affidavit from a member of our Bar, etc.

If the need for a uniform meaning is apparent even with respect to ordinary statutory deadlines, and indeed even with respect to court-created rules that can be amended at the judges' discretion, it is even more apparent when a statutory deadline bearing upon the very jurisdiction of the courts is at issue. In that context, allowing courts to give different meanings from case to case allows them to expand and contract the scope of their own competence. That this is not envisioned is plain (if any citation is needed) from Rule 26(b) of the Federal Rules of Appellate Procedure, which specifically excepts from the courts' broad equitable power to "suspend the requirements or provisions of any of these rules in a particular case," Fed.Rule App.Proc. 2, the power to "enlarge the time for filing a notice of appeal." When we adopted Rules 3 and 4 of the Federal Rules of Appellate Procedure we delayed, as required by law, their effective date until 90 days after they were "reported to Congress by the Chief Justice," 28 U.S.C. § 2072, so that Congress might consider whether it wished to legislate any changes in them. Surely Congress could not have imagined that "filing ... with the clerk" in Rule 3(a) and "filed with the clerk" in Rule 4(a)(1) could have a meaning as remote from plain English as "delivered to the warden of a prison"-or whatever else might be held in the future to fit today's announced "rationale ... that the appellant has no control over delays," *ante*, at 2384.

The Court seeks to have it both ways, at one and the same time abandoning a unitary interpretation of "filed" for purposes of the present decision, yet purporting "not [to] disturb" the many cases stating that a notice of appeal is filed when received, "[t]o the extent these cases state the general rule." *Ante*, at 2384. See, *e.g.*, *Parissi v. Telechron, Inc.*, 349 U.S. 46, 47, 75 S.Ct. 577, 577, 99 L.Ed. 867 (1955) (holding that timely receipt satisfies 28 U.S.C. § 2107); *United States v. Lombardo*, 241 U.S.

73, 76, 36 S.Ct. 508, 509, 60 L.Ed. 897 (1916) ("A paper is filed when it is delivered to the proper official and by him received and filed"); *Haney v. Mizell Memorial Hospital,* 744 F.2d 1467, 1472 (CA11 1984); *In re LBL Sports Center, Inc.,* 684 F.2d 410, 413 (CA6 1982); *In re Robinson,* 640 F.2d 737, 738 (CA5 1981); *In re Ramsey,* 612 F.2d 1220, 1223 (CA9 1980); *In re Bad Bubba Racing Products, Inc.,* 609 F.2d 815, 816 (CA5 1980); *Ward v. Atlantic Coast Line R. Co.,* 265 F.2d 75, 80 (CA5 1959), rev'd on other grounds, 362 U.S. 396, 80 S.Ct. 789, 4 L.Ed.2d 820 (1960); *Allen v. Schnuckle,* 253 F.2d 195, 197 (CA9 1958). It seems to me that to leave them undisturbed only "to the extent [they] state the general rule" is to disturb them profoundly. The rationale of today's decision is that any of various theoretically possible meanings of "filed with the clerk" may be adopted-even one as remote as "addressed to the clerk and given to the warden"-depending upon what equity requires. It may turn out that we will not often agree that equity requires anything other than "received by the clerk," but parties will often argue it, and the lower courts will sometimes hold it. Thus is wasteful litigation in our appellate courts multiplied.

Petitioner Prentiss Houston's notice of appeal in this case was stamped received 31 days after the District Court's judgment was entered-that is, one day after the expiration of the 30-day filing period set out in Federal Rule of Appellate Procedure 4(a)(1) . Since there is no legal warrant for creating a special exception to the rule of receipt for the benefit of incarcerated *pro se* appellants, I cannot join the Court in reversing the judgment on that basis.

II

Petitioner advanced several additional arguments supporting reversal which the Court did not have to reach. *Ante,* at

2385, n. 4. I must consider them, and, having done so, find that none of them has merit.

First, petitioner asserts that his untimeliness in filing his notice of appeal should be excused because he "did all he could under the circumstances," as required by *Fallen v. United States,* 378 U.S. 139, 144, 84 S.Ct. 1689, 1692–1693, 12 L.Ed.2d 760 (1964). This argument fails because there is no warrant for equitable tolling of filing deadlines in the civil context of this habeas corpus proceeding as there was in the criminal context that was at issue in *Fallen.* The bar erected by § 2107 in civil cases is jurisdictional, and this Court is without power to waive it, no matter what the equities of a particular case. As noted above, this is made explicit in Rule 26(b) of the Federal Rules of Appellate Procedure. In *Fallen,* by contrast, there was no jurisdictional statute at issue, and the relevant Federal Rule of Criminal Procedure 2 provided that a "just determination" should be achieved. See 378 U.S., at 142, 84 S.Ct., at 1691–1692.

Second, petitioner maintains that he was lulled into thinking that his appeal was timely by the issuance of a certificate of probable cause and briefing schedule, and thus did not move for an extension of time within the 30-day grace period, see Fed.Rule App.Proc. 4(a)(5). This, he suggests, constitutes a "unique circumstance" of the sort recognized in *Harris Truck Lines, Inc. v. Cherry Meat Packers, Inc.,* 371 U.S. 215, 217, 83 S.Ct. 283, 285, 9 L.Ed.2d 261 (1962); *Thompson v. INS,* 375 U.S. 384, 387, 84 S.Ct. 397, 398–399, 11 L.Ed.2d 404 (1964); and *Wolfsohn v. Hankin,* 376 U.S. 203, 84 S.Ct. 699, 11 L.Ed.2d 636 (1964). Petitioner asserts that those cases establish an equitable doctrine that sometimes permits the late filing of notices of appeal. Our later cases, however, effectively repudiate the *Harris Truck Lines* approach, affirming that the timely filing of a notice of appeal is "mandatory and jurisdictional." *Griggs v. Provident Consumer Discount Co.,* 459 U.S. 56, 58, 61, 103 S.Ct.

400, 402, 403, 74 L.Ed.2d 225 (1982); see also *Browder v. Director, Dept. of Corrections of Illinois,* 434 U.S. 257, 98 S.Ct. 556, 54 L.Ed.2d 521 (1978). As we observed in *United States v. Locke,* 471 U.S. 84, 100-101, 105 S.Ct. 1785, 1796, 85 L.Ed.2d 64 (1985):

> "Filing deadlines, like statutes of limitations, necessarily operate harshly and arbitrarily with respect to individuals who fall just on the other side of them, but if the concept of a filing deadline is to have any content, the deadline must be enforced. 'Any less rigid standard would risk encouraging a lax attitude toward filing dates,' *United States v. Boyle,* 469 U.S. [241,] 249 [105 S.Ct. 687, 691–692, 83 L.Ed.2d 622] [(1985)]. A filing deadline cannot be complied with, substantially or otherwise, by filing late-even by one day."

Finally, petitioner asserts that his notice of appeal should be treated as a motion for extension of time under Federal Rule of Appellate Procedure 4(a)(5). That Rule, however, was specifically amended to require that *a motion* must be filed with the district court to obtain an extension, and its text precludes treating a late filed notice as being a motion. As revised, the Rule explicitly states:

> "The district court, upon a showing of excusable neglect or good cause, may extend the time for filing a notice of appeal *upon motion* filed not later than 30 days after the expiration of the time prescribed by this Rule 4(a)" (emphasis added).

The Advisory Committee's Notes on Appellate Rule 4(a)(5) explain:

> "Under the present rule there is a possible implication that prior to the time the initial appeal time has run, the district court may extend the time on the basis of an informal appli-

> cation. The amendment would require that the application must be made by motion, though the motion may be made ex parte. After the expiration of the initial time a motion for the extension of the time must be made in compliance with the F.R.C.P. and local rules of the district court." 28 U.S.C.App., p. 469.

The courts below were therefore without power to treat petitioner's late filed notice of appeal as a motion for extension of time under Federal Rule of Appellate Procedure 4(a)(5).

* * *

Twenty-four years ago Justice Clark, joined by Justices Harlan, Stewart, and White, said in the dissent in *Thompson:*

> "Rules of procedure are a necessary part of an orderly system of justice. Their efficacy, however, depends upon the willingness of the courts to enforce them according to their terms. Changes in rules whose inflexibility has turned out to work hardship should be effected by the process of amendment, not by *ad hoc* relaxations by this Court in particular cases. Such dispensations in the long run actually produce mischievous results, undermining the certainty of the rules and causing confusion among the lower courts and the bar." 375 U.S., at 390, 84 S.Ct, at 400.

That could not be more correct, nor more applicable to the present case. The filing rule the Court supports today seems to me a good one, but it is fully within our power to adopt it by an amendment of the Rules. Doing so instead in the present fashion not only evades the statutory requirement that changes be placed before Congress so that it may reject them by legislation before they become effective, 28 U.S.C. § 2072, but destroys the most important characteristic of filing requirements, which is the certainty of their application. It is hard to understand why the Court felt the need to short-circuit the orderly process of rule amendment in order to provide immediate relief in the present case. Petitioner delivered his notice of appeal to the warden three days before it was due to be filed with the Clerk. It would have been imprudent even to place it in a mailbox with the deadline so close at hand.

For the reasons stated, I respectfully dissent.

Statutes are not weapons to be wielded by well-intentioned judges

Chisom v. Roemer, 501 U.S. 380 (1991)

Justice Scalia, with whom the Chief Justice and Justice Kennedy join, dissenting.

Section 2 of the Voting Rights Act of 1965 is not some all-purpose weapon for well-intentioned judges to wield as they please in the battle against discrimination. It is a statute. I thought we had adopted a regular method for interpreting the meaning of language in a statute: first, find the ordinary meaning of the language in its textual context; and second, using established canons of construction, ask whether there is any clear indication that some permissible meaning other than the ordinary one applies. If not—and especially if a good reason for the ordinary meaning appears plain—we apply that ordinary meaning. See, *e.g., West Virginia University Hospitals, Inc. v. Casey,* 499 U.S. 83, 98–99, 111 S.Ct. 1138, 1146–1147, 113 L.Ed.2d 68 (1991); *Demarest v. Manspeaker,* 498 U.S. 184, 190, 111 S.Ct. 599, 603, 112 L.Ed.2d 608 (1991); *United States v. Ron Pair Enterprises, Inc.,* 489 U.S. 235, 241, 109 S.Ct. 1026, 1030, 103 L.Ed.2d 290 (1989); *Pennsylvania Dept. of Public Welfare v. Davenport,* 495 U.S. 552, 557–558, 110 S.Ct. 2126, 2130–2131, 109 L.Ed.2d 588 (1990); *Caminetti v. United States,* 242 U.S. 470, 485, 37 S.Ct. 192, 194, 61 L.Ed. 442 (1917); *Public Citizen v. Department of Justice,* 491 U.S. 440, 470, 109 S.Ct. 2558, 2575, 105 L.Ed.2d 377 (1989) (Kennedy, J., concurring in judgment).

Today, however, the Court adopts a method quite out of accord with that usual practice. It begins not with what the statute says, but with an expectation about what the statute must mean absent particular phenomena ("[*W*]*e are convinced* that if Congress had ... an intent [to exclude judges] Congress would have made it explicit in the statute, or at least some of the Members would have identified or mentioned it at some point in the unusually extensive legislative history," *ante,* at 2364 (emphasis added)); and the Court then interprets the words of the statute to fulfill its expectation. Finding nothing in the legislative history affirming that judges were excluded from the coverage of § 2, the Court gives the phrase "to elect representatives" the quite extraordinary meaning that covers the election of judges.

As method, this is just backwards, and however much we may be attracted by the result it produces in a particular case, we should in every case resist it. Our job begins with a text that Congress has passed and the President has signed. We are to read the words of that text as any ordinary Member of Congress would have read them, see Holmes, "The Theory of Legal Interpretation," 12 *Harv.L.Rev.* 417 (1899), and apply the meaning so determined. In my view, that reading reveals that § 2 extends to vote dilution claims for the elections of representatives only, and judges are not representatives.

I

As the Court suggests, the 1982 amendments to the Voting Rights Act were adopted in response to our decision in *Mobile v. Bolden,* 446 U.S. 55, 100 S.Ct. 1490, 64 L.Ed.2d 47 (1980), which had held that the scope of the original Voting Rights Act was coextensive with the Fifteenth Amendment, and thus proscribed intentional discrimination only. I agree with the Court that that original legislation, directed toward intentional discrimination, applied to all elections, for it clearly said so:

> "No voting qualification or prerequisite to voting, or standard, practice, or procedure shall be imposed or applied by any State or political subdivision to deny or abridge the right of any citizen of the United States to vote on account of race or color." 79 Stat. 437.

The 1982 amendments, however, radically transformed the Act. As currently written, the statute proscribes intentional discrimination only if it has a discriminatory effect, but proscribes practices with discriminatory effect whether or not intentional. This new "results" criterion provides a powerful, albeit sometimes blunt, weapon with which to attack even the most subtle forms of discrimination. The question we confront here is how broadly the new remedy applies. The foundation of the Court's analysis, the itinerary for its journey in the wrong direction, is the following statement: "It is difficult to believe that Congress, in an express effort to broaden the protection afforded by the Voting Rights Act, withdrew, without comment, an important category of elections from that protection." *Ante,* at 2368. There are two things wrong with this. First is the notion that Congress cannot be credited with having achieved anything of major importance by simply saying it, in ordinary language, in the text of a statute, "without comment" in the legislative history. As the Court colorfully puts it, if the dog of legislative history has not barked nothing of great significance can have transpired. *Ante,* at 2364, n. 23. Apart from the questionable wisdom of assuming that dogs will bark when something important is happening, see 1 T. Livius, *The History of Rome* 411–413 (1892) (D. Spillan transl.), we have forcefully and explicitly rejected the Conan Doyle approach to statutory construction in the past. See *Harrison v. PPG Industries, Inc.,* 446 U.S. 578, 592, 100 S.Ct. 1889, 1897, 64 L.Ed.2d 525 (1980) ("In ascertaining the meaning of a statute, a court cannot, in the manner of Sherlock Holmes, pursue the theory of the dog that did not bark"). We are here to apply the statute, not legislative history, and certainly not the absence of legislative history. Statutes are the law though sleeping dogs lie. See, *e.g., Sedima, S.P.R.L. v. Imrex Co.,* 473 U.S. 479, 495–496, n. 13, 105 S.Ct. 3275, 3284–3285, n. 13, 87 L.Ed.2d 346 1985); *Williams v. United States,* 458 U.S. 279, 294–295, 102 S.Ct. 3088, 3096–3097, 73 L.Ed.2d 767 (1982) (Marshall, J., dissenting).

The more important error in the Court's starting point, however, is the assumption that the effect of excluding judges from the revised § 2 would be to "withdr[aw] ... an important category of elections from [the] protection [of the Voting Rights Act]." *Ante,* at 2368. There is absolutely no question here of *withdrawing* protection. Since the pre–1982 content of § 2 was coextensive with the Fifteenth Amendment, the entirety of that protection subsisted in the Constitution, and could be enforced through the other provisions of the Voting Rights Act. Nothing was lost from the prior coverage; *all* of the new "results" protection was an add-on. The issue is not, therefore, as the Court would have it, *ante,* at 2364, whether Congress has cut back on the coverage of the Voting Rights Act; the issue is how far it has extended it. Thus, even if a court's expectations were a proper basis for interpreting the text of a statute, while there would be reason to expect that Congress was not "withdrawing" protection, there is no particular reason to expect that the supplemental protection it provided was any more extensive than the text of the statute said.

What it said, with respect to establishing a violation of the amended § 2, is the following:

> "... A violation ... is established if ... it is shown that the political processes leading to nomination or election ... are not equally open to participation by members of a [protected] class ... in that its members have less opportunity than other members of the electorate *to participate in the political pro-*

cess and *to elect representatives of their choice.*" 42 U.S.C. § 1973(b) (emphasis added).

Though this text nowhere speaks of "vote dilution," *Thornburg v. Gingles,* 478 U.S. 30, 106 S.Ct. 2752, 92 L.Ed.2d 25 (1986), understood it to proscribe practices which produce that result, identifying as the statutory basis for a dilution claim the second of the two phrases highlighted above—"to elect representatives of their choice." Under this interpretation, the other highlighted phrase—"to participate in the political process"—is left for other, *nondilution* § 2 violations. If, for example, a county permitted voter registration for only three hours one day a week, and that made it more difficult for blacks to register than whites, blacks would have less opportunity "*to participate* in the political process" than whites, and § 2 would therefore be violated—even if the number of potential black voters was so small that they would on no hypothesis be able *to elect* their own candidate, see Blumstein, "Proving Race Discrimination," 69 *Va.L.Rev.* 633, 706–707 (1983).

The Court, however, now rejects *Thornburg*'s reading of the statute, and asserts that before a violation of § 2 can be made out, *both* conditions of § 2(b) must be met. As the Court explains,

> "As the statute is written, ... the inability to elect representatives of their choice is not sufficient to establish a violation unless, under the totality of the circumstances, it can also be said that the members of the protected class have less opportunity to participate in the political process. The statute does not create two separate and distinct rights.... It would distort the plain meaning of the sentence to substitute the word 'or' for the word 'and.' Such radical surgery would be required to separate the opportunity to participate from the opportunity to elect." *Ante,* at 2365.

This is unquestionably wrong. If both conditions must be violated before there is any § 2 violation, then minorities who form such a small part of the electorate in a particular jurisdiction that they could on no conceivable basis "elect representatives of their choice" would be entirely without § 2 protection. Since, as the Court's analysis suggests, the "results" test of § 2 judges a violation of the "to elect" provision on the basis of whether the practice in question prevents actual election, then a protected class that with or without the practice will be unable to elect its candidate can be denied equal opportunity "to participate in the political process" with impunity. The Court feels compelled to reach this implausible conclusion of a "singular right" because the "to participate" clause and the "to elect" clause are joined by the conjunction "and." It is unclear to me why the rules of English usage require that conclusion here, any more than they do in the case of the First Amendment—which reads "Congress shall make no law ... abridging ... the right of the people peaceably to assemble, and to petition the Government for a redress of grievances." This has not generally been thought to protect the right peaceably to assemble only when the purpose of the assembly is to petition the Government for a redress of grievances. So also here, one is deprived of an equal "opportunity ... to participate ... and to elect" if *either* the opportunity to participate *or* the opportunity to elect is unequal. The point is in any event not central to the present case—and it is sad to see the Court repudiate *Thornburg*, create such mischief in the application of § 2, and even cast doubt upon the First Amendment, merely to deprive the State of the argument that elections for judges *remain* covered by § 2 *even though* they are not subject to vote dilution claims.

The Court, petitioners, and petitioners' *amici* have labored mightily to establish that there is *a* meaning of "representatives" that would include judges, see, *e.g.*, Brief for Lawyers

Committee for Civil Rights as *Amicus Curiae* 10–11, and no doubt there is. But our job is not to scavenge the world of English usage to discover whether there is any possible meaning of "representatives" which suits our preconception that the statute includes judges; our job is to determine whether the *ordinary* meaning includes them, and if it does not, to ask whether there is any solid indication in the text or structure of the statute that something other than ordinary meaning was intended.

There is little doubt that the ordinary meaning of "representatives" does not include judges, see Webster's *Second New International Dictionary* 2114 (1950). The Court's feeble argument to the contrary is that "representatives" means those who "are chosen by popular election." *Ante,* at 2366. On that hypothesis, the fan-elected members of the baseball all-star teams are "representatives"—hardly a common, if even a permissible, usage. Surely the word "representative" connotes one who is not only *elected by* the people, but who also, at a minimum, *acts on behalf of* the people. Judges do that in a sense—but not in the ordinary sense. As the captions of the pleadings in some States still display, it is the prosecutor who represents "the People"; the judge represents the Law—which often requires him to rule against the People. It is precisely because we do not *ordinarily* conceive of judges as representatives that we held judges not within the Fourteenth Amendment's requirement of "one person, one vote." *Wells v. Edwards,* 347 F.Supp. 453 (MD La.1972), aff'd, 409 U.S. 1095, 93 S.Ct. 904, 34 L.Ed.2d 679 (1973). The point is not that a State could not make judges in some senses representative, or that all judges must be conceived of in the Article III mold, but rather, that giving "representatives" its ordinary meaning, the ordinary speaker in 1982 would not have applied the word to judges, see Holmes, "The Theory of Legal Interpretation," 12 *Harv.L.Rev.*

417 (1899). It remains only to ask whether there is good indication that ordinary meaning does not apply.

There is one canon of construction that might be applicable to the present cases which, in some circumstances, would counter ordinary meaning—but here it would only have the effect of *reinforcing* it. We apply that canon to another case today, concerning, curiously enough, the very same issue of whether state judges are covered by the provisions of a federal statute. In *Gregory v. Ashcroft,* 501 U.S. 452, 111 S.Ct. 2395, 115 L.Ed.2d 410 we say that unless it is *clear* that the term "appointee[s] on the policymaking level" does not include judges we will construe it to include them, since the contrary construction would cause the statute to intrude upon the structure of state government, establishing a federal qualification for state judicial office. Such intrusion, we say, requires a "plain statement" before we will acknowledge it. See also *Will v. Michigan Dept. of State Police,* 491 U.S. 58, 65, 109 S.Ct. 2304, 2308, 105 L.Ed.2d 45 (1989); *Atascadero State Hospital v. Scanlon,* 473 U.S. 234, 242, 105 S.Ct. 3142, 3147, 87 L.Ed.2d 171 (1985); *Pennhurst State School and Hospital v. Halderman,* 465 U.S. 89, 99, 104 S.Ct. 900, 907, 79 L.Ed.2d 67 (1984). If the same principle were applied here, we would have double reason to give "representatives" its ordinary meaning. It is true, however, that in *Gregory* interpreting the statute to include judges would make them the only high-level state officials affected, whereas here the question is whether judges were excluded from a general imposition upon state elections that unquestionably exists; and in *Gregory* it was questionable whether Congress was invoking its powers under the Fourteenth Amendment (rather than merely the Commerce Clause), whereas here it is obvious. Perhaps those factors suffice to distinguish the two cases. Moreover, we tacitly rejected a "plain statement" rule as applied to the unamended § 2 in *City of Rome v. United States,* 446 U.S. 156, 178–180, 100 S.Ct. 1548, 1562–1563, 64 L.Ed.2d 119 (1980), though arguably that was before the rule had developed the significance it currently has. I am content to dispense with the "plain statement" rule in the present cases, cf. *Pennsylvania v. Union Gas Co.,* 491 U.S. 1, 41–42, 109 S.Ct. 2273, 2302–2303, 105 L.Ed.2d 1 (1989) (opinion of Scalia, J.)—but it says something about the Court's approach to this decision that the possibility of applying that rule never crossed its mind.

While the "plain statement" rule may not be applicable, there is assuredly nothing whatever that points in the opposite direction, indicating that the ordinary meaning here should *not* be applied. Far from that, in my view the ordinary meaning of "representatives" gives clear purpose to congressional action that otherwise would seem pointless. As an initial matter, it is evident that Congress paid particular attention to the scope of elections covered by the "to elect" language. As the Court suggests, that language for the most part tracked this Court's opinions in *White v. Regester,* 412 U.S. 755, 766, 93 S.Ct. 2332, 2339, 37 L.Ed.2d 314 (1973), and *Whitcomb v. Chavis,* 403 U.S. 124, 149, 91 S.Ct. 1858, 1872, 29 L.Ed.2d 363 (1971), but the word "legislators" was not copied. Significantly, it was replaced not with the more general term "candidates" used repeatedly elsewhere in the Act, see, *e.g.,* 42 U.S.C. §§ 1971(b), (e); 1973i(c); 1973*l*(c)(1); 1973ff–2; 1974; 1974e, but with the term "representatives," which appears nowhere else in the Act (except as a proper noun referring to Members of the federal lower House, or designees of the Attorney General). The normal meaning of this term is broader than "legislators" (it includes, for example, school boards and city councils as well as senators and representatives) but narrower than "candidates."

The Court says that the seemingly significant refusal to use the term "candidate" and selection of the distinctive term "representative" are really inconsequential, because "candidate" could not have been used. According to the Court, since "candidate" refers to one who has been nominated but *not yet* elected, the phrase "to elect candidates" would be a contradiction in terms. *Ante,* at 2366. The only flaw in this argument is that it is not true, as repeated usage of the formulation "to elect candidates" by this Court itself amply demonstrates. See, *e.g.,* *Davis v. Bandemer,* 478 U.S. 109, 131, 106 S.Ct. 2797, 2809, 92 L.Ed.2d 85 (1986); *Rogers v. Lodge,* 458 U.S. 613, 624, 102 S.Ct. 3272, 3279, 73 L.Ed.2d 1012 (1982); *id.,* at 639, n. 18, 641, n. 22, 649, 102 S.Ct., at 3287, n. 18, 3288, n. 22, 3292 (STEVENS, J., dissenting); *Mobile v. Bolden,* 446 U.S., at 75, 100 S.Ct., at 1504; *United Jewish Organizations of Williamsburgh, Inc. v. Carey,* 430 U.S. 144, 158, 97 S.Ct. 996, 1006, 51 L.Ed.2d 229 (1977); *Moore v. Ogilvie,* 394 U.S. 814, 819, 89 S.Ct. 1493, 1496, 23 L.Ed.2d 1 (1969); *Allen v. State Bd. of Elections,* 393 U.S. 544, 569, 89 S.Ct. 817, 833, 22 L.Ed.2d 1 (1969). We even used the phrase repeatedly in *Thornburg. Thornburg v. Gingles,* 478 U.S., at 40, 44, 50, 54, 80, 106 S.Ct., at 2760, 2762, 2766, 2768, 2781; *id.,* at 86, 103, 106 S.Ct., at 2785, 2793 (O'CONNOR, J., concurring in judgment); *id.,* at 107, 106 S.Ct., at 2795 (STEVENS, J., concurring in part and dissenting in part). And the phrase is used in the complaint of the minority plaintiffs in the other § 2 case decided today. *Houston Lawyers' Assn. v. Attorney General of Texas,* 501 U.S. 419, 111 S.Ct. 2376, 115 L.Ed.2d 379 (1991). App. in Nos. 90–813, 90–974, p. 22a. In other words, far from being an impermissible choice, "candidates" would have been the natural choice, even if it had not been used repeatedly elsewhere in the statute. It is quite absurd to think that Congress went out of its way to replace that term with "representatives," in order to convey what "candidates" naturally suggests (viz., coverage of *all* elections) and what "representatives" naturally does not.

A second consideration confirms that "representatives" in § 2 was meant in its ordinary sense. When given its ordinary meaning, it causes the statute to reproduce an established, eminently logical, and perhaps practically indispensable limitation upon the availability of vote dilution claims. Whatever other requirements may be applicable to elections for "representatives" (in the sense of those who are not only elected by but act on behalf of the electorate), those elections, unlike elections for *all* officeholders, must be conducted in accordance with the equal protection principle of "one person, one vote." And it so happens—more than coincidentally, I think—that in every case in which, prior to the amendment of § 2, we recognized the possibility of a vote dilution claim, the principle of "one person, one vote" was applicable. See, *e.g., Fortson v. Dorsey,* 379 U.S. 433, 436, 85 S.Ct. 498, 500, 13 L.Ed.2d 401 (1965); *Burns v. Richardson,* 384 U.S. 73, 88, 86 S.Ct. 1286, 1294, 16 L.Ed.2d 376 (1966); *Whitcomb v. Chavis, supra,* 403 U.S., at 149–150, 91 S.Ct., at 1872–1873; *White v. Regester, supra,* 412 U.S., at 765–767, 93 S.Ct., at 2339–2340; see also *Davis v. Bandemer, supra,* 478 U.S., at 131–132, 106 S.Ct., at 2809–2810. Indeed, it is the principle of "one person, one vote" that gives meaning to the concept of "dilution." One's vote is diluted if it is not, *as it should be,* of the same practical effect as everyone else's. Of course the mere fact that an election practice satisfies the constitutional requirement of "one person, one vote" does not establish that there has been no vote dilution for Voting Rights Act purposes, since that looks not merely to equality of individual votes but also to equality of minority blocs of votes. (*White* itself, which dealt with a multimember district, demonstrates this point. See also *Mobile v. Bolden, supra,* 446 U.S., at 65, 100 S.Ct., at 1498.) But "one person, one vote" has been the premise and the necessary condition of a vote dilution claim, since it establishes the baseline for computing the voting strength that the minority bloc *ought to have.* As we have suggested, the first question in a dilution case is whether the "one-person, one-vote" standard is met, and if it is, the second is whether voting structures nonetheless operate to "'minimize or cancel out the voting strength of racial or political elements of the voting population.'" *Burns v. Richardson, supra,* 384 U.S., at 88, 86 S.Ct., at 1294. See also Note, "Fair and Effective Voting Strength Under Section 2 of the Voting Rights Act: The Impact of Thornburg v. Gingles on Minority Vote Dilution Litigation," 34 *Wayne L.Rev.* 303, 323–324 (1987).

Well before Congress amended § 2, we had held that the principle of "one person, one vote" does not apply to the election of judges, *Wells v. Edwards,* 347 F.Supp. 453 (MD La.1972), aff'd, 409 U.S. 1095, 93 S.Ct. 904, 34 L.Ed.2d 679 (1973). If Congress was (through use of the extremely inapt word "representatives") making vote dilution claims available with respect to the election of judges, it was, for the first time, extending that remedy to a context in which "one person, one vote" did not apply. *That* would have been a significant change in the law, and given the need to identify some other baseline for computing "dilution," *that* is a matter which those who believe in barking dogs should be astounded to find unmentioned in the legislative history. If "representatives" is given its normal meaning, on the other hand, there is no change in the law (except elimination of the intent requirement) and the silence is entirely understandable.

I frankly find it very difficult to conceive how it is to be determined whether "dilution" has occurred, once one has eliminated *both* the requirement of actual intent to disfavor minorities, *and* the principle that 10,000 minority votes throughout the State should have as much practical "electability" effect as 10,000 nonminority votes. How does one begin to decide, in such a system, how much elective strength a minority bloc *ought* to have? I do not assert that it is utterly impossible to impose "vote dilution" restrictions upon an electoral regime that is not based on the "one-person, one-vote" principle. Congress can define "vote dilution" to be whatever it will, within constitutional bounds. But my point is that "one person, one vote" is inherent in the normal concept of "vote dilution," and was an essential element of the pre-existing, judicially crafted definition under § 2; that Congress did *not* adopt any new definition; that creating a new definition is a seemingly standardless task; and that the word Congress selected ("representative") seems specifically designed to avoid these problems. The Court is stoic about the difficulty of defining "dilution" without a standard of purity, expressing its resolve to stand up to that onerous duty inescapably thrust upon it: "Even if serious problems lie ahead in applying the 'totality of the circumstances' standard described in § 2(b), that task, difficult as it may prove to be, cannot justify a judicially created limitation on the coverage of the broadly worded statute, as enacted and amended by Congress." *Ante*, at 2368. One would think that Congress had said "candidates," rather than "representatives." In reality, however, it is the Court rather than Congress that leads us—quite unnecessarily and indeed with stubborn persistence—into this morass of unguided and perhaps unguidable judicial interference in democratic elections. The Court attributes to Congress not only the intent to mean something other than what it said, but also the intent to let district courts invent (for there is no precedent where "one person, one vote" did not apply that Congress could have been consulting) what in the world constitutes dilution of a vote that does not have to be equal.

Finally, the Court suggests that there is something "anomalous" about extending coverage under § 5 of the Voting Rights Act to the election of judges, while not extending coverage under § 2 to the same elections. *Ante,* at 2367. This simply misconceives the different roles of § 2 and § 5. The latter requires certain jurisdictions to preclear changes in election methods before those changes are implemented; it is a means of assuring in advance the absence of all electoral illegality, not only that which violates the Voting Rights Act but that which violates the Constitution as well. In my view, judges *are* within the scope of § 2 for nondilution claims, and thus for those claims, § 5 preclearance would enforce the Voting Rights Act with respect to judges. Moreover, intentional discrimination in the election of judges, whatever its form, is constitutionally prohibited, and the preclearance provision of § 5 gives the Government a method by which to prevent that. The scheme makes entire sense without the need to bring judges within the "to elect" provision.

All this is enough to convince me that there is sense to the ordinary meaning of "representative" in § 2(b)—that there is reason to Congress' choice—and since there is, then, under our normal presumption, that ordinary meaning prevails. I would read § 2 as extending vote dilution claims to elections for "representatives," but not to elections for judges. For other claims under § 2, however—those resting on the "to participate in the political process" provision rather than the "to elect" provision—no similar restriction would apply. Since the claims here are exclusively claims of dilution, I would affirm the judgment of the Fifth Circuit.

* * *

As I said at the outset, these cases are about method. The Court transforms the meaning of § 2, not because the ordinary meaning is irrational, or inconsistent with other parts of the statute, see, *e.g., Green v. Bock Laundry Machine Co.,* 490 U.S. 504, 510–511, 109 S.Ct. 1981, 1985, 104 L.Ed.2d 557 (1989); *Public*

Citizen v. Department of Justice, 491 U.S., at 470, 109 S.Ct., at 2574 (Kennedy, J., concurring in judgment), but because it does not fit the Court's conception of what Congress must have had in mind. When we adopt a method that psychoanalyzes Congress rather than reads its laws, when we employ a tinkerer's toolbox, we do great harm. Not only do we reach the wrong result with respect to the statute at hand, but we poison the well of future legislation, depriving legislators of the assurance that ordinary terms, used in an ordinary context, will be given a predictable meaning. Our highest responsibility in the field of statutory construction is to read the laws in a consistent way, giving Congress a sure means by which it may work the people's will. We have ignored that responsibility today. I respectfully dissent.

The rules are the rules
PGA Tour, Inc. v. Martin,
532 U.S. 661 (2001)

Justice Scalia, with whom Justice Thomas joins, dissenting.

In my view today's opinion exercises a benevolent compassion that the law does not place it within our power to impose. The judgment distorts the text of Title III, the structure of the ADA, and common sense. I respectfully dissent.

I

The Court holds that a professional sport is a place of public accommodation and that respondent is a "custome[r]" of "competition" when he practices his profession. *Ante,* at 1891–1892. It finds, *ante,* at 1892, that this strange conclusion is compelled by the "literal text" of Title III of the Americans with Disabilities Act of 1990(ADA), 42 U.S.C. § 12101 *et seq.*, by the "expansive purpose" of the ADA, and by the fact that Title II of the Civil Rights Act of 1964, 42 U.S.C. § 2000a(a), has been applied to an amusement park and public golf courses. I disagree.

The ADA has three separate titles: Title I covers employment discrimination, Title II covers discrimination by government entities, and Title III covers discrimination by places of public accommodation. Title II is irrelevant to this case. Title I protects only "employees" of employers who have 15 or more employees, §§ 12112(a), 12111(5)(A). It does not protect independent contractors. See, *e.g., Birchem v. Knights of Columbus,* 116 F.3d 310, 312–313 (C.A.8 1997); cf. *Nationwide Mut. Ins. Co. v. Darden,* 503 U.S. 318, 322–323, 112 S.Ct. 1344, 117 L.Ed.2d 581 (1992). Respondent claimed employment discrimination under Title I, but the District Court found him to be an independent contractor rather than an employee.

Respondent also claimed protection under § 12182 of Title III. That section applies only to particular places and persons. The place must be a "place of public accommodation," and the person must be an "individual" seeking "enjoyment of the goods, services, facilities, privileges, advantages, or accommodations" of the covered place. § 12182(a). Of course a court indiscriminately invoking the "sweeping" and "expansive" purposes of the ADA, *ante,* at 1889, 1892, could argue that when a place of public accommodation denied *any* "individual," on the basis of his disability, *anything* that might be called a "privileg[e]," the individual has a valid Title III claim. Cf. *ante,* at 1890. On such an interpretation, the employees and independent contractors of every place of public accommodation come within Title III: The employee enjoys the "privilege" of employment, the contractor the "privilege" of the contract.

For many reasons, Title III will not bear such an interpretation. The provision of Title III at issue here (§ 12182, its principal provision) is a public-accommodation law, and it is the traditional understanding of public-accommodation laws that they provide rights for *customers.* "At common law, innkeepers, smiths, and others who made profession of a public employment, were prohibited from refusing, without good reason, to serve a customer." *Hurley v. Irish-American Gay, Lesbian and Bisexual Group of Boston, Inc.,* 515 U.S. 557, 571, 115 S.Ct. 2338, 132 L.Ed.2d 487 (1995) (internal quotation marks omitted). See also *Heart of Atlanta Motel, Inc. v. United States,* 379 U.S. 241, 85 S.Ct. 348, 13 L.Ed.2d 258 (1964). This understanding is clearly reflected in the text of Title III itself. Section 12181(7) lists 12 specific types of entities that qualify as "public accommodations," with a follow-on expansion that makes it clear what the "enjoyment of the goods, services, etc.," of those entities consists of—and it plainly envisions that the person "enjoying" the "public accommodation" will be a *customer.* For example, Title III is said to cover an "auditorium" or "other place of public gathering," § 12181(7)(D). Thus, "gathering" is the distinctive enjoyment derived from an auditorium; the persons "gathering" at an auditorium are presumably covered by Title III, but those contracting to clean the auditorium are not. Title III is said to cover a "zoo" or "other place of recreation," § 12181(7)(I). The persons "recreat[ing]" at a "zoo" are presumably covered, but the animal handlers bringing in the latest panda are not. The one place where Title III specifically addresses discrimination by places of public accommodation through "contractual" arrangements, it makes clear that discrimination against the other party to the contract is not covered, but only discrimination against "clients or customers of the covered public accommodation that enters into the contractual, licensing or other arrangement." § 12182(b)(1)

(A)(iv). And finally, the regulations promulgated by the Department of Justice reinforce the conclusion that Title III's protections extend only to customers. "The purpose of the ADA's public accommodations requirements," they say, "is to ensure accessibility to the goods offered by a public accommodation." 28 CFR, ch. 1, pt. 36, App. B, p. 650 (2000). Surely this has nothing to do with employees and independent contractors.

If there were any doubt left that § 12182 covers only clients and customers of places of public accommodation, it is eliminated by the fact that a contrary interpretation would make a muddle of the ADA as a whole. The words of Title III must be read "in their context and with a view to their place in the overall statutory scheme." *Davis v. Michigan Dept. of Treasury,* 489 U.S. 803, 809, 109 S.Ct. 1500, 103 L.Ed.2d 891 (1989). Congress expressly excluded employers of fewer than 15 employees from Title I. The mom-and-pop grocery store or laundromat need not worry about altering the nonpublic areas of its place of business to accommodate handicapped employees—or about the litigation that failure to do so will invite. Similarly, since independent contractors are not covered by Title I, the small business (or the large one, for that matter) need not worry about making special accommodations for the painters, electricians, and other independent workers whose services are contracted for from time to time. It is an entirely unreasonable interpretation of the statute to say that these exemptions so carefully crafted in Title I are entirely eliminated by Title III (for the many businesses that are places of public accommodation) because employees and independent contractors "enjoy" the employment and contracting that such places provide. The only *distinctive* feature of places of public accommodation is that they accommodate the *public,* and Congress could have no conceivable reason for according the employees and independent contractors of such businesses protections that employees and independent contractors of other businesses do not enjoy.

The United States apparently agrees that employee claims are not cognizable under Title III, see Brief for United States as *Amicus Curiae* 18–19, n. 17, but despite the implications of its own regulations, see 28 CFR, ch. 1, pt. 36, App. B, at 650, appears to believe (though it does not explicitly state) that claims of independent contractors are cognizable. In a discussion littered with entirely vague statements from the legislative history, cf. *ante,* at 1889, the United States argues that Congress presumably wanted independent contractors with private entities covered under Title III because independent contractors with governmental entities are covered by Title II, see Brief for United States as *Amicus Curiae* 18, and n. 17—a line of reasoning that does not commend itself to the untutored intellect. But since the United States does not provide (and I cannot conceive of) any possible construction of the *terms* of Title III that will exclude employees while simultaneously covering independent contractors, its concession regarding employees effectively concedes independent contractors as well. Title III applies only to customers.

The Court, for its part, assumes that conclusion for the sake of argument, *ante,* at 1891–1892, but pronounces respondent to be a "customer" of the PGA Tour or of the golf courses on which it is played. That seems to me quite incredible. The PGA Tour is a professional sporting event, staged for the entertainment of a live and TV audience, the receipts from whom (the TV audience's admission price is paid by advertisers) pay the expenses of the tour, including the cash prizes for the winning golfers. The professional golfers on the tour are no more "enjoying" (the statutory term) the entertainment that the tour provides, or the facilities of the golf courses on which it is held, than professional baseball players "enjoy" the baseball games in which they play or the facilities of Yankee Stadium. To be sure, professional ballplayers *participate* in the games, and *use* the ballfields, but no one in his right mind would think that they are *customers* of the American League or of Yankee Stadium. They are themselves the entertainment that the customers pay to watch. And professional golfers are no different. It makes not a bit of difference, insofar as their "customer" status is concerned, that the remuneration for their performance (unlike most of the remuneration for ballplayers) is not fixed but contingent—viz., the purses for the winners in the various events, and the compensation from product endorsements that consistent winners are assured. The compensation of *many* independent contractors is contingent upon their success—real estate brokers, for example, or insurance salesmen.

As the Court points out, the ADA specifically identifies golf courses as one of the covered places of public accommodation. See § 12181(7)(L) ("a gymnasium, health spa, bowling alley, golf course, or other place of exercise or recreation"); and the distinctive "goo[d], servic[e], facilit[y], privileg [e], advantag[e], or accommodatio[n]" identified by that provision as distinctive to that category of place of public accommodation is "exercise or recreation." Respondent did not seek to "exercise" or "recreate" at the PGA Tour events; he sought to make money (which is why he is called a *professional* golfer). He was not a customer *buying* recreation or entertainment; he was a professional athlete *selling* it. That is the reason (among others) the Court's reliance upon Civil Rights Act cases like *Daniel v. Paul,* 395 U.S. 298, 89 S.Ct. 1697, 23 L.Ed.2d 318 (1969), see *ante,* at 1892, is misplaced. A professional golfer's practicing his profession is not comparable to John Q. Public's frequenting "a 232-acre amusement area with swimming, boating, sun bathing, picnicking, miniature golf, dancing facilities, and a snack bar." *Daniel, supra,* at 301, 89 S.Ct. 1697.

The Court relies heavily upon the Q-School. It says that petitioner offers the golfing public the "privilege" of "competing in the Q-School and playing in the tours; indeed, the former is a privilege for which thousands of individuals from the general public pay, and the latter is one for which they vie." *Ante,* at 1890. But the Q-School is no more a "privilege" offered for the general public's "enjoyment" than is the California Bar Exam. It is a competition for entry into the PGA Tour—an open tryout, no different in principle from open casting for a movie or stage production, or walk-on tryouts for other professional sports, such as baseball. See, *e.g.*, "Amateurs Join Pros for New Season of HBO's 'Sopranos,'" *Detroit News,* Dec. 22, 2000, p. 2 (20,000 attend open casting for "The Sopranos"); Bill Zack, "Atlanta Braves," *Sporting News,* Feb. 6, 1995

(1,300 would-be players attended an open tryout for the Atlanta Braves). It may well be that some amateur golfers enjoy trying to make the grade, just as some amateur actors may enjoy auditions, and amateur baseball players may enjoy open tryouts (I hesitate to say that amateur lawyers may enjoy taking the California Bar Exam). But the purpose of holding those tryouts is not to provide entertainment; it is to hire. At bottom, open tryouts for performances to be held at a place of public accommodation are no different from open bidding on contracts to cut the grass at a place of public accommodation, or open applications for any job at a place of public accommodation. Those bidding, those applying—and those trying out—are not converted into customers. By the Court's reasoning, a business exists not only to sell goods and services to the public, but to provide the "privilege" of employment to the public; wherefore it follows, like night the day, that everyone who seeks a job is a customer.

II

Having erroneously held that Title III applies to the "customers" of professional golf who consist of its practitioners, the Court then erroneously answers—or to be accurate simply ignores—a second question. The ADA requires covered businesses to make such reasonable modifications of "policies, practices, or procedures" as are necessary to "afford" goods, services, and privileges to individuals with disabilities; but it explicitly does not require "modifications [that] would fundamentally alter the nature" of the goods, services, and privileges. § 12182(b)(2)(A)(ii). In other words, disabled indivi-duals must be given *access* to the same goods, services, and privileges that others enjoy. The regulations state that Title III "does not require a public accommodation to alter its inventory to include accessible or special goods with accessibility features that are designed for, or facilitate use by, individuals with disabilities." 28 CFR § 36.307 (2000); see also 28 CFR, ch. 1, pt. 36, App. B, at 650. As one Court of Appeals has explained:

> "The common sense of the statute is that the content of the goods or services offered by a place of public accommodation is not regulated. A camera store may not refuse to sell cameras to a disabled person, but it is not required to stock cameras specially designed for such persons. Had Congress purposed to impose so enormous a burden on the retail sector of the economy and so vast a supervisory responsibility on the federal courts, we think it would have made its intention clearer and would at least have imposed some standards. It is hardly a feasible judicial function to decide whether shoe stores should sell single shoes to one-legged persons and if so at what price, or how many Braille books the Borders or Barnes and Noble bookstore chains should stock in each of their stores." *Doe v. Mutual of Omaha Ins. Co.*, 179 F.3d 557, 560 (C.A.7 1999).

Since this is so, even if respondent here is a consumer of the "privilege" of the PGA Tour competition, see *ante*, at 1890, I see no basis for considering whether the rules of that competition must be altered. It is as irrelevant to the PGA Tour's compliance with the statute whether walking is essential to the game of golf as it is to the shoe store's compliance whether "pairness" is essential to the nature of shoes. If a shoe store wishes to sell shoes only in pairs it may; and if a golf tour (or a golf course) wishes to provide only walk-around golf, it may. The PGA Tour cannot deny respondent *access* to that game because of his disability, but it need not provide him a game different (whether in its essentials or in its details) from that offered to everyone else.

Since it has held (or assumed) professional golfers to be customers "enjoying" the "privilege" that consists of PGA Tour golf; and since it inexplicably regards the rules of PGA Tour golf as merely "policies, practices, or procedures" by which access to PGA Tour golf is provided, the Court must then confront the question whether respondent's requested modification of the supposed policy, practice, or procedure of walking would "fundamentally alter the nature" of the PGA Tour game, § 12182(b)(2)(A)(ii). The Court attacks this "fundamental alteration" analysis by asking two questions: first, whether the "essence" or an "essential aspect" of the sport of golf has been altered; and second, whether the change, even if not essential to the game, would give the disabled player an advantage over others and thereby "fundamentally alter the character of the competition." *Ante*, at 1893. It answers no to both.

Before considering the Court's answer to the first question, it is worth pointing out that the assumption which underlies that question is false. Nowhere is it writ that PGA Tour golf must be classic "essential" golf. Why cannot the PGA Tour, if it wishes, promote a new game, with distinctive rules (much as the American League promotes a game of baseball in which the pitcher's turn at the plate can be taken by a "designated hitter")? If members of the public do not like the new rules—if they feel that these rules do not truly test the individual's skill at "real golf" (or the team's skill at "real baseball") they can withdraw their patronage. But the rules are the rules. They are (as in all games) entirely arbitrary, and there is no basis on which anyone—not even the Supreme Court of the United States—can pronounce one or another of them to be "nonessential" if the rulemaker (here the PGA Tour) deems it to be essential.

If one assumes, however, that the PGA Tour has some legal obligation to play classic, Platonic golf—and if one assumes the correctness of all the other wrong turns the Court has made to get to this point—then we Justices must confront what is indeed an awesome responsibility. It has been rendered the solemn duty of the Supreme Court of the United States, laid upon it by Congress in pursuance of the Federal Government's power "[t]o regulate Commerce with foreign Nations, and among the several States," U.S. Const., Art. I, § 8, cl. 3, to decide What Is Golf. I am sure that the Framers of the Constitution, aware of the 1457 edict of King James II of Scotland prohibiting golf because it interfered with the practice of archery, fully expected that sooner or later the paths of golf and government, the law and the links, would once again cross, and that the judges of this august Court would some day have to wrestle with that age-old jurisprudential question, for which their years of study in the law have so well prepared them: Is someone riding around a golf course from shot to shot *really* a golfer? The answer, we learn, is yes. The Court ultimately concludes, and it will henceforth be the Law of the Land, that walking is not a "fundamental" aspect of golf.

Either out of humility or out of self-respect (one or the other) the Court should decline to answer this incredibly difficult and incredibly silly question. To say that something is "essential" is ordinarily to say that it is necessary to the achievement of a certain object. But since it is the very nature of a game to have no object except amusement (that is what distinguishes games from productive activity), it is quite impossible to say that any of a game's arbitrary rules is "essential." Eighteen-hole golf courses, 10-foot-high basketball hoops, 90-foot baselines, 100-yard football fields—all are arbitrary and none is essential. The only support for any of them is tradition and (in more modern times) insistence by what has come to be regarded as the ruling body of the sport—both of which factors support the PGA Tour's position in the present case. (Many, indeed, consider walking to be *the central feature* of the game of golf—hence Mark Twain's classic criticism of the sport: "a good walk spoiled.") I suppose there is some point at which the rules of a well-known game are changed to such a degree that no reasonable person would call it the same game. If the PGA Tour competitors were required to dribble a large, inflated ball and put it through a round hoop, the game could no longer reasonably be called golf. But this criterion—destroying recognizability as the same generic game—is surely not the test of "essentialness" or "fundamentalness" that the Court applies, since it apparently thinks that merely changing the diameter of the *cup* might "fundamentally alter" the game of golf, *ante,* at 1893.

Having concluded that dispensing with the walking rule would not violate federal-Platonic "golf" (and, implicitly, that it is federal-Platonic golf, and no other, that the PGA Tour can insist upon), the Court moves on to the second part of its test: the competitive effects of waiving this nonessential rule. In this part of its analysis, the Court first finds that the effects of the change are "mitigated" by the fact that in the game of golf weather, a "lucky bounce," and "pure chance" provide different conditions for each competitor and individual ability may not "be the sole determinant of the outcome." *Ante,* at 1895. I guess that is why those who follow professional golfing consider Jack Nicklaus the *luckiest* golfer of all time, only to be challenged of late by the phenomenal *luck* of Tiger Woods. The Court's empiricism is unpersuasive. "Pure chance" is randomly distributed among the players, but allowing respondent to use a cart gives him a "lucky" break every time he plays. Pure chance also only matters at the margin—a stroke here or there; the cart substantially improves this respondent's competitive prospects beyond a couple of strokes. But even granting that there are significant nonhuman variables affecting competition, that fact does not justify adding another variable that always favors one player.

In an apparent effort to make its opinion as narrow as possible, the Court relies upon the District Court's finding that even with a cart, respondent will be at least as fatigued as everyone else. *Ante,* at 1897. This, the Court says, *proves* that competition will not be affected. Far from thinking that reliance on this finding cabins the effect of today's opinion, I think it will prove to be its most expansive and destructive feature. Because step one of the Court's two-part inquiry into whether a requested change in a sport will "fundamentally alter [its] nature," § 12182(b)(2)(A)(ii), consists of an utterly unprincipled ontology of sports (pursuant to which the Court is not even sure whether golf's "essence" requires a 3-inch hole), there is every reason to think that in future cases involving requests for special treatment by would-be athletes the second step of the analysis will be determinative. In resolving that second step—determining whether waiver of the "nonessential" rule will have an impermissible "competitive effect"—by measuring the athletic capacity of the requesting individual, and asking whether the special dispensation would do no more than place him on a par (so to speak) with other competitors, the Court guarantees that future cases of this sort will have to be decided on the basis of individualized factual findings. Which means that future cases of this sort will be numerous, and a rich source of lucrative litigation. One can envision the parents of a Little League player with attention deficit disorder trying to convince a judge that their son's disability makes it at least 25% more difficult to hit a pitched ball. (If they are successful, the only thing that could prevent a court order giving the kid four strikes would be a judicial determination that, in baseball, three strikes are metaphysically necessary, which is quite absurd.)

The statute, of course, provides no basis for this individualized analysis that is the Court's last step on a long and misguided journey. The statute seeks to assure that a disabled person's disability will not deny him *equal access* to (among other things) competitive sporting events—not that his disability will not deny him an *equal chance to win* competitive sporting events. The latter is quite impossible, since the very *nature* of competitive sport is the measurement, by uniform rules, of unevenly distributed excellence. This unequal distribution is precisely what determines the winners and losers—and artificially to "even out" that distribution, by giving one or another player exemption from a rule that emphasizes his particular weakness, is to destroy the game. That is why the "handicaps" that are customary in social games of golf—which, by adding strokes to the scores of the good players and subtracting them from scores of the bad ones, "even out" the varying abilities—are *not* used in professional golf. In the Court's world, there is one set of rules that is "fair with respect to the able-bodied" but "individualized" rules, mandated by the ADA, for "talented but disabled athletes." *Ante,* at 1897. The ADA mandates no such ridiculous thing. Agility, strength, speed, balance, quickness of mind, steadiness of nerves, intensity of concentration—these talents are not evenly distributed. No wild-eyed dreamer has ever suggested that the managing bodies of the competitive sports that test precisely these qualities should try to take account of the uneven distribution of God-given gifts when writing and enforcing the rules of competition. And I have no doubt Congress did not authorize misty-eyed judicial supervision of such a revolution.

* * *

My belief that today's judgment is clearly in error should not be mistaken for a belief that the PGA Tour clearly *ought not* allow respondent to use a golf cart. *That* is a close question, on which even those who compete in the PGA Tour are apparently divided; but it is a *different* question from the one before the Court. Just as it is a different question whether the Little League *ought* to give disabled youngsters a fourth strike, or some other waiver from the rules that makes up for their disabilities. In both cases, whether they *ought* to do so depends upon (1) how central to the game that they have organized (and over whose rules they are the master) they deem the waived provision to be, and (2) how competitive—how strict a test of raw athletic ability in all aspects of the competition—they want their game to be. But whether Congress has said they *must* do so depends upon the answers to the legal questions I have discussed above—not upon what this Court sententiously decrees to be "'decent, tolerant, [and] progressive,'" *ante,* at 1889 (quoting *Board of Trustees of Univ. of Ala. v. Garrett,* 531 U.S. 356, 375, 121 S.Ct. 955, 148 L.Ed.2d 866 (2001) (Kennedy, J., concurring)).

And it should not be assumed that today's decent, tolerant, and progressive judgment will, in the long run, accrue to the benefit of sports competitors with disabilities. Now that it is clear courts will review the rules of sports for "fundamentalness," organizations that value their autonomy have every incentive to defend vigorously the necessity of every regulation. They may still be second-guessed in the end as to the Platonic requirements of the sport, but they will *assuredly* lose if they have at all wavered in their enforcement. The lesson the PGA Tour and other sports organizations should take from this case is to make sure that the same written rules are set forth for all levels of play, and never voluntarily to grant any modifications. The second lesson is to end open tryouts. I doubt that, in the long run, even disabled athletes will be well served by these incentives that the Court has created.

Complaints about this case are not "properly directed to Congress," *ante,* at 1897, n. 51. They are properly directed to this Court's Kafkaesque determination that professional sports organizations, and the fields they rent for their exhibitions, are "places of public accommodation" to the competing athletes, and the athletes themselves "customers" of the organization that pays them; its Alice in Wonderland determination that there are such things as judicially determinable "essential" and "nonessential" rules of a made-up game; and its Animal Farm determination that fairness and the ADA mean that everyone gets to play by individualized rules which will assure that no one's lack of ability (or at least no one's lack of ability so pronounced that it amounts to a disability) will be a handicap. The year was 2001, and "everybody was finally equal." K. Vonnegut, "Harrison Bergeron," in *Animal Farm and Related Readings* 129 (1997).

Statutory interpretation 101: begin with the text

Zuni Public School Dist. No. 89 v. Department of Educ., 550 U.S. 81 (2007)

Justice Scalia, with whom the Chief Justice and Justice Thomas join, and with whom Justice Souter joins as to Part I, dissenting.

In *Church of the Holy Trinity v. United States,* 143 U.S. 457, 12 S.Ct. 511, 36 L.Ed. 226 (1892), this Court conceded that a church's act of contracting with a prospective rector fell within the plain meaning of a federal labor statute, but nevertheless did not apply the statute to the church: "It is a familiar rule," the Court pronounced, "that a thing may be within the letter of the statute and yet not within the statute, because not within its spirit, nor within the intention of its makers." *Id.,* at 459, 12 S.Ct. 511. That is a judge-empowering proposition if there ever was one, and in the century since, the Court has wisely retreated from it, in words if not always in actions. But today *Church of the Holy Trinity* arises, Phoenix-like, from the ashes. The Court's contrary assertions aside, today's decision is nothing other than the elevation of judge-supposed legislative intent over clear statutory text. The plain language of the federal Impact Aid statute clearly and unambiguously forecloses the Secretary of Education's preferred methodology for determining whether a State's school-funding system is equalized. Her selection of that methodology is therefore entitled to zero deference under *Chevron U.S.A. Inc. v. Natural Resources Defense Council, Inc.,* 467 U.S. 837, 104 S.Ct. 2778, 81 L.Ed.2d 694 (1984).

I

The very structure of the Court's opinion provides an obvious clue as to what is afoot. The opinion purports to place a premium on the plain text of the Impact Aid statute, *ante,* at 1543, but it first takes us instead on a roundabout tour of "[c]onsiderations *other* than language," *ante,* at 1541 (emphasis added)—page after page of unenacted congressional intent and judicially perceived statutory purpose, Part II-A, *ante.* Only after we are shown "why Zuni concentrates its argument upon language alone," *ante,* at 1541 (impliedly a shameful practice, or at least indication of a feeble case), are we informed how the statute's plain text does not unambiguously *preclude* the interpretation the Court thinks best. Part II-B, *ante* (beginning "But what of the provision's literal language? The matter is important ..."). This is a most suspicious order of proceeding, since our case law is full of statements such as "We begin, as always, with the language of the statute," *Duncan v. Walker,* 533 U.S. 167, 172, 121 S.Ct. 2120, 150 L.Ed.2d 251 (2001), and replete with the affirmation that, when "[g]iven [a] straightforward statutory command, there is no reason to resort to legislative history," *United States v. Gonzales,* 520 U.S. 1, 6, 117 S.Ct. 1032, 137 L.Ed.2d 132 (1997). Nor is this cart-before-the-horse approach justified by the Court's excuse that the statute before us is, after all, a technical one, *ante,* at 1540–1541. This Court, charged with interpreting, among other things, the Internal Revenue Code, the Employee Retirement Income Security Act of 1974, and the Clean Air Act, confronts technical language all the time, but we never see fit to pronounce upon what we think Congress *meant* a statute to say, and what we think sound policy would *counsel* it to say, before considering what it *does* say. As almost a majority of today's majority worries, "[w]ere the inversion [of inquiry] to become systemic, it would create the impression that agency policy concerns, rather than the traditional tools of statutory construction, are shaping the judicial interpretation of statutes." *Ante,* at 1551 (Kennedy, J., joined by Alito, J., concurring). True enough—except I see no reason to wait for the distortion to become systemic before concluding that that is precisely what is happening in the present case. For some, policy-driven interpretation is apparently just fine. See *ante,* at 1549–1550 (Stevens, J., concurring). But for everyone else, let us return to Statutory Interpretation 101.

We must begin, as we always do, with the text. See, *e.g., Gonzales, supra,* at 4, 117 S.Ct. 1032. Under the federal Impact Aid program, 20 U.S.C. § 7701 *et seq.* (2000 ed. and Supp. IV), States distributing state aid to local school districts (referred to in the statute as "local educational agencies," or "LEAs") may not take into account the amount of federal Impact Aid that its LEAs receive. See § 7709(a). But the statute makes an exception if the Secretary of Education certifies that a State "has in effect a program of State aid that equalizes expenditures for free public education among local educational agencies in the State." § 7709(b)(1) (2000 ed., Supp. IV). Congress has specified a formula for the Secretary to use when making this equalization determination:

> "[A] program of State aid equalizes expenditures among local educational agencies if ... the amount of per-pupil expenditures made by, or per-pupil revenues available to, the local educational agency in the State with the highest such per-pupil expenditures or revenues did not exceed the amount of such per-pupil expenditures made by, or per-pupil revenues available to, the local educational agency in the State with the lowest such expenditures or revenues by more than 25 percent." § 7709(b)(2)(A).

The Secretary is further instructed, however, that when

making this determination, she shall "disregard local educational agencies with per-pupil expenditures or revenues above the 95th percentile or below the 5th percentile of such expenditures or revenues in the State." § 7709(b)(2)(B)(i). It is this latter subsection which concerns us here.

The casual observer will notice that the Secretary's implementing regulations do not look much like the statute. The regulations first require the Secretary to rank all of the LEAs in a State (New Mexico has 89) according to their per-pupil expenditures or revenues. 34 CFR pt. 222, subpt. K, App., ¶ (1)(a)(i) (2006). So far so good. But critically here, the Secretary must then "[i]dentif[y] those LEAs ... that fall at the 95th and 5th percentiles *of the total number of pupils in attendance* in the schools of those LEAs." *Id.*, ¶ (1)(a)(ii) (emphasis added). Finally, the Secretary compares the per-pupil figures of *those two* LEAs for the purpose of assessing whether a State exceeds the 25% disparity measure. *Id.*, ¶ (1)(a)(iii). The majority concludes that this method of calculation, with its focus on student population, is a permissible interpretation of the statute.

It most assuredly is not. To understand why, one first must look beyond the smokescreen that the Court lays down with its repeated apologies for inexperience in statistics, and its endless recitation of technical mathematical definitions of the word "percentile." See, *e.g.*, *ante*, at 1543–1544 ("'The *n*-th percentile is the value $^{xn/100}$ such that *n* per cent of the population is less than or equal to $^{xn/100}$'" (quoting C. Clapham & J. Nicholson, *The Concise Oxford Dictionary of Mathematics* 378 (3d ed.2005)). This case is not a scary math problem; it is a straightforward matter of statutory interpretation. And we do not need the Court's hypothetical cadre of number-crunching *amici*, *ante*, at 1546, to guide our way.

There is no dispute that for purposes relevant here "'percentile' refers to a division of a distribution of *some* population into 100 parts.'" *Ante,* at 1543. And there is further no dispute that the statute concerns the percentile of "per-pupil expenditures or revenues," for that is what the word "such" refers to. See 20 U.S.C. § 7709(b)(2)(B)(i) (Secretary shall "disregard local educational agencies with *per-pupil expenditures or revenues* above the 95th percentile or below the 5th percentile of *such* expenditures or revenues in the State" (emphasis added)). The question is: Whose per-pupil expenditures or revenues? Or, in the Court's terminology, what "population" is assigned the "characteristic" "per-pupil expenditure" or revenue? *Ante,* at 1544. At first blush, second blush, or twenty-second blush, the answer is abundantly clear: local educational agencies. The statute requires the Secretary to "disregard local educational agencies with" certain per-pupil figures above or below specified percentiles of those per-pupil figures. § 7709(b)(2)(B)(i). The attribute "per-pupil expenditur[e] or revenu[e]" is assigned to LEAs—there is no mention of student population whatsoever. And thus under the statute, "per-pupil expenditures or revenues" are to be arrayed using a population consisting of LEAs, so that percentiles are determined from a list of (in New Mexico) 89 per-pupil expenditures or revenues representing the 89 LEAs in the State. It is just that simple.

The Court makes little effort to defend the regulations as they are written. Instead, relying on a made-for-litigation theory that bears almost no relationship to the regulations themselves, the Court believes it has found a way to shoehorn those regulations into the statute. The Impact Aid statute is ambiguous, the Court says, because it "does not specify precisely what *population* is to be 'distributed' (*i.e.,* ranked according to the population's corresponding values for the relevant characteristic)." *Ante,* at 1544. Thus the Court finds that it is permissible for the Secretary to attribute the characteristic "per-pupil expenditure or revenue" to pupils, with the result that the Secretary may "us[e] ... the State's *students* as the relevant population for calculating the specified percentiles." *Ibid.* Under that interpretation, as the State manages to explain with a straight face, "[i]n New Mexico, during the time at issue, there were approximately 317,777 pupils in the [S]tate and thus there were 317,777 per-pupil revenues in the [S]tate." Brief for Respondent New Mexico Public Education Department 37; see also *id.*, at 36 ("Each and every student in an LEA and in a[S]tate may be treated as having his or her own 'per-pupil' expenditure or revenue amount"). The Court consequently concludes that "linguistically speaking, one may attribute the characteristic of per-pupil expenditure to each [student]." *Ante*, at 1545.

The sheer applesauce of this statutory interpretation should be obvious. It is of course true that every student in New Mexico causes an expenditure or produces a revenue that his LEA either enjoys (in the case of revenues) or is responsible for (in the case of expenditures). But it simply defies any semblance of normal English usage to say that every pupil has a "*per-pupil* expenditure or revenue." The word "per" *connotes* that the expenditure or revenue is a single average figure assigned to a unit the *composite members of which* are individual pupils. And the only such unit mentioned in the statute is the local educational agency. See 20 U.S.C. § 7709(b)(2)(B)(i). It is simply irrelevant that "[n]o dictionary definition ... suggests that there is any *single* logical, mathematical, or statistical link between [per-pupil expenditures or revenues] and ... the nature of the relevant population." *Ante*, at 1544–1545. Of course there is not. It is the *text* at issue which must identify the relevant population, and it does so here quite unambiguously: "*local educational agencies* with per-pupil expenditures or revenues." § 7709(b)(2)(B)(i) (emphasis added). That same phrase shows the utter irrelevance of the Court's excursus upon the meaning of the word "per." See *ante,* at 1545. It does indeed mean "'for each, or 'for every'"—and when it is contained in a clause that reads "local educational agencies with per-pupil expenditures or revenues" it refers to (and can only refer to) the average expenditure or revenue "for each" or "for every" student out of the total expenditures or revenues of the LEA.

The violence done to this statute would be severe enough if the Secretary *used* the actual expenditure or revenue for each individual pupil. But in fact the Secretary determines the per-pupil expenditure or revenue for each individual student by (guess what) *computing the per-pupil expenditure or revenue of each LEA!* As the New Mexico brief explains:

> "[A] per-pupil expenditure or revenue is an average number. It is not the amount actually spent on any given pupil, an amount which would be impossible to calculate in any meaningful way. It is roughly the total amount expended by an LEA divided by the number of pupils in that LEA." Brief for Respondent New Mexico Public Education Department 36.

The Secretary thus assigns an artificial number to each student that corresponds exactly to *his LEA's* per-pupil expenditure or revenue. In other words, at the end of the day the Secretary herself acknowledges that "per-pupil expenditures or revenues" pertains to LEAs, and not students. And she is interpreting "per-pupil expenditure or revenue" *not* as the Court suggests (an amount attributable to each student), but rather *as I suggest* (an average amount for the pupils in a particular LEA). But she then proceeds to take a step not at all permitted by the statutory formula—in effect applying "per-pupil expenditure or revenue" a *second* time (this time according to the Court's fanciful interpretation of "per-pupil") in order to reach the result she desires. Of course, if the Secretary did apply the "per-pupil expenditure or revenue" only once, arraying students by their actual expenditures or revenues, her entire system would collapse. Students from the same LEA, rather than appearing on the list with the same per-pupil figure, would be located at various points on the spectrum. And so long as an LEA had at least one student above the 95th or below the 5th percentile of pupil "per-pupil expenditures or revenues," that LEA would have to be excluded from the disparity analysis. The result would be a serious distortion of the disparity determination, excluding many more LEAs (in fact, perhaps all of them) from the disparity calculation. This would render the 25% disparity measure in § 7709(b)(2)(A) all but meaningless.

The Court makes one final attempt to rescue the Secretary's interpretation, appealing to "statutory context." "Context here tells us," it says, "that the instruction to identify school districts with 'per-pupil expenditures' above the 95th percentile 'of such expenditures' is ... ambiguous, because both students and school districts are of concern to the statute." *Ante*, at 1546. This is a complete non sequitur. Of course students are a concern to a statute dealing with school funding. But that does not create any ambiguity with respect to whether, under this statute, pupils can reasonably be said to have their own "per-pupil expenditures or revenues." It is simply irrational to say that the clear dispositions of a statute with regard to the entities that it regulates (here LEAs) are rendered ambiguous when those entities contain subunits that are the ultimate beneficiaries of the regulation (here students). Such a principle of interpretation—if it could be called that—would inject ambiguity into many statutes indeed.

The Court's reliance on statutory context is all the more puzzling since the context obviously favors petitioners. "The focus [of the Impact Aid statute] is upon LEAs, not upon the number of pupils." 393 F.3d 1158, 1172 (C.A.10 2004)

(O'Brien, J., dissenting), opinion vacated, 437 F.3d 1289, 1290 (2006) (en banc) *(per curiam).* In fact, the provisions at issue here make not the slightest mention of students. That is both sensible and predictable, since the Impact Aid program's equalization formula is designed to address funding disparities between *LEAs,* not between *students.* See 20 U.S.C. § 7709(b)(2)(A) (referring to "a program of State aid [that] equalizes expenditures among local educational agencies"); see also § 7709(d)(1). Indeed, the whole point of the equalization determination is to figure out whether States may reduce state aid to *LEAs.* See § 7709(a).

In sum, the plain language of the Impact Aid statute compels the conclusion that the Secretary's method of calculation is ultra vires. Employing the formula that the statute requires, New Mexico is not equalized. *Ante,* at 1540.

II

How then, if the text is so clear, are respondents managing to win this case? The answer can only be the return of that miraculous redeemer of lost causes, *Church of the Holy Trinity.* In order to contort the statute's language beyond recognition, the Court must believe Congress's intent so crystalline, the spirit of its legislation so glowingly bright, that the statutory text should simply not be read to say what it says. See Part II-A, *ante.* Justice Stevens is quite candid on the point: He is willing to contradict the text. See *ante,* at 1549–1550 (concurring opinion). But Justice Stevens' candor should not make his philosophy seem unassuming. He maintains that it is "a correct performance of the judicial function" to "override a strict interpretation of the text" so long as policy-driven interpretation "is faithful to the intent of Congress." *Ante,* at 1549. But once one departs from "strict interpretation of the text" (by which

Justice Stevens means the actual meaning of the text) fidelity to the intent of Congress is a chancy thing. The only thing we know for certain both Houses of Congress (and the President, if he signed the legislation) agreed upon is the text. Legislative history can never produce a "pellucidly clear" picture, *ante,* at 1550 (Stevens, J., concurring), of what a law was "intended" to mean, for the simple reason that it is never voted upon—or ordinarily even seen or heard—by the "intending" lawgiving entity, which consists of both Houses of Congress and the President (if he did not veto the bill). See U.S. Const., Art. I, §§ 1, 7. Thus, what judges believe Congress "meant" (apart from the text) has a disturbing but entirely unsurprising tendency to be whatever judges think Congress *must* have meant, *i.e., should* have meant. In *Church of the Holy Trinity,* every Justice on this Court disregarded the plain language of a statute that forbade the hiring of a clergyman from abroad because, after all (they thought), "this is a Christian nation," 143 U.S., at 471, 12 S.Ct. 511, so Congress could not have meant what it said. Is there any reason to believe that those Justices were lacking that "intellectua[l] honest[y]" that Justice Stevens "presume[s]" all our judges possess, *ante,* at 1550? Intellectual honesty does not exclude a blinding intellectual bias. And even if it did, the system of judicial amendatory veto over texts duly adopted by Congress bears no resemblance to the system of lawmaking set forth in our Constitution.

Justice Stevens takes comfort in the fact that this is a case in which he "cannot imagine anyone accusing any Member of the Court of voting one way or the other because of that Justice's own policy preferences." *Ante,* at 1550. I can readily imagine it, given that the Court's opinion begins with a lengthy description of why the system its judgment approves is the *better* one. But even assuming that, in this rare case, the Justices' departure from the enacted law has nothing to do with their policy view that it is a bad law, nothing in Justice Stevens' separate opinion limits his approach to such rarities. Why should we suppose that in matters more likely to arouse the judicial libido—voting rights, antidiscrimination laws, or environmental protection, to name only a few—a judge in the School of Textual Subversion would not find it convenient (yea, *righteous!*) to assume that Congress *must* have meant, not what it said, but what he knows to be best?

Lest there be any confusion on the point, I must discuss briefly the two cases Justice Stevens puts forward, *ante,* at 1549, as demonstrating this Court's recent endorsement of his unorthodox views. They demonstrate just the opposite. *Griffin v. Oceanic Contractors, Inc.,* 458 U.S. 564, 102 S.Ct. 3245, 73 L.Ed.2d 973 (1982), involved a maritime statute that required the master of a vessel to furnish unpaid wages to a seaman within a specified period after the seaman's discharge, and further provided that a master who failed to do so without sufficient cause "'shall pay to the seaman a sum equal to two days' pay for each and every day during which payment is delayed.'" *Id.,* at 570, 102 S.Ct. 3245 (quoting 46 U.S.C. § 596 (1976 ed.)). We explained that "Congress intended the statute to mean exactly what its plain language says," 458 U.S., at 574, 102 S.Ct. 3245, and held that the seaman was entitled to double wages for every day during which payment was delayed, even for the period in which he had obtained alternative employment. The result was that the seaman would receive approximately $300,000 for his master's improper withholding of $412.50, *id.,* at 575, 102 S.Ct. 3245, even though "[i]t [was] probably true that Congress did not precisely envision the grossness of the difference ... between the actual wages withheld and the amount of the award required by the statute," *id.,* at 576, 102 S.Ct. 3245. We suggested in dicta that there might be a "rare cas[e]" in which the Court could relax its steadfastness to statutory text, *id.*, at 571, 102 S.Ct. 3245, but if *Griffin* itself did not qualify, it is hard to imagine what would. The principle Justice Stevens would ascribe to *Griffin* is in fact the one he advocated in dissent. "[T]his is one of the cases in which the exercise of judgment dictates a departure from the literal text in order to be faithful to the legislative will." *Id.*, at 586, 102 S.Ct. 3245 (Stevens, J., dissenting).

The second case Justice Stevens relies upon, *United States v. Ron Pair Enterprises, Inc.*, 489 U.S. 235, 109 S.Ct. 1026, 103 L.Ed.2d 290 (1989), is equally inapt. The Court's opinion there (unlike the one here) explained that our analysis "must begin ... with the language of the statute itself," and concluded that that was "also where the inquiry should end, for where ... the statute's language is plain, 'the sole function of the courts is to enforce it according to its terms.'" *Id.*, at 241, 109 S.Ct. 1026 (quoting *Caminetti v. United States*, 242 U.S. 470, 485, 37 S.Ct. 192, 61 L.Ed. 442 (1917)). My "fifth vote" in *Ron Pair* was thus only "decisive," *ante*, at 1549 (Stevens, J., concurring), in reaffirming this Court's adherence to statutory text, decisively preventing it from falling off the precipice it plunges over today.

Contrary to the Court and Justice Stevens, I do not believe that what we are sure the Legislature *meant* to say can trump what it *did* say. Citizens arrange their affairs not on the basis of their legislators' unexpressed intent, but on the basis of the law as it is written and promulgated. I think it terribly unfair to expect that the two rural school districts that are petitioners here should have pored over some 30 years of regulatory history to divine Congress's "real" objective (and with it the "real" intent that a majority of Justices would find honest and true). To be governed by legislated text rather than legislators' intentions is what it means to be "a Government of laws, not of men." And in the last analysis the opposite approach is no more beneficial to the governors than it is to the governed. By "depriving legislators of the assurance that ordinary terms, used in an ordinary context, will be given a predictable meaning," we deprive Congress of "a sure means by which it may work the people's will." *Chisom v. Roemer,* 501 U.S. 380, 417, 111 S.Ct. 2354, 115 L.Ed.2d 348 (1991) (Scalia, J., dissenting).

I do not purport to know what Congress thought it was doing when it amended the Impact Aid program in 1994. But even indulging Justice Stevens' erroneous premise that there exists a "legislative intent" separate and apart from the statutory text, *ante,* at 1549 (concurring opinion), I do not see how the Court can possibly say, with any measure of confidence, that Congress wished one thing rather than another. There is ample evidence, for example, that at the time it amended the Impact Aid statute, Congress knew exactly how to incorporate student population into a disparity calculation. Most prominently, in the *very same* Act that added § 7709(b)(2)(B)(i) to the Impact Aid program, Congress established the Education Finance Incentive Program, known as EFIG. See Improving America's Schools Act of 1994, 108 Stat. 3575. That statute allocates grants to States based in part on an "equity factor" which requires a disparity calculation similar to that in the Impact Aid statute. See 20 U.S.C. § 6337(b)(1)(A) (2000 ed., Supp. IV). In EFIG, however, Congress specifically required the Secretary to take student population into account: "[T]he Secretary shall weigh the variation between per-pupil expenditures in each local educational agency ... *according to the number of pupils served by the local educational agency.*" § 6337(b)(3)(A)(ii)(II) (emphasis added); see also Brief for Federal Respondent 28–29. And there is more. In EFIG, Congress *expressly provided* that a State would be accorded a favorable "equity factor" rating if it was considered equalized under the Secretary's *Impact Aid regulations.* See § 6337(b)(3)(B) (2000 ed., Supp. IV). Congress thus explicitly incorporated the Impact Aid regulations into EFIG, but did no such thing with respect to the Impact Aid statute itself. All this on the very same day.

Nor do I see any significance in the fact that no legislator in 1994 expressed the view that § 7709(b)(2)(B)(i) was designed to upend the Secretary's equalization formula. *Ante,* at 1541 (majority opinion). It is quite plausible—indeed, eminently plausible—that the Members of Congress took the plain meaning of the language *which the Secretary himself had proposed* to be what the Secretary himself had previously been doing. It is bad enough for this Court to consider legislative materials beyond the statutory text in aid of resolving ambiguity, but it is truly unreasonable to *require* such extratextual evidence as a precondition for enforcing an *unambiguous* congressional mandate. See *Koons Buick Pontiac GMC, Inc. v. Nigh,* 543 U.S. 50, 73–74, 125 S.Ct. 460, 160 L.Ed.2d 389 (2004) (Scalia, J., dissenting). The Court points to the fact that "no Member of Congress has ever criticized the method the [Secretary's] regulation[s] sets forth." *Ante,* at 1541. But can it really be that this case turns, in the Court's view, on whether a freshman Congressman from New Mexico gave a floor speech that only late-night C–SPAN junkies would witness? The only fair inference from Congress's silence is that Congress had nothing further to say, its statutory text doing all of the talking.

Finally, the Court expresses its belief that Congress must have intended to adopt the Secretary's pre–1994 disparity test because that test is the more reasonable one, better able to account for States with small numbers of large LEAs, or large numbers of small ones. See *ante,* at 1541–1543. This, to tell the truth, is the core of the opinion. As I have suggested, it is no accident that the countertextual legislative intent judges perceive *invariably* accords with what judges think best. It seems to me, however, that this Court is no more capable of saying with certainty what is best in this area than it is of saying with certainty (apart from the text) what Congress intended. There is good reason to be concerned—in the implementation of a statute that makes a limited exception for States that have "in effect a program of State aid that equalizes expenditures for free public education *among local educational agencies,*" 20 U.S.C. § 7709(b)(1) (2000 ed., Supp. IV) (emphasis added)—that the Secretary's methodology eliminates from the disparity calculation *too many LEAs.* In the certification at issue in this very case, the Secretary excluded 23 of New Mexico's 89 LEAs, approximately 26%. Is this Court such an expert in school finance that it can affirm the desirability of excluding one in four of New Mexico's LEAs from consideration?

As for the Secretary's concerns about the discrepancy between large and small LEAs, does the Court have any basis for its apparent confidence that other parts of the Impact Aid statute do not adequately address the problem? Immediately after setting forth the 95th and 5th percentile cutoffs, § 7709(b)(2)(B)(i), the statute instructs the Secretary to "take into account the extent to which a program of State aid reflects the additional cost of providing free public education in particular types of local educational agencies, such as those that are geographically isolated, or to particular types of students, such as children with disabilities." § 7709(b)(2)(B)(ii). Respondents do not explain why the Secretary could not use § 7709(b)(2)(B)(ii) to temper any unintended effects of § 7709(b)(2)(B)(i). Respondents further maintain that States could take advantage of the statute's plain meaning by subdividing their LEAs. But again, the statute itself contains a remedy. Under § 7713(9)(B)(ii), "[t]he term 'local educational agency' does not include any agency or 'school authority that the Secretary determines on a case-by-case basis ... is not constituted or reconstituted for legitimate educational purposes."

* * *

The only sure indication of what Congress intended is what Congress enacted; and even if there is a difference between the two, the rule of law demands that the latter prevail. This case will live with *Church of the Holy Trinity* as an exemplar of judicial disregard of crystal-clear text. We must interpret the law as Congress has written it, not as we would wish it to be. I would reverse the judgment of the Court of Appeals.

When words no longer have meaning

King v. Burwell,

135 S.Ct. 2480 (2015)

Justice Scalia, with whom Justice Thomas and Justice Alito join, dissenting.

The Court holds that when the Patient Protection and Affordable Care Act says "Exchange established by the State" it means "Exchange established by the State or the Federal Government." That is of course quite absurd, and the Court's 21 pages of explanation make it no less so.

I

The Patient Protection and Affordable Care Act makes major reforms to the American health-insurance market. It provides, among other things, that every State "shall ... establish an American Health Benefit Exchange"—a marketplace where people can shop for health-insurance plans. 42 U.S.C. § 18031(b)(1). And it provides that if a State does not comply with this instruction, the Secretary of Health and Human Services must "establish and operate such Exchange within the State." § 18041(c)(1).

A separate part of the Act—housed in § 36B of the Internal Revenue Code—grants "premium tax credits" to subsidize certain purchases of health insurance made on Exchanges. The tax credit consists of "premium assistance amounts" for "coverage months." 26 U.S.C. § 36B(b)(1). An individual has a coverage month only when he is covered by an insurance plan "that was enrolled in through an Exchange established by the State under [§ 18031]." § 36B(c)(2)(A). And the law ties the size of the premium assistance amount to the premiums for health plans which cover the individual "and which were enrolled in through an Exchange established by the State under [§ 18031]." § 36B(b)(2)(A). The premium assistance amount further depends on the cost of certain other insurance plans "offered through the same Exchange." § 36B(b)(3)(B)(i).

This case requires us to decide whether someone who buys insurance on an Exchange established by the Secretary gets tax credits. You would think the answer would be obvious—so obvious there would hardly be a need for the Supreme Court to hear a case about it. In order to receive any money under § 36B, an individual must enroll in an insurance plan through an "Exchange established by the State." The Secretary of Health and Human Services is not a State. So an Exchange established by the Secretary is not an Exchange established by the State—which means people who buy health insurance through such an Exchange get no money under § 36B.

Words no longer have meaning if an Exchange that is *not* established by a State is "established by the State." It is hard to come up with a clearer way to limit tax credits to state Exchanges than to use the words "established by the State." And it is hard to come up with a reason to include the words "by the State" other than the purpose of limiting credits to state Exchanges. "[T]he plain, obvious, and rational meaning of a statute is always to be preferred to any curious, narrow, hidden sense that nothing but the exigency of a hard case and the ingenuity and study of an acute and powerful intellect would discover." *Lynch v. Alworth-Stephens Co.,* 267 U.S. 364, 370, 45 S.Ct. 274, 69 L.Ed. 660 (1925) (internal quotation marks omitted). Under all the usual rules of interpretation, in short, the Government should lose this case. But normal rules of interpretation seem always to yield to the overriding principle of the present Court: The Affordable Care Act must be saved.

II

The Court interprets § 36B to award tax credits on both federal and state Exchanges. It accepts that the "most natural sense" of the phrase "Exchange established by the State" is an Exchange established by a State. *Ante,* at 2502. (Understatement, thy name is an opinion on the Affordable Care Act!) Yet the opinion continues, with no semblance of shame, that "it is also possible that the phrase refers to *all* Exchanges—both State and Federal." *Ante,* at 2491. (Impossible possibility, thy name is an opinion on the Affordable Care Act!) The Court claims that "the context and structure of the Act compel [it] to depart from what would otherwise be the most natural reading of the pertinent statutory phrase." *Ante,* at 2495.

I wholeheartedly agree with the Court that sound interpretation requires paying attention to the whole law, not homing in on isolated words or even isolated sections. Context always matters. Let us not forget, however, *why* context matters: It is a tool for understanding the terms of the law, not an excuse for rewriting them.

Any effort to understand rather than to rewrite a law must accept and apply the presumption that lawmakers use words in "their natural and ordinary signification." *Pensacola Telegraph Co. v. Western Union Telegraph Co.,* 96 U.S. 1, 12, 24 L.Ed. 708 (1878). Ordinary connotation does not always prevail, but the more unnatural the proposed interpretation of a law, the more compelling the contextual evidence must be to show that it is correct. Today's interpretation is not merely unnatural; it is unheard of. Who would ever have dreamt that "Exchange established by the State" means "Exchange established by the State *or the Federal Government* "? Little short of an express statutory definition could justify adopting this singular reading. Yet the only pertinent definition here provides that "State" means "each of the 50 States and the District of Columbia." 42 U.S.C. § 18024(d). Because the Secretary is neither one of the 50 States nor the District of Columbia, that definition positively contradicts the eccentric theory that an Exchange established by the Secretary has been established by the State.

Far from offering the overwhelming evidence of meaning needed to justify the Court's interpretation, other contextual clues undermine it at every turn. To begin with, other parts of the Act sharply distinguish between the establishment of an Exchange by a State and the establishment of an Exchange by the Federal Government. The States' authority to set up Exchanges comes from one provision, § 18031(b); the Secretary's authority comes from an entirely different provision, § 18041(c). Funding for States to establish Exchanges comes from one part of the law, § 18031(a); funding for the Secretary to establish Exchanges comes from an entirely different part of the law, § 18121. States generally run state-created Exchanges; the Secretary generally runs federally created Exchanges. § 18041(b)-(c). And the Secretary's authority to set up an Exchange in a State depends upon the State's "[*f*]*ailure* to establish [an] Exchange." § 18041(c) (emphasis added). Provisions such as these destroy any pretense that a federal Exchange is in some sense also established by a State.

Reading the rest of the Act also confirms that, as relevant here, there are *only* two ways to set up an Exchange in a State: establishment by a State and establishment by the Secretary. §§ 18031(b), 18041(c). So saying that an Exchange established by the Federal Government is "established by the State" goes beyond giving words bizarre meanings; it leaves the limiting phrase "by the State" with no operative effect at all. That is a stark violation of the elementary principle that requires an interpreter "to give effect, if possible, to every clause and word of a statute." *Montclair v. Ramsdell,* 107 U.S. 147, 152, 2 S.Ct. 391,

27 L.Ed. 431 (1883). In weighing this argument, it is well to remember the difference between giving a term a meaning that duplicates another part of the law, and giving a term no meaning at all. Lawmakers sometimes repeat themselves—whether out of a desire to add emphasis, a sense of belt-and-suspenders caution, or a lawyerly penchant for doublets (aid and abet, cease and desist, null and void). Lawmakers do not, however, tend to use terms that "have no operation at all." *Marbury v. Madison,* 1 Cranch 137, 174, 2 L.Ed. 60 (1803). So while the rule against treating a term as a redundancy is far from categorical, the rule against treating it as a nullity is as close to absolute as interpretive principles get. The Court's reading does not merely give "by the State" a duplicative effect; it causes the phrase to have no effect whatever.

Making matters worse, the reader of the whole Act will come across a number of provisions beyond § 36B that refer to the establishment of Exchanges by States. Adopting the Court's interpretation means nullifying the term "by the State" not just once, but again and again throughout the Act. Consider for the moment only those parts of the Act that mention an "Exchange established by the State" in connection with tax credits:

- The formula for calculating the amount of the tax credit, as already explained, twice mentions "an Exchange established by the State." 26 U.S.C. § 36B(b)(2)(A), (c)(2)(A)(i).
- The Act directs States to screen children for eligibility for "[tax credits] under section 36B" and for "any other assistance or subsidies available for coverage obtained through" an "Exchange established by the State." 42 U.S.C. § 1396w–3(b)(1)(B)–(C).
- The Act requires "an Exchange established by the State" to use a "secure electronic interface" to determine eligibility for (among other things) tax credits. § 1396w–3(b)(1)(D).
- The Act authorizes "an Exchange established by the State"

to make arrangements under which other state agencies "determine whether a State resident is eligible for [tax credits] under section 36B." § 1396w–3(b)(2).

- The Act directs States to operate Web sites that allow anyone "who is eligible to receive [tax credits] under section 36B" to compare insurance plans offered through "an Exchange established by the State." § 1396w–3(b)(4).
- One of the Act's provisions addresses the enrollment of certain children in health plans "offered through an Exchange established by the State" and then discusses the eligibility of these children for tax credits. § 1397ee(d)(3)(B).

It is bad enough for a court to cross out "by the State" once. But seven times?

Congress did not, by the way, repeat "Exchange established by the State under [§ 18031]" by rote throughout the Act. Quite the contrary, clause after clause of the law uses a more general term such as "Exchange" or "Exchange established under [§ 18031]." See, *e.g.*, 42 U.S.C. §§ 18031(k), 18033; 26 U.S.C. § 6055. It is common sense that any speaker who says "Exchange" some of the time, but "Exchange established by the State" the rest of the time, probably means something by the contrast.

Equating establishment "by the State" with establishment by the Federal Government makes nonsense of other parts of the Act. The Act requires States to ensure (on pain of losing Medicaid funding) that any "Exchange established by the State" uses a "secure electronic interface" to determine an individual's eligibility for various benefits (including tax credits). 42 U.S.C. § 1396w-3(b)(1)(D). How could a State control the type of electronic interface used by a federal Exchange? The Act allows a State to control contracting decisions made by "an Exchange established by the State." § 18031(f)(3). Why would a State get to control the contracting decisions of a federal Exchange? The Act also provides "Assistance to States to establish

American Health Benefit Exchanges" and directs the Secretary to renew this funding "if the State ... is making progress ... toward ... establishing an Exchange." § 18031(a). Does a State that refuses to set up an Exchange still receive this funding, on the premise that Exchanges established by the Federal Government are really established by States? It is presumably in order to avoid these questions that the Court concludes that federal Exchanges count as state Exchanges only "for purposes of the tax credits." *Ante,* at 2491. (Contrivance, thy name is an opinion on the Affordable Care Act!)

It is probably piling on to add that the Congress that wrote the Affordable Care Act knew how to equate two different types of Exchanges when it wanted to do so. The Act includes a clause providing that "[a] *territory* that ... establishes ... an Exchange ... shall be treated as a State" for certain purposes. § 18043(a) (emphasis added). Tellingly, it does not include a comparable clause providing that the *Secretary* shall be treated as a State for purposes of § 36B when *she* establishes an Exchange.

Faced with overwhelming confirmation that "Exchange established by the State" means what it looks like it means, the Court comes up with argument after feeble argument to support its contrary interpretation. None of its tries comes close to establishing the implausible conclusion that Congress used "by the State" to mean "by the State or not by the State."

The Court emphasizes that if a State does not set up an Exchange, the Secretary must establish "such Exchange." § 18041(c). It claims that the word "such" implies that federal and state Exchanges are "the same." *Ante,* at 2491. To see the error in this reasoning, one need only consider a parallel provision from our Constitution: "The Times, Places and Manner of holding Elections for Senators and Representatives, shall be prescribed in each State by the Legislature thereof; but the Congress may at any time by Law make or alter *such Regula-*

tions." Art. I, § 4, cl. 1 (emphasis added). Just as the Affordable Care Act directs States to establish Exchanges while allowing the Secretary to establish "such Exchange" as a fallback, the Elections Clause directs state legislatures to prescribe election regulations while allowing Congress to make "such Regulations" as a fallback. Would anybody refer to an election regulation made by Congress as a "regulation prescribed by the state legislature"? Would anybody say that a federal election law and a state election law are in all respects equivalent? Of course not. The word "such" does not help the Court one whit. The Court's argument also overlooks the rudimentary principle that a specific provision governs a general one. Even if it were true that the term "such Exchange" in § 18041(c) implies that federal and state Exchanges are the same in general, the term "established by the State" in § 36B makes plain that they differ when it comes to tax credits in particular.

The Court's next bit of interpretive jiggery-pokery involves other parts of the Act that purportedly presuppose the availability of tax credits on both federal and state Exchanges. *Ante,* at 2491–2492. It is curious that the Court is willing to subordinate the express words of the section that grants tax credits to the mere implications of other provisions with only tangential connections to tax credits. One would think that interpretation would work the other way around. In any event, each of the provisions mentioned by the Court is perfectly consistent with limiting tax credits to state Exchanges. One of them says that the minimum functions of an Exchange include (alongside several tasks that have nothing to do with tax credits) setting up an electronic calculator that shows "the actual cost of coverage after the application of any premium tax credit." 42 U.S.C. § 18031(d)(4)(G). What stops a federal Exchange's electronic calculator from telling a customer that his tax credit is zero? Another provision requires an Exchange's outreach program to educate the public about health plans, to facilitate enrollment, and to "distribute fair and impartial information" about enrollment and "the availability of premium tax credits." § 18031(i)(3)(B). What stops a federal Exchange's outreach program from fairly and impartially telling customers that no tax credits are available? A third provision requires an Exchange to report information about each insurance plan sold—including level of coverage, premium, name of the insured, and "amount of any advance payment" of the tax credit. 26 U.S.C. § 36B(f)(3). What stops a federal Exchange's report from confirming that no tax credits have been paid out?

The Court persists that these provisions "would make little sense" if no tax credits were available on federal Exchanges. *Ante*, at 2492. Even if that observation were true, it would show only oddity, not ambiguity. Laws often include unusual or mismatched provisions. The Affordable Care Act spans 900 pages; it would be amazing if its provisions all lined up perfectly with each other. This Court "does not revise legislation ... just because the text as written creates an apparent anomaly." *Michigan v. Bay Mills Indian Community*, 572 U.S. ----, ----, 134 S.Ct. 2024, 2033, 188 L.Ed.2d 1071 (2014). At any rate, the provisions cited by the Court are not particularly unusual. Each requires an Exchange to perform a standardized series of tasks, some aspects of which relate in some way to tax credits. It is entirely natural for slight mismatches to occur when, as here, lawmakers draft "a single statutory provision" to cover "different kinds" of situations. *Robers v. United States*, 572 U.S. ----, ----, 134 S.Ct. 1854, 1858, 188 L.Ed.2d 885 (2014). Lawmakers need not, and often do not, "write extra language specifically exempting, phrase by phrase, applications in respect to which a portion of a phrase is not needed." *Ibid.*

Roaming even farther afield from § 36B, the Court turns to the Act's provisions about "qualified individuals." *Ante*, at

2489–2490. Qualified individuals receive favored treatment on Exchanges, although customers who are not qualified individuals may also shop there. See *Halbig v. Burwell,* 758 F.3d 390, 404–405 (C.A.D.C.2014). The Court claims that the Act must equate federal and state establishment of Exchanges when it defines a qualified individual as someone who (among other things) lives in the "State that established the Exchange," 42 U.S.C. § 18032(f)(1)(A). Otherwise, the Court says, there would be no qualified individuals on federal Exchanges, contradicting (for example) the provision requiring every Exchange to take the "'interests of qualified individuals'" into account when selecting health plans. *Ante,* at 2490 (quoting § 18031(e)(1)(b)). Pure applesauce. Imagine that a university sends around a bulletin reminding every professor to take the "interests of graduate students" into account when setting office hours, but that some professors teach only undergraduates. Would anybody reason that the bulletin implicitly presupposes that every professor has "graduate students," so that "graduate students" must really mean "graduate or undergraduate students"? Surely not. Just as one naturally reads instructions about graduate students to be inapplicable to the extent a particular professor has no such students, so too would one naturally read instructions about qualified individuals to be inapplicable to the extent a particular Exchange has no such individuals. There is no need to rewrite the term "State that established the Exchange" in the definition of "qualified individual," much less a need to rewrite the separate term "Exchange established by the State" in a separate part of the Act.

Least convincing of all, however, is the Court's attempt to uncover support for its interpretation in "the structure of Section 36B itself." *Ante,* at 2494. The Court finds it strange that Congress limited the tax credit to state Exchanges in the formula for calculating the *amount* of the credit, rather than in the provision defining the range of taxpayers *eligible* for the credit. Had the Court bothered to look at the rest of the Tax Code, it would have seen that the structure it finds strange is in fact quite common. Consider, for example, the many provisions that initially make taxpayers of all incomes eligible for a tax credit, only to provide later that the amount of the credit is zero if the taxpayer's income exceeds a specified threshold. See, *e.g.*, 26 U.S.C. § 24 (child tax credit); § 32 (earned-income tax credit); § 36 (first-time-homebuyer tax credit). Or consider, for an even closer parallel, a neighboring provision that initially makes taxpayers of all States eligible for a credit, only to provide later that the amount of the credit may be zero if the taxpayer's State does not satisfy certain requirements. See § 35 (health-insurance-costs tax credit). One begins to get the sense that the Court's insistence on reading things in context applies to "established by the State," but to nothing else.

For what it is worth, lawmakers usually draft tax-credit provisions the way they do—*i.e.*, the way they drafted § 36B—because the mechanics of the credit require it. Many Americans move to new States in the middle of the year. Mentioning state Exchanges in the definition of "coverage month"—rather than (as the Court proposes) in the provisions concerning taxpayers' eligibility for the credit—accounts for taxpayers who live in a State with a state Exchange for a part of the year, but a State with a federal Exchange for the rest of the year. In addition, § 36B awards a credit with respect to insurance plans "which cover the taxpayer, *the taxpayer's spouse, or any dependent ... of the taxpayer* and which were enrolled in through an Exchange established by the State." § 36B(b)(2)(A) (emphasis added). If Congress had mentioned state Exchanges in the provisions discussing taxpayers' eligibility for the credit, a taxpayer who buys insurance from a federal Exchange would get no money, even if he has a spouse or dependent who buys insurance from a state Exchange—say a child attending college in a different State. It thus makes perfect sense for "Exchange established by the State" to appear where it does, rather than where the Court suggests. Even if that were not so, of course, its location would not make it any less clear.

The Court has not come close to presenting the compelling contextual case necessary to justify departing from the ordinary meaning of the terms of the law. Quite the contrary, context only underscores the outlandishness of the Court's interpretation. Reading the Act as a whole leaves no doubt about the matter: "Exchange established by the State" means what it looks like it means.

III

For its next defense of the indefensible, the Court turns to the Affordable Care Act's design and purposes. As relevant here, the Act makes three major reforms. The guaranteed-issue and community-rating requirements prohibit insurers from considering a customer's health when deciding whether to sell insurance and how much to charge, 42 U.S.C. §§ 300gg, 300gg-1; its famous individual mandate requires everyone to maintain insurance coverage or to pay what the Act calls a "penalty," 26 U.S.C. § 5000A(b)(1), and what we have nonetheless called a tax, see *National Federation of Independent Business v. Sebelius,* 567 U.S. ----, ----, 132 S.Ct. 2566, 2597–2598, 183 L.Ed.2d 450 (2012); and its tax credits help make insurance more affordable. The Court reasons that Congress intended these three reforms to "work together to expand insurance coverage"; and because the first two apply in every State, so must the third. *Ante,* at 2493.

This reasoning suffers from no shortage of flaws. To begin with,

> "even the most formidable argument concerning the statute's purposes could not overcome the clarity [of] the statute's text." *Kloeckner v. Solis,* 568 U.S. ----, ----, n. 4, 133 S.Ct. 596, 607, n. 4, 184 L.Ed.2d 433 (2012).

Statutory design and purpose matter only to the extent they help clarify an otherwise ambiguous provision. Could anyone maintain with a straight face that § 36B is unclear? To mention just the highlights, the Court's interpretation clashes with a statutory definition, renders words inoperative in at least seven separate provisions of the Act, overlooks the contrast between provisions that say "Exchange" and those that say "Exchange established by the State," gives the same phrase one meaning for purposes of tax credits but an entirely different meaning for other purposes, and (let us not forget) contradicts the ordinary meaning of the words Congress used. On the other side of the ledger, the Court has come up with nothing more than a general provision that turns out to be controlled by a specific one, a handful of clauses that are consistent with either understanding of establishment by the State, and a resemblance between the tax-credit provision and the rest of the Tax Code. If that is all it takes to make something ambiguous, everything is ambiguous.

Having gone wrong in consulting statutory purpose at all, the Court goes wrong again in analyzing it. The purposes of a law must be "collected chiefly from its words," not "from extrinsic circumstances." *Sturges v. Crowninshield,* 4 Wheat. 122, 202, 4 L.Ed. 529 (1819) (Marshall, C.J.). Only by concentrating on the law's terms can a judge hope to uncover the scheme *of the statute,* rather than some other scheme that the judge thinks desirable. Like it or not, the express terms of the Affordable Care Act make only two of the three reforms mentioned by the Court applicable in States that do not establish Exchanges. It is perfectly possible for them to operate independently of tax credits. The guaranteed-issue and community-rating requirements continue to ensure that insurance companies treat all customers the same no matter their health, and the individual mandate continues to encourage people to maintain coverage, lest they be "taxed."

The Court protests that without the tax credits, the number of people covered by the individual mandate shrinks, and without a broadly applicable individual mandate the guaranteed-issue and community-rating requirements "would destabilize the individual insurance market." *Ante,* at 2493. If true, these projections would show only that the statutory scheme contains a flaw; they would not show that the statute means the opposite of what it says. Moreover, it is a flaw that appeared as well in other parts of the Act. A different title established a long-term-care insurance program with guaranteed-issue and community-rating requirements, but without an individual mandate or subsidies. §§ 8001–8002, 124 Stat. 828–847 (2010). This program never came into effect "only because Congress, in response to actuarial analyses predicting that the [program] would be fiscally unsustainable, repealed the provision in 2013." *Halbig,* 758 F.3d, at 410. How could the Court say that Congress would never dream of combining guaranteed-issue and community-rating requirements with a narrow individual mandate, when it combined those requirements with *no* individual mandate in the context of long-term-care insurance?

Similarly, the Department of Health and Human Services originally interpreted the Act to impose guaranteed-issue and community-rating requirements in the Federal Territories, even though the Act plainly does not make the individual mandate applicable there. *Ibid.*; see 26 U.S.C. § 5000A(f)(4); 42 U.S.C. § 201(f). "This combination, predictably, [threw] individual insurance markets in the territories into turmoil." *Halbig, supra,* at 410. Responding to complaints from the Territories, the Department at first insisted that it had "no statutory authority" to address the problem and suggested that the Territories "seek legislative relief from Congress" instead. Letter from G. Cohen, Director of the Center for Consumer Information and Insurance Oversight, to S. Igisomar, Secretary of Commerce of the Commonwealth of Northern Mariana Islands (July 12, 2013). The Department changed its mind a year later, after what it described as "a careful review of [the] situation and the relevant statutory language." Letter from M. Tavenner, Administrator of the Centers for Medicare and Medicaid Services, to G. Francis, Insurance Commissioner of the Virgin Islands (July 16, 2014). How could the Court pronounce it "implausible" for Congress to have tolerated instability in insurance markets in States with federal Exchanges, *ante*, at 2494, when even the Government maintained until recently that Congress did exactly that in American Samoa, Guam, the Northern Mariana Islands, Puerto Rico, and the Virgin Islands?

Compounding its errors, the Court forgets that it is no more appropriate to consider one of a statute's purposes in isolation than it is to consider one of its words that way. No law pursues just one purpose at all costs, and no statutory scheme encompasses just one element. Most relevant here, the Affordable Care Act displays a congressional preference for state participation in the establishment of Exchanges: Each State gets the first opportunity to set up its Exchange, 42 U.S.C. § 18031(b); States that take up the opportunity receive federal funding for "activities ... related to establishing" an Exchange, § 18031(a)(3); and the Secretary may establish an Exchange in a State only as a fallback, § 18041(c). But setting up and running an Exchange involve significant burdens—meeting strict deadlines, § 18041(b), implementing requirements related to the offering of insurance plans, § 18031(d)(4), setting up outreach programs, § 18031(i), and ensuring that the Exchange is self-sustaining by 2015, § 18031(d)(5)(A). A State would have much less reason to take on these burdens if its citizens could receive tax credits no matter who establishes its Exchange. (Now that the Internal Revenue Service has interpreted § 36B to authorize tax credits everywhere, by the way, 34 States have failed to set up their own Exchanges. *Ante,* at 2487.) So even if making credits available on all Exchanges advances the goal of improving healthcare markets, it frustrates the goal of encouraging state involvement in the implementation of the Act. *This* is what justifies going out of our way to read "established by the State" to mean "established by the State or not established by the State"?

Worst of all for the repute of today's decision, the Court's reasoning is largely self-defeating. The Court predicts that making tax credits unavailable in States that do not set up their own Exchanges would cause disastrous economic consequences there. If that is so, however, wouldn't one expect States to react by setting up their own Exchanges? And wouldn't that outcome satisfy two of the Act's goals rather than just one: enabling the Act's reforms to work *and* promoting state involvement in the Act's implementation? The Court protests that the very existence of a federal fallback shows that Congress expected that some States might fail to set up their own Exchanges. *Ante,* at 2495. So it does. It does not show, however, that Congress expected the number of recalcitrant States to be particularly large. The more accurate the Court's dire economic predictions, the smaller that number is likely to be. That reality destroys the Court's pretense that applying the law as written would imperil "the viability of the entire Affordable Care Act." *Ante,* at 2495. All in all, the Court's arguments about the law's purpose and design are no more convincing than its arguments about context.

IV

Perhaps sensing the dismal failure of its efforts to show that "established by the State" means "established by the State or the Federal Government," the Court tries to palm off the pertinent statutory phrase as "inartful drafting." *Ante,* at 2495. This Court, however, has no free-floating power "to rescue Congress from its drafting errors." *Lamie v. United States Trustee,* 540 U.S. 526, 542, 124 S.Ct. 1023, 157 L.Ed.2d 1024 (2004) (internal quotation marks omitted). Only when it is patently obvious to a reasonable reader that a drafting mistake has occurred may a court correct the mistake. The occurrence of a misprint may be apparent from the face of the law, as it is where the Affordable Care Act "creates three separate Section 1563s." *Ante,* at 2492. But the Court does not pretend that there is any such indication of a drafting error on the face of § 36B. The occurrence of a misprint may also be apparent because a provision decrees an absurd result—a consequence "so monstrous, that all mankind would, without hesitation, unite in rejecting the application." *Sturges,* 4 Wheat., at 203. But § 36B does not come remotely close to satisfying that demanding standard. It is entirely plausible that tax credits were restricted to state Exchanges deliberately—for example, in order to encourage States to establish their own Exchanges. We therefore have no authority to dismiss the terms of the law as a drafting fumble.

Let us not forget that the term "Exchange established by the State" appears twice in § 36B and five more times in other parts of the Act that mention tax credits. What are the odds, do you think, that the same slip of the pen occurred in seven separate places? No provision of the Act—none at all—contradicts the limitation of tax credits to state Exchanges. And as I have already explained, uses of the term "Exchange established by the State" beyond the context of tax credits look anything but accidental. *Supra,* at 2487. If there was a mistake here, context suggests it was a substantive mistake in designing this part of the law, not a technical mistake in transcribing it.

V

The Court's decision reflects the philosophy that judges should endure whatever interpretive distortions it takes in order to correct a supposed flaw in the statutory machinery. That philosophy ignores the American people's decision to give *Congress* "[a]ll legislative Powers" enumerated in the Constitution. Art. I, § 1. They made Congress, not this Court, responsible for both making laws and mending them. This Court holds only the judicial power—the power to pronounce the law as Congress has enacted it. We lack the prerogative to repair laws that do not work out in practice, just as the people lack the ability to throw us out of office if they dislike the solutions we concoct. We must always remember, therefore, that "[o]ur task is to apply the text, not to improve upon it." *Pavelic & LeFlore v. Marvel Entertainment Group, Div. of Cadence Industries Corp.*, 493 U.S. 120, 126, 110 S.Ct. 456, 107 L.Ed.2d 438 (1989).

Trying to make its judge-empowering approach seem respectful of congressional authority, the Court asserts that its decision merely ensures that the Affordable Care Act operates the way Congress "meant [it] to operate." *Ante*, at 2494. First of all, what makes the Court so sure that Congress "meant" tax credits to be available everywhere? Our only evidence of what Congress meant comes from the terms of the law, and those terms show beyond all question that tax credits are available only on state Exchanges. More importantly, the Court forgets that ours is a government of laws and not of men. That means we are governed by the terms of our laws, not by the unenacted will of our lawmakers. "If Congress enacted into law something different from what it intended, then it should amend the statute to conform to its intent." *Lamie, supra,* at 542, 124 S.Ct. 1023. In the meantime, this Court "has no roving license ... to disregard clear language simply on the view that ... Congress 'must have intended' something broader." *Bay Mills,* 572 U.S., at ----, 134 S.Ct., at 2034.

Even less defensible, if possible, is the Court's claim that its interpretive approach is justified because this Act "does not reflect the type of care and deliberation that one might expect of such significant legislation." *Ante,* at 2492 – 2493. It is not our place to judge the quality of the care and deliberation that went into this or any other law. A law enacted by voice vote with no deliberation whatever is fully as binding upon us as one enacted after years of study, months of committee hearings, and weeks of debate. Much less is it our place to make everything come out right when Congress does not do its job properly. It is up to Congress to design its laws with care, and it is up to the people to hold them to account if they fail to carry out that responsibility.

Rather than rewriting the law under the pretense of interpreting it, the Court should have left it to Congress to decide what to do about the Act's limitation of tax credits to state Exchanges. If Congress values above everything else the Act's applicability across the country, it could make tax credits available in every Exchange. If it prizes state involvement in the Act's implementation, it could continue to limit tax credits to state Exchanges while taking other steps to mitigate the economic consequences predicted by the Court. If Congress wants to accommodate both goals, it could make tax credits available everywhere while offering new incentives for States to set up their own Exchanges. And if Congress thinks that the present design of the Act works well enough, it could do nothing. Congress could also do something else altogether, entirely abandoning the structure of the Affordable Care Act. The

Court's insistence on making a choice that should be made by Congress both aggrandizes judicial power and encourages congressional lassitude.

Just ponder the significance of the Court's decision to take matters into its own hands. The Court's revision of the law authorizes the Internal Revenue Service to spend tens of billions of dollars every year in tax credits on federal Exchanges. It affects the price of insurance for millions of Americans. It diminishes the participation of the States in the implementation of the Act. It vastly expands the reach of the Act's individual mandate, whose scope depends in part on the availability of credits. What a parody today's decision makes of Hamilton's assurances to the people of New York: "The legislature not only commands the purse but prescribes the rules by which the duties and rights of every citizen are to be regulated. The judiciary, on the contrary, has no influence over ... the purse; no direction ... of the wealth of society, and can take no active resolution whatever. It may truly be said to have neither force nor will but merely judgment." *The Federalist* No. 78, p. 465 (C. Rossiter ed. 1961).

* * *

Today's opinion changes the usual rules of statutory interpretation for the sake of the Affordable Care Act. That, alas, is not a novelty. In *National Federation of Independent Business v. Sebelius,* 567 U.S. ----, 132 S.Ct. 2566, 183 L.Ed.2d 450 this Court revised major components of the statute in order to save them from unconstitutionality. The Act that Congress passed provides that every individual "shall" maintain insurance or else pay a "penalty." 26 U.S.C. § 5000A. This Court, however, saw that the Commerce Clause does not authorize a federal mandate to buy health insurance. So it rewrote the mandate-cum-penalty as a tax. 567 U.S., at ---- - ----, 132 S.Ct., at

2583–2601 (principal opinion). The Act that Congress passed also requires every State to accept an expansion of its Medicaid program, or else risk losing *all* Medicaid funding. 42 U.S.C. § 1396c. This Court, however, saw that the Spending Clause does not authorize this coercive condition. So it rewrote the law to withhold only the *incremental* funds associated with the Medicaid expansion. 567 U.S., at ---- - ----, 132 S.Ct., at 2601–2608 (principal opinion). Having transformed two major parts of the law, the Court today has turned its attention to a third. The Act that Congress passed makes tax credits available only on an "Exchange established by the State." This Court, however, concludes that this limitation would prevent the rest of the Act from working as well as hoped. So it rewrites the law to make tax credits available everywhere. We should start calling this law SCOTUScare.

Perhaps the Patient Protection and Affordable Care Act will attain the enduring status of the Social Security Act or the Taft–Hartley Act; perhaps not. But this Court's two decisions on the Act will surely be remembered through the years. The somersaults of statutory interpretation they have performed ("penalty" means tax, "further [Medicaid] payments to the State" means only incremental Medicaid payments to the State, "established by the State" means not established by the State) will be cited by litigants endlessly, to the confusion of honest jurisprudence. And the cases will publish forever the discouraging truth that the Supreme Court of the United States favors some laws over others, and is prepared to do whatever it takes to uphold and assist its favorites.

I dissent.

4

The Power of the Police

A hole in the Fourth Amendment
Ferguson v. City of Charleston, 532 U.S. 67 (2001)

The obfuscator of last resort
Michigan v. Bryant, 562 U.S. 344 (2011)

Open your mouth for inspection: grievous and oppressive searches
Maryland v. King, 133 S.Ct. 1958 (2013)

Do drunk drivers drive drunkenly?
Navarette v. California, 134 S.Ct. 1683 (2014)

Few more controversial subjects have come before the federal courts in recent decades than the powers and the constitutional limitations upon law enforcement. In these cases the Court was confronted with a series of scenarios in which police actions were challenged as violations of constitutional protections, particularly under the Fourth Amendment. Here, again, the Justices have been split in their reading of the Constitution—and the Fourth Amendment. The majority in these cases tends to read broadly and expansively. Justice Scalia, and the Justices who joined his dissents, reads the text strictly as he deems appropriate in a democracy. Indeed, in *Ferguson*, he makes clear the antidemocratic nature of majority's expansive readings of the Constitution and cases: "...the Constitution does not resolve all difficult social questions, but leaves the vast majority of them to resolution by debate and the democratic process—which would produce a decision by the citizens of Charleston, through their elected representatives, to forbid or permit the police action at issue here. The question before us is a narrower one: whether, whatever the desirability of this police conduct, it violates the Fourth Amendment's prohibition of unreasonable searches and seizures. In my view, it plainly does not."

A hole in the Fourth Amendment
Ferguson v. City of Charleston,
532 U.S. 67 (2001)

Justice Scalia, with whom the Chief Justice and Justice Thomas join as to Part II, dissenting.

There is always an unappealing aspect to the use of doctors and nurses, ministers of mercy, to obtain incriminating evidence against the supposed objects of their ministration—although here, it is correctly pointed out, the doctors and nurses were ministering not just to the mothers but also to the children whom their cooperation with the police was meant to protect. But whatever may be the correct social judgment concerning the desirability of what occurred here, that is not the issue in the present case. The Constitution does not resolve all difficult social questions, but leaves the vast majority of them to resolution by debate and the democratic process—which would produce a decision by the citizens of Charleston, through their elected representatives, to forbid or permit the police action at issue here. The question before us is a narrower one: whether, whatever the desirability of this police conduct, it violates the Fourth Amendment's prohibition of unreasonable searches and seizures. In my view, it plainly does not.

I

The first step in Fourth Amendment analysis is to identify the search or seizure at issue. What petitioners, the Court, and to a lesser extent the concurrence really object to is not the urine testing, but the hospital's reporting of positive drug-test results to police. But the latter is obviously not a search. At most it may be a "derivative use of the product of a past unlawful search," which, of course, "work[s] no new Fourth Amendment wrong" and "presents a question, not of rights, but of remedies." *United States v. Calandra,* 414 U.S. 338, 354, 94 S.Ct. 613, 38 L.Ed.2d 561 (1974). There is only one act that could conceivably be regarded as a search of petitioners in the present case: the *taking* of the urine sample. I suppose the *testing* of that urine for traces of unlawful drugs could be considered a search of sorts, but the Fourth Amendment protects only against searches of citizens' "persons, houses, papers, and effects"; and it is entirely unrealistic to regard urine as one of the "effects" (*i.e.,* part of the property) of the person who has passed and abandoned it. Cf. *California v. Greenwood,* 486 U.S. 35, 108 S.Ct. 1625, 100 L.Ed.2d 30 (1988) (garbage left at curb is not property protected by the Fourth Amendment). Some would argue, I suppose, that testing of the urine is prohibited by some generalized privacy right "emanating" from the "penumbras" of the Constitution (a question that is not before us); but it is not even arguable that the testing of urine that has been lawfully obtained is a Fourth Amendment search. (I may add that, even if it were, the factors legitimizing the taking of the sample, which I discuss below, would likewise legitimize the testing of it.)

It is rudimentary Fourth Amendment law that a search which has been consented to is not unreasonable. There is no contention in the present case that the urine samples were extracted forcibly. The only conceivable bases for saying that they were obtained without consent are the contentions (1) that the consent was coerced by the patients' need for medical treatment, (2) that the consent was uninformed because the patients were not told that the tests would include testing for drugs, and (3) that the consent was uninformed because the patients were not told that the results of the tests would be provided to the police. (When the court below said that it was reserving the factual issue of consent, see 186 F.3d 469, 476 (C.A.4 1999), it was referring at most to these three—and perhaps just to the last two.)

Under our established Fourth Amendment law, the last two contentions would not suffice, even without reference to the special-needs doctrine. The Court's analogizing of this case to *Miranda v. Arizona,* 384 U.S. 436, 86 S.Ct. 1602, 16 L.Ed.2d 694 (1966), and its claim that "standards of knowing waiver" apply, *ante,* at 1292, are flatly contradicted by our jurisprudence, which shows that using lawfully (but deceivingly) obtained material for purposes other than those represented, and giving that material or information derived from it to the police, is not unconstitutional. In *Hoffa v. United States,* 385 U.S. 293, 87 S.Ct. 408, 17 L.Ed.2d 374 (1966), "[t]he argument [was] that [the informant's] failure to disclose his role as a government informant vitiated the consent that the petitioner gave" for the agent's access to evidence of criminal wrongdoing, *id.,* at 300, 87 S.Ct. 408. We rejected that argument, because "the Fourth Amendment [does not protect] a wrongdoer's misplaced belief that a person to whom he voluntarily confides his wrongdoing will not reveal it." *Id.,* at 302, 87 S.Ct. 408. Because the defendant had voluntarily provided access to the evidence, there was no reasonable expectation of privacy to invade. Abuse of trust is surely a sneaky and ungentlemanly thing, and perhaps there should be (as there are) laws against such conduct by the government. See, *e.g.,* 50 U.S.C. § 403–7 (1994 ed., Supp. IV) (prohibiting the "Intelligence Community['s]" use of journalists as agents). That, however, is immaterial for Fourth Amendment purposes, for "*however strongly* a defendant may trust an apparent colleague, his expectations in this respect are not protected by the Fourth Amendment when it turns out that the colleague is a government agent regularly communicating with the authorities."

United States v. White, 401 U.S. 745, 749, 91 S.Ct. 1122, 28 L.Ed.2d 453 (1971) (emphasis added). The *Hoffa* line of cases, I may note, does not distinguish between operations meant to catch a criminal in the act, and those meant only to gather evidence of prior wrongdoing. See, *e.g., United States v. Miller,* 425 U.S. 435, 440–443, 96 S.Ct. 1619, 48 L.Ed.2d 71 (1976); cf. *Illinois v. Perkins,* 496 U.S. 292, 298, 110 S.Ct. 2394, 110 L.Ed.2d 243 (1990) (relying on *Hoffa* in holding the *Miranda* rule did not require suppression of an inmate confession given an agent posing as a fellow prisoner).

Until today, we have *never* held—or even suggested—that material which a person voluntarily entrusts to someone else cannot be given by that person to the police, and used for whatever evidence it may contain. Without so much as discussing the point, the Court today opens a hole in our Fourth Amendment jurisprudence, the size and shape of which is entirely indeterminate. Today's holding would be remarkable enough if the confidential relationship violated by the police conduct were at least one protected by state law. It would be surprising to learn, for example, that in a State which recognizes a spousal evidentiary privilege the police cannot use evidence obtained from a cooperating husband or wife. But today's holding goes even beyond that, since there does not exist any physician-patient privilege in South Carolina. See, *e.g., Peagler v. Atlantic Coast R.R. Co.,* 232 S.C. 274, 101 S.E.2d 821 (1958). Since the Court declines even to discuss the issue, it leaves law enforcement officials entirely in the dark as to when they can use incriminating evidence obtained from "trusted" sources. Presumably the lines will be drawn in the case-by-case development of a whole new branch of Fourth Amendment jurisprudence, taking yet another social judgment (which confidential relationships ought not be invaded by the police) out of democratic control, and confiding it to the uncontrolled judgment of this Court—uncontrolled because there is no common-law precedent to guide it. I would adhere to our established law, which says that information obtained through violation of a relationship of trust is obtained consensually, and is hence not a search.

There remains to be considered the first possible basis for invalidating this search, which is that the patients were coerced to produce their urine samples by their necessitous circumstances, to wit, their need for medical treatment of their pregnancy. If that was coercion, it was not coercion applied by the government—and if such nongovernmental coercion sufficed, the police would never be permitted to use the ballistic evidence obtained from treatment of a patient with a bullet wound. And the Fourth Amendment would invalidate those many state laws that require physicians to report gunshot wounds, evidence of spousal abuse, and (like the South Carolina law relevant here, see S.C.Code Ann. § 20–7–510 (2000)) evidence of child abuse.

II

I think it clear, therefore, that there is no basis for saying that obtaining of the urine sample was unconstitutional. The special-needs doctrine is thus quite irrelevant, since it operates only to validate searches and seizures that are otherwise unlawful. In the ensuing discussion, however, I shall assume (contrary to legal precedent) that the taking of the urine sample was (either because of the patients' necessitous circumstances, or because of failure to disclose that the urine would be tested for drugs, or because of failure to disclose that the results of the test would be given to the police) coerced. Indeed, I shall even assume (contrary to common sense) that the testing of the urine constituted an unconsented search of the patients' effects. On those assumptions, the special-needs doctrine *would* become relevant; and, properly applied, would validate what was done here.

The conclusion of the Court that the special-needs doctrine is inapplicable rests upon its contention that respondents "undert[ook] to obtain [drug] evidence from their patients" not for any medical purpose, but "*for the specific purpose of incriminating those patients.*" *Ante,* at 1292 (emphasis in original). In other words, the purported medical rationale was merely a pretext; there was no special need. See *Skinner v. Railway Labor Executives' Assn.,* 489 U.S. 602, 621, n. 5, 109 S.Ct. 1402, 103 L.Ed.2d 639 (1989). This contention contradicts the District Court's finding of fact that the goal of the testing policy "was not to arrest patients but to facilitate their treatment and protect both the mother and unborn child." App. to Pet. for Cert. A–38. This finding is binding upon us unless clearly erroneous, see Fed. Rule Civ. Proc. 52(a). Not only do I find it supportable; I think any other finding would have to be overturned.

The cocaine tests started in April 1989, *neither at police suggestion nor with police involvement.* Expectant mothers who tested positive were referred by hospital staff for substance-abuse treatment, *ante,* at 1284 (opinion of the Court)—an obvious health benefit to both mother and child. See App. 43 (testimony that a single use of cocaine can cause fetal damage). And, since "[i]nfants whose mothers abuse cocaine during pregnancy are born with a wide variety of physical and neurological abnormalities," *ante,* at 1294 (Kennedy, J., concurring in judgment), which require medical attention, see Brief in Opposition A76–A77, the tests were of additional medical benefit in predicting needed postnatal treatment for the child. Thus, in their origin—before the police were in any way involved—the tests had an immediate, not merely an "ultimate," *ante,* at 1291 (opinion of the Court), purpose of improving maternal and infant health. Several months after the testing had been initiated, a nurse discovered that local police were arresting pregnant users of cocaine for child abuse, the hospital's general counsel wrote the county solicitor to ask "what, if anything, our Medical Center needs to do to assist you in this matter," App. 499 (South Carolina law requires child abuse to be reported, see S.C.Code Ann. § 20–7–510), the police suggested ways to avoid tainting evidence, and the hospital and police in conjunction used the testing program as a means of securing what the Court calls the "ultimate" health benefit of coercing drug-abusing mothers into drug treatment. See *ante,* at 1284–1285, 1290–1291. Why would there be any reason to believe that, once this policy of using the drug tests for their "ultimate" health benefits had been adopted, use of them for their original, *immediate,* benefits somehow disappeared, and testing somehow became in its entirety nothing more than a "pretext" for obtaining grounds for arrest? On the face of it, this is incredible. The only evidence of the exclusively arrest-related purpose of the testing adduced by the Court is that the police-cooperation policy *itself* does not describe how to care for cocaine-exposed infants. See *ante,* at 1285, 1290–1291. But *of course* it does not, since that policy, adopted months after the cocaine testing was initiated, had as its only health object the "ultimate" goal of inducing drug treatment through threat of arrest. Does the Court really believe (or even *hope*) that, once invalidation of the program challenged here has been decreed, drug testing will cease?

In sum, there can be no basis for the Court's purported ability to "distinguis [h] this case from circumstances in which physicians or psychologists, in the course of ordinary medical procedures aimed at helping the patient herself, come across information that ... is subject to reporting requirements," *ante,* at 1290, unless it is this: That the *addition* of a law-enforcement-related purpose *to* a legitimate medical purpose destroys applicability of the "special-needs" doctrine. But that is quite impossible, since the special-needs doctrine was developed, and is ordinarily employed, precisely to enable searches *by law enforcement officials* who, of course, ordinarily have a law enforcement objective. Thus, in *Griffin v. Wisconsin,* 483 U.S. 868, 107 S.Ct. 3164, 97 L.Ed.2d 709 (1987), a probation officer received a tip from a detective that petitioner, a felon on probation, possessed a firearm. Accompanied by police, he conducted a warrantless search of petitioner's home. The weapon was found and used as evidence in the probationer's trial for unlawful possession of a firearm. See *id.,* at 870–872, 107 S.Ct. 3164. Affirming denial of a motion to suppress, we concluded that the "special need" of assuring compliance with terms of release justified a warrantless search of petitioner's home. Notably, we observed that a probation officer is not "the police officer who normally conducts searches against the ordinary citizen. He is an employee of the State Department of Health and Social Services who, while assuredly charged with protecting the public interest, is also supposed to have in mind the welfare of the probationer.... In such a setting, we think it reasonable to dispense with the warrant requirement." *Id.,* at 876–877, 107 S.Ct. 3164.

Like the probation officer, the doctors here do not "ordinarily conduc[t] searches against the ordinary citizen," and they are "supposed to have in mind the welfare of the [mother and child]." That they have in mind in addition the provision of evidence to the police should make no difference. The Court suggests that if police involvement in this case was in some way incidental and after-the-fact, that would make a difference in the outcome. See *ante,* at 1290–1292. But in *Griffin,* even more than here, police were involved in the search from the very beginning; indeed, the initial tip about the gun came from a detective. Under the factors relied upon by the Court, the use of evidence approved in *Griffin* would have been permitted only if the parole officer had been untrained in chain-of-custody procedures, had not known of the possibility a gun was present, and had been unaccompanied by police when he simply happened upon the weapon. Why any or all of these is constitutionally significant is baffling.

Petitioners seek to distinguish *Griffin* by observing that probationers enjoy a lesser expectation of privacy than does the general public. That is irrelevant to the point I make here, which is that the presence of a law enforcement purpose does not render the special-needs doctrine inapplicable. In any event, I doubt whether Griffin's reasonable expectation of privacy in his home was any less than petitioners' reasonable expectation of privacy in their urine taken, or in the urine tests performed, in a hospital—especially in a State such as South Carolina, which recognizes no physician-patient testimonial privilege and requires the physician's duty of confidentiality to yield to public policy, see *McCormick v. England,* 328 S.C. 627, 633, 640–642, 494 S.E.2d 431, 434, 438–439 (App.1997); and which requires medical conditions that indicate a violation of the law to be reported to authorities, see, *e.g.,* S.C.Code Ann. § 20–7–510 (2000) (child abuse). Cf. *Whalen v. Roe,* 429 U.S. 589, 597–598, 97 S.Ct. 869, 51 L.Ed.2d 64 (1977) (privacy interest does not forbid government to require hospitals to provide, for law enforcement purposes, names of patients receiving prescriptions of frequently abused drugs).

The concurrence makes essentially the same basic error as the Court, though it puts the point somewhat differently: "The special needs cases we have decided," it says, "do not sustain the active use of law enforcement ... as an integral part of a program which seeks to achieve legitimate, civil objectives."

Ante, at 1294. *Griffin* shows that is not true. Indeed, *Griffin* shows that there is not even any truth in the more limited proposition that our cases do not support application of the special-needs exception where the "legitimate, civil objectives" are sought only *through* the use of law enforcement means. (Surely the parole officer in *Griffin* was using threat of reincarceration to assure compliance with parole.) But even if this latter proposition *were* true, it would invalidate what occurred here only if the drug testing sought exclusively the "ultimate" health benefits achieved by coercing the mothers into drug treatment through threat of prosecution. But in fact the drug testing sought, independently of law enforcement involvement, the "immediate" health benefits of identifying drug-impaired mother and child for necessary medical treatment. The concurrence concedes that if the testing is conducted for medical reasons, the fact that "prosecuting authorities *then* adopt legitimate procedures to discover this information and prosecution follows ... ought not to invalidate the testing." *Ante,* at 1295 (emphasis added). But here the police involvement in each case did *take place after* the testing was conducted for independent reasons. Surely the concurrence cannot mean that no police-suggested procedures (such as preserving the chain of custody of the urine sample) can be applied until *after* the testing; or that the police-suggested procedures must have been *designed* after the testing. The facts in *Griffin* (and common sense) show that this cannot be so. It seems to me that the only real distinction between what the concurrence must reasonably be thought to be approving, and what we have here, is that here the police took the lesser step of initially *threatening* prosecution rather than bringing it.

* * *

As I indicated at the outset, it is not the function of this Court—at least not in Fourth Amendment cases—to weigh petitioners' privacy interest against the State's interest in meeting the crisis of "crack babies" that developed in the late 1980's. I cannot refrain from observing, however, that the outcome of a wise weighing of those interests is by no means clear. The initial goal of the doctors and nurses who conducted cocaine testing in this case was to refer pregnant drug addicts to treatment centers, and to prepare for necessary treatment of their possibly affected children. When the doctors and nurses agreed to the program providing test results to the police, they did so because (in addition to the fact that child abuse was required by law to be reported) they wanted to use the sanction of arrest as a strong incentive for their addicted patients to undertake drug-addiction treatment. And the police themselves used it for that benign purpose, as is shown by the fact that only 30 of 253 women testing positive for cocaine were ever arrested, and only 2 of those prosecuted. See App. 1125–1126. It would not be unreasonable to conclude that today's judgment, authorizing the assessment of damages against the county solicitor and individual doctors and nurses who participated in the program, proves once again that no good deed goes unpunished.

But as far as the Fourth Amendment is concerned: There was no unconsented search in this case. And if there was, it would have been validated by the special-needs doctrine. For these reasons, I respectfully dissent.

The obfuscator of last resort
Michigan v. Bryant,
562 U.S. 344 (2011)

Justice Scalia, dissenting.

Today's tale—a story of five officers conducting successive examinations of a dying man with the primary purpose, not of obtaining and preserving his testimony regarding his killer, but of protecting him, them, and others from a murderer somewhere on the loose—is so transparently false that professing to believe it demeans this institution. But reaching a patently incorrect conclusion on the facts is a relatively benign judicial mischief; it affects, after all, only the case at hand. In its vain attempt to make the incredible plausible, however—or perhaps as an intended second goal—today's opinion distorts our Confrontation Clause jurisprudence and leaves it in a shambles. Instead of clarifying the law, the Court makes itself the obfuscator of last resort. Because I continue to adhere to the Confrontation Clause that the People adopted, as described in *Crawford v. Washington,* 541 U.S. 36, 124 S.Ct. 1354, 158 L.Ed.2d 177 (2004), I dissent.

I

A

The Confrontation Clause of the Sixth Amendment, made binding on the States by the Fourteenth Amendment, *Pointer v. Texas,* 380 U.S. 400, 403, 85 S.Ct. 1065, 13 L.Ed.2d 923 (1965), provides that "[i]n all criminal prosecutions, the accused shall enjoy the right ... to be confronted with the witnesses against him." In *Crawford,* we held that this provision guarantees a defendant his common-law right to confront those "who 'bear testimony'" against him. 541 U.S., at 51, 124 S.Ct. 1354. A witness must deliver his testimony against the defendant in person, or the prosecution must prove that the witness is unavailable to appear at trial and that the defendant has had a prior opportunity for cross-examination. *Id.,* at 53–54, 124 S.Ct. 1354.

Not all hearsay falls within the Confrontation Clause's grasp. At trial a witness "bears testimony" by providing "'[a] solemn declaration or affirmation ... for the purpose of establishing or proving some fact.'" *Id.,* at 51, 124 S.Ct. 1354 (quoting 2 N. Webster, *An American Dictionary of the English Language* (1828)). The Confrontation Clause protects defendants only from hearsay statements that do the same. *Davis v. Washington,* 547 U.S. 813, 823–824, 126 S.Ct. 2266, 165 L.Ed.2d 224 (2006). In *Davis,* we explained how to identify testimonial hearsay prompted by police questioning in the field. A statement is testimonial "when the circumstances objectively indicate ... that the primary purpose of the interrogation is to establish or prove past events potentially relevant to later criminal prosecution." *Id.,* at 822, 126 S.Ct. 2266. When, however, the circumstances objectively indicate that the declarant's statements were "a cry for help [o]r the provision of information enabling officers immediately to end a threatening situation," *id.,* at 832, 126 S.Ct. 2266, they bear little resemblance to in-court testimony. "No 'witness' goes into court to proclaim an emergency and seek help." *Id.,* at 828, 126 S.Ct. 2266.

Crawford and *Davis* did not address whose perspective matters—the declarant's, the interrogator's, or both—when assessing "the primary purpose of [an] interrogation." In those cases the statements were testimonial from any perspective. I think the same is true here, but because the Court picks a perspective so will I: The declarant's intent is what counts. In-court testimony is more than a narrative of past events; it is a solemn declaration made in the course of a criminal trial. For an out-of-court statement to qualify as testimonial, the declarant must intend the statement to be a solemn declaration rather than an unconsidered or offhand remark; and he must make the statement with the understanding that it may be used to invoke the coercive machinery of the State against the accused. See Friedman, "Grappling with the Meaning of 'Testimonial,'" 71 *Brooklyn L.Rev.* 241, 259 (2005). That is what distinguishes a narrative told to a friend over dinner from a statement to the police. See *Crawford, supra,* at 51, 124 S.Ct. 1354. The hidden purpose of an interrogator cannot substitute for the declarant's intentional solemnity or his understanding of how his words may be used.

A declarant-focused inquiry is also the only inquiry that would work in every fact pattern implicating the Confrontation Clause. The Clause applies to volunteered testimony as well as statements solicited through police interrogation. See *Davis, supra,* at 822–823, n. 1, 126 S.Ct. 2266. An inquiry into an officer's purposes would make no sense when a declarant blurts out "Rick shot me" as soon as the officer arrives on the scene. I see no reason to adopt a different test—one that accounts for an officer's intent—when the officer asks "what happened" before the declarant makes his accusation. (This does not mean the interrogator is irrelevant. The identity of an interrogator, and the content and tenor of his questions, can bear upon whether a declarant intends to make a solemn statement, and envisions its use at a criminal trial. But none of this means that the interrogator's purpose matters.)

In an unsuccessful attempt to make its finding of emergency plausible, the Court instead adopts a test that looks to the purposes of both the police and the declarant. It claims that this is demanded by necessity, fretting that a domestic-violence victim may want her abuser briefly arrested—presumably to teach him a lesson—but not desire prosecution. See *ante,* at 1161–1162. I do not need to probe the purposes of the police to solve that problem. Even if a victim speaks to the police "to establish or prove past events" solely for the purpose of getting her abuser arrested, she surely knows her account is "potentially relevant to later criminal prosecution" should one ensue. *Davis, supra,* at 822, 126 S.Ct. 2266.

The Court also wrings its hands over the possibility that "a severely injured victim" may lack the capacity to form a purpose, and instead answer questions "reflexive[ly]." *Ante,* at 1161–1162. How to assess whether a declarant with diminished capacity bore testimony is a difficult question, and one I do not need to answer today. But the Court's proposed answer—to substitute the intentions of the police for the missing intentions of the declarant—cannot be the correct one. When the declarant has diminished capacity, focusing on the interrogators make less sense, not more. The inquiry under *Crawford* turns in part on the actions and statements of a declarant's audience only because they shape the declarant's perception of why his audience is listening and therefore influence *his purpose* in making the declaration. See 541 U.S., at 51, 124 S.Ct. 1354. But a person who cannot perceive his own purposes certainly cannot perceive why a listener might be interested in what he has to say. As far as I can tell, the Court's substituted-intent theory "has nothing to be said for it except that it can sometimes make our job easier," *Jerman v. Carlisle, McNellie, Rini, Kramer & Ulrich, L.P. A.,* 559 U.S. ----, ----, 130 S.Ct. 1605, 1626, 176 L.Ed.2d 519 (2010) (Scalia, J., concurring in part and concurring in judgment).

The Court claims one affirmative virtue for its focus on the purposes of both the declarant and the police: It "ameliorates problems that ... arise" when declarants have "mixed motives."

Ante, at 1161. I am at a loss to know how. Sorting out the primary purpose of a declarant with mixed motives is sometimes difficult. But adding in the mixed motives of the police only compounds the problem. Now courts will have to sort through two sets of mixed motives to determine the primary purpose of an interrogation. And the Court's solution creates a mixed-motive problem where (under the proper theory) it does not exist—viz., where the police and the declarant each have one motive, but those motives conflict. The Court does not provide an answer to this glaringly obvious problem, probably because it does not have one.

The only virtue of the Court's approach (if it can be misnamned a virtue) is that it leaves judges free to reach the "fairest" result under the totality of the circumstances. If the dastardly police trick a declarant into giving an incriminating statement against a sympathetic defendant, a court can focus on the police's intent and declare the statement testimonial. If the defendant "deserves" to go to jail, then a court can focus on whatever perspective is necessary to declare damning hearsay nontestimonial. And when all else fails, a court can mix-and-match perspectives to reach its desired outcome. Unfortunately, under this malleable approach "the guarantee of confrontation is no guarantee at all." *Giles v. California,* 554 U.S. 353, 375, 128 S.Ct. 2678, 171 L.Ed.2d 488 (2008) (plurality).

B

Looking to the declarant's purpose (as we should), this is an absurdly easy case. Roughly 25 minutes after Anthony Covington had been shot, Detroit police responded to a 911 call reporting that a gunshot victim had appeared at a neighborhood gas station. They quickly arrived at the scene, and in less than 10 minutes five different Detroit police officers questioned Covington about the shooting. Each asked him a similar battery of questions: "what happened" and when, App. 39, 126, "who shot the victim," *id.,* at 22, and "where" did the shooting take place, *id.,* at 132. See also *id.,* at 113. After Covington would answer, they would ask follow-up questions, such as "how tall is" the shooter, *id.,* at 134, "[h]ow much does he weigh," *ibid.* what is the exact address or physical description of the house where the shooting took place, and what chain of events led to the shooting. The battery relented when the paramedics arrived and began tending to Covington's wounds.

From Covington's perspective, his statements had little value except to ensure the arrest and eventual prosecution of Richard Bryant. He knew the "threatening situation," *Davis,* 547 U.S., at 832, 126 S.Ct. 2266, had ended six blocks away and 25 minutes earlier when he fled from Bryant's back porch. See 483 Mich. 132, 135–136, 768 N.W.2d 65, 67 (2009); App. 105. Bryant had not confronted him face-to-face before he was mortally wounded, instead shooting him through a door. See 483 Mich., at 136–137, 768 N.W.2d, at 67. Even if Bryant had pursued him (unlikely), and after seeing that Covington had ended up at the gas station was unable to confront him there before the police arrived (doubly unlikely), it was entirely beyond imagination that Bryant would again open fire while Covington was surrounded by five armed police officers. And Covington knew the shooting was the work of a drug dealer, not a spree killer who might randomly threaten others. *Id.,* at 135, 137, 768 N.W.2d, at 67.

Covington's knowledge that he had nothing to fear differs significantly from Michelle McCottry's state of mind during her "frantic" statements to a 911 operator at issue in *Davis,* 547 U.S., at 827, 126 S.Ct. 2266. Her "call was plainly a call for help against a bona fide physical threat" describing "events *as they were actually happening.*" *Ibid.* She did not have the luxuries of police protection and of time and space separating her from immediate danger that Covington enjoyed when he made his statements. See *id.*, at 831, 126 S.Ct. 2266.

Covington's pressing medical needs do not suggest that he was responding to an emergency, but to the contrary reinforce the testimonial character of his statements. He understood the police were focused on investigating a past crime, not his medical needs. None of the officers asked Covington how he was doing, attempted more than superficially to assess the severity of his wounds, or attempted to administer first aid. They instead primarily asked questions with little, if any, relevance to Covington's dire situation. Police, paramedics, and doctors do not need to know the address where a shooting took place, the name of the shooter, or the shooter's height and weight to provide proper medical care. Underscoring that Covington understood the officers' investigative role, he interrupted their interrogation to ask "when is EMS coming?" App. 57. When, in other words, would the focus shift to his medical needs rather than Bryant's crime?

Neither Covington's statements nor the colloquy between him and the officers would have been out of place at a trial; it would have been a routine direct examination. See *Davis*, 547 U.S., at 830, 126 S.Ct. 2266. Like a witness, Covington recounted in detail how a past criminal event began and progressed, and like a prosecutor, the police elicited that account through structured questioning. Preventing the admission of "weaker substitute[s] for live testimony at trial" such as this, *id.*, at 828, 126 S.Ct. 2266 (internal quotation marks omitted), is precisely what motivated the Framers to adopt the Confrontation Clause and what motivated our decisions in *Crawford* and in *Hammon v. Indiana*, decided with *Davis*. *Ex parte* examinations raise the same constitutional concerns whether they take place in a gas-station parking lot or in a police interrogation room.

C

Worse still for the repute of today's opinion, this is an absurdly easy case even if one (erroneously) takes the interrogating officers' purpose into account. The five officers interrogated Covington primarily to investigate past criminal events. None—absolutely none—of their actions indicated that they perceived an imminent threat. They did not draw their weapons, and indeed did not immediately search the gas station for potential shooters. To the contrary, all five testified that they questioned Covington *before conducting any investigation at the scene.* Would this have made any sense if they feared the presence of a shooter? Most tellingly, none of the officers started his interrogation by asking what would have been the obvious first question if any hint of such a fear existed: Where is the shooter?

But do not rely solely on my word about the officers' primary purpose. Listen to Sergeant Wenturine, who candidly admitted that he interrogated Covington because he "ha[d] a man here that [he] believe[d][was] dying [so he was] gonna find out who did this, period." App. 112. In short, he needed to interrogate Covington to solve a crime. Wenturine never mentioned an interest in ending an ongoing emergency.

At the very least, the officers' intentions *turned* investigative during their 10-minute encounter with Covington, and the conversation "evolve[d] into testimonial statements." *Davis,* 547 U.S., at 828, 126 S.Ct. 2266 (internal quotation marks omitted). The fifth officer to arrive at the scene did not need to run straight to Covington and ask a battery of questions "to determine the need for emergency assistance," *Ibid.* He could have asked his fellow officers, who presumably had a better sense of that than Covington—and a better sense of what he could do to assist. No, the value of asking the same battery of questions a fifth time was to ensure that Covington told a consistent story and to see if any new details helpful to the investigation and eventual prosecution would emerge. Having the testimony of five officers to recount Covington's consistent story undoubtedly helped obtain Bryant's conviction. (Which came, I may note, after the first jury could not reach a verdict. See 483 Mich., at 137, 768 N.W.2d, at 67.)

D

A final word about the Court's active imagination. The Court invents a world where an ongoing emergency exists whenever "an armed shooter, whose motive for and location after the shooting [are] unknown, ... mortally wound [s]" one individual "within a few blocks and [25] minutes of the location where the police" ultimately find that victim. *Ante,* at 1164. Breathlessly, it worries that a shooter could leave the scene armed and ready to pull the trigger again. See *ante,* at 1158–1159, 1164, 1166. Nothing suggests the five officers in this case shared the court's dystopian view of Detroit, where drug dealers hunt their shooting victim down and fire into a crowd of police officers to finish him off, see *ante,* at 1166, or where spree killers shoot through a door and then roam the streets leaving a trail of bodies behind. Because almost 90 percent of murders involve a single victim, it is much more likely—indeed, I think it certain—that the officers viewed their encounter with Covington for what it was: an investigation into a past crime with no ongoing or immediate consequences.

The Court's distorted view creates an expansive exception to the Confrontation Clause for violent crimes. Because Bryant posed a continuing threat to public safety in the Court's imagination, the emergency persisted for confrontation purposes at least until the police learned his "motive for and location after the shooting." *Ante,* at 1164. It may have persisted in this case until the police "secured the scene of the shooting" two-and-a-half hours later. *Ante,* at 1164–1165. (The relevance of securing the scene is unclear so long as the killer is still at large—especially if, as the Court speculates, he may be a spree-killer.) This is a dangerous definition of emergency. Many individuals who testify against a defendant at trial first offer their accounts to police in the hours after a violent act. If the police can plausibly claim that a "potential threat to ... the public" persisted through those first few hours, *ante,* at 1156 (and if the claim is plausible here it is always plausible) a defendant will have no constitutionally protected right to exclude the uncross-examined testimony of such witnesses. His conviction could rest (as perhaps it did here) solely on the officers' recollection at trial of the witnesses' accusations.

The Framers could not have envisioned such a hollow constitutional guarantee. No framing-era confrontation case that I know of, neither here nor in England, took such an enfeebled view of the right to confrontation. For example, *King v. Brasier,* 1 Leach 199, 200, 168 Eng. Rep. 202, 202–203 (K.B.1779), held inadmissible a mother's account of her young daughter's statements "immediately on her coming home" after being sexually assaulted. The daughter needed to testify herself. But today's majority presumably would hold the daughter's account to her mother a nontestimonial statement made during an ongoing emergency. She could not have known whether her attacker might reappear to attack again or attempt to silence the lone witness against him. Her mother likely listened to the account to assess the threat to her own safety and to decide whether the rapist posed a threat to the community that required the immediate intervention of the local authorities. Cf. *ante,* at 1165–1166. Utter nonsense.

The 16th- and 17th-century English treason trials that helped inspire the Confrontation Clause show that today's decision is a mistake. The Court's expansive definition of an "ongoing emergency" and its willingness to consider the perspective of the interrogator and the declarant cast a more favorable light on those trials than history or our past decisions suggest they deserve. Royal officials conducted many of the *ex parte* examinations introduced against Sir Walter Raleigh and Sir John Fenwick while investigating alleged treasonous conspiracies of unknown scope, aimed at killing or overthrowing the King. See Brief for National Association of Criminal Defense Lawyers as *Amicus Curiae* 21–22, and n. 11. Social stability in 16th- and 17th-century England depended mainly on the continuity of the ruling monarch, cf. 1 J. Stephen, *A History of the Criminal Law of England* 354 (1883), so such a conspiracy posed the most pressing emergency imaginable. Presumably, the royal officials investigating it would have understood the gravity of the situation and would have focused their interrogations primarily on ending the threat, not on generating testimony for trial. I therefore doubt that under the Court's test English officials acted improperly by denying Raleigh and Fenwick the opportunity to confront their accusers "face to face," *id.*, at 326.

Under my approach, in contrast, those English trials remain unquestionably infamous. Lord Cobham did not speak with royal officials to end an ongoing emergency. He was a traitor! He spoke, as Raleigh correctly observed, to establish Raleigh's guilt and to save his own life. See 1 D. Jardine, *Criminal Trials* 435 (1832). Cobham's statements, when assessed from his perspective, had only a testimonial purpose. The same is true of Covington's statements here.

II

A

But today's decision is not only a gross distortion of the facts. It is a gross distortion of the law—a revisionist narrative in which reliability continues to guide our Confrontation Clause jurisprudence, at least where emergencies and faux emergencies are concerned.

According to today's opinion, the *Davis* inquiry into whether a declarant spoke to end an ongoing emergency or rather to "prove past events potentially relevant to later criminal prosecution," 547 U.S., at 822, 126 S.Ct. 2266, is *not* aimed at answering whether the declarant acted as a witness. Instead, the *Davis* inquiry probes the *reliability* of a declarant's statements, "[i]mplicit[ly]" importing the excited-utterances hearsay exception into the Constitution. *Ante,* at 1157. A statement during an ongoing emergency is sufficiently reliable, the Court says, "because the prospect of fabrication ... is presumably significantly diminished," so it "does not [need] to be subject to the crucible of cross-examination." *Id.,* at 1157.

Compare that with the holding of *Crawford*: "Where testimonial statements are at issue, the only indicium of reliability sufficient to satisfy constitutional demands is the one the Constitution actually prescribes: confrontation." 541 U.S., at 68–69, 124 S.Ct. 1354. Today's opinion adopts, for emergencies and faux emergencies at least, the discredited logic of *White v. Illinois,* 502 U.S. 346, 355–356, and n. 8, 112 S.Ct. 736, 116 L.Ed.2d 848 (1992), and *Idaho v. Wright,* 497 U.S. 805, 819–820, 110 S.Ct. 3139, 111 L.Ed.2d 638 (1990). *White* is, of course, the decision that both *Crawford* and *Davis* found most incompatible with the text and history of the Confrontation Clause. See *Davis, supra,* at 825, 126 S.Ct. 2266; *Crawford, supra,* at 58, n. 8, 124 S.Ct. 1354. (This is not to say that that "reliability" logic can actually justify today's result: Twenty-five minutes is plenty of time for a shooting victim to reflect and fabricate a false story.)

The Court announces that in future cases it will look to "standard rules of hearsay, designed to identify some statements as reliable," when deciding whether a statement is testimonial. *Ante,* at 1155. *Ohio v. Roberts,* 448 U.S. 56, 100 S.Ct. 2531, 65 L.Ed.2d 597 (1980) said something remarkably similar: An out-of-court statement is admissible if it "falls within a firmly rooted hearsay exception" or otherwise "bears adequate 'indicia of reliability.'" *Id.,* at 66, 100 S.Ct. 2531. We tried that approach to the Confrontation Clause for nearly 25 years before *Crawford rejected* it as an unworkable standard unmoored from the text and the historical roots of the Confrontation Clause. See 541 U.S., at 54, 60, 63–65, 67–68, 124 S.Ct. 1354. The arguments in Raleigh's infamous 17th-century treason trial contained full debate about the reliability of Lord Cobham's *ex parte* accusations, see *Raleigh's Case,* 2 How. St. Tr. 1, 14, 17, 19–20, 22–23, 29 (1603); that case remains the canonical example of a Confrontation Clause violation, not because Raleigh should have won the debate but because he should have been allowed cross-examination.

The Court attempts to fit its resurrected interest in reliability into the *Crawford* framework, but the result is incoherent. Reliability, the Court tells us, is a good indicator of whether "a statement is ... an out-of-court substitute for trial testimony." *Ante,* at 1155. That is patently false. Reliability tells us *nothing* about whether a statement is testimonial. Testimonial and nontestimonial statements alike come in varying degrees of reliability. An eyewitness's statements to the police after a fender-bender, for example, are both reliable and testimonial. Statements to the police from one driver attempting to blame the other would be similarly testimonial but rarely reliable.

The Court suggests otherwise because it "misunderstands the relationship" between qualification for one of the standard hearsay exceptions and exemption from the confrontation requirement. *Melendez-Diaz v. Massachusetts,* 557 U.S. ----, ----, 129 S.Ct. 2527, 2539–2540, 174 L.Ed.2d 314 (2009). That relationship is not a causal one. Hearsay law exempts business records, for example, because businesses have a financial incentive to keep reliable records. See Fed. Rule Evid. 803(6). The Sixth Amendment also generally admits business records into evidence, but not because the records are reliable or because hearsay law says so. It admits them "because—having been created for the administration of an entity's affairs and not for the purpose of establishing or proving some fact at trial—they are not" weaker substitutes for live testimony. *Melendez-Diaz,* 557 U.S., at ----, 129 S.Ct., at 2539–2540. Moreover, the scope of the exemption from confrontation and that of the hearsay exceptions also are not always coextensive. The reliability logic of the business-record exception would extend to records maintained by neutral parties providing litigation-support services, such as evidence testing. The Confrontation Clause is not so forgiving. Business records prepared specifically for use at a criminal trial are testimonial and require confrontation. See *ibid.*

Is it possible that the Court does not recognize the contradiction between its focus on reliable statements and *Crawford*'s focus on testimonial ones? Does it not realize that the two cannot coexist? Or does it intend, by following today's illogical roadmap, to resurrect *Roberts* by a thousand unprincipled distinctions without ever explicitly overruling *Crawford?* After all, honestly overruling *Crawford* would destroy the illusion of judicial minimalism and restraint. And it would force the Court to explain how the Justices' preference comports with the meaning of the Confrontation Clause that the People adopted—or to confess that only the Justices' preference really matters.

B

The Court recedes from *Crawford* in a second significant way. It requires judges to conduct "open-ended balancing tests" and "amorphous, if not entirely subjective," inquiries into the totality of the circumstances bearing upon reliability. 541 U.S., at 63, 68, 124 S.Ct. 1354. Where the prosecution cries "emergency," the admissibility of a statement now turns on "a highly context-dependent inquiry," *ante,* at 1158, into the type of weapon the defendant wielded, see *ante,* at 1158–1159; the type of crime the defendant committed, see *ante,* at 1156, 1158–1159; the medical condition of the declarant, see *ante,* at 1158–1159; if the declarant is injured, whether paramedics have arrived on the scene, see *ante,* at 1160; whether the encounter takes place in an "exposed public area," *ibid.*; whether the encounter appears disorganized, see *ibid.*; whether the declarant is capable of forming a purpose, see *ante,* at 1161–1162; whether the police have secured the scene of the crime, see *ante,* at 1164–1165; the formality of the statement, see *ante,* at 1160; and finally, whether the statement strikes us as reliable, see *ante,* at 1155–1156, 1157. This is no better than the nine-factor balancing test we rejected in *Crawford,* 541 U.S., at 63, 124 S.Ct. 1354. I do not look forward to resolving conflicts in the future over whether knives and poison are more like guns or fists for Confrontation Clause purposes, or whether rape and armed robbery are more like murder or domestic violence.

It can be said, of course, that under *Crawford* analysis of whether a statement is testimonial requires consideration of all the circumstances, and so is also something of a multifactor balancing test. But the "reliability" test does not replace that analysis; it supplements it. As I understand the Court's opinion, even when it is determined that no emergency exists (or perhaps before that determination is made) the statement would be found admissible as far as the Confrontation Clause is concerned if it is not testimonial.

In any case, we did not disavow multifactor balancing for reliability in *Crawford* out of a preference for rules over standards. We did so because it "d[id] violence to" the Framers' design. *Id.,* at 68, 124 S.Ct. 1354. It was judges' open-ended determination of what was reliable that violated the trial rights of Englishmen in the political trials of the 16th and 17th centuries. See, *e.g., Throckmorton's Case,* 1 How. St. Tr. 869, 875–876 (1554); *Raleigh's Case,* 2 How. St. Tr., at 15–16, 24. The Framers placed the Confrontation Clause in the Bill of Rights to ensure that those abuses (and the abuses by the Admiralty courts in colonial America) would not be repeated in this country. Not even the least dangerous branch can be trusted to assess the reliability of uncross-examined testimony in politically charged trials or trials implicating threats to national security. See *Crawford, supra,* at 67–68, 124 S.Ct. 1354; cf. *Hamdi v. Rumsfeld,* 542 U.S. 507, 576–578, 124 S.Ct. 2633, 159 L.Ed.2d 578 (2004) (Scalia, J., dissenting).

* * *

Judicial decisions, like the Constitution itself, are nothing more than "parchment barriers," 5 *Writings of James Madison* 269, 272 (G. Hunt ed.1901). Both depend on a judicial culture that understands its constitutionally assigned role, has the courage to persist in that role when it means announcing unpopular decisions, and has the modesty to persist when it produces results that go against the judges' policy preferences. Today's opinion falls far short of living up to that obligation—short on the facts, and short on the law.

For all I know, Bryant has received his just deserts. But he surely has not received them pursuant to the procedures that our Constitution requires. And what has been taken away from him has been taken away from us all.

Open your mouth for inspection: grievous and oppressive searches

Maryland v. King, 133 S.Ct. 1958 (2013)

Justice Scalia, with whom Justice Ginsburg, Justice Sotomayor, and Justice Kagan join, dissenting.

The Fourth Amendment forbids searching a person for evidence of a crime when there is no basis for believing the person is guilty of the crime or is in possession of incriminating evidence. That prohibition is categorical and without exception; it lies at the very heart of the Fourth Amendment. Whenever this Court has allowed a suspicionless search, it has insisted upon a justifying motive apart from the investigation of crime.

It is obvious that no such noninvestigative motive exists in this case. The Court's assertion that DNA is being taken, not to solve crimes, but to *identify* those in the State's custody, taxes the credulity of the credulous. And the Court's comparison of Maryland's DNA searches to other techniques, such as fingerprinting, can seem apt only to those who know no more than today's opinion has chosen to tell them about how those DNA searches actually work.

I

A

At the time of the Founding, Americans despised the British use of so-called "general warrants"—warrants not grounded upon a sworn oath of a specific infraction by a particular individual, and thus not limited in scope and application. The first Virginia Constitution declared that "general warrants, whereby any officer or messenger may be commanded to search suspected places without evidence of a fact committed," or to search a person "whose offence is not particularly described and supported by evidence," "are grievous and oppressive, and ought not be granted." Va. Declaration of Rights § 10 (1776), in 1 B. Schwartz, *The Bill of Rights: A Documentary History* 234, 235 (1971). The Maryland Declaration of Rights similarly provided that general warrants were "illegal." Md. Declaration of Rights § XXIII (1776), in *id.*, at 280, 282.

In the ratification debates, Antifederalists sarcastically predicted that the general, suspicionless warrant would be among the Constitution's "blessings." "Blessings of the New Government," *Independent Gazetteer*, Oct. 6, 1787, in 13 *Documentary History of the Ratification of the Constitution* 345 (J. Kaminski & G. Saladino eds. 1981). "Brutus" of New York asked why the Federal Constitution contained no provision like Maryland's, "Brutus II," *N.Y. Journal*, Nov. 1, 1787, in *id.*, at 524, and Patrick Henry warned that the new Federal Constitution would expose the citizenry to searches and seizures "in the most arbitrary manner, without any evidence or reason." 3 *Debates on the Federal Constitution* 588 (J. Elliot 2d ed. 1854).

Madison's draft of what became the Fourth Amendment answered these charges by providing that the "rights of the people to be secured in their persons ... from all unreasonable searches and seizures, shall not be violated by warrants issued without probable cause ... or not particularly describing the places to be searched." 1 Annals of Cong. 434–435 (1789). As ratified, the Fourth Amendment's Warrant Clause forbids a warrant to "issue" except "upon probable cause," and requires that it be "particula[r]" (which is to say, *individualized*) to "the place to be searched, and the persons or things to be seized." And we have held that, even when a warrant is not constitutionally necessary, the Fourth Amendment's general prohibition of "unreasonable" searches imports the same requirement of individualized suspicion. See *Chandler v. Miller,* 520 U.S. 305, 308, 117 S.Ct. 1295, 137 L.Ed.2d 513 (1997).

Although there is a "closely guarded category of constitutionally permissible suspicionless searches," *id.,* at 309, 117 S.Ct. 1295, that has never included searches designed to serve "the normal need for law enforcement," *Skinner v. Railway Labor Executives' Assn.,* 489 U.S. 602, 619, 109 S.Ct. 1402, 103 L.Ed.2d 639 (1989) (internal quotation marks omitted). Even the common name for suspicionless searches—"special needs" searches—itself reflects that they must be justified, *always,* by concerns "other than crime detection." *Chandler, supra,* at 313–314, 117 S.Ct. 1295. We have approved random drug tests of railroad employees, yes—but only because the Government's need to "regulat[e] the conduct of railroad employees to ensure safety" is distinct from "normal law enforcement." *Skinner, supra,* at 620, 109 S.Ct. 1402. So too we have approved suspicionless searches in public schools—but only because there the government acts in furtherance of its "responsibilities ... as guardian and tutor of children entrusted to its care." *Vernonia School Dist. 47J v. Acton,* 515 U.S. 646, 665, 115 S.Ct. 2386, 132 L.Ed.2d 564 (1995).

So while the Court is correct to note (*ante,* at 1969–1970) that there are instances in which we have permitted searches without individualized suspicion, "[i]n none of these cases ... did we indicate approval of a [search] whose primary purpose was to detect evidence of ordinary criminal wrongdoing." *Indianapolis v. Edmond,* 531 U.S. 32, 38, 121 S.Ct. 447, 148 L.Ed.2d 333 (2000). That limitation is crucial. It is only when a governmental purpose aside from crime-solving is at stake that we engage in the free-form "reasonableness" inquiry that the Court indulges at length today. To put it another way, both the legitimacy of the Court's method and the correctness of its outcome hinge entirely on the truth of a single proposition: that the primary purpose of these DNA searches is something other than simply discovering evidence of criminal wrongdoing. As I detail below, that proposition is wrong.

B

The Court alludes at several points (see *ante,* at 1970–1971, 1978–1979) to the fact that King was an arrestee, and arrestees may be validly searched incident to their arrest. But the Court does not really *rest* on this principle, and for good reason: The objects of a search incident to arrest must be either (1) weapons or evidence that might easily be destroyed, or (2) evidence relevant to the crime of arrest. See *Arizona v. Gant,* 556 U.S. 332, 343–344, 129 S.Ct. 1710, 173 L.Ed.2d 485 (2009); *Thornton v. United States,* 541 U.S. 615, 632, 124 S.Ct. 2127, 158 L.Ed.2d 905 (2004) (Scalia, J., concurring in judgment). Neither is the object of the search at issue here.

The Court hastens to clarify that it does not mean to approve invasive surgery on arrestees or warrantless searches of their homes. *Ante,* at 1978–1979. That the Court feels the need to disclaim these consequences is as damning a criticism of its suspicionless-search regime as any I can muster. And the Court's attempt to distinguish those hypothetical searches from this real one is unconvincing. We are told that the "privacy-related concerns" in the search of a home "are weighty enough that the search may require a warrant, notwithstanding the diminished expectations of privacy of the arrestee." *Ante,* at 1979. But why are the "privacy-related concerns" not also "weighty" when an intrusion into the *body* is at stake? (The Fourth Amendment lists "persons" *first* among the entities protected against unreasonable searches and seizures.) And could the police engage, without any suspicion of wrongdoing, in a "brief and ... minimal" intrusion into the home of an arrestee—perhaps just peeking around the curtilage a bit? See *ante,* at 1979. Obviously not.

At any rate, all this discussion is beside the point. No matter the degree of invasiveness, suspicionless searches are *never* allowed if their principal end is ordinary crime-solving. A search incident to arrest either serves other ends (such as officer safety, in a search for weapons) or is not suspicionless (as when there is reason to believe the arrestee possesses evidence relevant to the crime of arrest).

Sensing (correctly) that it needs more, the Court elaborates at length the ways that the search here served the special purpose of "identifying" King. But that seems to me quite wrong—unless what one means by "identifying" someone is "searching for evidence that he has committed crimes unrelated to the crime of his arrest." At points the Court does appear to use "identifying" in that peculiar sense—claiming, for example, that knowing "an arrestee's past conduct is essential to an assessment of the danger he poses." *Ante,* at 1973. If identifying someone means finding out what unsolved crimes he has committed, then identification is indistinguishable from the ordinary law-enforcement aims that have never been thought to justify a suspicionless search. Searching every lawfully stopped car, for example, might turn up information about unsolved crimes the driver had committed, but no one would say that such a search was aimed at "identifying" him, and no court would hold such a search lawful. I will therefore assume that the Court means that the DNA search at issue here was useful to "identify" King in the normal sense of that word—in the sense that would identify the author of *Introduction to the Principles of Morals and Legislation* as Jeremy Bentham.

1

The portion of the Court's opinion that explains the identification rationale is strangely silent on the actual workings of the DNA search at issue here. To know those facts is to be instantly disabused of the notion that what happened had anything to do with identifying King.

King was arrested on April 10, 2009, on charges unrelated to the case before us. That same day, April 10, the police searched him and seized the DNA evidence at issue here. What happened next? Reading the Court's opinion, particularly its insistence that the search was necessary to know "who [had] been arrested," *ante*, at 1971, one might guess that King's DNA was swiftly processed and his identity thereby confirmed—perhaps against some master database of known DNA profiles, as is done for fingerprints. After all, was not the suspicionless search here crucial to avoid "inordinate risks for facility staff" or to "existing detainee population," *ante*, at 1972? Surely, then—*surely*—the State of Maryland got cracking on those grave risks immediately, by rushing to identify King with his DNA as soon as possible.

Nothing could be further from the truth. Maryland officials did not even begin the process of testing King's DNA that day. Or, actually, the next day. Or the day after that. And that was for a simple reason: Maryland law forbids them to do so. A "DNA sample collected from an individual charged with a crime ... *may not* be tested or placed in the statewide DNA data base system prior to the first scheduled arraignment date." Md. Pub. Saf. Code Ann. § 2-504(d)(1) (Lexis 2011) (emphasis added). And King's first appearance in court was not until three days after his arrest. (I suspect, though, that they did not wait three days to ask his name or take his fingerprints.)

This places in a rather different light the Court's solemn declaration that the search here was necessary so that King could be identified at "every stage of the criminal process." *Ante,* at 1974. I hope that the Maryland officials who read the Court's opinion do not take it seriously. Acting on the Court's misperception of Maryland law could lead to jail time. See Md. Pub. Saf. Code Ann. § 2-512(c)–(e) (punishing by up to five years' imprisonment anyone who obtains or tests DNA information except as provided by statute). Does the Court really believe that Maryland did not know whom it was arraigning? The Court's response is to imagine that release on bail could take so long that the DNA results are returned in time, or perhaps that bail could be revoked if the DNA test turned up incriminating information. *Ante,* at 1973–1974. That is no answer at all. If the purpose of this Act is to assess "whether [King] should be released on bail," *ante,* at 1973, why would it *possibly* forbid the DNA testing process to *begin* until King was arraigned? Why would Maryland resign itself to simply hoping that the bail decision will drag out long enough that the "identification" can succeed before the arrestee is released? The truth, known to Maryland and increasingly to the reader: this search had nothing to do with establishing King's identity.

It gets worse. King's DNA sample was not received by the Maryland State Police's Forensic Sciences Division until April 23, 2009—two weeks after his arrest. It sat in that office, ripening in a storage area, until the custodians got around to mailing it to a lab for testing on June 25, 2009—two months after it was received, and nearly *three* since King's arrest. After it was mailed, the data from the lab tests were not available for several more weeks, until July 13, 2009, which is when the test results were entered into Maryland's DNA database, *together with information identifying the person from whom the sample was taken.* Meanwhile, bail had been set, King had engaged in discovery, and he had requested a speedy trial—presumably not a trial of John Doe. It was not until August 4, 2009—four months after King's arrest—that the forwarded sample transmitted (*without* identifying information) from the Maryland DNA database to the Federal Bureau of Investigation's national database was matched with a sample taken from the scene of an unrelated crime years earlier.

A more specific description of exactly what happened at this point illustrates why, by definition, King could not have been *identified* by this match. The FBI's DNA database (known as CODIS) consists of two distinct collections. FBI, CODIS and NDIS Fact Sheet, http://www.fbi.gov/about-us/lab/codis/codis-and-ndis-fact-sheet (all Internet materials as visited May 31, 2013, and available in Clerk of Court's case file). One of them, the one to which King's DNA was submitted, consists of DNA samples taken from known convicts or arrestees. I will refer to this as the "Convict and Arrestee Collection." The other collection consists of samples taken from crime scenes; I will refer to this as the "Unsolved Crimes Collection." The Convict and Arrestee Collection stores "no names or other personal identifiers of the offenders, arrestees, or detainees." *Ibid.* Rather, it contains only the DNA profile itself, the name of the agency that submitted it, the laboratory personnel who analyzed it, and an identification number for the specimen. *Ibid.* This is because the submitting state laboratories are expected *already* to know the identities of the convicts and arrestees from whom samples are taken. (And, of course, they do.)

Moreover, the CODIS system works by checking to see whether any of the samples in the Unsolved Crimes Collection match any of the samples in the Convict and Arrestee Collection. *Ibid.* That is sensible, if what one wants to do is solve those cold cases, but note what it requires: that the identity of the people whose DNA has been entered in the Convict and Arrestee Collection *already be known*. If one wanted to identify someone in custody using his DNA, the logical thing to do would be to compare that DNA against the Convict and Arrestee Collection: to search, in other words, the collection that could be used (by checking back with the submitting state agency) to identify people, rather than the collection of evidence from unsolved crimes, whose perpetrators are by definition unknown. But that is not what was done. And that is because this search had nothing to do with identification.

In fact, if anything was "identified" at the moment that the DNA database returned a match, it was not King—his identity was already known. (The docket for the original criminal charges lists his full name, his race, his sex, his height, his weight, his date of birth, and his address.) Rather, what the August 4 match "identified" was *the previously-taken sample from the earlier crime.* That sample was genuinely mysterious to Maryland; the State knew that it had probably been left by the victim's attacker, but nothing else. King was not identified by his association with the sample; rather, the sample was identified by its association with King. The Court effectively destroys its own "identification" theory when it acknowledges that the object of this search was "to see what [was] already known about [King]." King was who he was, and volumes of his biography could not make him any more or any less King. No minimally competent speaker of English would say, upon noticing a known arrestee's similarity "to a wanted poster of a previously unidentified suspect," *ante,* at 1972, that the *arrestee* had thereby been identified. It was the previously unidentified suspect who had been identified—just as, here, it was the previously unidentified rapist.

2

That taking DNA samples from arrestees has nothing to do with identifying them is confirmed not just by actual practice (which the Court ignores) but by the enabling statute itself (which the Court also ignores). The Maryland Act at issue has a section helpfully entitled "Purpose of collecting and testing DNA samples." Md. Pub. Saf. Code Ann. § 2-505. (One would expect such a section to play a somewhat larger role in the Court's analysis of the Act's purpose—which is to say, at least *some* role.) That provision lists five purposes for which DNA samples may be tested. By this point, it will not surprise the reader to learn that the Court's imagined purpose is not among them.

Instead, the law provides that DNA samples are collected and tested, as a matter of Maryland law, "as part of an official investigation into a crime." § 2-505(a)(2). (Or, as our suspicionless-search cases would put it: for ordinary law-enforcement purposes.) That is certainly how everyone has always understood the Maryland Act until today. The Governor of Maryland, in commenting on our decision to hear this case, said that he was glad, because "[a]llowing law enforcement to collect DNA samples ... is absolutely critical to our efforts to continue driving down crime," and "bolsters our efforts to resolve open investigations and bring them to a resolution." Marbella, "Supreme Court Will Review Md. DNA Law," *Baltimore Sun*, Nov. 10, 2012, pp. 1, 14. The attorney general of Maryland remarked that he "look[ed] forward to the opportunity to defend this important crime-fighting tool," and praised the DNA database for helping to "bring to justice violent perpetrators." *Ibid.* Even this Court's order staying the decision below states that the statute "provides a valuable tool for investigating unsolved crimes and thereby helping to remove violent offenders from the general population"—with, unsurprisingly, no mention of identity. 567 U.S. ----, ----, 133 S.Ct. 1, 3, 183 L.Ed.2d 667 (2012) (ROBERTS, C.J., in chambers).

More devastating still for the Court's "identification" theory, the statute *does* enumerate two instances in which a DNA sample may be tested for the purpose of identification: "to help identify *human remains,*" § 2-505(a)(3) (emphasis added), and "to help identify *missing individuals,*" § 2-505(a)(4) (emphasis added). No mention of identifying arrestees. *Inclusio unius est exclusio alterius.* And note again that Maryland forbids using DNA records "for any purposes other than those specified"—it is actually a crime to do so. § 2-505(b)(2).

The Maryland regulations implementing the Act confirm what is now monotonously obvious: These DNA searches have nothing to do with identification. For example, if someone is arrested and law enforcement determines that "a convicted offender Statewide DNA Data Base sample already exists" for that arrestee, "the agency is not required to obtain a new sample." Code of Md. Regs., tit. 29, § 05.01.04(B)(4) (2011). But how could the State know if an arrestee has already had his DNA sample collected, if the point of the sample is to identify who he is? Of course, if the DNA sample is instead taken in order to investigate crimes, this restriction makes perfect sense: Having previously placed an identified someone's DNA on file to check against available crime-scene evidence, there is no sense in going to the expense of taking a new sample. Maryland's regulations further require that the "individual collecting a sample ... verify the identity of the individual from whom a sample is taken by name and, if applicable, State identification (SID) number." § 05.01.04(K). (But how?) And after the sample is taken, it continues to be identified *by* the individual's name, fingerprints, etc., see § 05.01.07(B)—rather than (as the Court believes) being used *to identify* individuals. See § 05.01.07(B)(2) ("Records and specimen information shall *be identified by* ... [the] [n]ame of the donor" (emphasis added)).

So, to review: DNA testing does not even begin until after arraignment and bail decisions are already made. The samples sit in storage for months, and take weeks to test. When they are tested, they are checked against the Unsolved Crimes Collection—rather than the Convict and Arrestee Collection, which could be used to identify them. The Act forbids the Court's purpose (identification), but prescribes as its purpose what our suspicionless-search cases forbid ("official investigation into a crime"). Against all of that, it is safe to say that if the Court's identification theory is not wrong, there is no such thing as error.

II

The Court also attempts to bolster its identification theory with a series of inapposite analogies. See *ante,* at 1974–1977.

Is not taking DNA samples the same, asks the Court, as taking a person's photograph? No—because that is not a Fourth Amendment search at all. It does not involve a physical intrusion onto the person, see *Florida v. Jardines,* 569 U.S. 1, ----, 133 S.Ct. 1409, 1413–1414, 185 L.Ed.2d 495 (2013), and we have never held that merely taking a person's photograph invades any recognized "expectation of privacy," see *Katz v. United States,* 389 U.S. 347, 88 S.Ct. 507, 19 L.Ed.2d 576 (1967). Thus, it is unsurprising that the cases the Court cites as authorizing photo-taking do not even mention the Fourth Amendment. See *State ex rel. Bruns v. Clausmier,* 154 Ind. 599, 57 N.E. 541 (1900) (libel), *Shaffer v. United States,* 24 App.D.C. 417 (1904) (Fifth Amendment privilege against self-incrimination).

But is not the practice of DNA searches, the Court asks, the same as taking "Bertillon" measurements—noting an arrestee's height, shoe size, and so on, on the back of a photograph? No, because that system was not, in the ordinary case, used to solve unsolved crimes. It is possible, I suppose, to imagine situations in which such measurements might be useful to generate leads. (If witnesses described a very tall burglar, all the "tall man" cards could then be pulled.) But the obvious primary purpose of such measurements, as the Court's description of them makes clear, was to verify that, for example, the person arrested today is the same person that was arrested a year ago. Which is to say, Bertillon measurements were *actually* used as a system of identification, and drew their primary usefulness from that task.

It is on the fingerprinting of arrestees, however, that the Court relies most heavily. *Ante,* at 1975–1977. The Court does not actually say whether it believes that taking a person's fingerprints is a Fourth Amendment search, and our cases provide no ready answer to that question. Even assuming so, however, law enforcement's post-arrest use of fingerprints could not be more different from its post-arrest use of DNA. Fingerprints of arrestees are taken primarily to identify them (though that process sometimes solves crimes); the DNA of arrestees is taken to solve crimes (and nothing else). Contrast CODIS, the FBI's nationwide DNA database, with IAFIS, the FBI's Integrated Automated Fingerprint Identification System. See FBI, Integrated Automated Fingerprint Identification System, http://www.fbi.gov/about-us/cjis/fingerprints_biometrics/iafis/iafis (hereinafter *IAFIS*).

Fingerprints	DNA Samples
The "average response time for an electronic criminal fingerprint submission is about 27 minutes." *IAFIS.*	DNA analysis can take months—far too long to be useful for identifying someone.
IAFIS includes detailed identification information, including "criminal histories; mug shots; scars and tattoo photos; physical characteris tics like height, weight, and hair and eye color."	CODIS contains "[n]o names or other personal identifiers of the offenders, arrestees, or detainees." See CODIS and NDIS Fact Sheet.
"Latent prints" recovered from crime scenes are not systematically compared against the database of known fingerprints, since that requires further forensic work.	The entire *point* of the DNA database is to check crime scene evidence against the profiles of arrestees and convicts as they come in.

The Court asserts that the taking of fingerprints was "constitutional for generations prior to the introduction" of the FBI's rapid computer-matching system. *Ante,* at 1977. This bold statement is bereft of citation to authority because there is none for it. The "great expansion in fingerprinting came before the modern era of Fourth Amendment jurisprudence," and so we were never asked to decide the legitimacy of the practice. *United States v. Kincade,* 379 F.3d 813, 874 (C.A.9 2004) (Kozinski, J., dissenting). As fingerprint databases expanded from convicted criminals, to arrestees, to civil servants, to immigrants, to everyone with a driver's license, Americans simply "became accustomed to having our fingerprints on file in some government database." *Ibid.* But it is wrong to suggest that this was uncontroversial at the time, or that this Court blessed universal fingerprinting for "generations" before it was possible to use it effectively for identification.

The Court also assures us that "the delay in processing DNA from arrestees is being reduced to a substantial degree by rapid technical advances." *Ante,* at 1977. The idea, presumably, is that the snail's pace in this case is atypical, so that DNA is now readily usable for identification. The Court's proof, however, is nothing but a pair of press releases—each of which turns out to undercut this argument. We learn in them that reductions in backlog have enabled Ohio and Louisiana crime labs to analyze a submitted DNA sample in twenty days. But that is *still longer* than the *eighteen* days that Maryland needed to analyze King's sample, once it worked its way through the State's labyrinthine bureaucracy. What this illustrates is that these times do not take into account the many other sources of delay. So if the Court means to suggest that Maryland is unusual, that may be right—it may qualify in this context as a paragon of efficiency. (Indeed, the Governor of Maryland was hailing the elimination of that State's backlog more than five years ago. See Wheeler, "O'Malley Wants to Expand DNA Testing," *Baltimore Sun,* Jan. 11, 2008, p. 5B.) Meanwhile, the Court's holding will result in the dumping of a large number of arrestee samples—many from minor offenders—onto an already overburdened system: Nearly one-third of Americans will be arrested for some offense by age 23. See Brame, Turner, Paternoster, & Bushway, "Cumulative Prevalence of Arrest From Ages 8 to 23 in a National Sample," 129 *Pediatrics* 21 (2011).

The Court also accepts uncritically the Government's representation at oral argument that it is developing devices that will be able to test DNA in mere minutes. At most, this demonstrates that it may one day be possible to design a program that uses DNA for a purpose other than crime-solving—not that Maryland has in fact designed such a program today. And that is the main point, which the Court's discussion of the brave new world of instant DNA analysis should not obscure. The issue before us is not whether DNA can *some day* be used for identification; nor even whether it can *today* be used for identification; but whether it *was used for identification here.*

Today, it can fairly be said that fingerprints really are used to identify people—so well, in fact, that there would be no need for the expense of a separate, wholly redundant DNA confirmation of the same information. What DNA adds—what makes it a valuable weapon in the law-enforcement arsenal—is the ability to solve unsolved crimes, by matching old crime-scene evidence against the profiles of people whose identities are already known. That is what was going on when King's DNA was taken, and we should not disguise the fact. Solving unsolved crimes is a noble objective, but it occupies a lower place in the American pantheon of noble objectives than the protection of our people from suspicionless law-enforcement searches. The Fourth Amendment must prevail.

* * *

The Court disguises the vast (and scary) scope of its holding by promising a limitation it cannot deliver. The Court repeatedly says that DNA testing, and entry into a national DNA registry, will not befall thee and me, dear reader, but only those arrested for "serious offense[s]." *Ante,* at 1979–1980; see also *ante,* at 1965, 1969–1970, 1972–1973, 1974, 1976–1977, 1977, 1977–1978 (repeatedly limiting the analysis to "serious offenses"). I cannot imagine what principle could possibly justify this limitation, and the Court does not attempt to suggest any. If one believes that DNA will "identify" someone arrested for assault, he must believe that it will "identify" someone arrested for a traffic offense. This Court does not base its judgments on senseless distinctions. At the end of the day, *logic will out.* When there comes before us the taking of DNA from an arrestee for a traffic violation, the Court will predictably (and quite rightly) say, "We can find no significant difference between this case and *King.*" Make no mistake about it: As an entirely predictable consequence of today's decision, your DNA can be taken and entered into a national DNA database if you are ever arrested, rightly or wrongly, and for whatever reason.

The most regrettable aspect of the suspicionless search that occurred here is that it proved to be quite unnecessary. All parties concede that it would have been entirely permissible, as far as the Fourth Amendment is concerned, for Maryland to take a sample of King's DNA as a consequence of his conviction for second-degree assault. So the ironic result of the Court's error is this: The only arrestees to whom the outcome here will ever make a difference are those who *have been acquitted* of the crime of arrest (so that their DNA could not have been taken upon conviction). In other words, this Act manages to burden uniquely the sole group for whom the Fourth Amendment's protections ought to be most jealously guarded: people who are innocent of the State's accusations.

Today's judgment will, to be sure, have the beneficial effect of solving more crimes; then again, so would the taking of DNA samples from anyone who flies on an airplane (surely the Transportation Security Administration needs to know the "identity" of the flying public), applies for a driver's license, or attends a public school. Perhaps the construction of such a genetic panopticon is wise. But I doubt that the proud men who wrote the charter of our liberties would have been so eager to open their mouths for royal inspection.

I therefore dissent, and hope that today's incursion upon the Fourth Amendment, like an earlier one, will someday be repudiated.

Do drunk drivers drive drunkenly?

Navarette v. California,

134 S.Ct. 1683 (2014)

Justice Scalia, with whom Justice Ginsburg, Justice Sotomayor, and Justice Kagan join, dissenting.

The California Court of Appeal in this case relied on jurisprudence from the California Supreme Court (adopted as well by other courts) to the effect that "an anonymous and uncorroborated tip regarding a possibly intoxicated highway driver" provides without more the reasonable suspicion necessary to justify a stop. *People v. Wells,* 38 Cal.4th 1078, 1082, 45 Cal.Rptr.3d 8, 136 P.3d 810, 812 (2006). See also, *e.g., United States v. Wheat,* 278 F.3d 722, 729–730 (C.A.8 2001); *State v. Walshire,* 634 N.W.2d 625, 626–627, 630 (Iowa 2001). Today's opinion does not explicitly adopt such a departure from our normal Fourth Amendment requirement that anonymous tips must be corroborated; it purports to adhere to our prior cases, such as *Florida v. J. L.,* 529 U.S. 266, 120 S.Ct. 1375, 146 L.Ed.2d 254 (2000), and *Alabama v. White,* 496 U.S. 325, 110 S.Ct. 2412, 110 L.Ed.2d 301 (1990). Be not deceived.

Law enforcement agencies follow closely our judgments on matters such as this, and they will identify at once our new rule: So long as the caller identifies where the car is, anonymous claims of a single instance of possibly careless or reckless driving, called in to 911, will support a traffic stop. This is not my concept, and I am sure would not be the Framers', of a people secure from unreasonable searches and seizures. I would reverse the judgment of the Court of Appeal of California.

I

The California Highway Patrol in this case knew nothing about the tipster on whose word—and that alone—they seized Lorenzo and José Prado Navarette. They did not know her name. They did not know her phone number or address. They did not even know where she called from (she may have dialed in from a neighboring county, App. 33a–34a).

The tipster said the truck had "[run her] off the roadway," *id.,* at 36a, but the police had no reason to credit that charge and many reasons to doubt it, beginning with the peculiar fact that the accusation was anonymous. "[E]liminating accountability ... is ordinarily the very purpose of anonymity." *McIntyre v. Ohio Elections Comm'n,* 514 U.S. 334, 385, 115 S.Ct. 1511, 131 L.Ed.2d 426 (1995) (Scalia, J., dissenting). The unnamed tipster "can lie with impunity," *J. L., supra,* at 275, 120 S.Ct. 1375 (Kennedy, J., concurring). Anonymity is especially suspicious with respect to the call that is the subject of the present case. When does a victim complain to the police about an arguably criminal act (running the victim off the road) without giving his identity, so that he can accuse and testify when the culprit is caught?

The question before us, the Court agrees, *ante,* at 1690 – 1691, is whether the "content of information possessed by police and its degree of reliability," *White,* 496 U.S., at 330, 110 S.Ct. 2412, gave the officers reasonable suspicion that the driver of the truck (Lorenzo) was committing an ongoing crime. When the only source of the government's information is an informant's tip, we ask whether the tip bears sufficient "'indicia of reliability,'" *id.,* at 328, 110 S.Ct. 2412, to establish "a particularized and objective basis for suspecting the particular person stopped of criminal activity," *United States v. Cortez,* 449 U.S. 411, 417–418, 101 S.Ct. 690, 66 L.Ed.2d 621 (1981).

The most extreme case, before this one, in which an anonymous tip was found to meet this standard was *White, supra.* There the reliability of the tip was established by the fact that it predicted the target's behavior in the finest detail—a detail that could be known only by someone familiar with the target's business: She would, the tipster said, leave a particular apartment building, get into a brown Plymouth station wagon with a broken right tail light, and drive immediately to a particular motel. *Id.,* at 327, 110 S.Ct. 2412. Very few persons would have such intimate knowledge, and hence knowledge of the unobservable fact that the woman was carrying unlawful drugs was plausible. *Id.,* at 332, 110 S.Ct. 2412. Here the Court makes a big deal of the fact that the tipster was dead right about the fact that a silver Ford F-150 truck (license plate 8D94925) was traveling south on Highway 1 somewhere near mile marker 88. But everyone in the world who saw the car would have that knowledge, and anyone who wanted the car stopped would have to provide that information. Unlike the situation in *White,* that generally available knowledge in no way makes it plausible that the tipster saw the car run someone off the road.

The Court says, *ante,* at 1689, that "[b]y reporting that she had been run off the road by a specific vehicle ... the caller necessarily claimed eyewitness knowledge." So what? The issue is not how she claimed to know, but whether what she claimed to know was true. The claim to "eyewitness knowledge" of being run off the road supports *not at all* its veracity; nor does the amazing, mystifying prediction (so far short of what existed in *White*) that the petitioners' truck *would be heading south on Highway 1.*

The Court finds "reason to think" that the informant "was telling the truth" in the fact that police observation confirmed that the truck had been driving near the spot at which, and at the approximate time at which, the tipster alleged she had been run off the road. *Ante,* at 1689. According to the Court, the statement therefore qualifies as a "'present sense impression'" or "'excited utterance,'" kinds of hearsay that the law deems categorically admissible given their low likelihood of reflecting "'deliberate or conscious misrepresentation.'" *Ibid.* (quoting Advisory Committee's Notes on Fed. Rule Evid. 803(1), 28 U.S.C.App., p. 371). So, the Court says, we can fairly suppose that the accusation was true.

No, we cannot. To begin with, it is questionable whether either the "present sense impression" or the "excited utterance" exception to the hearsay rule applies here. The classic "present sense impression" is the recounting of an event that is occurring before the declarant's eyes, as the declarant is speaking ("I am watching the Hindenburg explode!"). See 2 K. Broun, *McCormick on Evidence* 362 (7th ed. 2013) (hereinafter *McCormick*). And the classic "excited utterance" is a statement elicited, almost involuntarily, by the shock of what the declarant is immediately witnessing ("My God, those people will be killed!"). See *id.*, at 368–369. It is the immediacy that gives the statement some credibility; the declarant has not had time to dissemble or embellish. There is no such immediacy here. The declarant had time to observe the license number of the offending vehicle, 8D94925 (a difficult task if she was forced off the road and the vehicle was speeding away), to bring her car to a halt, to copy down the observed license number (presumably), and (if she was using her own cell phone) to dial a call to the police from the stopped car. Plenty of time to dissemble or embellish.

Moreover, even assuming that less than true immediacy will suffice for these hearsay exceptions to apply, the tipster's statement would run into additional barriers to admissibility and acceptance. According to the very Advisory Committee's Notes from which the Court quotes, cases addressing an unidentified declarant's present sense impression "indicate hesitancy in upholding the statement alone as sufficient" proof of the reported event. 28 U.S.C.App., at 371; see also 7 M. Graham, *Handbook of Federal Evidence* 19–20 (7th ed.2012). For excited utterances as well, the "knotty theoretical" question of statement-alone admissibility persists—seemingly even when the declarant is known. 2 *McCormick* 368. "Some courts ... have taken the position that an excited utterance is admissible only if other proof is presented which supports a finding of fact that the exciting event did occur. The issue has not yet been resolved under the Federal Rules." *Id.,* at 367–368 (footnote omitted). It is even unsettled whether excited utterances of an unknown declarant are *ever* admissible. A leading treatise reports that "the courts have been reluctant to admit such statements, principally because of uncertainty that foundational requirements, including the impact of the event on the declarant, have been satisfied." *Id.,* at 372. In sum, it is unlikely that the law of evidence would deem the mystery caller in this case "especially trustworthy," *ante,* at 1689.

Finally, and least tenably, the Court says that another "indicator of veracity" is the anonymous tipster's mere "use of the 911 emergency system," *ante,* at 1689. Because, you see, recent "technological and regulatory developments" suggest that the identities of unnamed 911 callers are increasingly less likely to remain unknown. *Ibid.* Indeed, the systems are able to identify "the caller's geographic location with increasing specificity." *Ibid. Amici* disagree with this, see Brief for National Association of Criminal Defense Lawyers et al. 8–12, and the present case surely suggests that *amici* are right—since we know neither the identity of the tipster nor even the county from which the call was made. But assuming the Court is right about the ease of identifying 911 callers, it proves absolutely nothing in the present case unless the anonymous caller was *aware* of that fact. "It is the tipster's *belief* in anonymity, not its *reality*, that will control his behavior." *Id.*, at 10 (emphasis added). There is no reason to believe that your average anonymous 911 tipster is aware that 911 callers are readily identifiable.

II

All that has been said up to now assumes that the anonymous caller made, at least in effect, an accusation of drunken driving. But in fact she did not. She said that the petitioners' truck "'[r]an [me] off the roadway.'" App. 36a. That neither asserts that the driver was drunk nor even raises the *likelihood* that the driver was drunk. The most it conveys is that the truck did some apparently nontypical thing that forced the tipster off the roadway, whether partly or fully, temporarily or permanently. Who really knows what (if anything) happened? The truck might have swerved to avoid an animal, a pothole, or a jaywalking pedestrian.

But let us assume the worst of the many possibilities: that it was a careless, reckless, or even intentional maneuver that forced the tipster off the road. Lorenzo might have been distracted by his use of a hands-free cell phone, see Strayer, Drews, & Crouch, "A Comparison of the Cell Phone Driver and the Drunk Driver," 48 *Human Factors* 381, 388 (2006), or distracted by an intense sports argument with Jose, see D. Strayer et al., AAA Foundation for Traffic Safety, Measuring Cognitive Distraction in the Automobile 28 (June 2013), online at https://www.aaafoundation.org/sites/default/files/MeasuringCognitiveDistractions.pdf as visited Apr. 17, 2014, and available in Clerk of Court's case file). Or, indeed, he might have intentionally forced the tipster off the road because of some personal animus, or hostility to her "Make Love, Not War" bumper sticker. I fail to see how reasonable suspicion of a *discrete instance* of irregular or hazardous driving generates a reasonable suspicion of *ongoing intoxicated driving.* What proportion of the hundreds of thousands—perhaps millions—of careless, reckless, or intentional traffic violations committed each day is attributable to drunken drivers? I say 0.1 percent. I have no basis for that except my own guesswork. But unless the Court has some basis in reality to believe that the proportion is many orders of magnitude above that—say 1 in 10 or at least 1 in 20—it has no grounds for its unsupported assertion that the tipster's report in this case gave rise to a *reasonable suspicion* of drunken driving.

Bear in mind that that is the only basis for the stop that has been asserted in this litigation. The stop required suspicion of an ongoing crime, not merely suspicion of having run someone off the road earlier. And driving while being a careless or reckless person, unlike driving while being a drunk person, is not an ongoing crime. In other words, in order to stop the petitioners the officers here not only had to assume without basis the accuracy of the anonymous accusation but also had to posit an unlikely reason (drunkenness) for the accused behavior.

In sum, at the moment the police spotted the truck, it was more than merely "*possib*[*le*]" that the petitioners were not committing an ongoing traffic crime. *United States v. Arvizu,* 534 U.S. 266, 277, 122 S.Ct. 744, 151 L.Ed.2d 740 (2002) (emphasis added). It was overwhelmingly likely that they were not.

III

It gets worse. Not only, it turns out, did the police have no good reason *at first* to believe that Lorenzo was driving drunk, they had very good reason *at last* to know that he was not. The Court concludes that the tip, plus confirmation of the truck's location, produced reasonable suspicion that the truck not only had been *but still was* barreling dangerously and drunkenly down Highway 1. *Ante,* at 1690–1692. In fact, alas, it was not, and the officers knew it. They followed the truck for five minutes, presumably to see if it was being operated recklessly. And *that* was good police work. While the anonymous tip was not enough to support a stop for drunken driving under *Terry v. Ohio,* 392 U.S. 1, 88 S.Ct. 1868, 20 L.Ed.2d 889 (1968), it was surely enough to counsel observation of the truck to see if it was driven by a drunken driver. But the pesky little detail left out of the Court's reasonable-suspicion equation is that, for the five minutes that the truck was being followed (five minutes is a *long* time), Lorenzo's driving was irreproachable. Had the officers witnessed the petitioners violate a single traffic law, they would have had cause to stop the truck, *Whren v. United States,* 517 U.S. 806, 810, 116 S.Ct. 1769, 135 L.Ed.2d 89 (1996), and this case would not be before us. And not only was the driving *irreproachable,* but the State offers no evidence to suggest that the petitioners even did anything *suspicious,* such as suddenly slowing down, pulling off to the side of the road, or turning somewhere to see whether they were being followed. Cf. *Arvizu, supra,* at 270–271, 277, 122 S.Ct. 744 (concluding that an officer's suspicion of criminality was enhanced when the driver, upon seeing that he was being followed, "slowed dramatically," "appeared stiff," and "seemed to be trying to pretend" that the patrol car was not there). Consequently, the tip's suggestion of ongoing drunken driving (if it could be deemed to suggest that) not only went uncorroborated; it was affirmatively undermined.

A hypothetical variation on the facts of this case illustrates the point. Suppose an anonymous tipster reports that, while following near mile marker 88 a silver Ford F-150, license plate 8D949925, traveling southbound on Highway 1, she saw in the truck's open cab several five-foot-tall stacks of what was unmistakably baled cannabis. Two minutes later, a highway patrolman spots the truck exactly where the tip suggested it would be, begins following it, but sees nothing in the truck's cab. It is not enough to say that the officer's observation merely failed to corroborate the tipster's accusation. It is more precise to say that the officer's observation *discredited* the informant's accusation: The crime was supposedly occurring (and would continue to occur) in plain view, but the police saw nothing. Similarly, here, the crime supposedly suggested by the tip was ongoing intoxicated driving, the hallmarks of which are many, readily identifiable, and difficult to conceal. That the officers witnessed nary a minor traffic violation nor any other "sound indici [um] of drunk driving," *ante*, at 1690, strongly suggests that the suspected crime was *not* occurring after all. The tip's implication of continuing criminality, already weak, grew even weaker.

Resisting this line of reasoning, the Court curiously asserts that, since drunk drivers who see marked squad cars in their rearview mirrors may evade detection simply by driving "more careful[ly]," the "absence of additional suspicious conduct" is "hardly surprising" and thus largely irrelevant. *Ante*, at 1691–1692. Whether a drunk driver drives drunkenly, the Court seems to think, is up to him. That is not how I understand the influence of alcohol. I subscribe to the more traditional view that the dangers of intoxicated driving are the intoxicant's impairing effects on the body—effects that no mere act of the will can resist. See, *e.g.*, A. Dasgupta, *The Science of Drinking: How Alcohol Affects Your Body and Mind* 39 (2011) (explaining that the physiological effect of a blood alcohol content between 0.08 and 0.109, for example, is "sever[e] impair[ment]" of "[b]alance, speech, hearing, and reaction time," as well as one's general "ability to drive a motor vehicle"). Consistent with this view, I take it as a fundamental premise of our intoxicated-driving laws that a driver soused enough to swerve once can be expected to swerve again—and soon. If he does not, and if the only evidence of his first episode of irregular driving is a mere inference from an uncorroborated, vague, and nameless tip, then the Fourth Amendment requires that he be left alone.

* * *

The Court's opinion serves up a freedom-destroying cocktail consisting of two parts patent falsity: (1) that anonymous 911 reports of traffic violations are reliable so long as they correctly identify a car and its location, and (2) that a single instance of careless or reckless driving necessarily supports a reasonable suspicion of drunkenness. All the malevolent 911 caller need do is assert a traffic violation, and the targeted car will be stopped, forcibly if necessary, by the police. If the driver turns out not to be drunk (which will almost always be the case), the caller need fear no consequences, even if 911 knows his identity. After all, he never alleged drunkenness, but merely called in a traffic violation—and on that point his word is as good as his victim's.

Drunken driving is a serious matter, but so is the loss of our freedom to come and go as we please without police interference. To prevent and detect murder we do not allow searches without probable cause or targeted *Terry* stops without reasonable suspicion. We should not do so for drunken driving either. After today's opinion all of us on the road, and not just drug dealers, are at risk of having our freedom of movement curtailed on suspicion of drunkenness, based upon a phone tip, true or false, of a single instance of careless driving. I respectfully dissent.

5

SPEECH

No such thing as too much speech
Austin v. Michigan Chamber of Commerce, 494 U.S. 652 (1990)

Mother, may I?
Morse v. Republican Party of Virginia, 517 U.S. 186 (1996)

No sanctuary in the First Amendment
U.S. v. Playboy Entertainment Group, Inc., 529 U.S. 803 (2000)

An Equal Protection Clause for ideas
Williams-Yulee v. Florida Bar, 135 S.Ct. 1656 (2015)

The cases included in this chapter forced the Court to determine the extent and meaning of the First Amendment's guarantee of "free speech." The Constitution prohibits Congress from passing laws "abridging the freedom of speech," but does not state to whom this right belongs nor the extent to which it may be limited. In recent years, in some cases, the Court has taken an expansive view of the First Amendment's coverage and extended it to corporations and other fictional entities, while in others it has taken a more restrictive view and has allowed it to be limited in such cases as *Playboy* and Williams-Yulee. Justice Scalia's dissents contained herein illustrate his vision of the First Amendment, his broad view of its coverage in the political arena and a narrower view of it when dealing with commercial, potentially obscene speech. Justice Scalia encapsulated his views on the breadth of coverage of the

First Amendment in *Austin* when he wrote "that government cannot be trusted to assure, through censorship, the 'fairness' of political debate" and in *Yulee-Williams* when he stated: "The first axiom of the First Amendment is this: As a general rule, the state has no power to ban speech on the basis of its content."

No such thing as too much speech
Austin v. Michigan Chamber of Commerce, 494 U.S. 652 (1990)

Justice Scalia, dissenting.

"Attention all citizens. To assure the fairness of elections by preventing disproportionate expression of the views of any single powerful group, your Government has decided that the following associations of persons shall be prohibited from speaking or writing in support of any candidate: _____." In permitting Michigan to make private corporations the first object of this Orwellian announcement, the Court today endorses the principle that too much speech is an evil that the democratic majority can proscribe. I dissent because that principle is contrary to our case law and incompatible with the absolutely central truth of the First Amendment: that government cannot be trusted to assure, through censorship, the "fairness" of political debate.

I

A

The Court's opinion says that political speech of corporations can be regulated because "[s]tate law grants [them] special advantages," *ante,* at 1397, and because this "unique state-conferred corporate structure ... facilitates the amassing of large treasuries," *ante,* at 1397–1398. This analysis seeks to create one good argument by combining two bad ones. Those individuals who form that type of voluntary association known as a corporation are, to be sure, given special advantages—notably, the immunization of their personal fortunes from liability for the actions of the association—that the State is under no obligation to confer. But so are other associations and private individuals given all sorts of special advantages that the State need not confer, ranging from tax breaks to contract awards to public employment to outright cash subsidies. It is rudimentary that the State cannot exact as the price of those special advantages the forfeiture of First Amendment rights. See *Pickering v. Board of Education of Township High School Dist. No. 205, Will County,* 391 U.S. 563, 88 S.Ct. 1731, 20 L.Ed.2d 811 (1968); *Speiser v. Randall,* 357 U.S. 513, 78 S.Ct. 1332, 2 L.Ed.2d 1460 (1958). The categorical suspension of the right of any person, or of any association of persons, to speak out on political matters must be justified by a compelling state need. See *Buckley v. Valeo,* 424 U.S. 1, 44–45, 96 S.Ct. 612, 646–647, 46 L.Ed.2d 659 (1976) (*per curiam*). That is why the Court puts forward its second bad argument, the fact that corporations "amas[s] large treasuries." But that alone is also not sufficient justification for the suppression of political speech, unless one thinks it would be lawful to prohibit men and women whose net worth is above a certain figure from endorsing political candidates. Neither of these two flawed arguments is improved by combining them and saying, as the Court in effect does, that "since the State gives special advantages to these voluntary associations, and since they thereby amass vast wealth, they may be required to abandon their right of political speech."

The Court's extensive reliance upon the fact that the objects of this speech restriction, corporations, receive "special advantages" is in stark contrast to our opinion issued just six years ago in *FCC v. League of Women Voters of California,* 468 U.S. 364, 104 S.Ct. 3106, 82 L.Ed.2d 278 (1984). In that decision, striking down a congressionally imposed ban upon editorializing by noncommercial broadcasting stations that receive federal funds, the *only* respect in which we considered the receipt of that "special advantage" relevant was in determining whether the speech limitation could be justified under Congress' spending power, as a means of assuring that the subsidy was devoted only to the purposes Congress intended, which did not include political editorializing. We held it could not be justified on that basis, since "a noncommercial educational station that receives only 1% of its overall income from [federal] grants is barred absolutely from all editorializing.... The station has no way of limiting the use of its federal funds to all noneditorializing activities, and, more importantly, it is barred from using even wholly private funds to finance its editorial activity." *Id.*, at 400, 104 S.Ct., at 3127. Of course the same is true here, even assuming that tax exemptions and other benefits accorded to incorporated associations constitute an exercise of the spending power. It is not just that portion of the corporation's assets attributable to the gratuitously conferred "special advantages" that is prohibited from being used for political endorsements, but *all* of the corporation's assets. I am at a loss to explain the vast difference between the treatment of the present case and *League of Women Voters.* Commercial corporations may not have a public *persona* as sympathetic as that of public broadcasters, but they are no less entitled to this Court's concern.

As for the second part of the Court's argumentation, the fact that corporations (or at least some of them) possess "massive wealth": Certain uses of "massive wealth" in the electoral process—whether or not the wealth is the result of "special advantages" conferred by the State—pose a substantial risk of corruption which constitutes a compelling need for the regulation of speech. Such a risk plainly exists when the wealth is given directly to the political candidate, to be used under his direction and control. We held in *Buckley v. Valeo, supra,* however, that independent expenditures to express the political views of individuals and associations do not raise a sufficient threat of corruption to justify prohibition. *Id.,* at 45, 96 S.Ct., at 647. Neither the Court's opinion nor either of the concurrences makes any effort to distinguish that case—except, perhaps, by misdescribing the case as involving "federal laws regulating individual donors," *ante,* at 1397, or as involving "individual expenditures," *ante,* at 1407 (Stevens, J., concurring). Section 608(e)(1) of the Federal Election Campaign Act of 1971, 18 U.S.C. § 608(e)(1) (1970 ed., Supp. V), which we found unconstitutional in *Buckley,* was directed, like the Michigan law before us here, to expenditures made for the purpose of advocating the election or defeat of a particular candidate, see 424 U.S., at 42, 96 S.Ct., at 645. It limited to $1,000 (a *lesser* restriction than the absolute prohibition at issue here) such expenditures not merely by "individuals," but by "persons," specifically defined to include corporations. See *id.,* at 187, 96 S.Ct., at 712 (setting forth § 591(g) of the statute). The plaintiffs in the case included corporations, see *id.,* at 8, 96 S.Ct., at 629, and we specifically discussed § 608(e)(1) as a restriction addressed not just to individuals but to "individuals and groups," *id.,* at 39, 48, 96 S.Ct., at 648, "persons and groups," *id.,* at 45, 96 S.Ct., at 647, "persons and organizations," *ibid.,* "person[s] [and] association[s]," *id.,* at 50, 96 S.Ct., at 650. In support of our determination that the restriction was "wholly at odds with the guarantees of the First Amendment" we cited *Miami Herald Publishing Co. v. Tornillo,* 418 U.S. 241, 94 S.Ct. 2831, 41 L.Ed.2d 730 (1974), which involved limitations upon a corporation. 424 U.S., at 50, 96 S.Ct., at 650. Of course, *if* § 608(e)(1) had been unconstitutional only as applied to individuals and not as applied to corporations, we might nonetheless have invalidated it *in toto* for substantial overbreadth, see *Broadrick v. Oklahoma,* 413 U.S. 601, 611–613, 93 S.Ct. 2908, 2915–2916, 37 L.Ed.2d 830 (1973), but there is not a hint of that doctrine in our opinion.

Our First Amendment law is much less certain than I had thought it to be if we are free to recharacterize each clear holding as a disguised "overbreadth" determination.

Buckley v. Valeo should not be overruled, because it is entirely correct. The contention that prohibiting overt advocacy for or against a political candidate satisfies a "compelling need" to avoid "corruption" is easily dismissed. As we said in *Buckley,* "[i]t would naively underestimate the ingenuity and resourcefulness of persons and groups desiring to buy influence to believe that they would have much difficulty devising expenditures that skirted the restriction on express advocacy of election or defeat but nevertheless benefited the candidate's campaign." 424 U.S., at 45, 96 S.Ct., at 647. Independent advocacy, moreover, unlike contributions, "may well provide little assistance to the candidate's campaign and indeed may prove counterproductive," thus reducing the danger that it will be exchanged "as a *quid pro quo* for improper commitments from the candidate." *Id.,* at 47, 96 S.Ct., at 648. The latter point seems even more plainly true with respect to corporate advocates than it is with respect to individuals. I expect I could count on the fingers of one hand the candidates who would generally welcome, much less negotiate for, a formal endorsement by AT & T or General Motors. The advocacy of such entities that have "amassed great wealth" will be effective only to the extent that it brings to the people's attention *ideas* which—despite the invariably self-interested and probably uncongenial source—strike them as true.

The Court does not try to defend the proposition that independent advocacy poses a substantial risk of political "corruption," as English speakers understand that term. Rather, it asserts that that concept (which it defines as "'financial *quid pro quo* 'corruption,'" *ante,* at 1397) is really just a narrow subspecies of a hitherto unrecognized genus of political corruption. "Michigan's regulation," we are told, "aims at a different type of corruption in the political arena: the corrosive and distorting effects of immense aggregations of wealth that are accumulated with the help of the corporate form and that have little or no correlation to the public's support for the corporations's political ideas." *Ibid.* Under this mode of analysis, virtually anything the Court deems politically undesirable can be turned into political corruption—by simply describing its effects as politically "corrosive," which is close enough to "corruptive" to qualify. It is sad to think that the First Amendment will ultimately be brought down not by brute force but by poetic metaphor.

The Court's opinion ultimately rests upon that proposition whose violation constitutes the "New Corruption": Expenditures must "reflect actual public support for the political ideas espoused." *Ibid.* This illiberal free-speech principle of "one man, one minute" was proposed and soundly rejected in *Buckley:*

> "It is argued, however, that the ancillary governmental interest in equalizing the relative ability of individuals and groups to influence the outcome of elections serves to justify the limitation on express advocacy of the election or defeat of candidates imposed by § 608(e)(1)'s expenditure ceiling. But the concept that government may restrict the speech of some elements of our society in order to enhance the relative voice of others is wholly foreign to the First Amendment, which was designed 'to secure "the widest possible dissemination of information from diverse and antagonistic sources,"' and '"to assure unfettered interchange of ideas for the bringing about of political and social changes desired by the people."' 424 U.S., at 48–49, 96 S.Ct., at 648–649 (citations omitted).

But it can be said that I have not accurately quoted today's decision. It does not endorse the proposition that government may ensure that expenditures "reflect actual public support for the political ideas espoused," but only the more limited proposition that government may ensure that expenditures "reflect actual public support for the political ideas espoused *by corporations.*" *Ante,* at 1397 (emphasis added). The limitation is of course entirely irrational. Why is it perfectly all right if advocacy by an individual billionaire is out of proportion with "actual public support" for his positions? There is no explanation, except the effort I described at the outset of this discussion to make one valid proposition out of two invalid ones: When the vessel labeled "corruption" begins to founder under weight too great to be logically sustained, the argumentation jumps to the good ship "special privilege"; and when that in turn begins to go down, it returns to "corruption." Thus hopping back and forth between the two, the argumentation may survive but makes no headway towards port, where its conclusion waits in vain.

B

Justice Brennan's concurrence would have us believe that the prohibition adopted by Michigan and approved by the Court is a paternalistic measure to protect the corporate shareholders of America. It is designed, we are told, "to avert [the] danger" that "corporate funds drawn from the general treasury—which represents, after all, [the shareholder's] money," might be used on behalf of a political candidate he opposes. *Ante,* at 1403 (Brennan, J., concurring). But such solicitude is a most implausible explanation for the Michigan statute, inasmuch as it permits corporations to take as many ideological and political positions as they please, so long as they are not "in assistance of, or in opposition to, the nomination or election of a candidate." Mich.Comp. Laws § 169.206(1) (1979). That is indeed the Court's sole basis for distinguishing *First National Bank of Boston v. Bellotti,* 435 U.S. 765, 98 S.Ct. 1407, 55

L.Ed.2d 707 (1978), which invalidated restriction of a corporation's general political speech. The Michigan law appears to be designed, in other words, neither to protect shareholders, nor even (impermissibly) to "balance" general political debate, but to protect political candidates. Given the degree of political sophistication that ought to attend the exercise of our constitutional responsibilities, it is regrettable that this should come as a surprise.

But even if the object of the prohibition could plausibly be portrayed as the protection of shareholders (which the Court's opinion, at least, does not even assert), that would not suffice as a "compelling need" to support this blatant restriction upon core political speech. A person becomes a member of that form of association known as a for-profit corporation in order to pursue economic objectives, *i.e.*, to make money. Some corporate charters may specify the line of commerce to which the company is limited, but even that can be amended by shareholder vote. Thus, in joining such an association, the shareholder knows that management may take any action that is ultimately in accord with what the majority (or a specified supermajority) of the shareholders wishes, so long as that action is designed to make a profit. That is the deal. The corporate actions to which the shareholder exposes himself, therefore, include many things that he may find politically or ideologically uncongenial: investment in South Africa, operation of an abortion clinic, publication of a pornographic magazine, or even publication of a newspaper that adopts absurd political views and makes catastrophic political endorsements. His only protections against such assaults upon his ideological commitments are (1) his ability to persuade a majority (or the requisite minority) of his fellow shareholders that the action should not be taken, and ultimately (2) his ability to sell his stock. (The latter course, by the way, does not ordinarily involve the severe psychic trauma or economic disaster that Justice Brennan's opinion suggests.) It seems to me entirely fanciful, in other words, to suggest that the Michigan statute makes any significant contribution toward insulating the exclusively profit-motivated shareholder from the rude world of politics and ideology.

But even if that were not fanciful, it would be fanciful to think, as Justice Brennan's opinion assumes, that there is any difference between for-profit and not-for-profit corporations insofar as the need for protection of the individual member's ideological psyche is concerned. Would it be any more upsetting to a shareholder of General Motors that it endorsed the election of Henry Wallace (to stay comfortably in the past) than it would be to a member of the American Civil Liberties Union that it endorsed the election of George Wallace? I should think much less so. Yet in the one case as in the other, the only protection against association-induced trauma is the will of the majority and, in the last analysis, withdrawal from membership.

C

In Part V of its opinion, the Court accurately sets forth our longstanding First Amendment law as follows:

> "Because the right to engage in political expression is fundamental to our constitutional system, statutory classifications impinging upon that right must be narrowly tailored to serve a compelling governmental interest." *Ante,* at 1401.

The Court finds this requirement fully met for the following reason:

> "As we explained in the context of our discussions of whether the statute was overinclusive, *supra,* at 1397–1398, or underinclusive, *supra,* at 1400–1401, the State's decision to regulate only corporations is precisely tailored to serve the compelling state interest of eliminating from the political process the corrosive effect of political 'war chests' amassed with the aid of the legal advantages given to corporations." *Ibid.*

That state interest (assuming it is compelling) does indeed explain why the State chose to silence "only corporations" rather than wealthy individuals as well. But it does not explain (what "narrow tailoring" pertains to) why the State chose to silence *all* corporations, rather than just those that possess great wealth. If narrow tailoring means anything, surely it must mean that action taken to counter the effect of amassed "war chests" must be targeted, if possible, at amassed "war chests." And surely such targeting is possible—either in the manner accomplished by the provision that we invalidated in *Buckley, i.e.,* by limiting the prohibition to independent expenditures above a certain amount, or in some other manner, *e.g.,* by limiting the expenditures of only those corporations with more than a certain amount of net worth or annual profit.

No more satisfactory explanation for the obvious lack of "narrow tailoring" is to be found in the Court's discussion of overinclusiveness, to which the above-quoted passage refers. That discussion asserts that we "rejected a similar argument" in *FEC v. National Right to Work Comm.,* 459 U.S. 197, 103 S.Ct. 552, 74 L.Ed.2d 364 (1982) (*NRWC*), where we said that "'we accept Congress' judgment'" that "'the special characteristics of the corporate structure'" create a "'*potential* for ... influence that demands regulation.'" *Ante,* at 1398, quoting 459 U.S., at 209–210, 103 S.Ct., at 560 (emphasis added by the Court). Today's opinion then continues: "Although some closely held corporations, just as some publicly held ones, may not have accumulated significant amounts of wealth, they receive from the State the special benefits conferred by the corporate structure and present the potential for distorting the political process. This potential for distortion justifies § 54(1)'s general applicability to all corporations." *Ante,* at 1398.

The Court thus holds, for the first time since Justice Holmes left the bench, that a direct restriction upon speech is narrowly enough tailored if it extends to speech that has the mere *potential* for producing social harm. *NRWC* (which in any event involved not a direct restriction upon corporate speech but a restriction upon corporate solicitation of funds for candidates) is no authority for that startling proposition, since it *did not purport* to be applying the First Amendment narrow-tailoring requirement. The principle the Court abandons today—that the mere potential for harm does not justify a restriction upon speech—had its origin in the "clear and present danger" test devised by Justice Holmes in 1919, see *Schenck v. United States,* 249 U.S. 47, 49–51, 39 S.Ct. 247, 248, 63 L.Ed. 470, and championed by him and Justice Brandeis over the next decade in a series of famous opinions opposing the affirmance of convictions for subversive speech, see *Abrams v. United States,* 250 U.S. 616, 624, 40 S.Ct. 17, 20, 63 L.Ed. 1173 (1919) (Holmes, J., dissenting); *Gitlow v. New York,* 268 U.S. 652, 672, 45 S.Ct. 625, 632, 69 L.Ed. 1138 (1925) (Holmes, J., dissenting); *Whitney v. California,* 274 U.S. 357, 374, 47 S.Ct. 641, 647, 71 L.Ed. 1095 (1927) (Brandeis, J., concurring). The Court finally adopted their view in 1937, see *Herndon v. Lowry,* 301 U.S. 242, 258, 57 S.Ct. 732, 739, 81 L.Ed. 1066; see also *Bridges v. California,* 314 U.S. 252, 263, 62 S.Ct. 190, 194, 86 L.Ed. 192 (1941); *Thornhill v. Alabama,* 310 U.S. 88, 105, 60 S.Ct. 736, 745, 84 L.Ed. 1093 (1940); *West Virginia Board of Education v. Barnette,* 319 U.S. 624, 639, 63 S.Ct.

1178, 1186, 87 L.Ed. 1628 (1943); *Terminiello v. Chicago,* 337 U.S. 1, 4–5, 69 S.Ct. 894, 895–896, 93 L.Ed. 1131 (1949). Today's reversal of field will require adjustment of a fairly large number of significant First Amendment holdings. Presumably the State may now convict individuals for selling books found to have a potentially harmful influence on minors, *Butler v. Michigan,* 352 U.S. 380, 77 S.Ct. 524, 1 L.Ed.2d 412 (1957), ban indecent telephone communications that have the potential for reaching minors, *Sable Communications of California v. FCC,* 492 U.S. 115, 109 S.Ct. 2829, 106 L.Ed.2d 93 (1989), restrain the press from publishing information that has the potential for jeopardizing a criminal defendant's right to a fair trial, *Nebraska Press Assn. v. Stuart,* 427 U.S. 539, 96 S.Ct. 2791, 49 L.Ed.2d 683 (1976), or the potential for damaging the reputation of the subject of an investigation, *Landmark Communications, Inc. v. Virginia,* 435 U.S. 829, 98 S.Ct. 1535, 56 L.Ed.2d 1 (1978), compel publication of the membership lists of organizations that have a potential for illegal activity, see *NAACP v. Alabama ex rel. Patterson,* 357 U.S. 449, 464, 78 S.Ct. 1163, 1172, 2 L.Ed.2d 1488 (1958), and compel an applicant for bar membership to reveal her political beliefs and affiliations to eliminate the potential for subversive activity, *Baird v. State Bar of Arizona,* 401 U.S. 1, 91 S.Ct. 702, 27 L.Ed.2d 639 (1971).

It is perplexing, or perhaps revealing, to compare the Court's cavalier treatment of the narrow-tailoring requirement today with its elaborate discussion of that issue six years ago in *League of Women Voters.* See 468 U.S., at 392–395, 397–398, 104 S.Ct. 3106, 3126, 82 L.Ed.2d 278. As my earlier discussion makes clear, it would make no difference if the law *were* narrowly tailored to serve its goal, since that goal is not compelling. But the fact that, even having made that first error, the Court must make yet a second in order to reach today's judgment suggests what an impregnable fortress our First Amendment jurisprudence has been. The Court's explicit acceptance of "potential danger" as adequate to establish narrow tailoring, even more than its recognition of an insubstantial interests as "compelling," greatly weakens those defenses.

D

Finally, a few words are in order concerning the Court's approval of the Michigan law's exception for "media corporations." This is all right, we are told, because of "the unique role that the press plays in 'informing and educating the public, offering criticism, and providing a forum for discussion and debate.'" *Ante,* at 1402 (citation omitted). But if one believes in the Court's rationale of "compelling state need" to prevent amassed corporate wealth from skewing the political debate, surely that "unique role" of the press does not give Michigan justification for *excluding* media corporations from coverage, but provides especially strong reason to *include* them. Amassed corporate wealth that regularly sits astride the ordinary channels of information is much more likely to produce the New Corruption (too much of one point of view) than amassed corporate wealth that is generally busy making money elsewhere. Such media corporations not only have vastly greater power to perpetrate the evil of overinforming, they also have vastly greater opportunity. General Motors, after all, will risk a stockholder suit if it makes a political endorsement that is not plausibly tied to its ability to make money for its shareholders. But media corporations make money *by* making political commentary, including endorsements. For them, unlike any other corporations, the whole world of politics and ideology is fair game. Yet the Court tells us that it is reasonable to *exclude* media corporations, rather than target them specially.

Members of the institutional press, despite the Court's approval of their illogical exemption from the Michigan law, will find little reason for comfort in today's decision. The theory of New Corruption it espouses is a dagger at their throats. The Court today holds merely that media corporations *may* be excluded from the Michigan law, not that they *must* be. We have consistently rejected the proposition that the institutional press has any constitutional privilege beyond that of other speakers. See *Bellotti,* 435 U.S., at 782, 98 S.Ct., at 1418, and cases cited. Thus, the Court's holding on this point must be put in the following unencouraging form: "Although the press' unique societal role may not entitle the press to greater protection under the Constitution, *Bellotti, supra,* at 782, 98 S.Ct., at 1418, and n. 18, it does provide a compelling reason for the State to exempt media corporations from the scope of political expenditure limitations." *Ante,* at 1402. One must hope, I suppose, that Michigan will continue to provide this generous and voluntary exemption.

II

I would not do justice to the significance of today's decision to discuss only its lapses from case precedent and logic. Infinitely more important than that is its departure from long-accepted premises of our political system regarding the benevolence that can be expected of government in managing the arena of public debate, and the danger that is to be anticipated from powerful private institutions that compete with government, and with one another, within that arena.

Perhaps the Michigan law before us here has an unqualifiedly noble objective—to "equalize" the political debate by preventing disproportionate expression of corporations' points of view. But governmental abridgment of liberty is always undertaken with the very best of announced objectives (dictators promise to bring order, not tyranny), and often with the very best of genuinely intended objectives (zealous policemen conduct unlawful searches in order to put dangerous felons behind bars). The premise of our Bill of Rights, however, is that there are some things—even some seemingly *desirable* things—that government cannot be trusted to do. The very first of these is establishing the restrictions upon speech that will assure "fair" political debate. The incumbent politician who says he welcomes full and fair debate is no more to be believed than the entrenched monopolist who says he welcomes full and fair competition. Perhaps the Michigan Legislature was genuinely trying to assure a "balanced" presentation of political views; on the other hand, perhaps it was trying to give unincorporated unions (a not insubstantial force in Michigan) political advantage over major employers. Or perhaps it was trying to assure a "balanced" presentation because it knows that with evenly balanced speech incumbent officeholders generally win. The fundamental approach of the First Amendment, I had always thought, was to assume the worst, and to rule the regulation of political speech "for fairness' sake" simply out of bounds.

I doubt that those who framed and adopted the First Amendment would agree that avoiding the New Corruption, that is, calibrating political speech to the degree of public opinion that supports it, is even a *desirable* objective, much less one that is important enough to qualify as a compelling state interest. Those Founders designed, of course, a system in which popular ideas would ultimately prevail; but also, through the First Amendment, a system in which true ideas could readily become popular. For the latter purpose, the calibration that the Court today endorses is precisely backwards: To the extent a valid proposition has scant public support, it should have wider rather than narrower public circulation. I am confident, in other words, that Jefferson and Madison would not have sat at these controls; but if they did, they would have turned them in the opposite direction.

Ah, but then there is the special element of corporate wealth: What would the Founders have thought of that? They would have endorsed, I think, what Tocqueville wrote in 1835:

> "When the members of an aristocratic community adopt a new opinion or conceive a new sentiment, they give it a station, as it were, beside themselves, upon the lofty platform where they stand; and opinions or sentiments so conspicuous to the eyes of the multitude are easily introduced into the minds or hearts of all around. In democratic countries the governing power alone is naturally in a condition to act in this manner; but it is easy to see that its action is always inadequate, and often dangerous.... No sooner does a government attempt to go beyond its political sphere and to enter upon this new track than it exercises, even unintentionally, an insupportable tyranny.... Worse still will be the case if the government really believes itself interested in preventing all circulation of ideas; it will then stand motionless and oppressed by the heaviness of voluntary torpor. Governments, therefore, should not be the only active powers; associations ought, in democratic nations, to stand in lieu of those powerful private individuals whom the equality of conditions has swept away." 2 A. de Tocqueville, *Democracy in America* 109 (P. Bradley ed. 1948).

While Tocqueville was discussing "circulation of ideas" in general, what he wrote is also true of candidate endorsements in particular. To eliminate voluntary associations—not only including powerful ones, but *especially* including powerful ones—from the public debate is either to augment the always dominant power of government or to impoverish the public debate. The case at hand is a good enough example. Why should the Michigan voters in the 93d House District be deprived of the information that private associations owning and operating a vast percentage of the industry of the State, and employing a large number of its citizens, believe that the election of a particular candidate is important to their prosperity? Contrary to the Court's suggestion, the same point cannot effectively be made through corporate PACs to which individuals may voluntarily contribute. It is important to the message that it represents the views of Michigan's leading corporations *as corporations,* occupying the "lofty platform" that they do within the economic life of the State—not just the views of some *other* voluntary associations to which some of the corporations' shareholders belong.

Despite all the talk about "corruption and the appearance of corruption"—evils that are not significantly implicated and that can be avoided in many other ways—it is entirely obvious that the object of the law we have approved today is not to prevent wrongdoing but to prevent speech. Since those private associations known as corporations have so much money, they will speak so much more, and their views will be given inordinate prominence in election campaigns. This is not an argument that our democratic traditions allow—neither with respect to individuals associated in corporations nor with respect to other categories of individuals whose speech may be "unduly" extensive (because they are rich) or "unduly" persuasive (because they are movie stars) or "unduly" respected (because they are clergymen). The premise of our system is that there is no such thing as too much speech—that the people are not foolish but intelligent, and will separate the wheat from the chaff. As conceded in Lincoln's aphorism about fooling "all of the people some of the time," that premise will not invariably accord with reality; but it will assuredly do so much more frequently than the premise the Court today embraces:

that a healthy democratic system can survive the legislative power to prescribe how much political speech is too much, who may speak, and who may not.

* * *

Because today's decision is inconsistent with unrepudiated legal judgments of our Court, but even more because it is incompatible with the unrepealable political wisdom of our First Amendment, I dissent.

Morse: Mother, may I?

Morse v. Republican Party of Virginia, 517 U.S. 186 (1996)

Justice Scalia, with whom Justice Thomas joins, dissenting.

> "Any interference with the freedom of a party is simultaneously an interference with the freedom of its adherents." *Sweezy v. New Hampshire,* 354 U.S. 234, 250, 77 S.Ct. 1203, 1212, 1 L.Ed.2d 1311 (1957). For that reason, we have always treated government assertion of control over the internal affairs of political parties—which, after all, are simply groups of like-minded individual voters—as a matter of the utmost constitutional consequence. See, *e.g., Democratic Party of United States v. Wisconsin ex rel. La Follette,* 450 U.S. 107, 121–122, 101 S.Ct. 1010, 1018–1019, 67 L.Ed.2d 82 (1981); *Cousins v. Wigoda,* 419 U.S. 477, 487–488, 95 S.Ct. 541, 547–548, 42 L.Ed.2d 595 (1975); *O'Brien v. Brown,* 409 U.S. 1, 4–5, 92 S.Ct. 2718, 2720–2721, 34 L.Ed.2d 1 (1972) *(per curiam).* What is at issue in this case, therefore, is not merely interpretation of § 5 of the Voting Rights Act, 42 U.S.C. § 1973c, but, inextricably bound up with that interpretation, the First Amendment freedom of political association.

There are several respects in which both Justice Stevens' opinion and Justice Breyer's opinion concurring in the judgment constitute remarkable departures from the settled course of our First Amendment jurisprudence. The most obvious, perhaps, is their refusal to consider the present application of § 5 unconstitutional on the basis of "hypothetical cases unrelated to the facts of this case [that] might implicate First Amendment concerns." Stevens, J., *ante,* at 1210. Instead, they "leave consideration of hypothetical concerns for another day," *ante,* at 1210–1211, and reserve such "difficult" questions "for a case that squarely presents them," Breyer, J., *ante*, at 1215. That is a luxury our precedents do not allow. It has been a constant of our free-speech jurisprudence that claimants whose First Amendment rights are affected may challenge a statute, not merely on the ground that its specific application to them is unconstitutional, but also on the ground that its application is void in a substantial number of other contexts that arguably fall within its scope. This principle of "overbreadth" has been applied not only in the context of freedom of speech narrowly speaking, but also in the context of the freedom to associate for the purpose of political speech. See, *e.g., United States v. Robel,* 389 U.S. 258, 265–266, 88 S.Ct. 419, 424–425, 19 L.Ed.2d 508 (1967); *Elfbrandt v. Russell,* 384 U.S. 11, 18–19, 86 S.Ct. 1238, 1241–1242, 16 L.Ed.2d 321 (1966).

Thus, to satisfy oneself that the particular practice challenged here lies "well outside the area of greatest 'associational' concern," Breyer, J., *ante*, at 1215, is to take only the first and smallest step in treating the weighty constitutional question posed by application of § 5 to political parties. In this First Amendment context, to "go no further than necessary to decide the case at hand" means going far enough to assure against overbreadth. We must do that whenever "rights of association [are] ensnared in statutes which, by their broad sweep, might result in burdening innocent associations." *Broadrick v. Oklahoma,* 413 U.S. 601, 612, 93 S.Ct. 2908, 2916, 37 L.Ed.2d 830 (1973) (citing, *inter alia, Keyishian v. Board of Regents of Univ. of State of N. Y.,* 385 U.S. 589, 87 S.Ct. 675, 17 L.Ed.2d 629 (1967)). Justice Stevens does not assert that applying § 5 to party activity passes First Amendment muster except "in the case before us," *ante,* at 1210, and Justice Breyer acknowledges that the First Amendment may bar application of § 5 to other convention activity, see *ante,* at 1215. Yet despite these indications of overbreadth, neither opinion attempts to provide what our cases require: a "limiting construction or partial invalidation" that will "remove the seeming threat or deterrence to constitutionally protected expression," *Broadrick, supra,* at 613, 93 S.Ct., at 2916.

Besides flouting the doctrine of overbreadth, the opinions' refusal to provide "[f]urther definition" of § 5's application to political parties, Breyer, J., *ante*, at 1216, leaves political parties without guidance as to "when [their] activities are, in effect, substitutes for state nominating primaries," *ante,* at 1214, and as to "which party nominating convention practices fall within the scope of the Act," *ante* at 1215. Before today, this Court has not tolerated such uncertainty in rules bearing upon First Amendment activities, because it causes persons to refrain from engaging in constitutionally protected conduct for fear of violation. See, *e.g., Baggett v. Bullitt,* 377 U.S. 360, 372, 84 S.Ct. 1316, 1322–1323, 12 L.Ed.2d 377 (1964). Surely such an effect can be expected here. Party officials will at least abstain from proceeding with *certain* convention activities without notification; and in light of the high degree of uncertainty they may well decide to hold no conventions *at all.*

Another respect in which the Court today diverges from our free-speech jurisprudence is even more astounding, if possible, than its disregard of the doctrines of overbreadth and vagueness. From reading the majority's two opinions, one would surmise that the only constitutional question at issue is whether the First Amendment permits the Federal Government to make unlawful and set aside party rule changes designed to hinder racial minorities' full participation in election-related functions. But this statute does *not* present only that question, any more than a statute establishing a Board of Obscenity Censors, to which films or books must be submitted for approval before publication, presents only the question whether the First Amendment permits the prohibition of obscenity. See, *e.g.*, *Freedman v. Maryland*, 380 U.S. 51, 85 S.Ct. 734, 13 L.Ed.2d 649 (1965); *Bantam Books, Inc. v. Sullivan*, 372 U.S. 58, 83 S.Ct. 631, 9 L.Ed.2d 584 (1963). A point entirely ignored by Justices Stevens and Breyer is that this case involves a *classic prior restraint.*

Our cases have heavily disfavored all manner of prior restraint upon the exercise of freedoms guaranteed by the First Amendment. Although most often imposed upon speech, prior restraints are no less noxious, and have been no less condemned, when directed against associational liberty (with which, we have said, freedom of speech "overlap[s] and blend[s]," *Citizens Against Rent Control/Coalition for Fair Housing v. Berkeley*, 454 U.S. 290, 300, 102 S.Ct. 434, 439, 70 L.Ed.2d 492 (1981)). See *Thomas v. Collins*, 323 U.S. 516, 539–540, 65 S.Ct. 315, 326–327, 89 L.Ed. 430 (1945); *Carroll v. President and Comm'rs of Princess Anne*, 393 U.S. 175, 180–185, 89 S.Ct. 347, 351–354, 21 L.Ed.2d 325 (1968); cf. *Healy v. James*, 408 U.S. 169, 184, 92 S.Ct. 2338, 2347–2348, 33 L.Ed.2d 266 (1972). Today, however, a majority of the Court readily accepts the proposition that § 5 can subject this First Amendment freedom *to a permit system,* requiring its exercise to be "precleared" with the Government even when it is not being used unlawfully. The Court thus makes citizens supplicants in the exercise of their First Amendment rights.

As the five Justices who support the judgment of the Court choose to read this statute, a political party (or at least one that the State has awarded a place on the ballot) can make *no* change in its practices or procedures that might affect a voter's capacity to have his candidate elected—no matter how race neutral in purpose and effect—*unless it first obtains prior clearance by the Government,* see Stevens, J., *ante*, at 1198–1200; Breyer, J., *ante*, at 1214–1215. Any change not precleared—after a proceeding in which the burden rests *on the party* to show *absence* of discriminatory purpose and effect, see *City of Rome v. United States,* 446 U.S. 156, 172–173, 183, n. 18, 100 S.Ct. 1548, 1559–1560, 1565 n. 18, 64 L.Ed.2d 119 (1980)—can be enjoined. Given that political parties are organized with the near-exclusive purpose of influencing the outcomes of elections, I think it obvious that as construed today, § 5 requires political parties to submit for prior Government approval, and bear the burden of justifying, virtually every decision of consequence regarding their internal operations. That is the most outrageous tyranny. A freedom of political association that must await the Government's favorable response to a "Mother, may I?" is no freedom of political association at all.

There would be reason enough for astonishment and regret if today's judgment upheld a statute clearly imposing a prior restraint upon private, First Amendment conduct. But what makes today's action astonishing and regrettable beyond belief is that this Court itself is the architect of a prior restraint that the law does not clearly express. And here is yet another respect in which today's opinions ignore established law: their total disregard of the doctrine that, where ambiguity exists, statutes should be construed to avoid substantial constitutional questions. That has been our practice because we presume that "Congress, which also has sworn to protect the Constitution, would intend to err on the side of fundamental constitutional liberties when its legislation implicates those liberties." *Regan v. Time, Inc.,* 468 U.S. 641, 697, 104 S.Ct. 3262, 3292, 82 L.Ed.2d 487 (1984) (Stevens, J., concurring in judgment in part and dissenting in part). We have in the past relied upon this canon to construe statutes narrowly, so as not to impose suspect prior restraints. For example, in *Lowe v. SEC,* 472 U.S. 181, 105 S.Ct. 2557, 86 L.Ed.2d 130 (1985), we held that a statute requiring all "investment advisors" to register with the

Securities and Exchange Commission, see 15 U.S.C. § 80b–3, does not extend to persons who publish "nonpersonalized" investment advice such as periodic market commentary—thereby avoiding the question whether Congress could constitutionally require such persons to register. *Lowe, supra,* at 190, 204–205, and n. 50, 105 S.Ct., at 2562–2563, 2569–2570, and n. 50. How insignificant that prior restraint when compared with the requirement for preclearance of all changes in self-governance by political parties.

What drives a majority of the Court to find a prior restraint where the text does not demand (or even suggest) it is the notion that it "strains credulity" to think that Congress would enact a Voting Rights Act that did *not* reach political-party activity, Stevens, J., *ante,* at 1205. Congress, the majority believes, "could not have intended" such a result, Breyer, J., *ante,* at 1215. I doubt the validity of that perception; the assumption it rests upon—that a legislature never adopts half-way measures, never attacks the easy part of a problem without attacking the more sensitive part as well—seems to me quite false. Indeed, the one-step-at-a-time doctrine that we regularly employ in equal protection cases is based on precisely the opposite assumption. See, *e.g., Williamson v. Lee Optical of Okla., Inc.,* 348 U.S. 483, 488–489, 75 S.Ct. 461, 464–465, 99 L.Ed. 563 (1955).

Moreover, even if one were to accept the majority's question-begging assumption that Congress *must* have covered political-party activity, and even if one were to credit their sole textual support for such coverage, today's decision to impose a prior restraint upon purely private, political-party activity would still be incomprehensible. The sole textual support adduced by the two opinions consists of § 14's reference to elections for "party office," and § 2's reference to "the political processes leading to nomination or election." See Stevens, J., *ante,* at 1200–1201; Breyer, J., *ante,* at 1214. Justice Thomas gives compelling reasons why these phrases cannot bear the meaning the majority would ascribe, see *post,* at 1234–1236. But even accepting that they mean what Justices Stevens and Breyer say, all that the phrase in § 14 shows is that *some portion of the Act* reaches private, political-party conduct; and all that the phrase in § 2 shows is that (at least in some circumstances) *§ 2* does so. *Nothing* in the text, nor anything in the assumption that Congress *must* have addressed political-party activity, compels the conclusion that Congress addressed political-party activity *in the preclearance, prior-restraint scheme of § 5,* which is of course the only question immediately before us. Thus, the only real credulity strainer involved here is the notion that Congress would impose a restraint bearing a "heavy presumption against its constitutional validity," *Bantam Books,* 372 U.S., at 70, 83 S.Ct., at 639, in such a backhanded fashion—saying simply "State[s]" and "political subdivision[s]" in § 5, but meaning political parties as well. Because I find that impossible to believe, I respectfully dissent.

No sanctuary in the First Amendment
U.S. v. Playboy Entertainment Group, Inc., 529 U.S. 803 (2000)

Justice Scalia, dissenting.

I agree with the principal dissent in this case that § 505 of the Telecommunications Act of 1996, Pub.L. 104-104, 110 Stat. 136, 47 U.S.C. § 561 (1994 ed., Supp. III), is supported by a compelling state interest and is narrowly tailored. I write separately to express my view that § 505 can be upheld in simpler fashion: by finding that it regulates the business of obscenity.

To be sure, § 505 and the Federal Communications Commission's implementing regulation, see 47 CFR § 76.227 (1999), purport to capture programming that is indecent rather than merely that which is obscene. And I will assume for purposes of this discussion (though it is a highly fanciful assumption) that none of the transmissions at issue independently crosses the boundary we have established for obscenity, see *Miller v. California,* 413 U.S. 15, 24, 93 S.Ct. 2607, 37 L.Ed.2d 419 (1973), so that the individual programs themselves would enjoy First Amendment protection. In my view, however, that assumption does not put an end to the inquiry.

We have recognized that commercial entities which engage in "the sordid business of pandering" by "deliberately emphasiz[ing] the sexually provocative aspects of [their nonobscene products], in order to catch the salaciously disposed," engage in constitutionally unprotected behavior. *Ginzburg v. United States,* 383 U.S. 463, 467, 472, 86 S.Ct. 942, 16 L.Ed.2d 31 (1966); see also *FW/PBS, Inc. v. Dallas,* 493 U.S. 215, 257-258, 110 S.Ct. 596, 107 L.Ed.2d 603 (1990) (Scalia, J., concurring in part and dissenting in part); *Pinkus v. United States,* 436 U.S. 293, 303-304, 98 S.Ct. 1808, 56 L.Ed.2d 293 (1978); *Splawn v.*

California, 431 U.S. 595, 597–599, 97 S.Ct. 1987, 52 L.Ed.2d 606 (1977); *Hamling v. United States,* 418 U.S. 87, 130, 94 S.Ct. 2887, 41 L.Ed.2d 590 (1974). Cf. *Jacobellis v. Ohio,* 378 U.S. 184, 201, 84 S.Ct. 1676, 12 L.Ed.2d 793 (1964) (Warren, C. J., dissenting) ("In my opinion, the use to which various materials are put-not just the words and pictures themselves-must be considered in determining whether or not the materials are obscene"). This is so whether or not the products in which the business traffics independently meet the high hurdle we have established for delineating the obscene, viz., that they contain no "serious literary, artistic, political, or scientific value." *Miller, supra,* at 24, 93 S.Ct. 2607. See *Ginzburg,* 383 U.S., at 471, 86 S.Ct. 942. We are more permissive of government regulation in these circumstances because it is clear from the context in which exchanges between such businesses and their customers occur that neither the merchant nor the buyer is interested in the work's literary, artistic, political, or scientific value. "The deliberate representation of petitioner's publications as erotically arousing ... stimulate[s] the reader to accept them as prurient; he looks for titillation, not for saving intellectual content." *Id.,* at 470, 86 S.Ct. 942. Thus, a business that "(1) offer [s] ... hardcore sexual material, (2) as a constant and intentional objective of [its] business, [and] (3) seek[s] to promote it as such" finds no sanctuary in the First Amendment. *FW/PBS, supra,* at 261, 110 S.Ct. 596 (Scalia J., concurring in part and dissenting in part).

Section 505 regulates just this sort of business. Its coverage is limited to programming that "describes or depicts sexual or excretory activities or organs *in a patently offensive manner* as measured by contemporary community standards [for cable television]." 47 CFR § 76.227(d) (1999) (emphasis added). It furthermore applies only to those channels that are "*primarily dedicated* to sexually-oriented programming." § 505(a) (emphasis added). It is conceivable, I suppose, that a channel which is primarily dedicated to sex might not *hold itself forth* as primarily dedicated to sex-in which case its productions which contain "serious literary, artistic, political, or scientific value" (if any) would be as entitled to First Amendment protection as the statuary rooms of the National Gallery. But in the competitive world of cable programming, the possibility that a channel devoted to sex would not advertise itself as such is sufficiently remote, and the number of such channels sufficiently small (if not indeed nonexistent), as not to render the provision substantially overbroad.

Playboy itself illustrates the type of business § 505 is designed to reach. Playboy provides, through its networks—Playboy Television, AdulTVision, Adam & Eve, and Spice—"virtually 100% sexually explicit adult programming." 30 F.Supp.2d 702, 707 (D.Del.1998). For example, on its Spice network, Playboy describes its own programming as depicting such activities as "female masturbation/external," "girl/girl sex," and "oral sex/cunnilingus." 1 Record, Exh. 73, p. TWC00132. As one would expect, given this content, Playboy advertises accordingly, with calls to "Enjoy the sexiest, hottest adult movies in the privacy of your own home." 6 *id.*, Exh. 136, at 2P009732. An example of the promotion for a particular movie is as follows: "Little miss country girls are aching for a quick roll in the hay! Watch southern hospitality pull out all the stops as these ravin' nymphos tear down the barn and light up the big country sky." 7 *id.*, Exh. 226, at 2P009187. One may doubt whether—or marvel that—this sort of embarrassingly juvenile promotion really attracts what Playboy assures us is an "adult" audience. But it is certainly marketing sex.

Thus, while I agree with Justice Breyer's child-protection analysis, it leaves me with the same feeling of true-but-inadequate as the conclusion that Al Capone did not accurately report his income. It is not only children who can be protected from occasional uninvited exposure to what appellee calls "adult-oriented programming"; we can all be. Section 505 covers only businesses that engage in the "commercial exploitation of erotica solely for the sake of their prurient appeal," *Ginzburg,* 383 U.S., at 466, 86 S.Ct. 942—which, as Playboy's own advertisements make plain, is what "adult" programming is all about. In most contexts, contemporary American society has chosen to permit such commercial exploitation. That may be a wise democratic choice, if only because of the difficulty in many contexts (though not this one) of identifying the panderer to sex. It is, however, not a course compelled by the Constitution. Since the Government is entirely free to *block* these transmissions, it may certainly take the less drastic step of dictating how, and during what times, they may occur.

An Equal Protection Clause for ideas
Williams-Yulee v. Florida Bar,
135 S.Ct. 1656 (2015)

Justice Scalia, with whom Justice Thomas joins, dissenting.

An ethics canon adopted by the Florida Supreme Court bans a candidate in a judicial election from asking anyone, under any circumstances, for a contribution to his campaign. Faithful application of our precedents would have made short work of this wildly disproportionate restriction upon speech. Intent upon upholding the Canon, however, the Court flattens one settled First Amendment principle after another.

I

The first axiom of the First Amendment is this: As a general rule, the state has no power to ban speech on the basis of its content. One need not equate judges with politicians to see that this principle does not grow weaker merely because the censored speech is a judicial candidate's request for a campaign contribution. Our cases hold that speech enjoys the full protection of the First Amendment unless a widespread and longstanding tradition ratifies its regulation. *Brown v. Entertainment Merchants Assn.,* 564 U.S. ----, ----, 131 S.Ct. 2729, 2733–2734, 180 L.Ed.2d 708 (2011). No such tradition looms here. Georgia became the first State to elect its judges in 1812, and judicial elections had spread to a large majority of the States by the time of the Civil War. *Republican Party of Minn. v. White,* 536 U.S. 765, 785, 122 S.Ct. 2528, 153 L.Ed.2d 694 (2002). Yet there appears to have been no regulation of judicial candidates' speech throughout the 19th and early 20th centuries. *Ibid.* The American Bar Association first proposed ethics rules concerning speech of judicial candidates in 1924, but these rules did not achieve widespread adoption until after the Second World War. *Id.*, at 786, 122 S.Ct. 2528.

Rules against soliciting campaign contributions arrived more recently still. The ABA first proposed a canon advising against it in 1972, and a canon prohibiting it only in 1990. See Brief for American Bar Association as *Amicus Curiae* 2–4. Even now, 9 of the 39 States that elect judges allow judicial candidates to ask for campaign contributions. See *id.*, at 4. In the absence of any long-settled custom about judicial candidates' speech in general or their solicitations in particular, we have no basis for relaxing the rules that normally apply to laws that suppress speech because of content.

One likewise need not equate judges with politicians to see that the electoral setting calls for all the more vigilance in ensuring observance of the First Amendment. When a candidate asks someone for a campaign contribution, he tends (as the principal opinion acknowledges) also to talk about his qualifications for office and his views on public issues. *Ante*, at 1664–1665 (plurality opinion). This expression lies at the heart of what the First Amendment is meant to protect. In addition, banning candidates from asking for money personally "favors some candidates over others—incumbent judges (who benefit from their current status) over non-judicial candidates, the well-to-do (who may not need to raise any money at all) over lower-income candidates, and the well-connected (who have an army of potential fundraisers) over outsiders." *Carey v. Wolnitzek*, 614 F.3d 189, 204 (C.A.6 2010). This danger of legislated (or judicially imposed) favoritism is the very reason the First Amendment exists.

Because Canon 7C(1) restricts fully protected speech on the basis of content, it presumptively violates the First Amendment. We may uphold it only if the State meets its burden of showing that the Canon survives strict scrutiny—that is to say, only if it shows that the Canon is narrowly tailored to serve a compelling interest. I do not for a moment question the Court's conclusion that States have different compelling interests when regulating judicial elections than when regulating political ones. Unlike a legislator, a judge must be impartial—without bias for or against any party or attorney who comes before him. I accept for the sake of argument that States have a compelling interest in ensuring that its judges are *seen* to be impartial. I will likewise assume that a judicial candidate's request to a litigant or attorney presents a danger of coercion that a political candidate's request to a constituent does not. But Canon 7C(1) does not narrowly target concerns about impartiality or its appearance; it applies even when the person asked for a financial contribution has no chance of ever appearing in the candidate's court. And Florida does not invoke concerns about coercion, presumably because the Canon bans solicitations regardless of whether their object is a lawyer, litigant, or other person vulnerable to judicial pressure. So Canon 7C(1) fails exacting scrutiny and infringes the First Amendment. This case should have been just that straightforward.

II

The Court concludes that Florida may prohibit personal solicitations by judicial candidates as a means of preserving "public confidence in the integrity of the judiciary." *Ante,* at 1666. It purports to reach this destination by applying strict scrutiny, but it would be more accurate to say that it does so by applying the appearance of strict scrutiny.

A

The first sign that mischief is afoot comes when the Court describes Florida's compelling interest. The State must first identify its objective with precision before one can tell whether that interest is compelling and whether the speech restriction narrowly targets it. In *White,* for example, the Court did not allow a State to invoke hazy concerns about judicial impartiality in justification of an ethics rule against judicial candidates' announcing their positions on legal issues. 536 U.S., at 775, 122 S.Ct. 2528. The Court instead separately analyzed the State's concerns about judges' bias against parties, preconceptions on legal issues, and openmindedness, and explained why each concern (and each for a different reason) did not suffice to sustain the rule. *Id.,* at 775–780, 122 S.Ct. 2528.

In stark contrast to *White,* the Court today relies on Florida's invocation of an ill-defined interest in "public confidence in judicial integrity." The Court at first suggests that "judicial integrity" involves the "ability to administer justice without fear or favor." *Ante,* at 1666. As its opinion unfolds, however, today's concept of judicial integrity turns out to be "a mere thing of wax in the hands of the judiciary, which they may twist, and shape into any form they please." 12 The Works of Thomas Jefferson 137 (P. Ford ed. 1905). When the Court explains how solicitation undermines confidence in judicial integrity, integrity starts to sound like saintliness. It involves independence from any "'*possible* temptation'" that "'*might* lead'" the judge, "even unknowingly," to favor one party. *Ante,* at 1667 (emphasis added). When the Court turns to distinguishing in-person solicitation from solicitation by proxy, the any-possible-temptation standard no longer helps and thus drops out. The critical factors instead become the "pressure" a listener feels during a solicitation and the "appearance that the candidate will remember who says yes, and who says no." *Ante,* at 1669. But when it comes time to explain Florida's decision to allow candidates to write thank-you notes, the "appearance that the candidate ... remember[s] who says yes" gets nary a mention. *Ante,* at 1669. And when the Court confronts Florida's decision to prohibit mass-mailed solicitations, concern about pressure fades away. *Ante,* at 1671. More outrageous still, the Court at times molds the interest in the perception that judges have integrity into an interest in the perception that judges do not solicit—for example when it says, "all personal solicitations by judicial candidates create a public appearance that undermines confidence in the integrity of the judiciary; banning all personal solicitations by judicial candidates is narrowly tailored to address that concern." *Ante,* at 1671. This is not strict scrutiny; it is sleight of hand.

B

The Court's twistifications have not come to an end; indeed, they are just beginning. In order to uphold Canon 7C(1) under strict scrutiny, Florida must do more than point to a vital public objective brooding overhead. The State must also meet a difficult burden of demonstrating that the speech restriction substantially advances the claimed objective. The State "bears the risk of uncertainty," so "ambiguous proof will not suffice." *Entertainment Merchants,* 564 U.S., at ----, 131 S.Ct., at 2739. In an arresting illustration, this Court held that a law punishing lies about winning military decorations like the Congressional Medal of Honor failed exacting scrutiny, because the Government could not satisfy its "heavy burden" of proving that "the public's general perception of military awards is diluted by false claims." *United States v. Alvarez,* 567 U.S. ----, ----, 132 S.Ct. 2537, 2549, 183 L.Ed.2d 574 (2012) (plurality opinion).

Now that we have a case about the public's perception of judicial honor rather than its perception of military honors, the Justices of this Court change the rules. The Court announces, on the basis of its "intuiti[on]," that allowing personal solicitations will make litigants worry that "'judges' decisions may be motivated by the desire to repay campaign contributions.'" *Ante,* at 1667. But this case is not about whether Yulee has the right to receive campaign contributions. It is about whether she has the right to *ask* for campaign contributions that Florida's statutory law already allows her to receive. Florida bears the burden of showing that banning *requests* for lawful contributions will improve public confidence in judges—not just a little bit, but significantly, because "the Government does not have a compelling interest in each marginal percentage point by which its goals are advanced." *Entertainment Merchants, supra,* at ----, n. 9, 131 S.Ct., at 2741, n. 9.

Neither the Court nor the State identifies the slightest evidence that banning requests for contributions will substantially improve public trust in judges. Nor does common sense make this happy forecast obvious. The concept of judicial integrity "dates back at least eight centuries," *ante,* at 1666, and judicial elections in America date back more than two centuries, *supra,* at 1676—but rules against personal solicitations date back only to 1972, *supra,* at 1676. The peaceful coexistence of judicial elections and personal solicitations for most of our history calls into doubt any claim that allowing personal solicitations would imperil public faith in judges. Many States allow judicial candidates to ask for contributions even today, but nobody suggests that public confidence in judges fares worse in these jurisdictions than elsewhere. And in any event, if candidates' appeals for money are "'characteristically intertwined'" with discussion of qualifications and views on public issues, *ante,* at 1665 (plurality opinion), how can the Court be so sure that the public will regard them as improprieties rather than as legitimate instances of campaigning? In the final analysis, Florida comes nowhere near making the convincing demonstration required by our cases that the speech restriction in this case substantially advances its objective.

C

But suppose we play along with the premise that prohibiting solicitations will significantly improve the public reputation of judges. Even then, Florida must show that the ban restricts no more speech than necessary to achieve the objective. See *Sable Communications of Cal., Inc. v. FCC,* 492 U.S. 115, 126, 109 S.Ct. 2829, 106 L.Ed.2d 93 (1989).

Canon 7C(1) falls miles short of satisfying this requirement. The Court seems to accept Florida's claim that solicitations erode public confidence by creating the perception that judges are selling justice to lawyers and litigants. *Ante,* at 1666. Yet the Canon prohibits candidates from asking for money from *anybody*—even from someone who is neither lawyer nor litigant, even from someone who (because of recusal rules) cannot possibly appear before the candidate as lawyer or litigant. Yulee thus may not call up an old friend, a cousin, or even her parents to ask for a donation to her campaign. The State has not come up with a plausible explanation of how soliciting someone who has no chance of appearing in the candidate's court will diminish public confidence in judges.

No less important, Canon 7C(1) bans candidates from asking for contributions even in messages that do not target any listener in particular—mass-mailed letters, flyers posted on telephone poles, speeches to large gatherings, and Web sites addressed to the general public. Messages like these do not share the features that lead the Court to pronounce personal solicitations a menace to public confidence in the judiciary. Consider online solicitations. They avoid "'the spectacle of lawyers or potential litigants directly handing over money to judicial candidates,'" *ante,* at 1667. People who come across online solicitations do not feel "pressure" to comply with the request, *ante,* at 1669. Nor does the candidate's signature on the online solicitation suggest "that the candidate will remember who says yes, and who says no," *ibid.* Yet Canon 7C(1) prohibits these and similar solicitations anyway. This tailoring is as narrow as the Court's scrutiny is strict.

Perhaps sensing the fragility of the initial claim that *all* solicitations threaten public confidence in judges, the Court argues that "the lines Yulee asks [it] to draw are unworkable." *Ante,* at 1671. That is a difficulty of the Court's own imagination. In reality, the Court could have chosen from a whole spectrum of workable rules. It could have held that States may regulate no more than solicitation of participants in pending cases, or solicitation of people who are likely to appear in the candidate's court, or even solicitation of any lawyer or litigant. And it could have ruled that candidates have the right to make fundraising appeals that are not directed to any particular listener (like requests in mass-mailed letters), or at least fundraising appeals plainly directed to the general public (like requests placed online). The Supreme Court of Florida has made similar accommodations in other settings. It allows sitting judges to solicit memberships in civic organizations if (among other things) the solicitee is not "likely ever to appear before the court on which the judge serves." Code of Judicial Conduct for the State of Florida 23 (2014) (Judicial Conduct Code). And it allows sitting judges to accept gifts if (among other things) "the donor is not a party or other person ... whose interests have come or are likely to come before the judge." *Id.,* at 24. It is not too much to ask that the State show election speech similar consideration.

The Court's accusation of unworkability also suffers from a bit of a pot-kettle problem. Consider the many real-world questions left open by today's decision. Does the First Amendment permit restricting a candidate's appearing at an event where somebody *else* asks for campaign funds on his behalf? See Florida Judicial Ethics Advisory Committee Opinion

No. 2012-14 (JEAC Op.). Does it permit prohibiting the candidate's *family* from making personal solicitations? See *ibid.* Does it allow prohibiting the candidate from participating in the creation of a Web site that solicits funds, even if the candidate's name does not appear next to the request? See JEAC Op. No. 2008-2011. More broadly, could Florida ban thank-you notes to donors? Cap a candidate's campaign spending? Restrict independent spending by people other than the candidate? Ban independent spending by corporations? And how, by the way, are judges supposed to decide whether these measures promote public confidence in judicial integrity, when the Court does not even have a consistent theory about what it means by "judicial integrity"? For the Court to wring its hands about workability under these circumstances is more than one should have to bear.

D

Even if Florida could show that banning all personal appeals for campaign funds is necessary to protect public confidence in judicial integrity, the Court must overpower one last sentinel of free speech before it can uphold Canon 7C(1). Among its other functions, the First Amendment is a kind of Equal Protection Clause for ideas. The state ordinarily may not regulate one message because it harms a government interest yet refuse to regulate other messages that impair the interest in a comparable way. Applying this principle, we invalidated a law that prohibited picketing dwellings but made an exception for picketing about labor issues; the State could not show that labor picketing harmed its asserted interest in residential privacy any less than other kinds of picketing. *Carey v. Brown,* 447 U.S. 455, 464–465, 100 S.Ct. 2286, 65 L.Ed.2d 263 (1980). In another case, we set aside a ban on showing movies containing nudity in drive-in theaters, because the government did not demonstrate that movies with nude scenes would distract passing drivers any more than, say, movies with violent scenes. *Erznoznik v. Jacksonville,* 422 U.S. 205, 214–215, 95 S.Ct. 2268, 45 L.Ed.2d 125 (1975).

The Court's decision disregards these principles. The Court tells us that "all personal solicitations by judicial candidates create a public appearance that undermines confidence in the integrity of the judiciary." *Ante,* at 1671. But Canon 7C(1) does not restrict *all* personal solicitations; it restricts only personal solicitations related to campaigns. The part of the Canon challenged here prohibits personal pleas for "campaign funds," and the Canon elsewhere prohibits personal appeals to attorneys for "publicly stated support." Judicial Conduct Code 38. So although Canon 7C(1) prevents Yulee from asking a lawyer for a few dollars to help her buy campaign pamphlets, it does not prevent her asking the same lawyer for a personal loan, access to his law firm's luxury suite at the local football stadium, or even a donation to help her fight the Florida Bar's charges. What could possibly justify these distinctions? Surely the Court does not believe that requests for campaign favors erode public confidence in a way that requests for favors unrelated to elections do not. Could anyone say with a straight face that it looks *worse* for a candidate to say "please give my campaign $25" than to say "please give *me* $25"?

Fumbling around for a fig-leaf, the Court says that "the First Amendment imposes no freestanding 'underinclusiveness limitation.'" *Ante,* at 1668. This analysis elides the distinction between selectivity on the basis of content and selectivity on other grounds. Because the First Amendment does not prohibit underinclusiveness as such, lawmakers may target a problem only at certain times or in certain places. Because the First Amendment *does* prohibit content discrimination as such, lawmakers may *not* target a problem only in certain messages.

Explaining this distinction, we have said that the First Amendment would allow banning obscenity "only in certain media or markets" but would preclude banning "only that obscenity which includes offensive political messages." *R.A.V. v. St. Paul,* 505 U.S. 377, 387–388, 112 S.Ct. 2538, 120 L.Ed.2d 305 (1992) (emphasis deleted). This case involves selectivity on the basis of content. The Florida Supreme Court has decided to eliminate the appearances associated with "personal appeals for money," *ante,* at 1671, when the appeals seek money for a campaign but not when the appeals seek money for other purposes. That distinction violates the First Amendment. See *Erznoznik, supra,* at 215, 95 S.Ct. 2268.

Even on the Court's own terms, Canon 7C(1) cannot stand. The Court concedes that "underinclusiveness can raise 'doubts about whether the government is in fact pursuing the interest it invokes.'" *Ante,* at 1668. Canon 7C(1)'s scope suggests that it has nothing to do with the appearances created by judges' asking for money, and everything to do with hostility toward judicial campaigning. How else to explain the Florida Supreme Court's decision to ban *all* personal appeals for campaign funds (even when the solicitee could never appear before the candidate), but to tolerate appeals for other kinds of funds (even when the solicitee will surely appear before the candidate)? It should come as no surprise that the ABA, whose model rules the Florida Supreme Court followed when framing Canon 7C(1), opposes judicial elections—preferring instead a system in which (surprise!) a committee of lawyers proposes candidates from among whom the Governor must make his selection. See *White,* 536 U.S., at 787, 122 S.Ct. 2528.

The Court tries to strike a pose of neutrality between appointment and election of judges, but no one should be deceived. A Court that sees impropriety in a candidate's request for *any* contributions to his election campaign does not much like judicial selection by the people. One cannot have judicial elections without judicial campaigns, and judicial campaigns without funds for campaigning, and funds for campaigning without asking for them. When a society decides that its judges should be elected, it necessarily decides that selection by the people is more important than the oracular sanctity of judges, their immunity from the (shudder!) indignity of begging for funds, and their exemption from those shadows of impropriety that fall over the proletarian public officials who must run for office. A free society, accustomed to electing its rulers, does not much care whether the rulers operate through statute and executive order, or through judicial distortion of statute, executive order, and constitution. The prescription that judges be elected probably springs from the people's realization that their judges can become their rulers—and (it must be said) from just a deep-down feeling that members of the Third Branch will profit from a hearty helping of humble pie, and from a severe reduction of their great remove from the (ugh!) People. (It should not be thought that I myself harbor such irreverent and revolutionary feelings; but I think it likely—and year by year more likely—that those who favor the election of judges do so.) In any case, hostility to campaigning by judges entitles the people of Florida to amend their Constitution to replace judicial elections with the selection of judges by lawyers' committees; it does not entitle the Florida Supreme Court to adopt, or this Court to endorse, a rule of judicial conduct that abridges candidates' speech in the judicial elections that the Florida Constitution prescribes.

* * *

This Court has not been shy to enforce the First Amendment in recent Terms—even in cases that do not involve election speech. It has accorded robust protection to depictions of animal torture, sale of violent video games to children, and lies about having won military medals. See *United States v. Stevens,* 559 U.S. 460, 130 S.Ct. 1577, 176 L.Ed.2d 435 (2010); *Entertainment Merchants,* 564 U.S. ----, 131 S.Ct. 2729, 180 L.Ed.2d 708; *Alvarez,* 567 U.S. ----, 132 S.Ct. 2537, 183 L.Ed.2d 574. Who would have thought that the same Court would today exert such heroic efforts to save so plain an abridgment of the freedom of speech? It is no great mystery what is going on here. The judges of this Court, like the judges of the Supreme Court of Florida who promulgated Canon 7C(1), evidently consider the preservation of public respect for the courts a policy objective of the highest order. So it is—but so too are preventing animal torture, protecting the innocence of children, and honoring valiant soldiers. The Court did not relax the Constitution's guarantee of freedom of speech when legislatures pursued those goals; it should not relax the guarantee when the Supreme Court of Florida pursues this one. The First Amendment is not abridged for the benefit of the Brotherhood of the Robe.

I respectfully dissent.

6

Religion

Our wonderfully flexible but embarrassing Establishment Clause jurisprudence
Edwards v. Aguillard, 482 U.S. 578 (1987)

The Constitution is not a bulldozer of social engineering
Lee v. Weisman, 505 U.S. 577 (1992)

The principle of not applying any principle
Locke v. Davey, 540 U.S. 712 (2004)

The dictatorship of a shifting Supreme Court majority
McCreary County, Ky. v. American Civil Liberties Union of Ky., 545 U.S. 844 (2005)

The First Amendment provides that Congress shall "make no law respecting an establishment of religion, or prohibiting the free exercise thereof." Since the beginnings of our nation, the definition of a "law respecting an establishment of religion" and what constitutes "the free exercise" of religion has led to multifarious lawsuits and puzzled some of the country's greatest legal minds. That Justice Scalia, who enjoyed a traditional Catholic upbringing and education, should have involved himself deeply in cases dealing with religion must come as no surprise. That he brought to his opinions in religion cases, both in the majority and in dissent, his greatest textual and analytical skills can also not be doubted. In addition, during the past century the religion cases confronted by the federal courts also brought the Courts into difficult areas such as the proper balance between religion and science and the proper role of prayer in public schools. The cases presented in this chapter show the interplay of the Justices' differing views on the *Establishment Clause*, and the *Free Exercise Clause.*

Our wonderfully flexible but embarrassing Establishment Clause jurisprudence

Edwards v. Aguillard,
482 U.S. 578 (1987)

Justice Scalia, with whom the Chief Justice joins, dissenting.

Even if I agreed with the questionable premise that legislation can be invalidated under the Establishment Clause on the basis of its motivation alone, without regard to its effects, I would still find no justification for today's decision. The Louisiana legislators who passed the "Balanced Treatment for Creation-Science and Evolution-Science Act" (Balanced Treatment Act), La.Rev.Stat.Ann. §§ 17:286.1–17:286.7 (West 1982), each of whom had sworn to support the Constitution, were well aware of the potential Establishment Clause problems and considered that aspect of the legislation with great care. After seven hearings and several months of study, resulting in substantial revision of the original proposal, they approved the Act overwhelmingly and specifically articulated the secular purpose they meant it to serve. Although the record contains abundant evidence of the sincerity of that purpose (the only issue pertinent to this case), the Court today holds, essentially on the basis of "its visceral knowledge regarding what *must* have motivated the legislators," 778 F.2d 225, 227 (CA5 1985) (Gee, J., dissenting) (emphasis added), that the members of the Louisiana Legislature knowingly violated their oaths and then lied about it. I dissent. Had requirements of the Balanced Treatment Act that are not apparent on its face been clarified by an interpretation of the Louisiana Supreme Court, or by the manner of its implementation, the Act might well be found unconstitutional; but the question of its constitutionality cannot rightly be disposed of on the gallop, by impugning the motives of its supporters.

I

This case arrives here in the following posture: The Louisiana Supreme Court has never been given an opportunity to interpret the Balanced Treatment Act, State officials have never attempted to implement it, and it has never been the subject of a full evidentiary hearing. We can only guess at its meaning. We know that it forbids instruction in either "creation-science" or "evolution-science" without instruction in the other, § 17:286.4A, but the parties are sharply divided over what creation science consists of. Appellants insist that it is a collection of educationally valuable scientific data that has been censored from classrooms by an embarrassed scientific establishment. Appellees insist it is not science at all but thinly veiled religious doctrine. Both interpretations of the intended meaning of that phrase find considerable support in the legislative history.

At least at this stage in the litigation, it is plain to me that we must accept appellants' view of what the statute means. To begin with, the statute itself *defines* "creation-science" as "the *scientific evidences* for creation and inferences from those *scientific evidences*." § 17:286.3(2) (emphasis added). If, however, that definition is not thought sufficiently helpful, the means by which the Louisiana Supreme Court will give the term more precise content is quite clear—and again, at this stage in the litigation, favors the appellants' view. "Creation science" is unquestionably a "term of art," see Brief for 72 Nobel Laureates et al. as *Amici Curiae* 20, and thus, under Louisiana law, is "to be interpreted according to [its] received meaning and acceptation with the learned in the art, trade or profession to which

[it] refer[s]." La.Civ.Code Ann., Art. 15 (West 1952). The only evidence in the record of the "received meaning and acceptation" of "creation science" is found in five affidavits filed by appellants. In those affidavits, two scientists, a philosopher, a theologian, and an educator, all of whom claim extensive knowledge of creation science, swear that it is essentially a collection of scientific data supporting the theory that the physical universe and life within it appeared suddenly and have not changed substantially since appearing. See App. to Juris.Statement A-19 (Kenyon); *id.,* at A-36 (Morrow); *id.,* at A-41 (Miethe). These experts insist that creation science is a strictly scientific concept that can be presented without religious reference. See *id.,* at A-19–A-20, A-35 (Kenyon); *id.,* at A-36–A-38 (Morrow); *id.,* at A-40, A-41, A-43 (Miethe); *id.,* at A-47, A-48 (Most); *id.,* at A-49 (Clinkert). At this point, then, we must assume that the Balanced Treatment Act does *not* require the presentation of religious doctrine.

Nothing in today's opinion is plainly to the contrary, but what the statute means and what it requires are of rather little concern to the Court. Like the Court of Appeals, 765 F.2d 1251, 1253, 1254 (CA5 1985), the Court finds it necessary to consider only the motives of the legislators who supported the Balanced Treatment Act, *ante,* at 2578, 2583, 2584. After examining the statute, its legislative history, and its historical and social context, the Court holds that the Louisiana Legislature acted without "a secular legislative purpose" and that the Act therefore fails the "purpose" prong of the three-part test set forth in *Lemon v. Kurtzman,* 403 U.S. 602, 612, 91 S.Ct. 2105, 2111, 29 L.Ed.2d 2105 (1971). As I explain below, *infra,* at --- - - ----, I doubt whether that "purpose" requirement of *Lemon* is a proper interpretation of the Constitution; but even if it were, I could not agree with the Court's assessment that the requirement was not satisfied here.

This Court has said little about the first component of the *Lemon* test. Almost invariably, we have effortlessly discovered a secular purpose for measures challenged under the Establishment Clause, typically devoting no more than a sentence or two to the matter. See, *e.g.*, *Witters v. Washington Dept. of Services for Blind,* 474 U.S. 481, 485–486, 106 S.Ct. 748, 750–751, 88 L.Ed.2d 846 (1986); *Grand Rapids School District v. Ball,* 473 U.S. 373, 383, 105 S.Ct. 3216, 3222, 87 L.Ed.2d 267 (1985); *Mueller v. Allen,* 463 U.S. 388, 394–395, 103 S.Ct. 3062, 3066–3067, 77 L.Ed.2d 721 (1983); *Larkin v. Grendel's Den, Inc.,* 459 U.S. 116, 123–124, 103 S.Ct. 505, 510–511, 74 L.Ed.2d 297 (1982); *Widmar v. Vincent,* 454 U.S. 263, 271, 102 S.Ct. 269, 275, 70 L.Ed.2d 440 (1981); *Committee for Public Education & Religious Liberty v. Regan,* 444 U.S. 646, 654, 657, 100 S.Ct. 840, 846, 848, 63 L.Ed.2d 94 (1980); *Wolman v. Walter,* 433 U.S. 229, 236, 97 S.Ct. 2593, 2599, 53 L.Ed.2d 714 (1977) (plurality opinion); *Meek v. Pittenger,* 421 U.S. 349, 363, 95 S.Ct. 1753, 1762, 44 L.Ed.2d 217 (1975); *Committee for Public Education & Religious Liberty v. Nyquist,* 413 U.S. 756, 773, 93 S.Ct. 2955, 2965, 37 L.Ed.2d 948 (1973); *Levitt v. Committee for Public Education & Religious Liberty,* 413 U.S. 472, 479–480, n. 7, 93 S.Ct. 2814, 2818–2819, n. 7, 37 L.Ed.2d 736 (1973); *Tilton v. Richardson,* 403 U.S. 672, 678–679, 91 S.Ct. 2091, 2095–2096, 29 L.Ed.2d 790 (1971) (plurality opinion); *Lemon v. Kurtzman, supra,* 403 U.S., at 613, 91 S.Ct., at 2111. In fact, only once before deciding *Lemon,* and twice since, have we invalidated a law for lack of a secular purpose. See *Wallace v. Jaffree,* 472 U.S. 38, 105 S.Ct. 2479, 86 L.Ed.2d 29 (1985); *Stone v. Graham,* 449 U.S. 39, 101 S.Ct. 192, 66 L.Ed.2d 199 (1980) (*per curiam*); *Epperson v. Arkansas,* 393 U.S. 97, 89 S.Ct. 266, 21 L.Ed.2d 228 (1968).

Nevertheless, a few principles have emerged from our cases, principles which should, but to an unfortunately large extent do not, guide the Court's application of *Lemon* today. It is clear, first of all, that regardless of what "legislative purpose" may mean in other contexts, for the purpose of the *Lemon* test it means the "actual" motives of those responsible for the challenged action. The Court recognizes this, see *ante,* at 2578, as it has in the past, see, *e.g., Witters v. Washington Dept. of Services for Blind, supra,* 474 U.S., at 486, 106 S.Ct., at 751; *Wallace v. Jaffree, supra,* 472 U.S., at 56, 105 S.Ct., at 2489. Thus, if those legislators who supported the Balanced Treatment Act *in fact* acted with a "sincere" secular purpose, *ante,* at 2579, the Act survives the first component of the *Lemon* test, regardless of whether that purpose is likely to be achieved by the provisions they enacted.

Our cases have also confirmed that when the *Lemon* Court referred to "a secular ... purpose," 403 U.S., at 612, 91 S.Ct., at 2111, it meant "*a* secular purpose." The author of *Lemon,* writing for the Court, has said that invalidation under the purpose prong is appropriate when "there [is] *no question* that the statute or activity was motivated *wholly* by religious considerations." *Lynch v. Donnelly,* 465 U.S. 668, 680, 104 S.Ct. 1355, 1362, 79 L.Ed.2d 604 (1984) (Burger, C.J.) (emphasis added); see also *id.,* at 681, n. 6, 104 S.Ct., at 1363, n. 6; *Wallace v. Jaffree, supra,* 472 U.S., at 56, 105 S.Ct., at 2489 ("[T]he First Amendment requires that a statute must be invalidated if it is *entirely* motivated by a purpose to advance religion") (emphasis added; footnote omitted). In all three cases in which we struck down laws under the Establishment Clause for lack of a secular purpose, we found that the legislature's sole motive was to promote religion. See *Wallace v. Jaffree, supra,* at 56, 57, 60, 105 S.Ct., at 2489, 2490, 2491; *Stone v. Graham, supra,* 449 U.S., at 41, 43, n. 5, 101 S.Ct., at 193, 194, n. 5; *Epperson v. Arkansas, supra,* 393 U.S., at 103, 107–108, 89 S.Ct., at 269, 272–273; see also *Lynch v. Donnelly, supra,* 465 U.S., at 680, 104

S.Ct., at 1362 (describing *Stone* and *Epperson* as cases in which we invalidated laws "motivated wholly by religious considerations"). Thus, the majority's invalidation of the Balanced Treatment Act is defensible only if the record indicates that the Louisiana Legislature had *no* secular purpose.

It is important to stress that the purpose forbidden by *Lemon* is the purpose to "advance religion." 403 U.S., at 613, 91 S.Ct., at 2111; accord, *ante,* at 2578 ("promote" religion); *Witters v. Washington Dept. of Services for Blind, supra,* 474 U.S., at 486, 106 S.Ct., at 751 ("endorse religion"); *Wallace v. Jaffree,* 472 U.S., at 56, 105 S.Ct., at 2490 ("advance religion"); *ibid.* ("endorse ... religion"); *Committee for Public Education & Religious Liberty v. Nyquist, supra,* 413 U.S., at 788, 93 S.Ct., at 2973 (" 'advancing' ... religion"); *Levitt v. Committee for Public Education & Religious Liberty, supra,* 413 U.S., at 481, 93 S.Ct., at 2820 ("advancing religion"); *Walz v. Tax Comm'n of New York City,* 397 U.S. 664, 674, 90 S.Ct. 1409, 1414, 25 L.Ed.2d 697 (1970) ("establishing, sponsoring, or supporting religion"); *Board of Education v. Allen,* 392 U.S. 236, 243, 88 S.Ct. 1923, 1926, 20 L.Ed.2d 1060 (1968) (" 'advancement or inhibition of religion'") (quoting *Abington School Dist. v. Schempp,* 374 U.S. 203, 222, 83 S.Ct. 1560, 1571, 10 L.Ed.2d 844 (1963)). Our cases in no way imply that the Establishment Clause forbids legislators merely to act upon their religious convictions. We surely would not strike down a law providing money to feed the hungry or shelter the homeless if it could be demonstrated that, but for the religious beliefs of the legislators, the funds would not have been approved. Also, political activism by the religiously motivated is part of our heritage. Notwithstanding the majority's implication to the contrary, *ante,* at 2580–2581, we do not presume that the sole purpose of a law is to advance religion merely because it was supported strongly by organized religions or by adherents of particular faiths. See *Walz v. Tax*

Comm'n of New York City, supra, 397 U.S., at 670, 90 S.Ct., at 1412; cf. *Harris v. McRae,* 448 U.S. 297, 319–320, 100 S.Ct. 2671, 2689–2690, 65 L.Ed.2d 784 (1980). To do so would deprive religious men and women of their right to participate in the political process. Today's religious activism may give us the Balanced Treatment Act, but yesterday's resulted in the abolition of slavery, and tomorrow's may bring relief for famine victims.

Similarly, we will not presume that a law's purpose is to advance religion merely because it "'happens to coincide or harmonize with the tenets of some or all religions,'" *Harris v. McRae, supra,* at 319, 100 S.Ct., at 2689 (quoting *McGowan v. Maryland,* 366 U.S. 420, 442, 81 S.Ct. 1101, 1113, 6 L.Ed.2d 393 (1961)), or because it benefits religion, even substantially. We have, for example, turned back Establishment Clause challenges to restrictions on abortion funding, *Harris v. McRae, supra,* and to Sunday closing laws, *McGowan v. Maryland, supra,* despite the fact that both "agre[e] with the dictates of [some] Judaeo-Christian religions," *id.,* at 442, 81 S.Ct., at 1114. "In many instances, the Congress or state legislatures conclude that the general welfare of society, wholly apart from any religious considerations, demands such regulation." *Ibid.* On many past occasions we have had no difficulty finding a secular purpose for governmental action far more likely to advance religion than the Balanced Treatment Act. See, *e.g., Mueller v. Allen,* 463 U.S., at 394–395, 103 S.Ct., at 3066–3067 (tax deduction for expenses of religious education); *Wolman v. Walter,* 433 U.S., at 236, 97 S.Ct., at 2599 (plurality opinion) (aid to religious schools); *Meek v. Pittenger,* 421 U.S., at 363, 95 S.Ct., at 1762 (same); *Committee for Public Education & Religious Liberty v. Nyquist,* 413 U.S., at 773, 93 S.Ct., at 2965 (same); *Lemon v. Kurtzman,* 403 U.S., at 613, 91 S.Ct., at 2111 (same); *Walz v. Tax Comm'n of New York City, supra,* 397 U.S., at 672, 90 S.Ct., at 1413 (tax exemption for church property); *Board of*

Education v. Allen, supra, 392 U.S., at 243, 88 S.Ct., at 1926 (textbook loans to students in religious schools). Thus, the fact that creation science coincides with the beliefs of certain religions, a fact upon which the majority relies heavily, does not itself justify invalidation of the Act.

Finally, our cases indicate that even certain kinds of governmental actions undertaken with the specific intention of improving the position of religion do not "advance religion" as that term is used in *Lemon.* 403 U.S., at 613, 91 S.Ct., at 2111. Rather, we have said that in at least two circumstances government *must* act to advance religion, and that in a third it *may* do so.

First, since we have consistently described the Establishment Clause as forbidding not only state action motivated by the desire to *advance* religion, but also that intended to "disapprove," "inhibit," or evince "hostility" toward religion, see, *e.g., ante,* at 2578 ("'disapprove'") (quoting *Lynch v. Donnelly, supra,* 465 U.S., at 690, 104 S.Ct., at 1368 (O'Connor, J., concurring)); *Lynch v. Donnelly, supra,* at 673, 104 S.Ct., at 1359 ("hostility"); *Committee for Public Education & Religious Liberty v. Nyquist, supra,* 413 U.S., at 788, 93 S.Ct., at 2973 ("'inhibi[t]'"); and since we have said that governmental "neutrality" toward religion is the preeminent goal of the First Amendment, see, *e.g., Grand Rapids School District v. Ball,* 473 U.S., at 382, 105 S.Ct., at 3221–3222; *Roemer v. Maryland Public Works Bd.,* 426 U.S. 736, 747, 96 S.Ct. 2337, 2345, 49 L.Ed.2d 179 (1976) (plurality opinion); *Committee for Public Education & Religious Liberty v. Nyquist, supra,* 413 U.S., at 792–793, 93 S.Ct., at 2975–2976; a State which discovers that its employees are inhibiting religion must take steps to prevent them from doing so, even though its purpose would clearly be to advance religion. Cf. *Walz v. Tax Comm'n of New York City, supra,* 397 U.S., at 673, 90 S.Ct., at 1413. Thus, if the Louisiana

Legislature sincerely believed that the State's science teachers were being hostile to religion, our cases indicate that it could act to eliminate that hostility without running afoul of *Lemon*'s purpose test.

Second, we have held that intentional governmental advancement of religion is sometimes required by the Free Exercise Clause. For example, in *Hobbie v. Unemployment Appeals Comm'n of Fla.,* 480 U.S. 136, 107 S.Ct. 1046, 94 L.Ed.2d 190 (1987); *Thomas v. Review Bd., Indiana Employment Security Div.,* 450 U.S. 707, 101 S.Ct. 1425, 67 L.Ed.2d 624 (1981); *Wisconsin v. Yoder,* 406 U.S. 205, 92 S.Ct. 1526, 32 L.Ed.2d 15 (1972); and *Sherbert v. Verner,* 374 U.S. 398, 83 S.Ct. 1790, 10 L.Ed.2d 965 (1963), we held that in some circumstances States must accommodate the beliefs of religious citizens by exempting them from generally applicable regulations. We have not yet come close to reconciling *Lemon* and our Free Exercise cases, and typically we do not really try. See, *e.g., Hobbie v. Unemployment Appeals Comm'n of Fla., supra,* 480 U.S., at 144–145, 107 S.Ct., at ----; *Thomas v. Review Bd., Indiana Employment Security Div., supra,* 450 U.S., at 719–720, 101 S.Ct., at 1432–1433. It is clear, however, that members of the Louisiana Legislature were not impermissibly motivated for purposes of the *Lemon* test if they believed that approval of the Balanced Treatment Act was *required* by the Free Exercise Clause.

We have also held that in some circumstances government may act to accommodate religion, even if that action is not required by the First Amendment. See *Hobbie v. Unemployment Appeals Comm'n of Fla., supra,* 480 U.S., at 144–145, 107 S.Ct., at ----. It is well established that "[t]he limits of permissible state accommodation to religion are by no means co-extensive with the noninterference mandated by the Free Exercise Clause." *Walz v. Tax Comm'n of New York City, supra,* 397

U.S., at 673, 90 S.Ct., at 1413; see also *Gillette v. United States,* 401 U.S. 437, 453, 91 S.Ct. 828, 838, 28 L.Ed.2d 168 (1971). We have implied that voluntary governmental accommodation of religion is not only permissible, but desirable. See, *e.g., ibid.* Thus, few would contend that Title VII of the Civil Rights Act of 1964, which both forbids religious discrimination by private-sector employers, 78 Stat. 255, 42 U.S.C. § 2000e-2(a)(1), and requires them reasonably to accommodate the religious practices of their employees, § 2000e(j), violates the Establishment Clause, even though its "purpose" is, of course, to advance religion, and even though it is almost certainly not required by the Free Exercise Clause. While we have warned that at some point, accommodation may devolve into "an unlawful fostering of religion," *Hobbie v. Unemployment Appeals Comm'n of Fla., supra,* 480 U.S., at 145, 107 S.Ct., at 1051, we have not suggested precisely (or even roughly) where that point might be. It is possible, then, that even if the sole motive of those voting for the Balanced Treatment Act was to advance religion, and its passage was not actually required, or even believed to be required, by either the Free Exercise or Establishment Clauses, the Act would nonetheless survive scrutiny under *Lemon's* purpose test.

One final observation about the application of that test: Although the Court's opinion gives no hint of it, in the past we have repeatedly affirmed "our reluctance to attribute unconstitutional motives to the States." *Mueller v. Allen, supra,* 463 U.S., at 394, 103 S.Ct., at 3066; see also *Lynch v. Donnelly,* 465 U.S., at 699, 104 S.Ct., at 1373 (BRENNAN, J., dissenting). We "presume that legislatures act in a constitutional manner." *Illinois v. Krull,* 480 U.S. 340–351, 107 S.Ct. 1160, 1168, 94 L.Ed.2d 364 (1987); see also *Clements v. Fashing,* 457 U.S. 957, 963, 102 S.Ct. 2836, 2843, 73 L.Ed.2d 508 (1982) (plurality opinion); *Rostker v. Goldberg,* 453 U.S. 57, 64, 101 S.Ct. 2646,

2651, 69 L.Ed.2d 478 (1981); *McDonald v. Board of Election Comm'rs of Chicago,* 394 U.S. 802, 809, 89 S.Ct. 1404, 1408, 22 L.Ed.2d 739 (1969). Whenever we are called upon to judge the constitutionality of an act of a state legislature, "we must have 'due regard to the fact that this Court is not exercising a primary judgment but is sitting in judgment upon those who also have taken the oath to observe the Constitution and who have the responsibility for carrying on government.'" *Rostker v. Goldberg, supra,* 453 U.S., at 64, 101 S.Ct., at 2651 (quoting *Joint Anti-Fascist Refugee Committee v. McGrath,* 341 U.S. 123, 164, 71 S.Ct. 624, 644, 95 L.Ed. 817 (1951) (Frankfurter, J., concurring)). This is particularly true, we have said, where the legislature has specifically considered the question of a law's constitutionality. *Ibid.*

With the foregoing in mind, I now turn to the purposes underlying adoption of the Balanced Treatment Act.

II

A

We have relatively little information upon which to judge the motives of those who supported the Act. About the only direct evidence is the statute itself and transcripts of the seven committee hearings at which it was considered. Unfortunately, several of those hearings were sparsely attended, and the legislators who were present revealed little about their motives. We have no committee reports, no floor debates, no remarks inserted into the legislative history, no statement from the Governor, and no postenactment statements or testimony from the bill's sponsor or any other legislators. Cf. *Wallace v. Jaffree,* 472 U.S., at 43, 56–57, 105 S.Ct., at 2482, 2489–2490. Nevertheless, there is ample evidence that the majority is wrong in holding that the Balanced Treatment Act is without secular purpose.

At the outset, it is important to note that the Balanced Treatment Act did not fly through the Louisiana Legislature on wings of fundamentalist religious fervor—which would be unlikely, in any event, since only a small minority of the State's citizens belong to fundamentalist religious denominations. See B. Quinn, H. Anderson, M. Bradley, P. Goetting, & P. Shriver, *Churches and Church Membership in the United States* 16 (1982). The Act had its genesis (so to speak) in legislation introduced by Senator Bill Keith in June 1980. After two hearings before the Senate Committee on Education, Senator Keith asked that his bill be referred to a study commission composed of members of both Houses of the Louisiana Legislature. He expressed hope that the joint committee would give the bill careful consideration and determine whether his arguments were "legitimate." 1 App. E-29–E-30. The committee met twice during the interim, heard testimony (both for and against the bill) from several witnesses, and received staff reports. Senator Keith introduced his bill again when the legislature reconvened. The Senate Committee on Education held two more hearings and approved the bill after substantially amending it (in part over Senator Keith's objection). After approval by the full Senate, the bill was referred to the House Committee on Education. That committee conducted a lengthy hearing, adopted further amendments, and sent the bill on to the full House, where it received favorable consideration. The Senate concurred in the House amendments and on July 20, 1981, the Governor signed the bill into law.

Senator Keith's statements before the various committees that considered the bill hardly reflect the confidence of a man preaching to the converted. He asked his colleagues to "keep an open mind" and not to be "biased" by misleading characterizations of creation science. *Id.*, at E-33. He also urged them to "look at this subject on its merits and not on some preconceived idea." *Id.,* at E-34; see also 2 *id.,* at E-491. Senator Keith's reception was not especially warm. Over his strenuous objection, the Senate Committee on Education voted 5–1 to amend his bill to deprive it of any force; as amended, the bill merely gave teachers *permission* to balance the teaching of creation science or evolution with the other. 1 *id.,* at E-442–E-461. The House Committee restored the "mandatory" language to the bill by a vote of only 6–5, 2 *id.,* at E-626–E-627, and both the full House (by vote of 52–35), *id.,* at E-700–E-706, and full Senate (23–15), *id.,* at E-735–E-738, had to repel further efforts to gut the bill.

The legislators understood that Senator Keith's bill involved a "unique" subject, 1 *id.,* at E-106 (Rep. M. Thompson), and they were repeatedly made aware of its potential constitutional problems, see, *e.g., id.,* at E-26–E-28 (McGehee); *id.,* at E-38–E-39 (Sen. Keith); *id.,* at E-241–E-242 (Rossman); *id.,* at E-257 (Probst); *id.,* at E-261 (Beck); *id.,* at E-282 (Sen. Keith). Although the Establishment Clause, including its secular purpose requirement, was of substantial concern to the legislators, they eventually voted overwhelmingly in favor of the Balanced Treatment Act: The House approved it 71–19 (with 15 members absent), 2 *id.,* at E-716–E-722; the Senate 26–12 (with all members present), *id.,* at E-741–E-744. The legislators specifically designated the protection of "academic freedom" as the purpose of the Act. La.Rev.Stat.Ann. § 17:286.2 (West 1982). We cannot accurately assess whether this purpose is a "sham," *ante,* at 2579, until we first examine the evidence presented to the legislature far more carefully than the Court has done.

Before summarizing the testimony of Senator Keith and his supporters, I wish to make clear that I by no means intend to endorse its accuracy. But my views (and the views of this Court) about creation science and evolution are (or should be) beside the point. Our task is not to judge the debate about teaching the origins of life, but to ascertain what the members of the Louisiana Legislature believed. The vast majority of them voted to approve a bill which explicitly stated a secular purpose; what is crucial is not their *wisdom* in believing that purpose would be achieved by the bill, but their *sincerity* in believing it would be.

Most of the testimony in support of Senator Keith's bill came from the Senator himself and from scientists and educators he presented, many of whom enjoyed academic credentials that may have been regarded as quite impressive by members of the Louisiana Legislature. To a substantial extent, their testimony was devoted to lengthy, and, to the layman, seemingly expert scientific expositions on the origin of life. See, *e.g.*, 1 App. E-11–E-18 (Sunderland); *id.*, at E-50–E-60 (Boudreaux); *id.*, at E-86–E-89 (Ward); *id.*, at E-130–E-153 (Boudreaux paper); *id.*, at E-321–E-326 (Boudreaux); *id.*, at E-423–E-428 (Sen. Keith). These scientific lectures touched upon, *inter alia,* biology, paleontology, genetics, astronomy, astrophysics, probability analysis, and biochemistry. The witnesses repeatedly assured committee members that "hundreds and hundreds" of highly respected, internationally renowned scientists believed in creation science and would support their testimony. See, *e.g.*, *id.*, at E-5 (Sunderland); *id.*, at E-76 (Sen. Keith); *id.*, at E-100–E-101 (Reiboldt); *id.*, at E-327–E-328 (Boudreaux); 2 *id.*, at E-503–E-504 (Boudreaux).

Senator Keith and his witnesses testified essentially as set forth in the following numbered paragraphs:

> (1) There are two and only two scientific explanations for the beginning of life—evolution and creation science. 1 *id.*, at E-6 (Sunderland); *id.*, at E–34 (Sen. Keith); *id.*, at E–280 (Sen. Keith); *id.*, at E-417–E-418 (Sen. Keith). Both are bona fide "sciences." *Id.*, at E-6–E-7 (Sunderland); *id.*, at E–12

(Sunderland); *id.*, at E-416 (Sen. Keith); *id.*, at E-427 (Sen. Keith); 2 *id.*, at E-491–E-492 (Sen. Keith); *id.*, at E-497–E-498 (Sen. Keith). Both posit a theory of the origin of life and subject that theory to empirical testing. Evolution posits that life arose out of inanimate chemical compounds and has gradually evolved over millions of years. Creation science posits that all life forms now on earth appeared suddenly and relatively recently and have changed little. Since there are only two possible explanations of the origin of life, any evidence that tends to disprove the theory of evolution necessarily tends to prove the theory of creation science, and vice versa. For example, the abrupt appearance in the fossil record of complex life, and the extreme rarityof transitional life forms in that record, are evidence for creation science. 1 *id.*, at E-7 (Sunderland); *id.*, at E-12–E-18 (Sunderland); *id.*, at E-45–E-60 (Boudreaux); *id.*, at E-67 (Harlow); *id.*, at E-130–E-153 (Boudreaux paper); *id.*, at E-423–E-428 (Sen. Keith).

(2) The body of scientific evidence supporting creation science is as strong as that supporting evolution. In fact, it may be *stronger*. *Id.*, at E-214 (Young statement); *id.*, at 310 (Sen. Keith); *id.*, at E-416 (Sen. Keith); 2 *id.*, at E-492 (Sen. Keith). The evidence for evolution is far less compelling than we have been led to believe. Evolution is not a scientific "fact," since it cannot actually be observed in a laboratory. Rather, evolution is merely a scientific theory or "guess." 1 *id.*, at E-20–E-21 (Morris); *id.*, at E-85 (Ward); *id.*, at E-100 (Reiboldt); *id.*, at E-328–E-329 (Boudreaux); 2 *id.*, at E-506 (Boudreaux). It is a very bad guess at that. The scientific problems with evolution are so serious that it could accurately be termed a "myth." 1 *id.*, at E-85 (Ward); *id.*, at E-92–E-93 (Kalivoda); *id.*, at E-95–E-97 (Sen. Keith); *id.*, at E-154 (Boudreaux paper); *id.*, at E-329 (Boudreaux); *id.*, at E-453 (Sen. Keith); 2 *id.*, at E-505–E-506 (Boudreaux); *id.*, at E-516 (Young).

(3) Creation science is educationally valuable. Students exposed to it better understand the current state of scientific evidence about the origin of life. 1 *id.*, at E-19 (Sunderland); *id.*, at E-39 (Sen. Keith); *id.*, at E-79 (Kalivoda); *id.*, at E-308 (Sen. Keith); 2 *id.*, at E-513–E-514 (Morris). Those students even have a better understanding of evolution. 1 *id.*, at E-19 (Sunderland). Creation science can and should be presented to children without any religious content. *Id.*, at E-12 (Sunderland); *id.*, at E-22 (Sanderford); *id.*, at E-35–E-36 (Sen. Keith); *id.*, at E-101 (Reiboldt); *id.*, at E-279–E-280 (Sen. Keith); *id.*, at E-282 (Sen. Keith).

(4) Although creation science is educationally valuable and strictly scientific, it is now being censored from or misrepresented in the public schools. *Id.*, at E-19 (Sunderland); *id.*, at E-21 (Morris); *id.*, at E-34 (Sen. Keith); *id.*, at E-37 (Sen. Keith); *id.*, at E-42 (Sen. Keith); *id.*, at E-92 (Kalivoda); *id.*, at E-97–E-98 (Reiboldt); *id.*, at E-214 (Young statement); *id.*, at E-218 (Young statement); *id.*, at E-280 (Sen. Keith); *id.*, at E-309 (Sen. Keith); 2 *id.*, at E-513 (Morris). Evolution, in turn, is misrepresented as an absolute truth. 1 *id.*, at E-63 (Harlow); *id.*, at E-74 (Sen. Keith); *id.*, at E-81 (Kalivoda); *id.*, at E-214 (Young statement); 2 *id.*, at E-507 (Harlow); *id.*, at E-513 (Morris); *id.*, at E–516 (Young). Teachers have been brainwashed by an entrenched scientific establishment composed almost exclusively of scientists to whom evolution is like a "religion." These scientists discriminate against creation scientists so as to prevent evolution's weaknesses from being exposed. 1 *id.*, at E-61 (Boudreaux); *id.*, at E-63–E-64 (Harlow); *id.*, at E-78–E-79 (Kalivoda); *id.*, at E-80 (Kalivoda); *id.*, at E-95–E-97 (Sen. Keith); *id.*, at E-129 (Boudreaux paper); *id.*, at E-218 (Young statement); *id.*, at E-357 (Sen. Keith); *id.*, at E-430 (Boudreaux).

(5) The censorship of creation science has at least two harmful effects. First, it deprives students of knowledge of one of

> the two scientific explanations for the origin of life and leads them to believe that evolution is proven fact; thus, their education suffers and they are wrongly taught that science has proved their religious beliefs false. Second, it violates the Establishment Clause. The United States Supreme Court has held that secular humanism is a religion. *Id.,* at E-36 (Sen. Keith) (referring to *Torcaso v. Watkins,* 367 U.S. 488, 495, n. 11, 81 S.Ct. 1680, 1683, n. 11, 6 L.Ed.2d 982 (1961)); 1 App. E-418 (Sen. Keith); 2 *id.*, at E-499 (Sen. Keith). Belief in evolution is a central tenet of that religion. 1 *id.,* at E-282 (Sen. Keith); *id.,* at E-312–E-313 (Sen. Keith); *id.,* at E-317 (Sen. Keith); *id.,* at E-418 (Sen. Keith); 2 *id.,* at E-499 (Sen. Keith). Thus, by censoring creation science and instructing students that evolution is fact, public school teachers are *now* advancing religion in violation of the Establishment Clause. 1 *id.,* at E-2–E-4 (Sen. Keith); *id.,* at E-36–E-37, E-39 (Sen. Keith); *id.,* at E-154–E-155 (Boudreaux paper); *id.,* at E-281–E-282 (Sen. Keith); *id.,* at E-313 (Sen. Keith); *id.,* at E-315–E-316 (Sen. Keith); *id.,* at E-317 (Sen. Keith); 2 *id.,* at E-499–E-500 (Sen. Keith).

Senator Keith repeatedly and vehemently denied that his purpose was to advance a particular religious doctrine. At the outset of the first hearing on the legislation, he testified: "We are not going to say today that you should have some kind of religious instructions in our schools.... We are not talking about religion today.... I am not proposing that we take the Bible in each science class and read the first chapter of Genesis." 1 *id.,* at E-35. At a later hearing, Senator Keith stressed: "[T]o ... teach religion and disguise it as creationism ... is not my intent. My intent is to see to it that our textbooks are not censored." *Id.,* at E-280. He made many similar statements throughout the hearings. See, *e.g., id.,* at E-41; *id.,* at E-282; *id.,* at E-310; *id.,* at E–417; see also *id.,* at E-44 (Boudreaux); *id.,* at E-80 (Kalivoda).

We have no way of knowing, of course, how many legislators believed the testimony of Senator Keith and his witnesses. But in the absence of evidence to the contrary, we have to assume that many of them did. Given that assumption, the Court today plainly errs in holding that the Louisiana Legislature passed the Balanced Treatment Act for exclusively religious purposes.

B

Even with nothing more than this legislative history to go on, I think it would be extraordinary to invalidate the Balanced Treatment Act for lack of a valid secular purpose. Striking down a law approved by the democratically elected representatives of the people is no minor matter. "The cardinal principle of statutory construction is to save and not to destroy. We have repeatedly held that as between two possible interpretations of a statute, by one of which it would be unconstitutional and by the other valid, our plain duty is to adopt that which will save the act." *NLRB v. Jones & Laughlin Steel Corp.*, 301 U.S. 1, 30, 57 S.Ct. 615, 621, 81 L.Ed. 893 (1937). So, too, it seems to me, with discerning statutory purpose. Even if the legislative history were silent or ambiguous about the existence of a secular purpose—and here it is not—the statute should survive *Lemon*'s purpose test. But even more validation than mere legislative history is present here. The Louisiana Legislature explicitly set forth its secular purpose ("protecting academic freedom") in the very text of the Act. La.Rev.Stat. § 17:286.2 (West 1982). We have in the past repeatedly relied upon or deferred to such expressions, see, *e.g., Committee for Public Education & Religious Liberty v. Regan,* 444 U.S., at 654, 100 S.Ct., at 846–847; *Meek v. Pittenger,* 421 U.S., at 363, 367–368, 95 S.Ct., at 1764–1765; *Committee for Public Education & Religious Liberty v. Nyquist,* 413 U.S., at 773, 93 S.Ct., at 2965–2966; *Levitt v. Committee for Public Education & Religious Liberty,* 413 U.S., at 479–480, n. 7, 93 S.Ct., at 2819

n. 7; *Tilton v. Richardson,* 403 U.S., at 678–679, 91 S.Ct., at 2095–2096 (plurality opinion); *Lemon v. Kurtzman,* 403 U.S., at 613, 91 S.Ct., at 2111; *Board of Education v. Allen,* 392 U.S., at 243, 88 S.Ct., at 1926.

The Court seeks to evade the force of this expression of purpose by stubbornly misinterpreting it, and then finding that the provisions of the Act do not advance that misinterpreted purpose, thereby showing it to be a sham. The Court first surmises that "academic freedom" means "enhancing the freedom of teachers to teach what they will," *ante,* at 2578—even though "academic freedom" in that sense has little scope in the structured elementary and secondary curriculums with which the Act is concerned. Alternatively, the Court suggests that it might mean "maximiz[ing] the comprehensiveness and effectiveness of science instruction," *ante,* at 2579—though that is an exceedingly strange interpretation of the words, and one that is refuted on the very face of the statute. See § 17:286.5. Had the Court devoted to this central question of the meaning of the legislatively expressed purpose a small fraction of the research into legislative history that produced its quotations of religiously motivated statements by individual legislators, it would have discerned quite readily what "academic freedom" meant: *students'* freedom from *indoctrination.* The legislature wanted to ensure that students would be free to decide for themselves how life began, based upon a fair and balanced presentation of the scientific evidence—that is, to protect "the right of each [student] voluntarily to determine what to believe (and what not to believe) free of any coercive pressures from the State." *Grand Rapids School District v. Ball,* 473 U.S., at 385, 105 S.Ct., at 3223. The legislature did not care *whether* the topic of origins was taught; it simply wished to ensure that *when* the topic was taught, students would receive "'all of the evidence.'" *Ante,* at 2579 (quoting Tr. of Oral Arg. 60).

As originally introduced, the "purpose" section of the Balanced Treatment Act read: "This Chapter is enacted for the purposes of protecting academic freedom ... *of students* ... and assisting *students* in their search for truth." 1 App. E–292 (emphasis added). Among the proposed findings of fact contained in the original version of the bill was the following: "Public school instruction in only evolution-science ... *violates the principle of academic freedom because it denies students a choice between scientific models and instead indoctrinates them in evolution science alone.*" *Id.*, at E-295 (emphasis added). Senator Keith unquestionably understood "academic freedom" to mean "freedom from indoctrination." See *id.*, at E-36 (purpose of bill is "to protect academic freedom by providing student choice"); *id.*, at E-283 (purpose of bill is to protect "academic freedom" by giving students a "choice" rather than subjecting them to "indoctrination on origins").

If one adopts the obviously intended meaning of the statutory term "academic freedom," there is no basis whatever for concluding that the purpose they express is a "sham." *Ante,* at 2579. To the contrary, the Act pursues that purpose plainly and consistently. It requires that, whenever the subject of origins is covered, evolution be "taught as a theory, rather than as proven scientific fact" and that scientific evidence inconsistent with the theory of evolution (viz., "creation science") be taught as well. La.Rev.Stat.Ann. § 17:286.4A (West 1982). Living up to its title of "*Balanced Treatment* for Creation-Science and Evolution-Science Act," § 17:286.1, it treats the teaching of creation the same way. It does *not* mandate instruction in creation science, § 17:286.5; *forbids* teachers to present creation science "as proven scientific fact," § 17:286.4A; and *bans* the teaching of creation science unless the theory is (to use the Court's terminology) "discredit[ed] '... at every turn'" with the teaching of evolution. *Ante,* at 2580 (quoting 765 F.2d, at

1257). It surpasses understanding how the Court can see in this a purpose "to restructure the science curriculum to conform with a particular religious viewpoint," *ante,* at 2582, "to provide a persuasive advantage to a particular religious doctrine," *ante,* at 2582, "to promote the theory of creation science which embodies a particular religious tenet," *ante,* at 2582, and "to endorse a particular religious doctrine," *ante,* at 2583.

The Act's reference to "creation" is not convincing evidence of religious purpose. The Act defines creation science as "*scientific evidenc*[*e*]," § 17:286.3(2) (emphasis added), and Senator Keith and his witnesses repeatedly stressed that the subject can and should be presented without religious content. See *supra,* at ----. We have no basis on the record to conclude that creation science need be anything other than a collection of scientific data supporting the theory that life abruptly appeared on earth. See n. 4, *supra.* Creation science, its proponents insist, no more must explain *whence* life came than evolution must explain whence came the inanimate materials from which it says life evolved. But even if that were not so, to posit a past creator is not to posit the eternal and personal God who is the object of religious veneration. Indeed, it is not even to posit the "*unmoved* mover" hypothesized by Aristotle and other notably nonfundamentalist philosophers. Senator Keith suggested this when he referred to "a creator *however you define a creator.*" 1 App. E–280 (emphasis added).

The Court cites three provisions of the Act which, it argues, demonstrate a "discriminatory preference for the teaching of creation science" and no interest in "academic freedom." *Ante,* at 2579. First, the Act prohibits discrimination only against creation scientists and those who teach creation science. § 17:286.4C. Second, the Act requires local school boards to develop and provide to science teachers "a curriculum guide on presentation of creation-science." § 17:286.7A.

Finally, the Act requires the Governor to designate seven creation scientists who shall, upon request, assist local school boards in developing the curriculum guides. § 17:286.7B. But none of these provisions casts doubt upon the sincerity of the legislators' articulated purpose of "academic freedom"—unless, of course, one gives that term the obviously erroneous meanings preferred by the Court. The Louisiana legislators had been told repeatedly that creation scientists were scorned by most educators and scientists, who themselves had an almost religious faith in evolution. It is hardly surprising, then, that in seeking to achieve a balanced, "nonindoctrinating" curriculum, the legislators protected from discrimination only those teachers whom they thought were *suffering* from discrimination. (Also, the legislators were undoubtedly aware of *Epperson v. Arkansas,* 393 U.S. 97, 89 S.Ct. 266, 21 L.Ed.2d 228 (1968), and thus could quite reasonably have concluded that discrimination against evolutionists was already prohibited.) The two provisions respecting the development of curriculum guides are also consistent with "academic freedom" as the Louisiana Legislature understood the term. Witnesses had informed the legislators that, because of the hostility of most scientists and educators to creation science, the topic had been censored from or badly misrepresented in elementary and secondary school texts. In light of the unavailability of works on creation science suitable for classroom use (a fact appellees concede, see Brief for Appellees 27, 40) and the existence of ample materials on evolution, it was entirely reasonable for the legislature to conclude that science teachers attempting to implement the Act would need a curriculum guide on creation science, but not on evolution, and that those charged with developing the guide would need an easily accessible group of creation scientists. Thus, the provisions of the Act of so much concern to the Court *support* the conclusion that the legislature acted to advance "academic freedom."

The legislative history gives ample evidence of the sincerity of the Balanced Treatment Act's articulated purpose. Witness after witness urged the legislators to support the Act so that students would not be "indoctrinated" but would instead be free to decide for themselves, based upon a fair presentation of the scientific evidence, about the origin of life. See, *e.g.*, 1 App. E-18 (Sunderland) ("all that we are advocating" is presenting "scientific data" to students and "letting [them] make up their own mind [s]"); *id.*, at E-19–E-20 (Sunderland) (Students are now being "indoctrinated" in evolution through the use of "censored school books.... All that we are asking for is [the] open unbiased education in the classroom ... your students deserve"); *id.*, at E-21 (Morris) ("A student cannot [make an intelligent decision about the origin of life] unless he is well informed about both [evolution and creation science]"); *id.*, at E–22 (Sanderford) ("We are asking very simply [that] ... creationism [be presented] alongside ... evolution and let people make their own mind[s] up"); *id.*, at E-23 (Young) (the bill would require teachers to live up to their "obligation to present all theories" and thereby enable "students to make judgments themselves"); *id.*, at E-44 (Boudreaux) ("Our intention is truth and as a scientist, I am interested in truth"); *id.*, at E-60–E-61 (Boudreaux) ("[W]e [teachers] are guilty of a lot of brainwashing.... We have a duty to.... [present the] truth" to students "at all levels from grade school on through the college level"); *id.*, at E-79 (Kalivoda) ("This [hearing] is being held I think to determine whether children will benefit from freedom of information or if they will be handicapped educationally by having little or no information about creation"); *id.*, at E–80 (Kalivoda) ("I am not interested in teaching religion in schools.... I am interested in the truth and [students] having the opportunity to hear more than one side"); *id.*, at E-98

(Reiboldt) ("The students have a right to know there is an alternate creationist point of view. They have a right to know the scientific evidences which suppor[t] that alternative"); *id.*, at E-218 (Young statement) (passage of the bill will ensure that "communication of scientific ideas and discoveries may be unhindered"); 2 *id.*, at E-514 (Morris) ("[A]re we going to allow [students] to look at evolution, to look at creationism, and to let one or the other stand or fall on its own merits, or will we by failing to pass this bill ... deny students an opportunity to hear another viewpoint?"); *id.*, at E-516–E-517 (Young) ("We want to give the children here in this state an equal opportunity to see both sides of the theories"). Senator Keith expressed similar views. See *e.g.*, 1 *id.*, at E-36; *id.*, at E-41; *id.*, at E-280; *id.*, at E-283.

Legislators other than Senator Keith made only a few statements providing insight into their motives, but those statements cast no doubt upon the sincerity of the Act's articulated purpose. The legislators were concerned primarily about the manner in which the subject of origins was presented in Louisiana schools—specifically, about whether scientifically valuable information was being censored and students misled about evolution. Representatives Cain, Jenkins, and F. Thompson seemed impressed by the scientific evidence presented in support of creation science. See 2 *id.*, at E-530 (Rep. F. Thompson); *id.*, at E-533 (Rep. Cain); *id.*, at E-613 (Rep. Jenkins). At the first study commission hearing, Senator Picard and Representative M. Thompson questioned Senator Keith about Louisiana teachers' treatment of evolution and creation science. See 1 *id.*, at E-71–E-74. At the close of the hearing, Representative M. Thompson told the audience:

"We as members of the committee will also receive from the staff information of what is currently being taught in the Louisiana public schools. We really want to see [it]. I ... have no idea in what manner [biology] is presented and in what manner the creationist theories [are] excluded in the public school [s]. We want to look at what the status of the situation is." *Id.,* at E-104.

Legislators made other comments suggesting a concern about censorship and misrepresentation of scientific information. See, *e.g., id.,* at E-386 (Sen. McLeod); 2 *id.,* at E-527 (Rep. Jenkins); *id.,* at E-528 (Rep. M. Thompson); *id.,* at E-534 (Rep. Fair).

It is undoubtedly true that what prompted the legislature to direct its attention to the misrepresentation of evolution in the schools (rather than the inaccurate presentation of other topics) was its awareness of the tension between evolution and the religious beliefs of many children. But even appellees concede that a valid secular purpose is not rendered impermissible simply because its pursuit is prompted by concern for religious sensitivities. Tr. of Oral Arg. 43, 56. If a history teacher falsely told her students that the bones of Jesus Christ had been discovered, or a physics teacher that the Shroud of Turin had been conclusively established to be inexplicable on the basis of natural causes, I cannot believe (despite the majority's implication to the contrary, see *ante,* at 2582) that legislators or school board members would be constitutionally prohibited from taking corrective action, simply because that action was prompted by concern for the religious beliefs of the misinstructed students.

In sum, even if one concedes, for the sake of argument, that a majority of the Louisiana Legislature voted for the Balanced Treatment Act partly in order to foster (rather than merely eliminate discrimination against) Christian fundamentalist beliefs, our cases establish that that alone would not suffice to invalidate the Act, so long as there was a genuine secular purpose as well. We have, moreover, no adequate basis for disbelieving the secular purpose set forth in the Act itself, or for concluding that it is a sham enacted to conceal the legislators' violation of their oaths of office. I am astonished by the Court's unprecedented readiness to reach such a conclusion, which I can only attribute to an intellectual predisposition created by the facts and the legend of *Scopes v. State,* 154 Tenn. 105, 289 S.W. 363 (1927)—an instinctive reaction that any governmentally imposed requirements bearing upon the teaching of evolution must be a manifestation of Christian fundamentalist repression. In this case, however, it seems to me the Court's position is the repressive one. The people of Louisiana, including those who are Christian fundamentalists, are quite entitled, as a secular matter, to have whatever scientific evidence there may be against evolution presented in their schools, just as Mr. Scopes was entitled to present whatever scientific evidence there was for it. Perhaps what the Louisiana Legislature has done is unconstitutional because there *is* no such evidence, and the scheme they have established will amount to no more than a presentation of the Book of Genesis. But we cannot say that on the evidence before us in this summary judgment context, which includes ample uncontradicted testimony that "creation science" is a body of scientific knowledge rather than revealed belief. *Infinitely less* can we say (or should we say) that the scientific evidence for evolution is so conclusive that no one could be gullible enough to believe that there is any real scientific evidence to the contrary, so that the legislation's stated purpose must be a lie. Yet that illiberal judgment, that *Scopes*-in-reverse, is ultimately the basis on which the Court's facile rejection of the Louisiana Legislature's purpose must rest.

Since the existence of secular purpose is so entirely clear, and thus dispositive, I will not go on to discuss the fact that, even if the Louisiana Legislature's purpose were exclusively to advance religion, some of the well-established exceptions to the impermissibility of that purpose might be applicable—the validating intent to eliminate a perceived discrimination against a particular religion, to facilitate its free exercise, or to accommodate it. See *supra,* at ----. I am not in any case enamored of those amorphous exceptions, since I think them no more than unpredictable correctives to what is (as the next Part of this opinion will discuss) a fundamentally unsound rule. It is surprising, however, that the Court does not address these exceptions, since the context of the legislature's action gives some reason to believe they may be applicable.

Because I believe that the Balanced Treatment Act had a secular purpose, which is all the first component of the *Lemon* test requires, I would reverse the judgment of the Court of Appeals and remand for further consideration.

III

I have to this point assumed the validity of the *Lemon* "purpose" test. In fact, however, I think the pessimistic evaluation that the Chief Justice made of the totality of *Lemon* is particularly applicable to the "purpose" prong: it is "a constitutional theory [that] has no basis in the history of the amendment it seeks to interpret, is difficult to apply and yields unprincipled results...." *Wallace v. Jaffree,* 472 U.S., at 112, 105 S.Ct., at 2519 (Rehnquist, J., dissenting).

Our cases interpreting and applying the purpose test have made such a maze of the Establishment Clause that even the most conscientious governmental officials can only guess what motives will be held unconstitutional. We have said essentially the following: Government may not act with the purpose of advancing religion, except when forced to do so by the Free Exercise Clause (which is now and then); or when eliminating existing governmental hostility to religion (which exists sometimes); or even when merely accommodating governmentally uninhibited religious practices, except that at some point (it is unclear where) intentional accommodation results in the fostering of religion, which is of course unconstitutional. See *supra*, at ----.

But the difficulty of knowing what vitiating purpose one is looking for is as nothing compared with the difficulty of knowing how or where to find it. For while it is possible to discern the objective "purpose" of a statute (*i.e.*, the public good at which its provisions appear to be directed), or even the formal motivation for a statute where that is explicitly set forth (as it was, to no avail, here), discerning the subjective motivation of those enacting the statute is, to be honest, almost always an impossible task. The number of possible motivations, to begin with, is not binary, or indeed even finite. In the present case, for example, a particular legislator need not have voted for the Act either because he wanted to foster religion or because he wanted to improve education. He may have thought the bill would provide jobs for his district, or may have wanted to make amends with a faction of his party he had alienated on another vote, or he may have been a close friend of the bill's sponsor, or he may have been repaying a favor he owed the majority leader, or he may have hoped the Governor would appreciate his vote and make a fundraising appearance for him, or he may have been pressured to vote for a bill he disliked by a wealthy contributor or by a flood of constituent mail, or he may have been seeking favorable publicity, or he may have been reluctant to hurt the feelings of a loyal staff member who worked on the bill, or he may have been settling an old score with a legislator who opposed the bill, or he may have been mad at his wife who opposed the bill, or he may have been intoxicated and utterly *un*motivated when the vote was called, or he may have accidentally voted "yes" instead of "no," or, of course, he may have had (and very likely did have) a combination of some of the above and many other motivations. To look for *the sole purpose* of even a single legislator is probably to look for something that does not exist.

Putting that problem aside, however, where ought we to look for the individual legislator's purpose? We cannot of course assume that every member present (if, as is unlikely, we know who or even how many they were) agreed with the motivation expressed in a particular legislator's pre-enactment floor or committee statement. Quite obviously, "[w]hat motivates one legislator to make a speech about a statute is not necessarily what motivates scores of others to enact it." *United States v. O'Brien,* 391 U.S. 367, 384, 88 S.Ct. 1673, 1683, 20 L.Ed.2d 672 (1968). Can we assume, then, that they all agree with the motivation expressed in the staff-prepared committee reports they might have read—even though we are unwilling to assume that they agreed with the motivation expressed in the very statute that they voted for? Should we consider postenactment floor statements? Or postenactment testimony from legislators, obtained expressly for the lawsuit? Should we consider media reports on the realities of the legislative bargaining? All of these sources, of course, are eminently manipulable. Legislative histories can be contrived and sanitized, favorable media coverage orchestrated, and postenactment recollections conveniently distorted. Perhaps most valuable of all would be more objective indications—for example, evidence regarding the individual legislators' religious affiliations. And if that, why not evidence regarding the fervor or tepidity of their beliefs?

Having achieved, through these simple means, an assessment of what individual legislators intended, we must still confront the question (yet to be addressed in any of our cases) how *many* of them must have the invalidating intent. If a state senate approves a bill by vote of 26 to 25, and only one of the

26 intended solely to advance religion, is the law unconstitutional? What if 13 of the 26 had that intent? What if 3 of the 26 had the impermissible intent, but 3 of the 25 voting against the bill were motivated by religious hostility or were simply attempting to "balance" the votes of their impermissibly motivated colleagues? Or is it possible that the intent of the bill's sponsor is alone enough to invalidate it—on a theory, perhaps, that even though everyone else's intent was pure, what they produced was the fruit of a forbidden tree?

Because there are no good answers to these questions, this Court has recognized from Chief Justice Marshall, see *Fletcher v. Peck,* 6 Cranch 87, 13 0, 3 L.Ed. 162 (1810), to Chief Justice Warren, *United States v. O'Brien, supra,* 391 U.S. at 383–384, 88 S.Ct. at 1682–83, that determining the subjective intent of legislators is a perilous enterprise. See also *Palmer v. Thompson,* 403 U.S. 217, 224–225, 91 S.Ct. 1940, 1944–1945, 29 L.Ed.2d 438 (1971); *Epperson v. Arkansas,* 393 U.S., at 113, 89 S.Ct., at 275 (Black, J., concurring). It is perilous, I might note, not just for the judges who will very likely reach the wrong result, but also for the legislators who find that they must assess the validity of proposed legislation—and risk the condemnation of having voted for an unconstitutional measure—not on the basis of what the legislation contains, nor even on the basis of what they themselves intend, but on the basis of what *others* have in mind.

Given the many hazards involved in assessing the subjective intent of governmental decisionmakers, the first prong of *Lemon* is defensible, I think, only if the text of the Establishment Clause demands it. That is surely not the case. The Clause states that "Congress shall make no law respecting an establishment of religion." One could argue, I suppose, that any time Congress acts with the *intent* of advancing religion, it has enacted a "law respecting an establishment of religion"; but far from being an unavoidable reading, it is quite an unnatural one. I doubt, for example, that the Clayton Act, 38 Stat. 730, as amended, 15 U.S.C. § 12 *et seq.*, could reasonably be described as a "law respecting an establishment of religion" if bizarre new historical evidence revealed that it lacked a secular purpose, even though it has no discernible nonsecular effect. It is, in short, far from an inevitable reading of the Establishment Clause that it forbids all governmental action intended to advance religion; and if not inevitable, any reading with such untoward consequences must be wrong.

In the past we have attempted to justify our embarrassing Establishment Clause jurisprudence on the ground that it "sacrifices clarity and predictability for flexibility." *Committee for Public Education & Religious Liberty v. Regan,* 444 U.S., at 662, 100 S.Ct., at 851. One commentator has aptly characterized this as "a euphemism ... for ... the absence of any principled rationale." Choper, *supra* n. 7, at 681. I think it time that we sacrifice some "flexibility" for "clarity and predictability." Abandoning *Lemon*'s purpose test—a test which exacerbates the tension between the Free Exercise and Establishment Clauses, has no basis in the language or history of the Amendment, and, as today's decision shows, has wonderfully flexible consequences—would be a good place to start.

The Constitution is not a bulldozer of social engineering

Lee v. Weisman, 505 U.S. 577 (1992)

Justice Scalia, with whom the Chief Justice, Justice White, and Justice Thomas join, dissenting.

Three Terms ago, I joined an opinion recognizing that the Establishment Clause must be construed in light of the "[g]overnment policies of accommodation, acknowledgment, and support for religion [that] are an accepted part of our political and cultural heritage." That opinion affirmed that "the meaning of the Clause is to be determined by reference to historical practices and understandings." It said that "[a] test for implementing the protections of the Establishment Clause that, if applied with consistency, would invalidate longstanding traditions cannot be a proper reading of the Clause." *County of Allegheny v. American Civil Liberties Union, Greater Pittsburgh Chapter,* 492 U.S. 573, 657, 670, 109 S.Ct. 3086, 3135, 3142, 106 L.Ed.2d 472 (1989) (Kennedy, J., concurring in judgment in part and dissenting in part).

These views of course prevent me from joining today's opinion, which is conspicuously bereft of any reference to history. In holding that the Establishment Clause prohibits invocations and benedictions at public-school graduation ceremonies, the Court—with nary a mention that it is doing so—lays waste a tradition that is as old as public-school graduation ceremonies themselves, and that is a component of an even more longstanding American tradition of nonsectarian prayer to God at public celebrations generally. As its instrument of destruction, the bulldozer of its social engineering, the Court invents a boundless, and boundlessly manipulable, test of psychological coercion, which promises to do for the Establishment Clause what the *Durham* rule did for the insanity defense. See *Durham v. United States,* 94 U.S.App.D.C. 228, 214 F.2d 862 (1954). Today's opinion shows more forcefully than volumes of argumentation why our Nation's protection, that fortress which is our Constitution, cannot possibly rest upon the changeable philosophical predilections of the Justices of this Court, but must have deep foundations in the historic practices of our people.

I

Justice Holmes' aphorism that "a page of history is worth a volume of logic," *New York Trust Co. v. Eisner,* 256 U.S. 345, 349, 41 S.Ct. 506, 507, 65 L.Ed. 963 (1921), applies with particular force to our Establishment Clause jurisprudence. As we have recognized, our interpretation of the Establishment Clause should "compor[t] with what history reveals was the contemporaneous understanding of its guarantees." *Lynch v. Donnelly,* 465 U.S. 668, 673, 104 S.Ct. 1355, 1359, 79 L.Ed.2d 604 (1984). "[T]he line we must draw between the permissible and the impermissible is one which accords with history and faithfully reflects the understanding of the Founding Fathers." *School Dist. of Abington v. Schempp,* 374 U.S. 203, 294, 83 S.Ct. 1560, 1609, 10 L.Ed.2d 844 (1963) (Brennan, J., concurring). "[H]istorical evidence sheds light not only on what the draftsmen intended the Establishment Clause to mean, but also on how they thought that Clause applied" to contemporaneous practices. *Marsh v. Chambers,* 463 U.S. 783, 790, 103 S.Ct. 3330, 3335, 77 L.Ed.2d 1019 (1983). Thus, "[t]he existence from the beginning of the Nation's life of a practice, [while] not conclusive of its constitutionality ...[,] is a fact of considerable import in the interpretation" of the Establishment Clause. *Walz v. Tax Comm'n of New York City,* 397 U.S. 664, 681, 90 S.Ct. 1409, 1417–1418, 25 L.Ed.2d 697 (1970) (Brennan, J., concurring).

The history and tradition of our Nation are replete with public ceremonies featuring prayers of thanksgiving and petition. Illustrations of this point have been amply provided in our prior opinions, see, *e.g., Lynch, supra,* 465 U.S., at 674–678, 104 S.Ct., at 1359–1361; *Marsh, supra,* 463 U.S., at 786–788, 103 S.Ct., at 3333–3334; see also *Wallace v. Jaffree,* 472 U.S. 38, 100–103, 105 S.Ct. 2479, 2512–2514, 86 L.Ed.2d 29 (1985) (Rehnquist, J., dissenting); *Engel v. Vitale,* 370 U.S. 421, 446–450, and n. 3, 82 S.Ct. 1261, 1275–1277, and n. 3, 8 L.Ed.2d 601 (1962) (Stewart, J., dissenting), but since the Court is so oblivious to our history as to suggest that the Constitution restricts "preservation and transmission of religious beliefs ... to the private sphere," *ante,* at 2656, it appears necessary to provide another brief account.

From our Nation's origin, prayer has been a prominent part of governmental ceremonies and proclamations. The Declaration of Independence, the document marking our birth as a separate people, "appeal[ed] to the Supreme Judge of the world for the rectitude of our intentions" and avowed "a firm reliance on the protection of divine Providence." In his first inaugural address, after swearing his oath of office on a Bible, George Washington deliberately made a prayer a part of his first official act as President:

> "[I]t would be peculiarly improper to omit in this first official act my fervent supplications to that Almighty Being who rules over the universe, who presides in the councils of nations, and whose providential aids can supply every human defect, that His benediction may consecrate to the liberties and happiness of the people of the United States a Govern-

ment instituted by themselves for these essential purposes." Inaugural Addresses of the Presidents of the United States, S.Doc. 101–10, p. 2 (1989).

Such supplications have been a characteristic feature of inaugural addresses ever since. Thomas Jefferson, for example, prayed in his first inaugural address: "[M]ay that Infinite Power which rules the destinies of the universe lead our councils to what is best, and give them a favorable issue for your peace and prosperity." *Id.*, at 17. In his second inaugural address, Jefferson acknowledged his need for divine guidance and invited his audience to join his prayer:

> "I shall need, too, the favor of that Being in whose hands we are, who led our fathers, as Israel of old, from their native land and planted them in a country flowing with all the necessaries and comforts of life; who has covered our infancy with His providence and our riper years with His wisdom and power, and to whose goodness I ask you to join in supplications with me that He will so enlighten the minds of your servants, guide their councils, and prosper their measures that whatsoever they do shall result in your good, and shall secure to you the peace, friendship, and approbation of all nations." *Id.*, at 22–23.

Similarly, James Madison, in his first inaugural address, placed his confidence

> "in the guardianship and guidance of that Almighty Being whose power regulates the destiny of nations, whose blessings have been so conspicuously dispensed to this rising Republic, and to whom we are bound to address our devout gratitude for the past, as well as our fervent supplications and best hopes for the future." *Id.*, at 28.

Most recently, President Bush, continuing the tradition established by President Washington, asked those attending his inauguration to bow their heads, and made a prayer his first official act as President. *Id.,* at 346.

Our national celebration of Thanksgiving likewise dates back to President Washington. As we recounted in *Lynch:*

> "The day after the First Amendment was proposed, Congress urged President Washington to proclaim 'a day of public thanksgiving and prayer, to be observed by acknowledging with grateful hearts the many and signal favours of Almighty God.' President Washington proclaimed November 26, 1789, a day of thanksgiving to 'offe[r] our prayers and supplications to the Great Lord and Ruler of Nations, and beseech Him to pardon our national and other transgressions....'" 465 U.S., at 675, n. 2, 104 S.Ct., at 1360, n. 2 (citations omitted).
>
> This tradition of Thanksgiving Proclamations—with their religious theme of prayerful gratitude to God—has been adhered to by almost every President. *Id.,* at 675, and nn. 2 and 3, 104 S.Ct., at 1360, and nn. 2 and 3; *Wallace v. Jaffree, supra,* 472 U.S., at 100–103, 105 S.Ct. at 2512–2514 (Rehnquist, J., dissenting).

The other two branches of the Federal Government also have a long-established practice of prayer at public events. As we detailed in *Marsh,* congressional sessions have opened with a chaplain's prayer ever since the First Congress. 463 U.S., at 787–788, 103 S.Ct., at 3334. And this Court's own sessions have opened with the invocation "God save the United States and this Honorable Court" since the days of Chief Justice Marshall. 1 C. Warren, *The Supreme Court in United States History* 469 (1922).

In addition to this general tradition of prayer at public ceremonies, there exists a more specific tradition of invocations and benedictions at public school graduation exercises. By one account, the first public high school graduation ceremony took place in Connecticut in July 1868—the very month, as it happens, that the Fourteenth Amendment (the vehicle by which the Establishment Clause has been applied against the States) was ratified—when "15 seniors from the Norwich Free Academy marched in their best Sunday suits and dresses into a church hall and waited through majestic music and long prayers." Brodinsky, "Commencement Rites Obsolete? Not At All, A 10-Week Study Shows," 10 *Updating School Board Policies*, No. 4, p. 3 (Apr. 1979). As the Court obliquely acknowledges in describing the "customary features" of high school graduations, *ante,* at 2653, and as respondents do not contest, the invocation and benediction have long been recognized to be "as traditional as any other parts of the [school] graduation program and are widely established." H. McKown, *Commencement Activities* 56 (1931); see also Brodinsky, *supra,* at 5.

II

The Court presumably would separate graduation invocations and benedictions from other instances of public "preservation and transmission of religious beliefs" on the ground that they involve "psychological coercion." I find it a sufficient embarrassment that our Establishment Clause jurisprudence regarding holiday displays, see *County of Allegheny v. American Civil Liberties Union, Greater Pittsburgh Chapter,* 492 U.S. 573, 109 S.Ct. 3086, 106 L.Ed.2d 472 (1989), has come to "requir[e] scrutiny more commonly associated with interior decorators than with the judiciary." *American Jewish Congress v. Chicago,* 827 F.2d 120, 129 (CA7 1987) (Easterbrook, J., dissenting). But interior decorating is a rock-hard science compared to psychology practiced by amateurs. A few citations of "[r]esearch in psychology" that have no particular bearing upon the precise issue here, *ante*, at 2659, cannot disguise the fact that the Court has gone beyond the realm where judges know what they are doing. The Court's argument that state officials have "coerced" students to take part in the invocation and benediction at graduation ceremonies is, not to put too fine a point on it, incoherent.

The Court identifies two "dominant facts" that it says dictate its ruling that invocations and benedictions at public school graduation ceremonies violate the Establishment Clause. *Ante*, at 2655. Neither of them is in any relevant sense true.

A

The Court declares that students' "attendance and participation in the [invocation and benediction] are in a fair and real sense obligatory." *Ibid.* But what exactly is this "fair and real sense"? According to the Court, students at graduation who want "to avoid the fact or appearance of participation," *ante*, at 2656, in the invocation and benediction are *psychologically* obligated by "public pressure, as well as peer pressure, ... to stand as a group or, at least, maintain respectful silence" during those prayers. *Ante*, at 2658. This assertion—*the very linchpin of the Court's opinion* —is almost as intriguing for what it does not say as for what it says. It does not say, for example, that students are psychologically coerced to bow their heads, place their hands in a Dürer-like prayer position, pay attention to the prayers, utter "Amen," or in fact pray. (Perhaps further intensive psychological research remains to be done on these matters.) It claims only that students are psychologically coerced "to stand ... *or*, at least, maintain respectful silence." *Ibid.* (emphasis added). Both halves of this disjunctive (*both* of which must amount to the fact or appearance of participation in prayer if the Court's analysis is to survive on its own terms) merit particular attention.

To begin with the latter: The Court's notion that a student who simply *sits* in "respectful silence" during the invocation and benediction (when all others are standing) has somehow joined—or would somehow be perceived as having joined—in the prayers is nothing short of ludicrous. We indeed live in a vulgar age. But surely "our social conventions," *ibid.*, have not coarsened to the point that anyone who does not stand on his chair and shout obscenities can reasonably be deemed to have assented to everything said in his presence. Since the Court does not dispute that students exposed to prayer at graduation ceremonies retain (despite "subtle coercive pressures," *ante*, at 2656) the free will to sit, cf. *ante*, at 2658, there is absolutely no basis for the Court's decision. It is fanciful enough to say that "a reasonable dissenter," standing head erect in a class of bowed heads, "could believe that the group exercise signified her own participation or approval of it," *ibid.* It is beyond the absurd to say that she could entertain such a belief while pointedly declining to rise.

But let us assume the very worst, that the nonparticipating graduate is "subtly coerced" ... to stand! Even that half of the disjunctive does not remotely establish a "participation" (or an "appearance of participation") in a religious exercise. The Court acknowledges that "in our culture standing ... can signify adherence to a view or simple respect for the views of others." *Ibid.* (Much more often the latter than the former, I think, except perhaps in the proverbial town meeting, where one votes by standing.) But if it is a permissible inference that one who is standing is doing so simply out of respect for the prayers of others that are in progress, then how can it possibly be said that a "reasonable dissenter ... could believe that the group exercise signified her own participation or approval" ? Quite obviously, it cannot. I may add, moreover, that maintaining respect for the religious observances of others is a fundamental civic virtue that government (including the public schools) can and should cultivate—so that even if it were the case that the displaying of such respect might be mistaken for taking part in the prayer, I would deny that the dissenter's interest in avoiding *even the false appearance of participation* constitutionally trumps the government's interest in fostering respect for religion generally.

The opinion manifests that the Court itself has not given careful consideration to its test of psychological coercion. For if it had, how could it observe, with no hint of concern or disapproval, that students stood for the Pledge of Allegiance, which immediately preceded Rabbi Gutterman's invocation? *Ante,* at 2653. The government can, of course, no more coerce political orthodoxy than religious orthodoxy. *West Virginia Bd. of Ed. v. Barnette,* 319 U.S. 624, 642, 63 S.Ct. 1178, 1187, 87 L.Ed. 1628 (1943). Moreover, since the Pledge of Allegiance has been revised since *Barnette* to include the phrase "under God," recital of the Pledge would appear to raise the same Establishment Clause issue as the invocation and benediction. If students were psychologically coerced to remain standing during the invocation, they must also have been psychologically coerced, moments before, to stand for (and thereby, in the Court's view, take part in or appear to take part in) the Pledge. Must the Pledge therefore be barred from the public schools (both from graduation ceremonies and from the classroom)? In *Barnette* we held that a public school student could not be compelled to *recite* the Pledge; we did not even hint that she could not be compelled to observe respectful silence—indeed, even to *stand* in respectful silence—when those who wished to recite it did so. Logically, that ought to be the next project for the Court's bulldozer.

I also find it odd that the Court concludes that high school graduates may not be subjected to this supposed psychological coercion, yet refrains from addressing whether "mature adults" may. *Ante,* at 2658. I had thought that the reason graduation from high school is regarded as so significant an event is that it is generally associated with transition from adolescence to young adulthood. Many graduating seniors, of course, are old enough to vote. Why, then, does the Court treat them as though they were first-graders? Will we soon have a jurisprudence that distinguishes between mature and immature adults?

B

The other "dominant fac[t]" identified by the Court is that "[s]tate officials direct the performance of a formal religious exercise" at school graduation ceremonies. *Ante,* at 2655. "Direct[ing] the performance of a formal religious exercise" has a sound of liturgy to it, summoning up images of the principal directing acolytes where to carry the cross, or showing the rabbi where to unroll the Torah. A Court professing to be engaged in a "delicate and fact-sensitive" line-drawing, *ante,* at 2661, would better describe what it means as "prescribing the content of an invocation and benediction." But even that would be false. All the record shows is that principals of the Providence public schools, acting within their delegated authority, have invited clergy to deliver invocations and benedictions at graduations; and that Principal Lee invited Rabbi Gutterman, provided him a two-page pamphlet, prepared by the National Conference of Christians and Jews, giving general advice on inclusive prayer for civic occasions, and advised him that his prayers at graduation should be nonsectarian. How these facts can fairly be transformed into the charges that Principal Lee "directed and controlled the content of [Rabbi Gutterman's] prayer," *ante,* at 2656, that school officials "monitor prayer," *ante,* at 2657, and attempted to "'compose official prayers,'" *ante,* at 2656, and that the "government involvement with religious activity in this case is pervasive," *ante,* at 2655, is difficult to fathom. The Court identifies nothing in the record remotely suggesting that school officials have ever drafted, edited, screened, or censored graduation prayers, or that Rabbi Gutterman was a mouthpiece of the school officials.

These distortions of the record are, of course, not harmless error: without them the Court's solemn assertion that the school officials could reasonably be perceived to be "enforc[ing] a religious orthodoxy," *ante,* at 2658, would ring as hollow as it ought.

III

The deeper flaw in the Court's opinion does not lie in its wrong answer to the question whether there was state-induced "peer-pressure" coercion; it lies, rather, in the Court's making violation of the Establishment Clause hinge on such a precious question. The coercion that was a hallmark of historical establishments of religion was coercion of religious orthodoxy and of financial support *by force of law and threat of penalty.* Typically, attendance at the state church was required; only clergy of the official church could lawfully perform sacraments; and dissenters, if tolerated, faced an array of civil disabilities. L. Levy, *The Establishment Clause* 4 (1986). Thus, for example, in the Colony of Virginia, where the Church of England had been established, ministers were required by law to conform to the doctrine and rites of the Church of England; and all persons were required to attend church and observe the Sabbath, were tithed for the public support of Anglican ministers, and were taxed for the costs of building and repairing churches. *Id.,* at 3–4.

The Establishment Clause was adopted to prohibit such an establishment of religion at the federal level (and to protect state establishments of religion from federal interference). I will further acknowledge for the sake of argument that, as some scholars have argued, by 1790 the term "establishment" had acquired an additional meaning—"financial support of religion generally, by public taxation"—that reflected the development of "general or multiple" establishments, not limited to a single church. *Id.*, at 8–9. But that would still be an establishment coerced *by force of law.* And I will further concede that our constitutional tradition, from the Declaration of Independence and the first inaugural address of Washington, quoted earlier, down to the present day, has, with a few aberrations, see *Church of Holy Trinity v. United States,* 143 U.S. 457, 12 S.Ct. 511, 36 L.Ed. 226 (1892), ruled out of order government-sponsored endorsement of religion—even when no legal coercion is present, and indeed even when no ersatz, "peer-pressure" psycho-coercion is present—where the endorsement is sectarian, in the sense of specifying details upon which men and women who believe in a benevolent, omnipotent Creator and Ruler of the world are known to differ (for example, the divinity of Christ). But there is simply no support for the proposition that the officially sponsored nondenominational invocation and benediction read by Rabbi Gutterman—with no one legally coerced to recite them—violated the Constitution of the United States. To the contrary, they are so characteristically American they could have come from the pen of George Washington or Abraham Lincoln himself.

Thus, while I have no quarrel with the Court's general proposition that the Establishment Clause "guarantees that government may not coerce anyone to support or participate in religion or its exercise," *ante,* at 2655, I see no warrant for expanding the concept of coercion beyond acts backed by threat of penalty—a brand of coercion that, happily, is readily discernible to those of us who have made a career of reading the disciples of Blackstone rather than of Freud. The Framers were indeed opposed to coercion of religious worship by the National Government; but, as their own sponsorship of non-sectarian prayer in public events demonstrates, they understood that "[s]peech is not coercive; the listener may do as he likes." *American Jewish Congress v. Chicago,* 827 F.2d, at 132 (Easterbrook, J., dissenting).

This historical discussion places in revealing perspective the Court's extravagant claim that the State has "for all practical purposes," *ante,* at 2656, and "in every practical sense," *ante,* at 2661, compelled students to participate in prayers at graduation. Beyond the fact, stipulated to by the parties, that attendance at graduation is voluntary, there is nothing in the record to indicate that failure of attending students to take part in the invocation or benediction was subject to any penalty or discipline. Contrast this with, for example, the facts of *Barnette*: Schoolchildren were required by law to recite the Pledge of Allegiance; failure to do so resulted in expulsion, threatened the expelled child with the prospect of being sent to a reformatory for criminally inclined juveniles, and subjected his parents to prosecution (and incarceration) for causing delinquency. 319 U.S., at 629–630, 63 S.Ct., at 1181. To characterize the "subtle coercive pressures," *ante,* at 2656, allegedly present here as the "practical" equivalent of the legal sanctions in *Barnette* is ... well, let me just say it is not a "delicate and fact-sensitive" analysis.

The Court relies on our "school prayer" cases, *Engel v. Vitale,* 370 U.S. 421, 82 S.Ct. 1261, 8 L.Ed.2d 601 (1962), and *School Dist. of Abington v. Schempp,* 374 U.S. 203, 83 S.Ct. 1560, 10 L.Ed.2d 844 (1963). *Ante,* at 2658. But whatever the merit of those cases, they do not support, much less compel, the Court's psycho-journey. In the first place, *Engel* and *Schempp* do not constitute an exception to the rule, distilled from historical practice, that public ceremonies may include prayer, see *supra,* at 2679–2681; rather, they simply do not fall within the scope of the rule (for the obvious reason that school instruction is not a public ceremony). Second, we have made clear our understanding that school prayer occurs within a framework in which legal coercion to attend school (*i.e.,* coercion under threat of penalty) provides the ultimate backdrop. In *Schempp,* for example, we emphasized that the prayers were "prescribed as part of the curricular activities of students who are *required by law* to attend school." 374 U.S., at 223, 83 S.Ct., at 1572 (emphasis added). *Engel*'s suggestion that the school prayer program at issue there—which permitted students "to remain silent or be excused from the room," 370 U.S., at 430, 82 S.Ct., at 1266—involved "indirect coercive pressure," *id.,* at 431, 82 S.Ct., at 1267, should be understood against this backdrop of legal coercion. The question whether the opt-out procedure in *Engel* sufficed to dispel the coercion resulting from the mandatory attendance requirement is quite different from the question whether forbidden coercion exists in an environment *utterly devoid of legal compulsion.* And finally, our school prayer cases turn in part on the fact that the classroom is inherently an instructional setting, and daily prayer there—where parents are not present to counter "the students' emulation of teachers as role models and the children's susceptibility to peer pressure," *Edwards v. Aguillard,* 482 U.S. 578, 584, 107 S.Ct. 2573, 2578, 96 L.Ed.2d 510 (1987)—might be thought to raise special concerns regarding state interference with the liberty of parents to direct the religious upbringing of their children: "Families entrust public schools with the education of their children, but condition their trust on the understanding that the classroom will not purposely be used to advance religious views that may conflict with the private beliefs of the student and his or her family." *Ibid.;* see *Pierce v. Society of Sis-*

ters, 268 U.S. 510, 534–535, 45 S.Ct. 571, 573, 69 L.Ed. 1070 (1925). Voluntary prayer at graduation—a one-time ceremony at which parents, friends, and relatives are present—can hardly be thought to raise the same concerns.

IV

Our Religion Clause jurisprudence has become bedeviled (so to speak) by reliance on formulaic abstractions that are not derived from, but positively conflict with, our long-accepted constitutional traditions. Foremost among these has been the so-called *Lemon* test, see *Lemon v. Kurtzman,* 403 U.S. 602, 612–613, 91 S.Ct. 2105, 2111, 29 L.Ed.2d 745 (1971), which has received well-earned criticism from many Members of this Court. See, *e.g., County of Allegheny,* 492 U.S., at 655–656, 109 S.Ct., at 3134 (opinion of Kennedy, J.); *Edwards v. Aguillard, supra,* 482 U.S., at 636–640, 107 S.Ct., at 2605–2607 (Scalia, J., dissenting); *Wallace v. Jaffree,* 472 U.S., at 108–112, 105 S.Ct., at 2516–2518 (Rehnquist, J., dissenting); *Aguilar v. Felton,* 473 U.S. 402, 426–430, 105 S.Ct. 3232, 3245–3247, 87 L.Ed.2d 290 (1985) (O'Connor, J., dissenting); *Roemer v. Board of Pub. Works of Md.,* 426 U.S. 736, 768–769, 96 S.Ct. 2337, 2355, 49 L.Ed.2d 179 (1976) (White, J., concurring in judgment). The Court today demonstrates the irrelevance of *Lemon* by essentially ignoring it, see *ante,* at 2655, and the interment of that case may be the one happy byproduct of the Court's otherwise lamentable decision. Unfortunately, however, the Court has replaced *Lemon* with its psycho-coercion test, which suffers the double disability of having no roots whatever in our people's historic practice, and being as infinitely expandable as the reasons for psychotherapy itself.

Another happy aspect of the case is that it is only a jurisprudential disaster and not a practical one. Given the odd basis for the Court's decision, invocations and benedictions will be able to be given at public school graduations next June, as they have for the past century and a half, so long as school authorities make clear that anyone who abstains from screaming in protest does not necessarily participate in the prayers. All that is seemingly needed is an announcement, or perhaps a written insertion at the beginning of the graduation program, to the effect that, while all are asked to rise for the invocation and benediction, none is compelled to join in them, nor will be assumed, by rising, to have done so. That obvious fact recited, the graduates and their parents may proceed to thank God, as Americans have always done, for the blessings He has generously bestowed on them and on their country.

* * *

The reader has been told much in this case about the personal interest of Mr. Weisman and his daughter, and very little about the personal interests on the other side. They are not inconsequential. Church and state would not be such a difficult subject if religion were, as the Court apparently thinks it to be, some purely personal avocation that can be indulged entirely in secret, like pornography, in the privacy of one's room. For most believers it is *not* that, and has never been. Religious men and women of almost all denominations have felt it necessary to acknowledge and beseech the blessing of God as a people, and not just as individuals, because they believe in the "protection of divine Providence," as the Declaration of Independence put it, not just for individuals but for societies; because they believe God to be, as Washington's first Thanksgiving Proclamation put it, the "Great Lord and Ruler of Nations." One can believe in the effectiveness of such public worship, or one can deprecate and deride it. But the longstanding American tradition of prayer at official ceremonies displays with unmistakable clarity that the Establishment Clause does not forbid the government to accommodate it.

The narrow context of the present case involves a community's celebration of one of the milestones in its young citizens' lives, and it is a bold step for this Court to seek to banish from that occasion, and from thousands of similar celebrations throughout this land, the expression of gratitude to God that a majority of the community wishes to make. The issue before us today is not the abstract philosophical question whether the alternative of frustrating this desire of a religious majority is to be preferred over the alternative of imposing "psychological coercion," or a feeling of exclusion, upon nonbelievers. Rather, the question is *whether a mandatory choice in favor of the former has been imposed by the United States Constitution.* As the age-old practices of our people show, the answer to that question is not at all in doubt.

I must add one final observation: The Founders of our Republic knew the fearsome potential of sectarian religious belief to generate civil dissension and civil strife. And they also knew that nothing, absolutely nothing, is so inclined to foster among religious believers of various faiths a toleration—no, an affection—for one another than voluntarily joining in prayer together, to the God whom they all worship and seek. Needless to say, no one should be compelled to do that, but it is a shame to deprive our public culture of the opportunity, and indeed the encouragement, for people to do it voluntarily. The Baptist or Catholic who heard and joined in the simple and inspiring prayers of Rabbi Gutterman on this official and patriotic occasion was inoculated from religious bigotry and prejudice in a manner that cannot be replicated. To deprive our society of that important unifying mechanism, in order to spare the nonbeliever what seems to me the minimal inconvenience of standing or even sitting in respectful nonparticipation, is as senseless in policy as it is unsupported in law.

For the foregoing reasons, I dissent.

The principle of not applying any principle
Locke v. Davey, 540 U.S. 712 (2004)

Justice Scalia, with whom Justice Thomas joins, dissenting.

In *Church of Lukumi Babalu Aye, Inc. v. Hialeah,* 508 U.S. 520, 113 S.Ct. 2217, 124 L.Ed.2d 472 (1993), the majority opinion held that "[a] law burdening religious practice that is not neutral ... must undergo the most rigorous of scrutiny," *id.,* at 546, 113 S.Ct. 2217, and that "the minimum requirement of neutrality is that a law not discriminate on its face," *id.,* at 533, 113 S.Ct. 2217. The concurrence of two Justices stated that "[w]hen a law discriminates against religion as such, ... it automatically will fail strict scrutiny." *Id.,* at 579, 113 S.Ct. 2217 (Blackmun, J., joined by O'Connor, J., concurring in judgment). And the concurrence of a third Justice endorsed the "noncontroversial principle" that "formal neutrality" is a "necessary conditio[n] for free-exercise constitutionality." *Id.,* at 563, 113 S.Ct. 2217 (SOUTER, J., concurring in part and concurring in judgment). These opinions are irreconcilable with today's decision, which sustains a public benefits program that facially discriminates against religion.

I

We articulated the principle that governs this case more than 50 years ago in *Everson v. Board of Ed. of Ewing,* 330 U.S. 1, 67 S.Ct. 504, 91 L.Ed. 711 (1947):

> "New Jersey cannot hamper its citizens in the free exercise of their own religion. Consequently, it cannot exclude individual Catholics, Lutherans, Mohammedans, Baptists, Jews,

> Methodists, Non-believers, Presbyterians, or the members of any other faith, because of their faith, or lack of it, from receiving the benefits of public welfare legislation." *Id.,* at 16, 67 S.Ct. 504 (emphasis deleted).

When the State makes a public benefit generally available, that benefit becomes part of the baseline against which burdens on religion are measured; and when the State withholds that benefit from some individuals solely on the basis of religion, it violates the Free Exercise Clause no less than if it had imposed a special tax.

That is precisely what the State of Washington has done here. It has created a generally available public benefit, whose receipt is conditioned only on academic performance, income, and attendance at an accredited school. It has then carved out a solitary course of study for exclusion: theology. Wash. Rev.Code Ann. § 28B.119.010(8) (West Supp.2004); Wash. Admin. Code § 250-80-020(12)(g) (2003). No field of study but religion is singled out for disfavor in this fashion. Davey is not asking for a special benefit to which others are not entitled. Cf. *Lyng v. Northwest Indian Cemetery Protective Assn.,* 485 U.S. 439, 453, 108 S.Ct. 1319, 99 L.Ed.2d 534 (1988). He seeks only *equal* treatment—the right to direct his scholarship to his chosen course of study, a right every other Promise Scholar enjoys.

The Court's reference to historical "popular uprisings against procuring taxpayer funds to support church leaders," *ante,* at 1313, is therefore quite misplaced. That history involved not the inclusion of religious ministers in public benefits programs like the one at issue here, but laws that singled them out for financial aid. For example, the Virginia bill at which Madison's Remonstrance was directed provided: "[F]or the support of Christian teachers ... [a] sum payable for tax on the property within this Commonwealth, is hereby assessed ... ." A Bill Establishing a Provision for Teachers of the Christian Religion (1784), reprinted in *Everson, supra,* at 72, 67 S.Ct. 504. Laws supporting the clergy in other States operated in a similar fashion. See S. Cobb, *The Rise of Religious Liberty in America* 131, 169, 270, 295, 304, 386 (1902). One can concede the Framers' hostility to funding the clergy *specifically,* but that says nothing about whether the clergy had to be excluded from benefits the State made available to all. No one would seriously contend, for example, that the Framers would have barred ministers from using public roads on their way to church.

The Court does not dispute that the Free Exercise Clause places some constraints on public benefits programs, but finds none here, based on a principle of "'play in the joints.'" *Ante,* at 1311. I use the term "principle" loosely, for that is not so much a legal principle as a refusal to apply *any* principle when faced with competing constitutional directives. There is nothing anomalous about constitutional commands that abut. A municipality hiring public contractors may not discriminate *against* blacks or *in favor of* them; it cannot discriminate a little bit each way and then plead "play in the joints" when haled into court. If the Religion Clauses demand neutrality, we must enforce them, in hard cases as well as easy ones.

Even if "play in the joints" were a valid legal principle, surely it would apply only when it was a close call whether complying with one of the Religion Clauses would violate the other. But that is not the case here. It is not just that "the State could, consistent with the Federal Constitution, permit Promise Scholars to pursue a degree in devotional theology." *Ibid.* The establishment question *would not even be close,* as is evident from the fact that this Court's decision in *Witters v. Washington Dept. of Servs. for Blind,* 474 U.S. 481, 106 S.Ct. 748, 88 L.Ed.2d 846 (1986), was unanimous. Perhaps some formally neutral public benefits programs are so gerrymandered and devoid of plausible secular purpose that they might raise specters of state aid to religion, but an evenhanded Promise Scholarship Program is not among them.

In any case, the State already has all the play in the joints it needs. There are any number of ways it could respect both its unusually sensitive concern for the conscience of its taxpayers *and* the Federal Free Exercise Clause. It could make the scholarships redeemable only at public universities (where it sets the curriculum), or only for select courses of study. Either option would replace a program that facially discriminates against religion with one that just happens not to subsidize it. The State could also simply abandon the scholarship program altogether. If that seems a dear price to pay for freedom of conscience, it is only because the State has defined that freedom so broadly that it would be offended by a program with such an incidental, indirect religious effect.

What is the nature of the State's asserted interest here? It cannot be protecting the pocketbooks of its citizens; given the tiny fraction of Promise Scholars who would pursue theology degrees, the amount of any citizen's tax bill at stake is *de minimis.* It cannot be preventing mistaken appearance of endorsement; where a State merely declines to penalize students for selecting a religious major, "[n]o reasonable observer is likely to draw ... an inference that the State itself is endorsing a religious practice or belief." *Id.*, at 493, 106 S.Ct. 748 (O'Connor, J., concurring in part and concurring in judgment). Nor can Washington's exclusion be defended as a means of assuring that the State will neither favor nor disfavor Davey in his religious calling. Davey will throughout his life contribute to the public fisc through sales taxes on personal purchases, property taxes on his home, and so on; and nothing in the Court's opinion turns on whether Davey winds up a net winner or loser in the State's tax-and-spend scheme.

No, the interest to which the Court defers is not fear of a conceivable Establishment Clause violation, budget constraints, avoidance of endorsement, or substantive neutrality—none of these. It is a pure philosophical preference: the State's opinion that it would violate taxpayers' freedom of conscience *not* to discriminate against candidates for the ministry. This sort of protection of "freedom of conscience" has no logical limit and can justify the singling out of religion for exclusion from public programs in virtually any context. The Court never says whether it deems this interest compelling (the opinion is devoid of any mention of standard of review) but, self-evidently, it is not.

II

The Court makes no serious attempt to defend the program's neutrality, and instead identifies two features thought to render its discrimination less offensive. The first is the lightness of Davey's burden. The Court offers no authority for approving facial discrimination against religion simply because its material consequences are not severe. I might understand such a test if we were still in the business of reviewing facially neutral laws that merely happen to burden some individual's religious exercise, but we are not. See *Employment Div., Dept. of Human Resources of Ore. v. Smith,* 494 U.S. 872, 885, 110 S.Ct. 1595, 108 L.Ed.2d 876 (1990). Discrimination *on the face of a statute* is something else. The indignity of being singled out for special burdens on the basis of one's religious calling is so profound that the concrete harm produced can never be dismissed as insubstantial. The Court has not required proof of "substantial" concrete harm with other forms of discrimination, see, *e.g., Brown v. Board of Education,* 347 U.S. 483, 493–495, 74 S.Ct. 686, 98 L.Ed. 873 (1954); cf. *Craig v. Boren,* 429 U.S. 190, 97 S.Ct. 451, 50 L.Ed.2d 397 (1976), and it should not do so here.

Even if there were some threshold quantum-of-harm requirement, surely Davey has satisfied it. The First Amendment, after all, guarantees *free* exercise of religion, and when the State exacts a financial penalty of almost $3,000 for religious exercise—whether by tax or by forfeiture of an otherwise available benefit—religious practice is anything *but* free. The Court's only response is that "Promise Scholars may still use their scholarship to pursue a secular degree at a different institution from where they are studying devotional theology." *Ante,* at 1313, n. 4. But part of what makes a Promise Scholarship attractive is that the recipient can apply it to his *preferred* course of study at his *preferred* accredited institution. That is part of the "benefit" the State confers. The Court distinguishes our precedents only by swapping the benefit to which Davey was actually entitled (a scholarship for his chosen course of study) with another, less valuable one (a scholarship for any course of study *but* his chosen one). On such reasoning, any facially discriminatory benefits program can be redeemed simply by redefining what it guarantees.

The other reason the Court thinks this particular facial discrimination less offensive is that the scholarship program was not motivated by animus toward religion. The Court does not explain why the legislature's motive matters, and I fail to see why it should. If a State deprives a citizen of trial by jury or passes an *ex post facto* law, we do not pause to investigate whether it was actually trying to accomplish the evil the Constitution prohibits. It is sufficient that the citizen's rights have been infringed. "[It does not] matter that a legislature consists entirely of the purehearted, if the law it enacts in fact singles out a religious practice for special burdens." *Lukumi,* 508 U.S., at 559, 113 S.Ct. 2217 (Scalia, J., concurring in part and concurring in judgment).

The Court has not approached other forms of discrimination this way. When we declared racial segregation unconstitutional, we did not ask whether the State had originally adopted the regime, not out of "animus" against blacks, but because of a well-meaning but misguided belief that the races would be better off apart. It was sufficient to note the current effect of segregation on racial minorities. See *Brown, supra,* at 493–95, 74 S.Ct. 686. Similarly, the Court does not excuse statutes that facially discriminate against women just because they are the vestigial product of a well-intentioned view of women's appropriate social role. See, *e.g., United States v. Virginia,* 518 U.S. 515, 549–551, 116 S.Ct. 2264, 135 L.Ed.2d 735 (1996); *Adkins v. Children's Hospital of D. C.,* 261 U.S. 525, 552–553, 43 S.Ct. 394, 67 L.Ed. 785 (1923). We do sometimes look to legislative intent to smoke out more subtle instances of discrimination, but we do so as a *supplement* to the core guarantee of facially equal treatment, not as a replacement for it. See *Hunt v. Cromartie,* 526 U.S. 541, 546, 119 S.Ct. 1545, 143 L.Ed.2d 731 (1999).

There is no need to rely on analogies, however, because we have rejected the Court's methodology in this very context. In *McDaniel v. Paty,* 435 U.S. 618, 98 S.Ct. 1322, 55 L.Ed.2d 593 (1978), we considered a Tennessee statute that disqualified clergy from participation in the state constitutional convention. That statute, like the one here, was based upon a state constitutional provision—a clause in the 1796 Tennessee Constitution that disqualified clergy from sitting in the legislature. *Id.,* at 621, and n. 1, 98 S.Ct. 1322 (plurality opinion). The State defended the statute as an attempt to be faithful to its constitutional separation of church and state, and we accepted that claimed benevolent purpose as bona fide. See *id.,* at 628, 98 S.Ct. 1322. Nonetheless, because it did not justify facial discrimination against religion, we invalidated the restriction. *Id.,* at 629, 98 S.Ct. 1322.

It may be that Washington's original purpose in excluding

the clergy from public benefits was benign, and the same might be true of its purpose in maintaining the exclusion today. But those singled out for disfavor can be forgiven for suspecting more invidious forces at work. Let there be no doubt: This case is about discrimination against a religious minority. Most citizens of this country identify themselves as professing some religious belief, but the State's policy poses no obstacle to practitioners of only a tepid, civic version of faith. Those the statutory exclusion actually affects—those whose belief in their religion is so strong that they dedicate their study and their lives to its ministry—are a far narrower set. One need not delve too far into modern popular culture to perceive a trendy disdain for deep religious conviction. In an era when the Court is so quick to come to the aid of other disfavored groups, see, *e.g., Romer v. Evans,* 517 U.S. 620, 635, 116 S.Ct. 1620, 134 L.Ed.2d 855 (1996), its indifference in this case, which involves a form of discrimination to which the Constitution actually speaks, is exceptional.

* * *

Today's holding is limited to training the clergy, but its logic is readily extendible, and there are plenty of directions to go. What next? Will we deny priests and nuns their prescription-drug benefits on the ground that taxpayers' freedom of conscience forbids medicating the clergy at public expense? This may seem fanciful, but recall that France has proposed banning religious attire from schools, invoking interests in secularism no less benign than those the Court embraces today. See Sciolino, "Chirac Backs Law to Keep Signs of Faith Out of School," *N.Y. Times,* Dec. 18, 2003, p. A17, col. 1. When the public's freedom of conscience is invoked to justify denial of equal treatment, benevolent motives shade into indifference and ultimately into repression. Having accepted the justification in this case, the Court is less well equipped to fend it off in the future. I respectfully dissent.

The dictatorship of a shifting Supreme Court majority
McCreary County, Ky. v. American Civil Liberties Union of Ky.,
545 U.S. 844 (2005)

Justice Scalia, with whom the Chief Justice and Justice Thomas join, and with whom Justice Kennedy joins as to Parts II and III, dissenting.

I would uphold McCreary County and Pulaski County, Kentucky's (hereinafter Counties) displays of the Ten Commandments. I shall discuss, first, why the Court's oft repeated assertion that the government cannot favor religious practice is false; second, why today's opinion extends the scope of that falsehood even beyond prior cases; and third, why even on the basis of the Court's false assumptions the judgment here is wrong.

I

A

On September 11, 2001, I was attending in Rome, Italy, an international conference of judges and lawyers, principally from Europe and the United States. That night and the next morning virtually all of the participants watched, in their hotel rooms, the address to the Nation by the President of the United States concerning the murderous attacks upon the Twin Towers and the Pentagon, in which thousands of Americans had been killed. The address ended, as Presidential addresses often do, with the prayer "God bless America." The next afternoon I was approached by one of the judges from a European country, who, after extending his profound condolences for my country's loss, sadly observed: "How I wish that the Head of State of my country, at a similar time of national tragedy and distress, could conclude his address 'God bless ______.' It is of course absolutely forbidden."

That is one model of the relationship between church and state—a model spread across Europe by the armies of Napoleon, and reflected in the Constitution of France, which begins, "France is [a] ... secular ... Republic." France Const., Art. 1, in 7 *Constitutions of the Countries of the World*, p. 1 (G. Flanz ed.2000). Religion is to be strictly excluded from the public forum. This is not, and never was, the model adopted by America. George Washington added to the form of Presidential oath prescribed by Art. II, § 1, cl. 8, of the Constitution, the concluding words "so help me God." See Blomquist, "The Presidential Oath, the American National Interest and a Call for Presiprudence," 73 *UMKC L.Rev.* 1, 34 (2004). The Supreme Court under John Marshall opened its sessions with the prayer, "God save the United States and this Honorable Court." 1 C. Warren, *The Supreme Court in United States History* 469 (rev. ed.1926) (internal quotation marks omitted). The First Congress instituted the practice of beginning its legislative sessions with a prayer. *Marsh v. Chambers*, 463 U.S. 783, 787–788, 103 S.Ct. 3330, 77 L.Ed.2d 1019 (1983). The same week that Congress submitted the Establishment Clause as part of the Bill of Rights for ratification by the States, it enacted legislation providing for paid chaplains in the House and Senate. *Id.*, at 788, 103 S.Ct. 3330. The day after the First Amendment was proposed, the same Congress that had proposed it requested the President to proclaim "a day of public thanksgiving and prayer, to be observed, by acknowledging, with grateful hearts, the many signal favours of Almighty God." H.R. Jour., 1st Cong., 1st Sess., 123 (1826 ed.); see also

Sen. Jour., 1st Sess., 88 (1820 ed.). President Washington offered the first Thanksgiving Proclamation shortly thereafter, devoting November 26, 1789, on behalf of the American people " 'to the service of that great and glorious Being who is the beneficent author of all the good that was, that is, or that will be,' " *Van Orden v. Perry, post,* 545 U.S., at 687, 125 S.Ct. at 2882, 2005 WL 1500276, *22 (plurality opinion) (quoting President Washington's first Thanksgiving Proclamation), thus beginning a tradition of offering gratitude to God that continues today. See *Wallace v. Jaffree,* 472 U.S. 38, 100–103, 105 S.Ct. 2479, 86 L.Ed.2d 29 (1985) (Rehnquist, J., dissenting). The same Congress also reenacted the Northwest Territory Ordinance of 1787, 1 Stat. 50, Article III of which provided: "Religion, morality, and knowledge, being necessary to good government and the happiness of mankind, schools and the means of education shall forever be encouraged." *Id.,* at 52, n. *(a).* And of course the First Amendment itself accords religion (and no other manner of belief) special constitutional protection.

These actions of our First President and Congress and the Marshall Court were not idiosyncratic; they reflected the beliefs of the period. Those who wrote the Constitution believed that morality was essential to the well-being of society and that encouragement of religion was the best way to foster morality. The "fact that the Founding Fathers believed devotedly that there was a God and that the unalienable rights of man were rooted in Him is clearly evidenced in their writings, from the Mayflower Compact to the Constitution itself." *School Dist. of Abington Township v. Schempp,* 374 U.S. 203, 213, 83 S.Ct. 1560, 10 L.Ed.2d 844 (1963). See Underkuffler-Freund, "The Separation of the Religious and the Secular: A Foundational Challenge to First-Amendment Theory," 36 *Wm. & Mary L.Rev.* 837, 896–918 (1995). President Washington opened his Presidency with a prayer, see Inaugural Addresses of the Presidents of the United States 1, 2 (1989), and reminded his fellow citizens at the conclusion of it that "reason and experience both forbid us to expect that National morality can prevail in exclusion of religious principle," Farewell Address (1796), reprinted in 35 *Writings of George Washington* 229 (J. Fitzpatrick ed.1940). President John Adams wrote to the Massachusetts Militia, "We have no government armed with power capable of contending with human passions unbridled by morality and religion.... Our Constitution was made only for a moral and religious people. It is wholly inadequate to the government of any other." Letter (Oct. 11, 1798), reprinted in 9 *Works of John Adams* 229 (C. Adams ed.1971). Thomas Jefferson concluded his second inaugural address by inviting his audience to pray:

> "I shall need, too, the favor of that Being in whose hands we are, who led our fathers, as Israel of old, from their native land and planted them in a country flowing with all the necessaries and comforts of life; who has covered our infancy with His providence and our riper years with His wisdom and power and to whose goodness I ask you to join in supplications with me that He will so enlighten the minds of your servants, guide their councils, and prosper their measures that whatsoever they do shall result in your good, and shall secure to you the peace, friendship, and approbation of all nations." *Inaugural Addresses of the Presidents of the United States*, at 18, 22–23.

James Madison, in his first inaugural address, likewise placed his confidence "in the guardianship and guidance of that Almighty Being whose power regulates the destiny of nations, whose blessings have been so conspicuously dispensed to this rising Republic, and to whom we are bound to address our devout gratitude for the past, as well as our fervent supplications and best hopes for the future." *Id.*, at 25, 28.

Nor have the views of our people on this matter significantly changed. Presidents continue to conclude the Presidential oath with the words "so help me God." Our legislatures, state and national, continue to open their sessions with prayer led by official chaplains. The sessions of this Court continue to open with the prayer "God save the United States and this Honorable Court." Invocation of the Almighty by our public figures, at all levels of government, remains commonplace. Our coinage bears the motto, "IN GOD WE TRUST." And our Pledge of Allegiance contains the acknowledgment that we are a Nation "under God." As one of our Supreme Court opinions rightly observed, "We are a religious people whose institutions presuppose a Supreme Being." *Zorach v. Clauson,* 343 U.S. 306, 313, 72 S.Ct. 679, 96 L.Ed. 954 (1952), repeated with approval in *Lynch v. Donnelly,* 465 U.S. 668, 675, 104 S.Ct. 1355, 79 L.Ed.2d 604 (1984); *Marsh,* 463 U.S., at 792, 103 S.Ct. 3330; *Abington Township, supra,* at 213, 83 S.Ct. 1560.

With all of this reality (and much more) staring it in the face, how can the Court *possibly* assert that the "'First Amendment mandates governmental neutrality between ... religion and nonreligion,'" *ante,* at 2733, and that "[m]anifesting a purpose to favor ... adherence to religion generally," *ibid.,* is unconstitutional? Who says so? Surely not the words of the Constitution. Surely not the history and traditions that reflect our society's constant understanding of those words. Surely not even the current sense of our society, recently reflected in an Act of Congress adopted *unanimously* by the Senate and with only five nays in the House of Representatives, see 148 Cong. Rec. 12041 (June 28, 2002); *id.,* at 19518 (Oct. 8, 2002), criticizing a Court of Appeals opinion that had held "under God" in the Pledge of Allegiance unconstitutional. See Act of Nov. 13, 2002, §§ 1(9), 2(a), 3(a), 116 Stat.2057, 2058, 2060–2061 (reaffirming the Pledge of Allegiance and the National Motto ("In God We Trust") and stating that the Pledge of Allegiance is "clearly consistent with the text and intent of the Constitution"). Nothing stands behind the Court's assertion that governmental affirmation of the society's belief in God is unconstitutional except the Court's own say-so, citing as support only the unsubstantiated say-so of earlier Courts going back no further than the mid-20th century. See *ante,* at 2733, citing *Corporation of Presiding Bishop of Church of Jesus Christ of Latter-day Saints v. Amos,* 483 U.S. 327, 335, 107 S.Ct. 2862, 97 L.Ed.2d 273 (1987), in turn citing *Lemon v. Kurtzman,* 403 U.S. 602, 612, 91 S.Ct. 2105, 29 L.Ed.2d 745 (1971), in turn citing *Board of Ed. of Central School Dist. No. 1 v. Allen,* 392 U.S. 236, 243, 88 S.Ct. 1923, 20 L.Ed.2d 1060 (1968), in turn quoting *Abington Township,* 374 U.S., at 222, 83 S.Ct. 1560, in turn citing *Everson v. Board of Ed. of Ewing,* 330 U.S. 1, 15, 67 S.Ct. 504, 91 L.Ed. 711 (1947). And it is, moreover, a thoroughly discredited say-so. It is discredited, to begin with, because a majority of the Justices on the current Court (including at least one Member of today's majority) have, in separate opinions, repudiated the brain-spun "*Lemon* test" that embodies the supposed principle of neutrality between religion and irreligion. See *Lamb's Chapel v. Center Moriches Union Free School Dist.,* 508 U.S. 384, 398–399, 113 S.Ct. 2141, 124 L.Ed.2d 352 (1993) (Scalia, J., concurring in judgment) (collecting criticism of *Lemon); Van Orden, post,* 545 U.S., at 692–693, 125 S.Ct., at 2865, 2867 (Thomas, J., concurring); *Board of Ed. of Kiryas Joel Village School Dist. v. Grumet,* 512 U.S. 687, 720, 114 S.Ct. 2481, 129 L.Ed.2d 546 (1994) (O'Connor, J., concurring in part and concurring in judgment); *County of Allegheny v. American Civil Liberties Union, Greater Pittsburgh Chapter,* 492 U.S. 573, 655–656, 672–673, 109 S.Ct. 3086, 106 L.Ed.2d 472 (1989) (Kennedy, J., concurring in judgment in part and dissenting in part); *Wallace,* 472 U.S., at 112, 105 S.Ct. 2479 (Rehnquist, J., dissenting); see also *Committee for Public Ed. and Religious Liberty v. Regan,* 444 U.S. 646, 671, 100 S.Ct. 840, 63 L.Ed.2d 94 (1980) (Stevens, J., dissenting) (disparaging "the sisyphean task of trying to patch together the 'blurred, indistinct, and variable barrier' described in *Lemon*"). And it is discredited because the Court has not had the courage (or the foolhardiness) to apply the neutrality principle consistently.

What distinguishes the rule of law from the dictatorship of a shifting Supreme Court majority is the absolutely indispensable requirement that judicial opinions be grounded in consistently applied principle. That is what prevents judges from ruling now this way, now that—thumbs up or thumbs down—as their personal preferences dictate. Today's opinion forthrightly (or actually, somewhat less than forthrightly) admits that it does not rest upon consistently applied principle. In a revealing footnote, *ante,* at 2733, n. 10, the Court acknowledges that the "Establishment Clause doctrine" it purports to be applying "lacks the comfort of categorical absolutes." What the Court means by this lovely euphemism is that sometimes the Court chooses to decide cases on the principle that government cannot favor religion, and sometimes it does not. The footnote goes on to say that "[i]n special instances we have found good reason" to dispense with the principle, but "[n]o such reasons present themselves here." *Ibid.* It does not identify all of those "special instances," much less identify the "good reason" for their existence.

I have cataloged elsewhere the variety of circumstances in which this Court—even *after* its embrace of *Lemon's* stated prohibition of such behavior—has approved government action "undertaken with the specific intention of improving the position of religion," *Edwards v. Aguillard,* 482 U.S. 578, 616, 107 S.Ct. 2573, 96 L.Ed.2d 510 (1987) (Scalia, J., dissenting). See *id.,* at 616–618, 107 S.Ct. 2573. Suffice it to say here that when the government relieves churches from the obligation to pay property taxes, when it allows students to absent themselves from public school to take religious classes, and when it exempts religious organizations from generally applicable prohibitions of religious discrimination, it surely means to bestow a benefit on religious practice—but we have approved it. See *Amos, supra,* at 338, 107 S.Ct. 2862 (exemption from federal prohibition of religious discrimination by employers); *Walz v. Tax Comm'n of City of New York,* 397 U.S. 664, 673, 90 S.Ct. 1409, 25 L.Ed.2d 697 (1970) (property tax exemption for church property); *Zorach, supra,* at 308, 315, 72 S.Ct. 679 (law permitting students to leave public school for the purpose of receiving religious education). Indeed, we have even approved (post-*Lemon*) government-led prayer to God. In *Marsh v. Chambers,* the Court upheld the Nebraska State Legislature's practice of paying a chaplain to lead it in prayer at the opening of legislative sessions. The Court explained that "[t]o invoke Divine guidance on a public body entrusted with making the laws is not ... an 'establishment' of religion or a step toward establishment; it is simply a tolerable acknowledgment of beliefs widely held among the people of this country." 463 U.S., at 792, 103 S.Ct. 3330. (Why, one wonders, is not respect for the Ten Commandments a tolerable acknowledgment of beliefs widely held among the people of this country?)

The only "good reason" for ignoring the neutrality principle set forth in any of these cases was the antiquity of the practice at issue. See *id.,* at 786–792, 794, 103 S.Ct. 3330; *Walz, supra,* at 676–680, 90 S.Ct. 1409. That would be a good reason for finding the neutrality principle a mistaken interpretation of the Constitution, but it is hardly a good reason for letting an unconstitutional practice continue. We did not hide behind that reason in *Reynolds v. Sims,* 377 U.S. 533, 84 S.Ct. 1362, 12 L.Ed.2d 506 (1964), which found unconstitutional bicameral state legislatures of a sort that had existed since the beginning of the Republic. And almost monthly, it seems, the Court has not shrunk from invalidating aspects of criminal procedure and penology of similar vintage. See, *e.g., Deck v. Missouri,* 544 U.S. 622, 633, 125 S.Ct. 2007, 2014–2015, 161 L.Ed.2d 953, 2005 WL 1200394 (2005) (invalidating practice of shackling defendants absent "special circumstances"); *id.,* at 641–645, 125 S.Ct., at 2020–2022 (Thomas, J., dissenting); *Roper v. Simmons,* 543 U.S. 551, 568, 125 S.Ct. 1183, 1194–1195, 161 L.Ed.2d 1, 2005 WL 464890 (2005) (invalidating practice of executing under-18-year-old offenders); *id.,* at 611, n. 2, 125 S.Ct., at 2018 n. 2, (Scalia, J., dissenting). What, then, could be the genuine "good reason" for occasionally ignoring the neutrality principle? I suggest it is the instinct for self-preservation, and the recognition that the Court, which "has no influence over either the sword or the purse," *The Federalist* No. 78, p. 412 (J. Pole ed.2005) (A. Hamilton), cannot go too far down the road of an enforced neutrality that contradicts both historical fact and current practice without losing all that sustains it: the willingness of the people to accept its interpretation of the Constitution as definitive, in preference to the contrary interpretation of the democratically elected branches.

Besides appealing to the demonstrably false principle that the government cannot favor religion over irreligion, today's opinion suggests that the posting of the Ten Commandments violates the principle that the government cannot favor one religion over another. See *ante,* at 2738; see also *Van Orden, post,* 545 U.S., at 717–718, 125 S.Ct. at 2879 (Stevens, J., dissenting). That is indeed a valid principle where public aid or assistance to religion is concerned, see *Zelman v. Simmons-Harris,* 536 U.S. 639, 652, 122 S.Ct. 2460, 153 L.Ed.2d 604 (2002), or where the free exercise of religion is at issue, *Church of Lukumi Babalu Aye, Inc. v. Hialeah,* 508 U.S. 520, 532–533,

113 S.Ct. 2217, 124 L.Ed.2d 472 (1993); *id.*, at 557–558, 113 S.Ct. 2217 (Scalia, J., concurring in part and concurring in judgment), but it necessarily applies in a more limited sense to public acknowledgment of the Creator. If religion in the public forum had to be entirely nondenom-inational, there could be no religion in the public forum at all. One cannot say the word "God," or "the Almighty," one cannot offer public supplication or thanksgiving, without contradicting the beliefs of some people that there are many gods, or that God or the gods pay no attention to human affairs. With respect to public acknowledgment of religious belief, it is entirely clear from our Nation's historical practices that the Establishment Clause permits this disregard of polytheists and believers in unconcerned deities, just as it permits the disregard of devout atheists. The Thanksgiving Proclamation issued by George Washington at the instance of the First Congress was scrupulously nondenominational—but it was monotheistic. In *Marsh v. Chambers, supra,* we said that the fact the particular prayers offered in the Nebraska Legislature were "in the Judeo-Christian tradition," *id.*, at 793, 103 S.Ct. 3330, posed no additional problem, because "there is no indication that the prayer opportunity has been exploited to proselytize or advance any one, or to disparage any other, faith or belief," *id.*, at 794–795, 103 S.Ct. 3330.

Historical practices thus demonstrate that there is a distance between the acknowledgment of a single Creator and the establishment of a religion. The former is, as *Marsh v. Chambers* put it, "a tolerable acknowledgment of beliefs widely held among the people of this country." *Id.*, at 792, 103 S.Ct. 3330. The three most popular religions in the United States, Christianity, Judaism, and Islam—which combined account for 97.7% of all believers—are monotheistic. See U.S. Dept. of Commerce, Bureau of Census, *Statistical Abstract of the United*

States: 2004–2005, p. 55 (124th ed. 2004) (Table No. 67). All of them, moreover (Islam included), believe that the Ten Commandments were given by God to Moses, and are divine prescriptions for a virtuous life. See 13 *Encyclopedia of Religion* 9074 (2d ed.2005); *The Qur'an* 104 (M. Haleem transl.2004). Publicly honoring the Ten Commandments is thus indistinguishable, insofar as discriminating against other religions is concerned, from publicly honoring God. Both practices are recognized across such a broad and diverse range of the population—from Christians to Muslims—that they cannot be reasonably understood as a government endorsement of a particular religious viewpoint.

B

A few remarks are necessary in response to the criticism of this dissent by the Court, as well as Justice Stevens' criticism in the related case of *Van Orden v. Perry, post,* 545 U.S. 677, 707, 125 S.Ct. 2854, 2873–2874. Justice Stevens' writing is largely devoted to an attack upon a straw man. "[R]eliance on early religious proclamations and statements made by the Founders is ... problematic," he says, "because those views were not espoused at the Constitutional Convention in 1787 nor enshrined in the Constitution's text." *Van Orden, post,* 545 U.S., at 724, 125 S.Ct., at 2882, 2005 WL 1500276, at *22 (dissenting opinion) (footnote omitted). But I have not relied upon (as he and the Court in this case do) mere "proclamations and statements" of the Founders. I have relied primarily upon official acts and official proclamations of the United States or of the component branches of its Government, including the First Congress's beginning of the tradition of legislative prayer to God, its appointment of congressional chaplains, its legislative proposal of a Thanksgiving Proclamation, and its reenactment of the Northwest Territory Ordinance; our first President's issuance of a Thanksgiving Proclamation; and invocation of God at the opening of sessions of the Supreme Court. The only mere "proclamations and statements" of the Founders I have relied upon were statements of Founders who occupied federal office, and spoke in at least a quasi-official capacity—Washington's prayer at the opening of his Presidency and his Farewell Address, President John Adams' letter to the Massachusetts Militia, and Jefferson's and Madison's inaugural addresses. The Court and Justice Stevens, by contrast, appeal to no official or even quasi-official action in support of their view of the Establishment Clause—only James Madison's Memorial and Remonstrance Against Religious Assessments, written before the Federal Constitution had even been proposed, two letters written by Madison long after he was President, and the quasi-official *inaction* of Thomas Jefferson in refusing to issue a Thanksgiving Proclamation. See *ante,* at 2743–2744; *Van Orden, post,* 545 U.S., at 724–25, 125 S.Ct., at 2884 (Stevens, J., dissenting). The Madison Memorial and Remonstrance, dealing as it does with enforced contribution to religion rather than public acknowledgment of God, is irrelevant; one of the letters is utterly ambiguous as to the point at issue here, and should not be read to contradict Madison's statements in his first inaugural address, quoted earlier; even the other letter does not disapprove public acknowledgment of God, unless one posits (what Madison's own actions as President would contradict) that reference to God contradicts "the equality of *all* religious sects." See Letter from James Madison to Edward Livingston (July 10, 1822), in 5 *The Founders' Constitution* 105–106 (P. Kurland & R. Lerner eds.1987). And as to Jefferson: The notoriously self-contradicting Jefferson did not choose to have his nonauthorship of a Thanksgiving Proclamation inscribed on his tombstone. What he did have inscribed was his authorship of the Virginia Statute for Religious Freedom, a governmental act which begins "Whereas, Almighty God hath created the mind free...." Va.Code Ann. § 57–1 (Lexis 2003).

It is no answer for Justice Stevens to say that the understanding that these official and quasi-official actions reflect was not "enshrined in the Constitution's text." *Van Orden, post,* 545 U.S., at 724, 125 S.Ct., at 2883 (dissenting opinion). The Establishment Clause, upon which Justice Stevens would rely, *was* enshrined in the Constitution's text, and these official actions show *what it meant.* There were doubtless some who thought it should have a broader meaning, but those views were plainly rejected. Justice Stevens says that reliance on these actions is "bound to paint a misleading picture," *ibid.,* but it is hard to see why. What is more probative of the meaning of the Establishment Clause than the actions of the very Congress that proposed it, and of the first President charged with observing it?

Justice Stevens also appeals to the undoubted fact that some in the founding generation thought that the Religion Clauses of the First Amendment should have a *narrower* meaning, protecting only the Christian religion or perhaps only Protestantism. See *Van Orden, post,* 545 U.S., at 725–728, 125 S.Ct., at 2884–2885. I am at a loss to see how this helps his case, except by providing a cloud of obfuscating smoke. (Since most thought the Clause permitted government invocation of monotheism, and some others thought it permitted government invocation of Christianity, he proposes that it be construed not to permit any government invocation of religion at all.) At any rate, those narrower views of the Establishment Clause were as clearly rejected as the more expansive ones. Washington's First Thanksgiving Proclamation is merely an example. *All* of the actions of Washington and the First Congress upon which I have relied, virtually all Thanksgiving Proclamations throughout our history, and *all* the other examples of our Government's favoring religion that I have cited, have invoked God, but not Jesus Christ. Rather than relying upon Justice Stevens' assurance that "[t]he original understanding of the type of 'religion' that qualified for constitutional protection under the Establishment Clause likely did not include ... followers of Judaism and Islam," *Van Orden, post,* 545 U.S., at 728, 125 S.Ct., at 2886, 2005 WL 1500276, at *24; see also *ante,* at 2745, I would prefer to take the word of George Washington, who, in his famous Letter to the Hebrew Congregation of Newport, Rhode Island, wrote:

> "All possess alike liberty of conscience and immunities of citizenship. It is now no more that toleration is spoken of, as if it was by the indulgence of one class of people, that another enjoyed the exercise of their inherent natural rights." 6 *The Papers of George Washington, Presidential Series* 285 (D. Twohig ed.1996).

The letter concluded, by the way, with an invocation of the one God:

> "May the father of all mercies scatter light and not darkness in our paths, and make us all in our several vocations useful here, and in his own due time and way everlastingly happy." *Ibid.*

Justice Stevens says that if one is serious about following the original understanding of the Establishment Clause, he must repudiate its incorporation into the Fourteenth Amendment, and hold that it does not apply against the States. See *Van Orden, post,* 545 U.S., at 729–731, 125 S.Ct., at 2887–2888 (dissenting opinion). This is more smoke. Justice Stevens did not feel that way last Term, when he joined an opinion insisting upon the original meaning of the Confrontation Clause, but nonetheless applying it against the State of Washington. See *Crawford v. Washington,* 541 U.S. 36, 124 S.Ct. 1354, 158 L.Ed.2d 177 (2004). The notion that incorporation empties the incorporated provisions of their original meaning has no support in either reason or precedent.

Justice Stevens argues that original meaning should not be the touchstone anyway, but that we should rather "expoun[d] the meaning of constitutional provisions with one eye toward our Nation's history and the other fixed on its democratic aspirations." *Van Orden, post,* 545 U.S., at 732, 125 S.Ct., at 2888–2889 (dissenting opinion). This is not the place to debate the merits of the "living Constitution," though I must observe that Justice Stevens' quotation from *McCulloch v. Maryland,* 4 Wheat. 316, 407, 4 L.Ed. 579 (1819), refutes rather than supports that approach. Even assuming, however, that the meaning of the Constitution ought to change according to "democratic aspirations," why are those aspirations to be found in Justices' notions of what the Establishment Clause ought to mean, rather than in the democratically adopted dispositions of our current society? As I have observed above, numerous provisions of our laws and numerous continuing practices of our people demonstrate that the government's invocation of God (and hence the government's invocation of the Ten Commandments) is unobjectionable—including a statute enacted by Congress almost unanimously less than three years ago, stating that "under God" in the Pledge of Allegiance is constitutional, see 116 Stat. 2058. To ignore all this is not to give effect to "democratic aspirations" but to frustrate them.

Finally, I must respond to Justice Stevens' assertion that I would "marginaliz[e] the belief systems of more than 7 million Americans" who adhere to religions that are not monotheistic. *Van Orden, post,* 545 U.S., at 719, n. 18, 125 S.Ct., at 2881, n. 18, 2005 WL 1500276, at *20 (dissenting opinion). Surely that is a gross exaggeration. The beliefs of those citizens are entirely protected by the Free Exercise Clause, and by those aspects of the Establishment Clause that do not relate to government acknowledgment of the Creator. Invocation of God despite their beliefs is permitted not because nonmonotheistic religions cease to be religions recognized by the Religion Clauses of the First Amendment, but because governmental invocation of God is not an establishment. Justice Stevens fails to recognize that in the context of public acknowledgments of God there are legitimate *competing* interests: On the one hand, the interest of that minority in not feeling "excluded"; but on the other, the interest of the overwhelming majority of religious believers in being able to give God thanks and supplication *as a people,* and with respect to our national endeavors. Our national tradition has resolved that conflict in favor of the majority. It is not for this Court to change a disposition that accounts, many Americans think, for the phenomenon remarked upon in a quotation attributed to various authors, including Bismarck, but which I prefer to associate with Charles de Gaulle: "God watches over little children, drunkards, and the United States of America."

II

As bad as the *Lemon* test is, it is worse for the fact that, since its inception, its seemingly simple mandates have been manipulated to fit whatever result the Court aimed to achieve. Today's opinion is no different. In two respects it modifies *Lemon* to ratchet up the Court's hostility to religion. First, the Court justifies inquiry into legislative purpose, not as an end itself, but as a means to ascertain the appearance of the government action to an "'objective observer.'" *Ante,* at 2734. Because in the Court's view the true danger to be guarded against is that the objective observer would feel like an "'outside[r]'" or "'not [a] full membe[r] of the political community,'" its inquiry focuses not on the *actual pur-*

pose of government action, but the "purpose apparent from government action." *Ante,* at 2733. Under this approach, even if a government could show that its actual purpose was not to advance religion, it would presumably violate the Constitution as long as the Court's objective observer would think otherwise. See *Capitol Square Review and Advisory Bd. v. Pinette,* 515 U.S. 753, 776–777, 115 S.Ct. 2440, 132 L.Ed.2d 650 (1995) (O'Connor, J., concurring in part and concurring in judgment) (stating that "when the reasonable observer would view a government practice as endorsing religion, ... it is our *duty* to hold the practice invalid," even if the law at issue was neutral and the benefit conferred on the religious entity was incidental).

I have remarked before that it is an odd jurisprudence that bases the unconstitutionality of a government practice that does not *actually* advance religion on the hopes of the government that it *would* do so. See *Edwards,* 482 U.S., at 639, 107 S.Ct. 2573. But that oddity pales in comparison to the one invited by today's analysis: the legitimacy of a government action with a wholly secular effect would turn on the *misperception* of an imaginary observer that the government officials behind the action had the intent to advance religion.

Second, the Court replaces *Lemon's* requirement that the government have "*a* secular ... purpose," 403 U.S., at 612, 91 S.Ct. 2105 (emphasis added), with the heightened requirement that the secular purpose "predominate" over any purpose to advance religion. *Ante,* at 2735–2736. The Court treats this extension as a natural outgrowth of the longstanding requirement that the government's secular purpose not be a sham, but simple logic shows the two to be unrelated. If the government's proffered secular purpose is not genuine, then the government has no secular purpose at all. The new demand that secular purpose predominate contradicts *Lemon's* more limited requirement, and finds no support in our cases. In all but one of the five cases in which this Court has invalidated a government practice on the basis of its purpose to benefit religion, it has first declared that the statute was motivated entirely by the desire to advance religion. See *Santa Fe Independent School Dist. v. Doe,* 530 U.S. 290, 308–309, 120 S.Ct. 2266, 147 L.Ed.2d 295 (2000) (dismissing the school district's proffered secular purposes as shams); *Wallace,* 472 U.S., at 56, 105 S.Ct. 2479 (finding "*no* secular purpose" (emphasis in original)); *Stone v. Graham,* 449 U.S. 39, 41, 101 S.Ct. 192, 66 L.Ed.2d 199 (1980) (*per curiam*) (finding that "Kentucky's statute requiring the posting of the Ten Commandments in public school rooms has *no secular legislative purpose*" (emphasis added)); *Epperson v. Arkansas,* 393 U.S. 97, 107–109, 89 S.Ct. 266, 21 L.Ed.2d 228 (1968). In *Edwards, supra,* the Court did say that the state action was invalid because its "primary" or "preeminent" purpose was to advance a particular religious belief, 482 U.S., at 590, 593, 594, 107 S.Ct. 2573, but that statement was unnecessary to the result, since the Court rejected the State's only proffered secular purpose as a sham. See *id.,* at 589, 107 S.Ct. 2573.

I have urged that *Lemon's* purpose prong be abandoned, because (as I have discussed in Part I) even an *exclusive* purpose to foster or assist religious practice is not necessarily invalidating. But today's extension makes things even worse. By shifting the focus of *Lemon's* purpose prong from the search for a genuine, secular motivation to the hunt for a predominantly religious purpose, the Court converts what has in the past been a fairly limited inquiry into a rigorous review of the full record. Those responsible for the adoption of the Religion Clauses would surely regard it as a bitter irony that the religious values they designed those Clauses to *protect* have now become so distasteful to this Court that if they constitute anything more than a subordinate motive for government action they will invalidate it.

III

Even accepting the Court's *Lemon*-based premises, the displays at issue here were constitutional.

A

To any person who happened to walk down the hallway of the McCreary or Pulaski County Courthouse during the roughly nine months when the Foundations Displays were exhibited, the displays must have seemed unremarkable—if indeed they were noticed at all. The walls of both courthouses were already lined with historical documents and other assorted portraits; each Foundations Display was exhibited in the same format as these other displays and nothing in the record suggests that either County took steps to give it greater prominence.

Entitled "The Foundations of American Law and Government Display," each display consisted of nine equally sized documents: the original version of the Magna Carta, the Declaration of Independence, the Bill of Rights, the Star Spangled Banner, the Mayflower Compact of 1620, a picture of Lady Justice, the National Motto of the United States ("In God We Trust"), the Preamble to the Kentucky Constitution, and the Ten Commandments. The displays did not emphasize any of the nine documents in any way: The frame holding the Ten Commandments was of the same size and had the same appearance as that which held each of the other documents. See 354 F.3d 438, 443 (C.A.6 2003).

Posted with the documents was a plaque, identifying the display, and explaining that it "'contains documents that played a significant role in the foundation of our system of law and government.'" *Ibid.* The explanation related to the Ten Commandments was third in the list of nine and did not serve to distinguish it from the other documents. It stated:

"'The Ten Commandments have profoundly influenced the formation of Western legal thought and the formation of our country. That influence is clearly seen in the Declaration of Independence, which declared that, "We hold these truths to be self-evident, that all men are created equal, that they are endowed by their Creator with certain unalienable Rights, that among these are Life, Liberty, and the pursuit of Happiness." The Ten Commandments provide the moral background of the Declaration of Independence and the foundation of our legal tradition.'" *Ibid.*

B

On its face, the Foundations Displays manifested the purely secular purpose that the Counties asserted before the District Court: "to display documents that played a significant role in the foundation of our system of law and government." Affidavit of Judge Jimmie Green in Support of Defendants' Opposition to Plaintiffs' Motion for Contempt or, in the Alternative, for Supplemental Preliminary Injunction in Civ. Action No. 99–507 (ED Ky.), p. 2, ¶ 4, App. 57. That the displays included the Ten Commandments did not transform their apparent secular purpose into one of impermissible advocacy for Judeo–Christian beliefs. Even an isolated display of the Decalogue conveys, at worst, "an equivocal message, perhaps of respect for Judaism, for religion in general, or for law." *Allegheny County,* 492 U.S., at 652, 109 S.Ct. 3086 (Stevens, J., concurring in part and dissenting in part). But when the Ten Commandments appear alongside other documents of secular significance in a display devoted to the foundations of American law and government, the context communicates that the Ten Commandments are included, not to teach their binding nature as a religious text, but to show their unique contribution to the development of the legal system. See *id.,* at 652–653,

109 S.Ct. 3086. This is doubly true when the display is introduced by a document that informs passersby that it "'contains documents that played a significant role in the foundation of our system of law and government.'" 354 F.3d, at 443.

The same result follows if the Ten Commandments display is viewed in light of the government practices that this Court has countenanced in the past. The acknowledgment of the contribution that religion in general, and the Ten Commandments in particular, have made to our Nation's legal and governmental heritage is surely no more of a step toward establishment of religion than was the practice of legislative prayer we approved in *Marsh v. Chambers,* 463 U.S. 783, 103 S.Ct. 3330, 77 L.Ed.2d 1019 (1983), and it seems to be on par with the inclusion of a crèche or a menorah in a "Holiday" display that incorporates other secular symbols, see *Lynch v. Donnelly,* 465 U.S., at 679–680, 104 S.Ct. 1355; *Allegheny County, supra,* at 621, 109 S.Ct. 3086 (Blackmun, J., concurring in part and dissenting in part). The parallels between this case and *Marsh* and *Lynch* are sufficiently compelling that they ought to decide this case, even under the Court's misguided Establishment Clause jurisprudence.

Acknowledgment of the contribution that religion has made to our Nation's legal and governmental heritage partakes of a centuries-old tradition. Members of this Court have themselves often detailed the degree to which religious belief pervaded the National Government during the founding era. See *Lynch, supra,* at 674–678, 104 S.Ct. 1355; *Marsh, supra,* at 786–788, 103 S.Ct. 3330; *Lee v. Weisman,* 505 U.S. 577, 633–636, 112 S.Ct. 2649, 120 L.Ed.2d 467 (1992) (Scalia, J., dissenting); *Wallace,* 472 U.S., at 100–106, 105 S.Ct. 2479 (Rehnquist, J., dissenting); *Engel v. Vitale,* 370 U.S. 421, 446–450, and n. 3, 82 S.Ct. 1261, 8 L.Ed.2d 601 (1962) (Stewart, J., dissenting). Display of the Ten Commandments is well within the mainstream of this practice of acknowledgment. Federal, state, and local governments across the Nation have engaged in such display. The Supreme Court Building itself includes depictions of Moses with the Ten Commandments in the Courtroom and on the east pediment of the building, and symbols of the Ten Commandments "adorn the metal gates lining the north and south sides of the Courtroom as well as the doors leading into the Courtroom." *Van Orden, post,* 545 U.S., at 688, 125 S.Ct., at 2861, 2005 WL 1500276, at *5 (plurality opinion). Similar depictions of the Decalogue appear on public buildings and monuments throughout our Nation's Capital. *Post,* 545 U.S., at 689, 125 S.Ct., at 2861. The frequency of these displays testifies to the popular understanding that the Ten Commandments are a foundation of the rule of law, and a symbol of the role that religion played, and continues to play, in our system of government.

Perhaps in recognition of the centrality of the Ten Commandments as a widely recognized symbol of religion in public life, the Court is at pains to dispel the impression that its decision will require governments across the country to sandblast the Ten Commandments from the public square. See *ante,* at 2741. The constitutional problem, the Court says, is with the Counties' *purpose* in erecting the Foundations Displays, not the displays themselves. The Court adds in a footnote: "One consequence of taking account of the purpose underlying past actions is that the same government action may be constitutional if taken in the first instance and unconstitutional if it has a sectarian heritage." *Ante,* at 2737, n. 14.

This inconsistency may be explicable in theory, but I suspect that the "objective observer" with whom the Court is so concerned will recognize its absurdity in practice. By virtue of details familiar only to the parties to litigation and their lawyers, McCreary and Pulaski Counties, Kentucky, and Rutherford County, Tennessee, have been ordered to remove the same display that appears in courthouses from Mercer County, Kentucky, to Elkhart County, Indiana. Compare *American Civil Liberties Union of Tenn. v. Rutherford County,* 209 F.Supp.2d 799, 808–809 (M.D.Tenn.2002) (holding Foundations Display to be unconstitutional based on prior actions of county commission), with *Books v. Elkhart County,* 401 F.3d 857, 869 (C.A.7 2005) (sustaining Foundations Display as "secular ... in its purpose and effect"); *American Civil Liberties Union of Ky. v. Mercer County,* 219 F.Supp.2d 777, 787–789 (E.D.Ky.2002) (rejecting Establishment Clause challenge to an identical Foundations Display and distinguishing *McCreary County* on the ground that the County's purpose had not been "tainted with any prior history"). Displays erected in silence (and under the direction of good legal advice) are permissible, while those hung after discussion and debate are deemed unconstitutional. Reduction of the Establishment Clause to such minutiae trivializes the Clause's protection against religious establishment; indeed, it may inflame religious passions by making the passing comments of every government official the subject of endless litigation.

C

In any event, the Court's conclusion that the Counties exhibited the Foundations Displays with the purpose of promoting religion is doubtful. In the Court's view, the impermissible motive was apparent from the initial displays of the Ten Commandments all by themselves: When that occurs, the Court says, "a religious object is unmistakable." *Ante,* at 2739. Surely that cannot be. If, as discussed above, the Commandments have a proper place in our civic history, even placing them by themselves can be civically motivated—especially when they are placed, not in a school (as they were in the *Stone* case upon which the Court places such reliance), but in a courthouse. Cf. *Van Orden, post,* 545 U.S., at 701, 125 S.Ct., at 2869–2870 (BREYER, J., concurring in judgment) ("The circumstances surrounding the display's placement on the capitol grounds and its physical setting suggest that the State itself intended the ... nonreligious aspects of the tablets' message to predominate"). And the fact that at the posting of the exhibit a clergyman was present is unremarkable (clergymen taking particular pride in the role of the Ten Commandments in our civic history); and even more unremarkable the fact that the clergyman "testified to the certainty of the existence of God," *ante,* at 2738.

The Court has in the past prohibited government actions that "proselytize or advance any one, or ... disparage any other, faith or belief," *Marsh,* 463 U.S., at 794–795, 103 S.Ct. 3330, or that apply some level of coercion (though I and others have disagreed about the form that coercion must take), see, *e.g., Lee v. Weisman,* 505 U.S., at 592, 112 S.Ct. 2649 (prayer at high-school graduation invalid because of "subtle coercive pressure"); *id.,* at 642, 112 S.Ct. 2649 (Scalia, J., dissenting). The passive display of the Ten Commandments, even standing alone, does not begin to do either. What Justice Kennedy said of the crèche in *Allegheny County* is equally true of the Counties' original Ten Commandments displays:

> "No one was compelled to observe or participate in any religious ceremony or activity. [T]he count[ies] [did not] contribut[e] significant amounts of tax money to serve the cause of one religious faith. [The Ten Commandments] are purely passive symbols of [the religious foundation for many of our laws and governmental institutions]. Passersby who disagree with the message conveyed by th[e] displays are free to ignore them, or even to turn their backs, just as they are free to do when they disagree with any other form

of government speech." 492 U.S., at 664, 109 S.Ct. 3086 (opinion concurring in judgment in part and dissenting in part).

Nor is it the case that a solo display of the Ten Commandments advances any one faith. They are assuredly a religious symbol, but they are not so closely associated with a single religious belief that their display can reasonably be understood as preferring one religious sect over another. The Ten Commandments are recognized by Judaism, Christianity, and Islam alike as divinely given. See 13 *Encyclopedia of Religion* 9074 (2d ed.2005).

The Court also points to the Counties' second displays, which featured a number of statements in historical documents reflecting a religious influence, and the resolutions that accompanied their erection, as evidence of an impermissible religious purpose. In the Court's view, "[t]he [second] display's unstinting focus ... on religious passages, show[s] that the Counties were posting the Commandments precisely because of their sectarian content." *Ante,* at 2739. No, all it necessarily shows is that the exhibit was meant to focus upon the historic role of religious belief in our national life—which is entirely permissible. And the same can be said of the resolution. To forbid any government focus upon this aspect of our history is to display what Justice Goldberg called "untutored devotion to the concept of neutrality," *Abington Township,* 374 U.S., at 306, 83 S.Ct. 1560 (concurring opinion), that would commit the Court (and the Nation) to a revisionist agenda of secularization.

Turning at last to the displays actually at issue in this case, the Court faults the Counties for not *repealing* the resolution expressing what the Court believes to be an impermissible intent. Under these circumstances, the Court says, "[n]o reasonable observer could swallow the claim that the Counties had cast off the objective so unmistakable in the earlier displays." *Ante,* at 2740. Even were I to accept all that the Court has said before, I would not agree with that assessment. To begin with, of course, it is unlikely that a reasonable observer *would even have been aware* of the resolutions, so there would be nothing to "cast off." The Court implies that the Counties may have been able to remedy the "taint" from the old resolutions by enacting a new one. See *ante,* at 2740. But that action would have been wholly unnecessary in light of the explanation that the Counties included *with the displays themselves*: A plaque next to the documents informed all who passed by that each display "contains documents that played a significant role in the foundation of our system of law and government." Additionally, there was no reason for the Counties to repeal or repudiate the resolutions adopted with the hanging of the second displays, since they related *only to the second displays.* After complying with the District Court's order to remove the second displays "immediately," and erecting new displays that in content and by express assertion reflected a *different* purpose from that identified in the resolutions, the Counties had no reason to believe that their previous resolutions would be deemed to be the basis for their actions. After the Counties discovered that the sentiments expressed in the resolutions could be attributed to their most recent displays (in oral argument before this Court), they repudiated them immediately.

In sum: The first displays did not necessarily evidence an intent to further religious practice; nor did the second displays, or the resolutions authorizing them; and there is in any event no basis for attributing whatever intent motivated the first and second displays to the third. Given the presumption of regularity that always accompanies our review of official action, see n. 9, *supra,* the Court has identified no evidence of a purpose to advance religion in a way that is inconsistent with our cases. The Court may well be correct in identifying the third displays as the fruit of a desire to display the Ten Commandments, *ante,* at 2740, but neither our cases nor our history support its assertion that such a desire renders the fruit poisonous.

* * *

For the foregoing reasons, I would reverse the judgment of the Court of Appeals.

7

Social Regulation

Lord Acton did not say power purifies
Planned Parenthood of Southeastern Pennsylvania v. Casey, 505 U.S. 833 (1992)

A democratic vote by nine lawyers
Stenberg v. Carhart, 530 U.S. 914 (2000)

Prize for most feeble effort
Atkins v. Virginia, 536 U.S. 304 (2002)

A lesson of life rather than law
Grutter v. Bollinger, 539 U.S. 306 (2003)

An exalted court
U.S. v. Windsor, 133 S.Ct. 2675 (2013)

Robbing the people of their most important liberty
Obergefell v. Hodges, 135 S.Ct. 2584 (2015)

The United States is a nation of laws and the law is ubiquitous throughout our nation. The impact of law is felt in every aspect of American Society. From where we send our children to school to how we are permitted to behave in the marital chamber, laws have their effect. The Supreme Court, as the highest arbiter of which laws are constitutionally permissible and which are not, issues decisions that shape society in many ways. Cases such as *Roe v. Wade* and *Brown v. Board of Education* radically changed the way Americans live. The cases presented in this chapter range from abortion rights to affirmative action to the definition of marriage to constitutional limits on capital punishment. All of the issues presented in these cases were extremely controversial and implicated firmly held beliefs on both sides of the issues. In his dissents in these cases, Justice Scalia not only showed his immense interpretative and literary skills, but, also revealed his own strongly felt beliefs.

Lord Acton did not say power purifies
Planned Parenthood of Southeastern Pennsylvania v. Casey,
505 U.S. 833 (1992)

Justice Scalia, with whom the Chief Justice, Justice White, and Justice Thomas join, concurring in the judgment in part and dissenting in part.

My views on this matter are unchanged from those I set forth in my separate opinions in *Webster v. Reproductive Health Services,* 492 U.S. 490, 532, 109 S.Ct. 3040, 3064, 106 L.Ed.2d 410 (1989) (opinion concurring in part and concurring in judgment), and *Ohio v. Akron Center for Reproductive Health,* 497 U.S. 502, 520, 110 S.Ct. 2972, 2984, 111 L.Ed.2d 405 (1990) (*Akron II*) (concurring opinion). The States may, if they wish, permit abortion on demand, but the Constitution does not *require* them to do so. The permissibility of abortion, and the limitations upon it, are to be resolved like most important questions in our democracy: by citizens trying to persuade one another and then voting. As the Court acknowledges, "where reasonable people disagree the government can adopt one position or the other." *Ante,* at 2806. The Court is correct in adding the qualification that this "assumes a state of affairs in which the choice does not intrude upon a protected liberty," *ante,* at 2807—but the crucial part of that qualification is the penultimate word. A State's choice between two positions on which reasonable people can disagree is constitutional even when (as is often the case) it intrudes upon a "liberty" in the absolute sense. Laws against bigamy, for example—with which entire societies of reasonable people disagree—intrude upon men and women's liberty to marry and live with one another. But bigamy happens not to be a liberty specially "protected" by the Constitution.

That is, quite simply, the issue in these cases: not whether the power of a woman to abort her unborn child is a "liberty" in the absolute sense; or even whether it is a liberty of great importance to many women. Of course it is both. The issue is whether it is a liberty protected by the Constitution of the United States. I am sure it is not. I reach that conclusion not because of anything so exalted as my views concerning the "concept of existence, of meaning, of the universe, and of the mystery of human life." *Ibid.* Rather, I reach it for the same reason I reach the conclusion that bigamy is not constitutionally protected—because of two simple facts: (1) the Constitution says absolutely nothing about it, and (2) the longstanding traditions of American society have permitted it to be legally proscribed. *Akron II, supra,* at 520, 110 S.Ct., at 2984 (Scalia, J., concurring).

The Court destroys the proposition, evidently meant to represent my position, that "liberty" includes "only those practices, defined at the most specific level, that were protected against government interference by other rules of law when the Fourteenth Amendment was ratified," *ante,* at 2805 (citing *Michael H. v. Gerald D.,* 491 U.S. 110, 127, n. 6, 109 S.Ct. 2333, 2344, n. 6, 105 L.Ed.2d 91 (1989) (opinion of Scalia, J.)). That is not, however, what *Michael H.* says; it merely observes that, in defining "liberty," we may not disregard a specific, "relevant tradition protecting, or denying protection to, the asserted right," *ibid.* But the Court does not wish to be fettered by any such limitations on its preferences. The Court's statement that it is "tempting" to acknowledge the authoritativeness of tradition in order to "cur[b] the discretion of federal judges," *ante,* at 2804, is of course rhetoric rather than reality; no government official is "tempted" to place restraints upon his own freedom of action, which is why Lord Acton did not say "Power tends to purify." The Court's temptation is in the quite opposite and more natural direction—towards systematically eliminating checks upon its own power; and it succumbs.

Beyond that brief summary of the essence of my position, I will not swell the United States Reports with repetition of what I have said before; and applying the rational basis test, I would uphold the Pennsylvania statute in its entirety. I must, however, respond to a few of the more outrageous arguments in today's opinion, which it is beyond human nature to leave unanswered. I shall discuss each of them under a quotation from the Court's opinion to which they pertain.

> "The inescapable fact is that adjudication of substantive due process claims may call upon the Court in interpreting the Constitution to exercise that same capacity which by tradition courts always have exercised: reasoned judgment." *Ante,* at 2806.

Assuming that the question before us is to be resolved at such a level of philosophical abstraction, in such isolation from the traditions of American society, as by simply applying "reasoned judgment," I do not see how that could possibly have produced the answer the Court arrived at in *Roe v. Wade,* 410 U.S. 113, 93 S.Ct. 705, 35 L.Ed.2d 147 (1973). Today's opinion describes the methodology of *Roe,* quite accurately, as weighing against the woman's interest the State's "'important and legitimate interest in protecting the potentiality of human life.'" *Ante,* at 2817 (quoting *Roe, supra,* at 162, 93 S.Ct., at 731). But "reasoned judgment" does not begin by begging the question, as *Roe* and subsequent cases unquestionably did by assuming that what the State is protecting is the mere "potentiality of human life." See, *e.g., Roe, supra,* at 162, 93 S.Ct., at 731; *Planned Parenthood of Central Mo. v. Danforth,* 428 U.S. 52, 61, 96 S.Ct. 2831, 2837, 49 L.Ed.2d 788 (1976); *Colautti v.*

Franklin, 439 U.S. 379, 386, 99 S.Ct. 675, 681, 58 L.Ed.2d 596 (1979); *Akron v. Akron Center for Reproductive Health, Inc.*, 462 U.S. 416, 428, 103 S.Ct. 2481, 2491, 76 L.Ed.2d 687 (1983) (*Akron I*); *Planned Parenthood Assn. of Kansas City, Mo., Inc. v. Ashcroft*, 462 U.S. 476, 482, 103 S.Ct. 2517, 2520, 76 L.Ed.2d 733 (1983). The whole argument of abortion opponents is that what the Court calls the fetus and what others call the unborn child *is a human life*. Thus, whatever answer *Roe* came up with after conducting its "balancing" is bound to be wrong, unless it is correct that the human fetus is in some critical sense merely potentially human. There is of course no way to determine that as a legal matter; it is in fact a value judgment. Some societies have considered newborn children not yet human, or the incompetent elderly no longer so.

The authors of the joint opinion, of course, do not squarely contend that *Roe v. Wade* was a *correct* application of "reasoned judgment"; merely that it must be followed, because of *stare decisis*. *Ante*, at 2808, 2812, 2817. But in their exhaustive discussion of all the factors that go into the determination of when *stare decisis* should be observed and when disregarded, they never mention "how wrong was the decision on its face?" Surely, if "[t]he Court's power lies ... in its legitimacy, a product of substance and perception," *ante*, at 2814, the "substance" part of the equation demands that plain error be acknowledged and eliminated. *Roe* was plainly wrong—even on the Court's methodology of "reasoned judgment," and even more so (of course) if the proper criteria of text and tradition are applied.

The emptiness of the "reasoned judgment" that produced *Roe* is displayed in plain view by the fact that, after more than 19 years of effort by some of the brightest (and most determined) legal minds in the country, after more than 10 cases upholding abortion rights in this Court, and after dozens upon dozens of *amicus* briefs submitted in these and other cases, the best the Court can do to explain how it is that the word "liberty" *must* be thought to include the right to destroy human fetuses is to rattle off a collection of adjectives that simply decorate a value judgment and conceal a political choice. The right to abort, we are told, inheres in "liberty" because it is among "a person's most basic decisions," *ante,* at 2806; it involves a "most intimate and personal choic[e]," *ante,* at 2807; it is "central to personal dignity and autonomy," *ibid.;* it "originate[s] within the zone of conscience and belief," *ibid.;* it is "too intimate and personal" for state interference, *ante,* at 2807; it reflects "intimate views" of a "deep, personal character," *ante,* at 2808; it involves "intimate relationships" and notions of "personal autonomy and bodily integrity," *ante,* at 2810; and it concerns a particularly " 'important decisio[n],'" *ante,* at 2811 (citation omitted). But it is obvious to anyone applying "reasoned judgment" that the same adjectives can be applied to many forms of conduct that this Court (including one of the Justices in today's majority, see *Bowers v. Hardwick,* 478 U.S. 186, 106 S.Ct. 2841, 92 L.Ed.2d 140 (1986)) has held are *not* entitled to constitutional protection—because, like abortion, they are forms of conduct that have long been criminalized in American society. Those adjectives might be applied, for example, to homosexual sodomy, polygamy, adult incest, and suicide, all of which are equally "intimate" and "deep[ly] personal" decisions involving "personal autonomy and bodily integrity," and all of which can constitutionally be proscribed because it is our unquestionable constitutional tradition that they are proscribable. It is not reasoned judgment that supports the Court's decision; only personal predilection. Justice Curtis's warning is as timely today as it was 135 years ago:

> "[W]hen a strict interpretation of the Constitution, according to the fixed rules which govern the interpretation of laws, is abandoned, and the theoretical opinions of individ-

> uals are allowed to control its meaning, we have no longer a Constitution; we are under the government of individual men, who for the time being have power to declare what the Constitution is, according to their own views of what it ought to mean." *Dred Scott v. Sandford,* 19 How. 393, 621, 15 L.Ed. 691 (1857) (dissenting opinion).

"Liberty finds no refuge in a jurisprudence of doubt." *Ante,* at 2803.

One might have feared to encounter this august and sonorous phrase in an opinion defending the real *Roe v. Wade,* rather than the revised version fabricated today by the authors of the joint opinion. The shortcomings of *Roe* did not include lack of clarity: Virtually all regulation of abortion before the third trimester was invalid. But to come across this phrase in the joint opinion—which calls upon federal district judges to apply an "undue burden" standard as doubtful in application as it is unprincipled in origin—is really more than one should have to bear.

The joint opinion frankly concedes that the amorphous concept of "undue burden" has been inconsistently applied by the Members of this Court in the few brief years since that "test" was first explicitly propounded by Justice O'Connor in her dissent in *Akron I,* 462 U.S. 416, 103 S.Ct. 2481, 76 L.Ed.2d 687 (1983). See *ante,* at 2820. Because the three Justices now wish to "set forth a standard of general application," the joint opinion announces that "it is important to clarify what is meant by an undue burden." *Ibid.* I certainly agree with that, but I do not agree that the joint opinion succeeds in the announced endeavor. To the contrary, its efforts at clarification make clear only that the standard is inherently manipulable and will prove hopelessly unworkable in practice.

The joint opinion explains that a state regulation imposes an "undue burden" if it "has the purpose or effect of placing a substantial obstacle in the path of a woman seeking an abortion of a nonviable fetus." *Ibid.*; see also *ante,* at 2820–2821. An obstacle is "substantial," we are told, if it is "calculated[,] [not] to inform the woman's free choice, [but to] hinder it." *Ante,* at 2820. This latter statement cannot possibly mean what it says. *Any* regulation of abortion that is intended to advance what the joint opinion concedes is the State's "substantial" interest in protecting unborn life will be "calculated [to] hinder" a decision to have an abortion. It thus seems more accurate to say that the joint opinion would uphold abortion regulations only if they do not *unduly* hinder the woman's decision. That, of course, brings us right back to square one: Defining an "undue burden" as an "undue hindrance" (or a "substantial obstacle") hardly "clarifies" the test. Consciously or not, the joint opinion's verbal shell game will conceal raw judicial policy choices concerning what is "appropriate" abortion legislation.

The ultimately standardless nature of the "undue burden" inquiry is a reflection of the underlying fact that the concept has no principled or coherent legal basis. As the Chief Justice points out, *Roe*'s strict-scrutiny standard "at least had a recognized basis in constitutional law at the time *Roe* was decided," *ante,* at 2866, while "[t]he same cannot be said for the 'undue burden' standard, which is created largely out of whole cloth by the authors of the joint opinion," *ibid.* The joint opinion is flatly wrong in asserting that "our jurisprudence relating to all liberties save perhaps abortion has recognized" the permissibility of laws that do not impose an "undue burden." *Ante,* at 2818. It argues that the abortion right is similar to other rights in that a law "not designed to strike at the right itself, [but which] has the incidental effect of making it more difficult or more expensive to [exercise the right,]" is not invalid. *Ante,* at 2819. I agree, indeed I have forcefully urged, that a law of general applicability which places only an incidental burden on a fundamental right does not infringe that right, see *R.A.V. v. St. Paul,* 505 U.S. 377, 389–390, 112 S.Ct. 2538, 2546–2547, 120 L.Ed.2d 305 (1992); *Employment Div., Dept. of Human Resources of Ore. v. Smith,* 494 U.S. 872, 878–882, 110 S.Ct. 1595, 1599–1602, 108 L.Ed.2d 876 (1990), but that principle does not establish the quite different (and quite dangerous) proposition that a law which *directly* regulates a fundamental right will not be found to violate the Constitution unless it imposes an "undue burden." It is that, of course, which is at issue here: Pennsylvania has *consciously and directly* regulated conduct that our cases have held is constitutionally protected. The appropriate analogy, therefore, is that of a state law requiring purchasers of religious books to endure a 24-hour waiting period, or to pay a nominal additional tax of 1¢. The joint opinion cannot possibly be correct in suggesting that we would uphold such legislation on the ground that it does not impose a "substantial obstacle" to the exercise of First Amendment rights. The "undue burden" standard is not at all the generally applicable principle the joint opinion pretends it to be; rather, it is a unique concept created specially for these cases, to preserve some judicial foothold in this ill-gotten territory. In claiming otherwise, the three Justices show their willingness to place all constitutional rights at risk in an effort to preserve what they deem the "central holding in *Roe.*" *Ante,* at 2818.

The rootless nature of the "undue burden" standard, a phrase plucked out of context from our earlier abortion decisions, see n. 3, *supra,* is further reflected in the fact that the joint opinion finds it necessary expressly to repudiate the more narrow formulations used in Justice O'Connor's earlier opinions. *Ante,* at 2820. Those opinions stated that a statute imposes an "undue burden" if it imposes "*absolute* obstacles or *severe* limitations on the abortion decision," *Akron I,* 462 U.S., at 464, 103 S.Ct., at 2510 (dissenting opinion) (emphasis added); see also *Thornburgh v. American College of Obstetricians and Gynecologists,* 476 U.S. 747, 828, 106 S.Ct. 2169, 2214, 90 L.Ed.2d 779 (1986) (dissenting opinion). Those strong adjectives are conspicuously missing from the joint opinion, whose authors have for some unexplained reason now determined that a burden is "undue" if it merely imposes a "substantial" obstacle to abortion decisions. See, *e.g., ante,* at 2830, 2833. Justice O'Connor has also abandoned (again without explanation) the view she expressed in *Planned Parenthood Assn. of Kansas City, Mo., Inc. v. Ashcroft,* 462 U.S. 476, 103 S.Ct. 2517, 76 L.Ed.2d 733 (1983) (dissenting opinion), that a medical regulation which imposes an "undue burden" could nevertheless be upheld if it "reasonably relate[s] to the preservation and protection of maternal health," *id.,* at 505, 103 S.Ct., at 2532 (citation and internal quotation marks omitted). In today's version, even health measures will be upheld only "*if they do not constitute an undue burden,*" *ante,* at 2821 (emphasis added). Gone too is Justice O'Connor's statement that "the State possesses *compelling* interests in the protection of potential human life ... throughout pregnancy," *Akron I, supra,* 462 U.S., at 461, 103 S.Ct., at 2509 (dissenting opinion) (emphasis added); see also *Ashcroft, supra,* 462 U.S., at 505, 103 S.Ct., at 2532 (O'Connor, J., concurring in judgment in part and dissenting in part); *Thornburgh, supra,* 476 U.S., at 828, 106 S.Ct., at 2214 (O'Connor, J., dissenting); instead, the State's interest in unborn human life is stealthily downgraded to a merely "substantial" or "profound" interest, *ante,* at 2820, 2821. (That had to be done, of course, since designating the interest as "compelling" throughout pregnancy would have been, shall we say, a "substantial obstacle" to the joint opinion's determined effort to reaffirm what it views as the "central holding" of *Roe.* See *Akron I,* 462 U.S., at 420, n. 1, 103 S.Ct., at 2487, n. 1.) And "viability" is no longer the "arbitrary" dividing line previously decried by Justice O'Connor in *Akron I, id.*, at 461, 103 S.Ct., at 2509; the Court now announces that "the attainment of viability may continue to serve as the critical fact," *ante*, at 2811. It is difficult to maintain the illusion that we are interpreting a Constitution rather than inventing one, when we amend its provisions so breezily.

Because the portion of the joint opinion adopting and describing the undue burden test provides no more useful guidance than the empty phrases discussed above, one must turn to the 23 pages applying that standard to the present facts for further guidance. In evaluating Pennsylvania's abortion law, the joint opinion relies extensively on the factual findings of the District Court, and repeatedly qualifies its conclusions by noting that they are contingent upon the record developed in these cases. Thus, the joint opinion would uphold the 24-hour waiting period contained in the Pennsylvania statute's informed consent provision, 18 Pa.Cons.Stat. § 3205 (1990), because "the record evidence shows that in the vast majority of cases, a 24-hour delay does not create any appreciable health risk," *ante*, at 2825. The three Justices therefore conclude that "on the record before us, ... we are not convinced that the 24-hour waiting period constitutes an undue burden." *Ante*, at 2826. The requirement that a doctor provide the information pertinent to informed consent would also be upheld because "there is no evidence on this record that [this requirement] would amount in practical terms to a substantial obstacle to a woman seeking an abortion." *Ante*, at 2824. Similarly, the joint opinion would uphold the reporting requirements of the Act, §§ 3207, 3214, because "there is no ... showing on the record before us" that these requirements constitute a "substantial obstacle" to abortion decisions. *Ante*, at 2833. But at the same time the opinion pointedly observes that these reporting requirements may increase the costs of abortions and that "at some point [that fact] could become a substantial obstacle." *Ibid.* Most significantly, the joint opinion's conclusion that the spousal notice requirement of the Act, see § 3209, imposes an "undue burden" is based in large measure on the District Court's "detailed findings of fact," which the joint opinion sets out at great length, *ante,* at 2826–2828.

I do not, of course, have any objection to the notion that, in applying legal principles, one should rely only upon the facts that are contained in the record or that are properly subject to judicial notice. But what is remarkable about the joint opinion's fact-intensive analysis is that it does not result in any measurable clarification of the "undue burden" standard. Rather, the approach of the joint opinion is, for the most part, simply to highlight certain facts in the record that apparently strike the three Justices as particularly significant in establishing (or refuting) the existence of an undue burden; after describing these facts, the opinion then simply announces that the provision either does or does not impose a "substantial obstacle" or an "undue burden." See, *e.g., ante,* at 2822, 2824, 2825–2826, 2828–2829, 2830, 2833. We do not know whether the same conclusions could have been reached on a different record, or in what respects the record would have had to differ before an opposite conclusion would have been appropriate. The inherently standardless nature of this inquiry invites the district judge to give effect to his personal preferences about abortion. By finding and relying upon the right facts, he can invalidate, it would seem, almost any abortion restriction that strikes him as "undue"—subject, of course, to the possibility of being reversed by a court of appeals or Supreme Court that is as unconstrained in reviewing his decision as he was in making it.

To the extent I can discern *any* meaningful content in the "undue burden" standard as applied in the joint opinion, it appears to be that a State may not regulate abortion in such a way as to reduce significantly its incidence. The joint opinion repeatedly emphasizes that an important factor in the "undue burden" analysis is whether the regulation "prevent[s] a significant number of women from obtaining an abortion," *ante,* at 2829; whether a "significant number of women ... are likely to be deterred from procuring an abortion," *ibid.;* and whether the regulation often "deters" women from seeking abortions, *ante,* at 2830–2831. We are not told, however, what forms of "deterrence" are impermissible or what degree of success in deterrence is too much to be tolerated. If, for example, a State required a woman to read a pamphlet describing, with illustrations, the facts of fetal development before she could obtain an abortion, the effect of such legislation might be to "deter" a "significant number of women" from procuring abortions, thereby seemingly allowing a district judge to invalidate it as an undue burden. Thus, despite flowery rhetoric about the State's "substantial" and "profound" interest in "potential human life," and criticism of *Roe* for undervaluing that interest, the joint opinion permits the State to pursue that interest only so long as it is not too successful. As Justice BLACKMUN recognizes (with evident hope), *ante,* at 2845, the "undue burden" standard may ultimately require the invalidation of each provision upheld today if it can be shown, on a better record, that the State is too effectively "express[ing] a preference for childbirth over abortion," *ante,* at 2824. Reason finds no refuge in this jurisprudence of confusion.

"While we appreciate the weight of the arguments ... that *Roe* should be overruled, the reservations any of us may have in reaffirming the central holding of *Roe* are outweighed by the explication of individual liberty we have given combined with the force of *stare decisis.*" *Ante,* at 2808.

The Court's reliance upon *stare decisis* can best be described as contrived. It insists upon the necessity of adhering not to all of *Roe,* but only to what it calls the "central holding." It seems to me that *stare decisis* ought to be applied even to the doctrine of *stare decisis,* and I confess never to have heard of this new, keep-what-you-want-and-throw-away-the-rest version. I wonder whether, as applied to *Marbury v. Madison,* 1 Cranch 137, 2 L.Ed. 60 (1803), for example, the new version of *stare decisis* would be satisfied if we allowed courts to review the constitutionality of only those statutes that (like the one in *Marbury*) pertain to the jurisdiction of the courts.

I am certainly not in a good position to dispute that the Court *has saved* the "central holding" of *Roe,* since to do that effectively I would have to know what the Court has saved, which in turn would require me to understand (as I do not) what the "undue burden" test means. I must confess, however, that I have always thought, and I think a lot of other people have always thought, that the arbitrary trimester framework, which the Court today discards, was quite as central to *Roe* as the arbitrary viability test, which the Court today retains. It seems particularly ungrateful to carve the trimester framework out of the core of *Roe,* since its very rigidity (in sharp contrast to the utter indeterminability of the "undue burden" test) is probably the only reason the Court is able to say, in urging *stare decisis,* that *Roe* "has in no sense proven 'unworkable,'" *ante,* at 2809. I suppose the Court is entitled to call a "central holding" whatever it wants to call a "central holding"—which is, come to think of it, perhaps one of the difficulties with this modified version of *stare decisis.* I thought I might note, however, that the following portions of *Roe* have not been saved:

- Under *Roe,* requiring that a woman seeking an abortion be provided truthful information about abortion before giving informed written consent is unconstitutional, if the information is designed to influence her choice. *Thornburgh,* 476 U.S., at 759–765, 106 S.Ct., at 2178–2181;

Akron I, 462 U.S., at 442–445, 103 S.Ct., at 2499–2500. Under the joint opinion's "undue burden" regime (as applied today, at least) such a requirement is constitutional. *Ante,* at 2822–2825.

- Under *Roe,* requiring that information be provided by a doctor, rather than by nonphysician counselors, is unconstitutional, *Akron I, supra,* at 446–449, 103 S.Ct., at 2501–2502. Under the "undue burden" regime (as applied today, at least) it is not. *Ante,* at 2824.

- Under *Roe,* requiring a 24-hour waiting period between the time the woman gives her informed consent and the time of the abortion is unconstitutional. *Akron I, supra,* at 449–451, 103 S.Ct., at 2502–2503. Under the "undue burden" regime (as applied today, at least) it is not. *Ante,* at 2825–2826.

- Under *Roe,* requiring detailed reports that include demographic data about each woman who seeks an abortion and various information about each abortion is unconstitutional. *Thornburgh, supra,* 476 U.S., at 765–768, 106 S.Ct., at 2181–2183. Under the "undue burden" regime (as applied today, at least) it generally is not. *Ante,* at 2832–2833.

"Where, in the performance of its judicial duties, the Court decides a case in such a way as to resolve the sort of intensely divisive controversy reflected in *Roe* ..., its decision has a dimension that the resolution of the normal case does not carry. It is the dimension present whenever the Court's interpretation of the Constitution calls the contending sides of a national controversy to end their national division by accepting a common mandate rooted in the Constitution." *Ante,* at 2815.

The Court's description of the place of *Roe* in the social history of the United States is unrecognizable. Not only did *Roe* not, as the Court suggests, *resolve* the deeply divisive issue of abortion; it did more than anything else to nourish it, by elevating it to the national level where it is infinitely more difficult to resolve. National politics were not plagued by abortion protests, national abortion lobbying, or abortion marches on Congress before *Roe v. Wade* was decided. Profound disagreement existed among our citizens over the issue—as it does over other issues, such as the death penalty—but that disagreement was being worked out at the state level. As with many other issues, the division of sentiment within each State was not as closely balanced as it was among the population of the Nation as a whole, meaning not only that more people would be satisfied with the results of state-by-state resolution, but also that those results would be more stable. Pre-*Roe*, moreover, political compromise was possible.

Roe's mandate for abortion on demand destroyed the compromises of the past, rendered compromise impossible for the future, and required the entire issue to be resolved uniformly, at the national level. At the same time, *Roe* created a vast new class of abortion consumers and abortion proponents by eliminating the moral opprobrium that had attached to the act. ("If the Constitution *guarantees* abortion, how can it be bad?"—not an accurate line of thought, but a natural one.) Many favor all of those developments, and it is not for me to say that they are wrong. But to portray *Roe* as the statesmanlike "settlement" of a divisive issue, a jurisprudential Peace of Westphalia that is worth preserving, is nothing less than Orwellian. *Roe* fanned into life an issue that has inflamed our national politics in general, and has obscured with its smoke the selection of Justices to this Court in particular, ever since. And by keeping us in the abortion-umpiring business, it is the perpetuation of that disruption, rather than of any *Pax Roeana,* that the Court's new majority decrees.

> "[T]o overrule under fire ... would subvert the Court's legitimacy....
>
> "... To all those who will be ... tested by following, the Court implicitly undertakes to remain steadfast.... The promise of constancy, once given, binds its maker for as long as the power to stand by the decision survives and ... the commitment [is not] obsolete....
>
> "[The American people's] belief in themselves as ... a people [who aspire to live according to the rule of law] is not readily separable from their understanding of the Court invested with the authority to decide their constitutional cases and speak before all others for their constitutional ideals. If the Court's legitimacy should be undermined, then, so would the country be in its very ability to see itself through its constitutional ideals." *Ante,* at 2815–2816.

The Imperial Judiciary lives. It is instructive to compare this Nietzschean vision of us unelected, life-tenured judges—leading a Volk who will be "tested by following," and whose very "belief in themselves" is mystically bound up in their "understanding" of a Court that "speak[s] before all others for their constitutional ideals"—with the somewhat more modest role envisioned for these lawyers by the Founders.

> "The judiciary ... has ... no direction either of the strength or of the wealth of the society, and can take no active resolution whatever. It may truly be said to have neither Force nor Will, but merely judgment...." *The Federalist* No. 78, pp. 393–394 (G. Wills ed. 1982).

Or, again, to compare this ecstasy of a Supreme Court in which there is, especially on controversial matters, no shadow of change or hint of alteration ("There is a limit to the amount of error that can plausibly be imputed to prior Courts," *ante,* at 2815), with the more democratic views of a more humble man:

> "[T]he candid citizen must confess that if the policy of the Government upon vital questions affecting the whole people is to be irrevocably fixed by decisions of the Supreme Court, ... the people will have ceased to be their own rulers, having to that extent practically resigned their Government into the hands of that eminent tribunal." A. Lincoln, First Inaugural Address (Mar. 4, 1861), reprinted in *Inaugural Addresses of the Presidents of the United States,* S. Doc. No. 101–10, p. 139 (1989).

It is particularly difficult, in the circumstances of the present decision, to sit still for the Court's lengthy lecture upon the virtues of "constancy," *ante,* at 2815, of "remain[ing] steadfast," *ibid.,* of adhering to "principle," *ante, passim.* Among the five Justices who purportedly adhere to *Roe,* at most three agree upon the *principle* that constitutes adherence (the joint opinion's "undue burden" standard)—and that principle is inconsistent with *Roe.* See 410 U.S., at 154–156, 93 S.Ct., at 727–728. To make matters worse, two of the three, in order thus to remain steadfast, had to abandon previously stated positions. See n. 4, *supra;* see *supra,* at 2878–2879. It is beyond me how the Court expects these accommodations to be accepted "as grounded truly in principle, not as compromises with social and political pressures having, as such, no bearing on the principled choices that the Court is obliged to make." *Ante,* at 2814. The only principle the Court "adheres" to, it seems to me, is the principle that the Court must be seen as standing by *Roe.* That is not a principle of law (which is what I thought the Court was talking about), but a principle of *Realpolitik*—and a wrong one at that.

I cannot agree with, indeed I am appalled by, the Court's suggestion that the decision whether to stand by an erroneous constitutional decision must be strongly influenced—*against* overruling, no less—by the substantial and continuing public opposition the decision has generated. The Court's judgment that any other course would "subvert the Court's legitimacy" must be another consequence of reading the error-filled history book that described the deeply divided country brought together by *Roe.* In my history-book, the Court was covered with dishonor and deprived of legitimacy by *Dred Scott v. Sandford,* 19 How. 393, 15 L.Ed. 691 (1857), an erroneous (and widely opposed) opinion that it did not abandon, rather than by *West Coast Hotel Co. v. Parrish,* 300 U.S. 379, 57 S.Ct. 578, 81 L.Ed. 703 (1937), which produced the famous "switch in time" from the Court's erroneous (and widely opposed) constitutional opposition to the social measures of the New Deal. (Both *Dred Scott* and one line of the cases resisting the New Deal rested upon the concept of "substantive due process" that the Court praises and employs today. Indeed, *Dred Scott* was "very possibly the first application of substantive due process in the Supreme Court, the original precedent for *Lochner v. New York* and *Roe v. Wade.*" D. Currie, *The Constitution in the Supreme Court* 271 (1985) (footnotes omitted).)

But whether it would "subvert the Court's legitimacy" or not, the notion that we would decide a case differently from the way we otherwise would have in order to show that we can stand firm against public disapproval is frightening. It is a bad enough idea, even in the head of someone like me, who believes that the text of the Constitution, and our traditions, say what they say and there is no fiddling with them. But when it is in the mind of a Court that believes the Constitution has an evolving meaning, see *ante,* at 2805; that the Ninth Amendment's reference to "othe [r]" rights is not a disclaimer, but a charter for action, *ibid.;* and that the function of this Court is to "speak before all others for [the people's] constitutional ideals" unrestrained by meaningful text or tradition—then the notion that the Court must adhere to a decision for as long as the decision faces "great opposition" and the Court is "under fire" acquires a character of almost czarist arrogance. We are offended by these marchers who descend upon us, every year on the anniversary of *Roe,* to protest our saying that the Constitution requires what our society has never thought the Constitution requires. These people who refuse to be "tested by following" must be taught a lesson. We have no Cossacks, but at least we can stubbornly refuse to abandon an erroneous opinion that we might otherwise change—to show how little they intimidate us.

Of course, as the Chief Justice points out, we have been subjected to what the Court calls "'political pressure'" by *both* sides of this issue. *Ante,* at 2865. Maybe today's decision *not* to overrule *Roe* will be seen as buckling to pressure from *that* direction. Instead of engaging in the hopeless task of predicting public perception—a job not for lawyers but for political campaign managers—the Justices should do what is *legally* right by asking two questions: (1) Was *Roe* correctly decided? (2) Has *Roe* succeeded in producing a settled body of law? If the answer to both questions is no, *Roe* should undoubtedly be overruled.

In truth, I am as distressed as the Court is—and expressed my distress several years ago, see *Webster,* 492 U.S., at 535, 109 S.Ct., at 3065—about the "political pressure" directed to the Court: the marches, the mail, the protests aimed at inducing us to change our opinions. How upsetting it is, that so many of our citizens (good people, not lawless ones, on both sides of this abortion issue, and on various sides of other issues as well) think that we Justices should properly take into account their views, as though we were engaged not in ascertaining an objective law but in determining some kind of social consensus. The Court would profit, I think, from giving less attention to the *fact* of this distressing phenomenon, and more attention to the *cause* of it. That cause permeates today's opinion: a new mode of constitutional adjudication that relies not upon text and traditional practice to determine the law, but upon what the Court calls "reasoned judgment," *ante,* at 2806, which turns out to be nothing but philosophical predilection and moral intuition. All manner of "liberties," the Court tells us, inhere in the Constitution and are enforceable by this Court—not just those mentioned in the text or established in the traditions of our society. *Ante,* at 2804–2806. Why even the Ninth Amendment—which says only that "[t]he enumeration in the Constitution, of certain rights, shall not be construed to deny or disparage others retained by the people"—is, despite our contrary understanding for almost 200 years, a literally boundless source of additional, unnamed, unhinted—at "rights," definable and enforceable by us, through "reasoned judgment." *Ante,* at 2805–2806.

What makes all this relevant to the bothersome application of "political pressure" against the Court are the twin facts that the American people love democracy and the American people are not fools. As long as this Court thought (and the people thought) that we Justices were doing essentially lawyers' work up here—reading text and discerning our society's traditional understanding of that text—the public pretty much left us alone. Texts and traditions are facts to study, not convictions to demonstrate about. But if in reality our process of constitutional adjudication consists primarily of making *value judgments*; if we can ignore a long and clear tradition clarifying an ambiguous text, as we did, for example, five days ago in declaring unconstitutional invocations and benedictions at public high school graduation ceremonies, *Lee v. Weisman,* 505 U.S.

577, 112 S.Ct. 2649, 120 L.Ed.2d 467 (1992); if, as I say, our pronouncement of constitutional law rests primarily on value judgments, then a free and intelligent people's attitude towards us can be expected to be (*ought* to be) quite different. The people know that their value judgments are quite as good as those taught in any law school—maybe better. If, indeed, the "liberties" protected by the Constitution are, as the Court says, undefined and unbounded, then the people *should* demonstrate, to protest that we do not implement *their* values instead of *ours*. Not only that, but confirmation hearings for new Justices *should* deteriorate into question-and-answer sessions in which Senators go through a list of their constituents' most favored and most disfavored alleged constitutional rights, and seek the nominee's commitment to support or oppose them. Value judgments, after all, should be voted on, not dictated; and if our Constitution has somehow accidently committed them to the Supreme Court, at least we can have a sort of plebiscite each time a new nominee to that body is put forward. Justice Blackmun not only regards this prospect with equanimity, he solicits it. *Ante*, at 2854–2855.

* * *

There is a poignant aspect to today's opinion. Its length, and what might be called its epic tone, suggest that its authors believe they are bringing to an end a troublesome era in the history of our Nation and of our Court. "It is the dimension" of authority, they say, to "cal[l] the contending sides of national controversy to end their national division by accepting a common mandate rooted in the Constitution." *Ante*, at 2815.

There comes vividly to mind a portrait by Emanuel Leutze that hangs in the Harvard Law School: Roger Brooke Taney, painted in 1859, the 82d year of his life, the 24th of his Chief Justiceship, the second after his opinion in *Dred Scott*. He is all in black, sitting in a shadowed red armchair, left hand resting upon a pad of paper in his lap, right hand hanging limply, almost lifelessly, beside the inner arm of the chair. He sits facing the viewer and staring straight out. There seems to be on his face, and in his deep-set eyes, an expression of profound sadness and disillusionment. Perhaps he always looked that way, even when dwelling upon the happiest of thoughts. But those of us who know how the lustre of his great Chief Justiceship came to be eclipsed by *Dred Scott* cannot help believing that he had that case—its already apparent consequences for the Court and its soon-to-be-played-out consequences for the Nation—burning on his mind. I expect that two years earlier he, too, had thought himself "call[ing] the contending sides of national controversy to end their national division by accepting a common mandate rooted in the Constitution."

It is no more realistic for us in this litigation, than it was for him in that, to think that an issue of the sort they both involved—an issue involving life and death, freedom and subjugation—can be "speedily and finally settled" by the Supreme Court, as President James Buchanan in his inaugural address said the issue of slavery in the territories would be. See *Inaugural Addresses of the Presidents of the United States*, S.Doc. No. 101–110, p. 126 (1989). Quite to the contrary, by foreclosing all democratic outlet for the deep passions this issue arouses, by banishing the issue from the political forum that gives all participants, even the losers, the satisfaction of a fair hearing and an honest fight, by continuing the imposition of a rigid national rule instead of allowing for regional differences, the Court merely prolongs and intensifies the anguish.

We should get out of this area, where we have no right to be, and where we do neither ourselves nor the country any good by remaining.

A democratic vote by nine lawyers
Stenberg v. Carhart,
530 U.S. 914 (2000)

Justice Scalia, dissenting.

I am optimistic enough to believe that, one day, *Stenberg v. Carhart* will be assigned its rightful place in the history of this Court's jurisprudence beside *Korematsu* and *Dred Scott.* The method of killing a human child—one cannot even accurately say an entirely unborn human child—proscribed by this statute is so horrible that the most clinical description of it evokes a shudder of revulsion. And the Court must know (as most state legislatures banning this procedure have concluded) that demanding a "health exception"—which requires the abortionist to assure himself that, in his expert medical judgment, this method is, in the case at hand, marginally safer than others (how can one prove the contrary beyond a reasonable doubt?)—is to give live-birth abortion free rein. The notion that the Constitution of the United States, designed, among other things, "to establish Justice, insure domestic Tranquility, ... and secure the Blessings of Liberty to ourselves and our Posterity," prohibits the States from simply banning this visibly brutal means of eliminating our half-born posterity is quite simply absurd.

Even so, I had not intended to write separately here until the focus of the other separate writings (including the one I have joined) gave me cause to fear that this case might be taken to stand for an error different from the one that it actually exemplifies. Because of the Court's practice of publishing dissents in the order of the seniority of their authors, this writing will appear in the United States Reports before those others, but the reader will not comprehend what follows unless he reads them first.

* * *

The two lengthy dissents in this case have, appropriately enough, set out to establish that today's result does not follow from this Court's most recent pronouncement on the matter of abortion, *Planned Parenthood of Southeastern Pa. v. Casey,* 505 U.S. 833, 112 S.Ct. 2791, 120 L.Ed.2d 674 (1992). It would be unfortunate, however, if those who disagree with the result were induced to regard it as merely a regrettable misapplication of *Casey.* It is not that, but is *Casey's* logical and entirely predictable consequence. To be sure, the Court's construction of this statute so as to make it include procedures other than live-birth abortion involves not only a disregard of fair meaning, but an abandonment of the principle that even ambiguous statutes should be interpreted in such fashion as to render them valid rather than void. *Casey* does not permit *that* jurisprudential novelty—which must be chalked up to the Court's inclination to bend the rules when any effort to limit abortion, or even to speak in opposition to abortion, is at issue. It is of a piece, in other words, with *Hill v. Colorado,* 530 U.S. 703, 120 S.Ct. 2480, also decided today.

But the Court gives a second and independent reason for invalidating this humane (not to say anti-barbarian) law: That it fails to allow an exception for the situation in which the abortionist believes that this live-birth method of destroying the child might be safer for the woman. (As pointed out by Justice Thomas, and elaborated upon by Justice Kennedy, there is no good reason to believe this is ever the case, but—who knows?—it sometime *might* be.)

I have joined Justice Thomas's dissent because I agree that today's decision is an "unprecedented expansio[n]" of our prior cases, *post,* at 2652, "is not mandated" by *Casey's* "undue-burden" test, *post,* at 2651, and can even be called (though this pushes me to the limit of my belief) "obviously irreconcilable with *Casey's* explication of what its undue-burden standard requires," *post,* at 2636. But I never put much stock in *Casey's* explication of the inexplicable. In the last analysis, my judgment that *Casey* does not support today's tragic result can be traced to the fact that what I consider to be an "undue burden" is different from what the majority considers to be an "undue burden"—a conclusion that cannot be demonstrated true or false by factual inquiry or legal reasoning. It is a value judgment, dependent upon how much one respects (or believes society ought to respect) the life of a partially delivered fetus, and how much one respects (or believes society ought to respect) the freedom of the woman who gave it life to kill it. Evidently, the five Justices in today's majority value the former less, or the latter more, (or both), than the four of us in dissent. Case closed. There is no cause for anyone who believes in *Casey* to feel betrayed by this outcome. It has been arrived at by precisely the process *Casey* promised—a democratic vote by nine lawyers, not on the question whether the text of the Constitution has anything to say about this subject (it obviously does not); nor even on the question (also appropriate for lawyers) whether the legal traditions of the American people would have sustained such a limitation upon abortion (they obviously would); but upon the pure policy question whether this limitation upon abortion is "undue"—*i.e.,* goes too far.

In my dissent in *Casey,* I wrote that the "undue burden" test made law by the joint opinion created a standard that was "as doubtful in application as it is unprincipled in origin," *Casey,* 505 U.S., at 985, 112 S.Ct. 2791; "hopelessly unworkable in practice," *id.,* at 986, 112 S.Ct. 2791; "ultimately standardless," *id.,* at 987, 112 S.Ct. 2791. Today's decision is the proof. As long as we are debating this issue of necessity for a health-of-the-mother exception on the basis of *Casey,* it is really quite impossible for us dissenters to contend that the majority is *wrong* on the law—any more than it could be said that one is *wrong in law* to support or oppose the death penalty, or to support or oppose mandatory minimum sentences. The most that we can honestly say is that we disagree with the majority on their policy-judgment-couched-as-law. And those who believe that a 5–to–4 vote on a policy matter by unelected lawyers should not overcome the judgment of 30 state legislatures have a problem, not with the *application* of *Casey,* but with its *existence. Casey* must be overruled.

While I am in an I-told-you-so mood, I must recall my bemusement, in *Casey,* at the majority opinion's expressed belief that *Roe v. Wade,* 410 U.S. 113, 93 S.Ct. 705, 35 L.Ed.2d 147 (1973), had "call[ed] the contending sides of a national controversy to end their national division by accepting a common mandate rooted in the Constitution," *Casey,* 505 U.S., at 867, 112 S.Ct. 2791, and that the decision in *Casey* would ratify that happy truce. It seemed to me, quite to the contrary, that "*Roe* fanned into life an issue that has inflamed our national politics in general, and has obscured with its smoke the selection of Justices to this Court in particular, ever since"; and that, "by keeping us in the abortion-umpiring business, it is the perpetuation of that disruption, rather than of any *Pax Roeana,* that the Court's new majority decrees." *Id.,* at 995–996, 112 S.Ct. 2791. Today's decision, that the Constitution of the United States prevents the prohibition of a horrible mode of abortion, will be greeted by a firestorm of criticism—as well it should. I cannot understand why those who *acknowledge* that, in the opening words of Justice O'Connor's concurrence, "[t]he issue of abortion is one of the most contentious and controversial in contemporary American society," *ante,* at 2617, persist in the belief that this Court, armed with neither constitutional text nor accepted tradition, can resolve that contention and controversy rather than be consumed by it. If only for the sake of its own preservation, the Court should return this matter to the people—where the Constitution, by its silence on the subject, left it—and let *them* decide, State by State, whether this practice should be allowed. *Casey* must be overruled.

Prize for most feeble effort
Atkins v. Virginia,
536 U.S. 304 (2002)

Justice Scalia, with whom the Chief Justice and Justice Thomas join, dissenting.

Today's decision is the pinnacle of our Eighth Amendment death-is-different jurisprudence. Not only does it, like all of that jurisprudence, find no support in the text or history of the Eighth Amendment; it does not even have support in current social attitudes regarding the conditions that render an otherwise just death penalty inappropriate. Seldom has an opinion of this Court rested so obviously upon nothing but the personal views of its Members.

I

I begin with a brief restatement of facts that are abridged by the Court but important to understanding this case. After spending the day drinking alcohol and smoking marijuana, petitioner Daryl Renard Atkins and a partner in crime drove to a convenience store, intending to rob a customer. Their victim was Eric Nesbitt, an airman from Langley Air Force Base, whom they abducted, drove to a nearby automated teller machine, and forced to withdraw $200. They then drove him to a deserted area, ignoring his pleas to leave him unharmed. According to the co-conspirator, whose testimony the jury evidently credited, Atkins ordered Nesbitt out of the vehicle and, after he had taken only a few steps, shot him one, two, three, four, five, six, seven, eight times in the thorax, chest, abdomen, arms, and legs.

The jury convicted Atkins of capital murder. At resentencing (the Virginia Supreme Court affirmed his conviction but remanded for resentencing because the trial court had used an improper verdict form, 257 Va. 160, 179, 510 S.E.2d 445, 457 (1999)), the jury heard extensive evidence of petitioner's alleged mental retardation. A psychologist testified that petitioner was mildly mentally retarded with an IQ of 59, that he was a "slow learner," App. 444, who showed a "lack of success in pretty much every domain of his life," *id.*, at 442, and that he had an "impaired" capacity to appreciate the criminality of his conduct and to conform his conduct to the law, *id.*, at 453. Petitioner's family members offered additional evidence in support of his mental retardation claim (*e.g.*, that petitioner is a "follower," *id.*, at 421). The Commonwealth contested the evidence of retardation and presented testimony of a psychologist who found "absolutely no evidence other than the IQ score ... indicating that [petitioner] was in the least bit mentally retarded" and concluded that petitioner was "of average intelligence, at least." *Id.*, at 476.

The jury also heard testimony about petitioner's 16 prior felony convictions for robbery, attempted robbery, abduction, use of a firearm, and maiming. *Id.*, at 491–522. The victims of these offenses provided graphic depictions of petitioner's violent tendencies: He hit one over the head with a beer bottle, *id.*, at 406; he slapped a gun across another victim's face, clubbed her in the head with it, knocked her to the ground, and then helped her up, only to shoot her in the stomach, *id.*, at 411–413. The jury sentenced petitioner to death. The Supreme Court of Virginia affirmed petitioner's sentence. 260 Va. 375, 534 S.E.2d 312 (2000).

II

As the foregoing history demonstrates, petitioner's mental retardation was a *central issue* at sentencing. The jury concluded, however, that his alleged retardation was not a compelling reason to exempt him from the death penalty in light of the brutality of his crime and his long demonstrated propensity for violence. "In upsetting this particularized judgment on the basis of a constitutional absolute," the Court concludes that no one who is even slightly mentally retarded can have sufficient "moral responsibility to be subjected to capital punishment for any crime. As a sociological and moral conclusion that is implausible; and it is doubly implausible as an interpretation of the United States Constitution." *Thompson v. Oklahoma,* 487 U.S. 815, 863–864, 108 S.Ct. 2687, 101 L.Ed.2d 702 (1988) (Scalia, J., dissenting).

Under our Eighth Amendment jurisprudence, a punishment is "cruel and unusual" if it falls within one of two categories: "those modes or acts of punishment that had been considered cruel and unusual at the time that the Bill of Rights was adopted," *Ford v. Wainwright,* 477 U.S. 399, 405, 106 S.Ct. 2595, 91 L.Ed.2d 335 (1986), and modes of punishment that are inconsistent with modern "'standards of decency,'" as evinced by objective indicia, the most important of which is "legislation enacted by the country's legislatures," *Penry v. Lynaugh,* 492 U.S. 302, 330–331, 109 S.Ct. 2934, 106 L.Ed.2d 256 (1989).

The Court makes no pretense that execution of the mildly mentally retarded would have been considered "cruel and unusual" in 1791. Only the *severely* or *profoundly* mentally retarded, commonly known as "idiots," enjoyed any special status under the law at that time. They, like lunatics, suffered a "deficiency in will" rendering them unable to tell right from wrong. 4 W. Blackstone, *Commentaries on the Laws of England*

24 (1769) (hereinafter *Blackstone*); see also *Penry,* 492 U.S., at 331–332, 109 S.Ct. 2934 ("[T]he term 'idiot' was generally used to describe persons who had a total lack of reason or understanding, or an inability to distinguish between good and evil"); *id.,* at 333, 109 S.Ct. 2934 (citing sources indicating that idiots generally had an IQ of 25 or below, which would place them within the "profound" or "severe" range of mental retardation under modern standards); 2 A. Fitzherbert, *Natura Brevium* 233B (9th ed. 1794) (originally published 1534) (An idiot is "such a person who cannot account or number twenty pence, nor can tell who was his father or mother, nor how old he is, etc., so as it may appear that he hath no understanding of reason what shall be for his profit, or what for his loss"). Due to their incompetence, idiots were "excuse[d] from the guilt, and of course from the punishment, of any criminal action committed under such deprivation of the senses." 4 *Blackstone* 25; see also *Penry, supra,* at 331, 109 S.Ct. 2934. Instead, they were often committed to civil confinement or made wards of the State, thereby preventing them from "go[ing] loose, to the terror of the king's subjects." 4 *Blackstone* 25; see also S. Brakel, J. Parry, & B. Weiner, *The Mentally Disabled and the Law* 12–14 (3d ed.1985); 1 *Blackstone* 292–296; 1 M. Hale, *Pleas of the Crown* 33 (1st Am. ed. 1847). Mentally retarded offenders with less severe impairments—those who were not "idiots"—suffered criminal prosecution and punishment, including capital punishment. See, *e.g.,* I. Ray, *Medical Jurisprudence of Insanity* 65, 87–92 (W. Overholser ed.1962) (recounting the 1834 trial and execution in Concord, New Hampshire, of an apparent "imbecile"—imbecility being a less severe form of retardation which "differs from idiocy in the circumstance that while in [the idiot] there is an utter destitution of every thing like reason, [imbeciles] possess some intellectual capacity, though infinitely less than is possessed by the great mass of

mankind"); A. Highmore, *Law of Idiocy and Lunacy* 200 (1807) ("The great difficulty in all these cases, is to determine where a person shall be said to be so far deprived of his sense and memory as not to have any of his actions imputed to him: or where notwithstanding some defects of this kind he still appears to have so much reason and understanding as will make him accountable for his actions ...").

The Court is left to argue, therefore, that execution of the mildly retarded is inconsistent with the "evolving standards of decency that mark the progress of a maturing society." *Trop v. Dulles,* 356 U.S. 86, 101, 78 S.Ct. 590, 2 L.Ed.2d 630 (1958) (plurality opinion) (Warren, C. J.). Before today, our opinions consistently emphasized that Eighth Amendment judgments regarding the existence of social "standards" "should be informed by objective factors to the maximum possible extent" and "should not be, or appear to be, merely the subjective views of individual Justices." *Coker v. Georgia,* 433 U.S. 584, 592, 97 S.Ct. 2861, 53 L.Ed.2d 982 (1977) (plurality opinion); see also *Stanford v. Kentucky,* 492 U.S. 361, 369, 109 S.Ct. 2969, 106 L.Ed.2d 306 (1989); *McCleskey v. Kemp,* 481 U.S. 279, 300, 107 S.Ct. 1756, 95 L.Ed.2d 262 (1987); *Enmund v. Florida,* 458 U.S. 782, 788, 102 S.Ct. 3368, 73 L.Ed.2d 1140 (1982). "First" among these objective factors are the "statutes passed by society's elected representatives," *Stanford v. Kentucky, supra,* at 370, 109 S.Ct. 2969; because it "will rarely if ever be the case that the Members of this Court will have a better sense of the evolution in views of the American people than do their elected representatives," *Thompson, supra,* at 865, 108 S.Ct. 2687 (Scalia, J., dissenting).

The Court pays lip service to these precedents as it miraculously extracts a "national consensus" forbidding execution of the mentally retarded, *ante,* at 2250, from the fact that 18 States—less than *half* (47%) of the 38 States that permit capital punishment (for whom the issue exists)—have very recently enacted legislation barring execution of the mentally retarded. Even that 47% figure is a distorted one. If one is to say, as the Court does today, that *all* executions of the mentally retarded are so morally repugnant as to violate our national "standards of decency," surely the "consensus" it points to must be one that has set its righteous face against *all* such executions. Not 18 States, but only 7—18% of death penalty jurisdictions—have legislation of that scope. Eleven of those that the Court counts enacted statutes prohibiting execution of mentally retarded defendants *convicted after, or convicted of crimes committed after, the effective date* of the legislation; those already on death row, or consigned there before the statute's effective date, or even (in those States using the date of the crime as the criterion of retroactivity) tried in the future for murders committed many years ago, could be put to death. That is not a statement of absolute moral repugnance, but one of current preference between two tolerable approaches. Two of these States permit execution of the mentally retarded in other situations as well: Kansas apparently permits execution of all except the *severely* mentally retarded; New York permits execution of the mentally retarded who commit murder in a correctional facility. N.Y.Crim. Proc. Law § 400.27.12(d) (McKinney 2001); N.Y. Penal Law § 125.27 (McKinney 2002).

But let us accept, for the sake of argument, the Court's faulty count. That bare number of States alone—*18*—should be enough to convince any reasonable person that no "national consensus" exists. How is it possible that agreement among 47% of the death penalty jurisdictions amounts to "consensus"? Our prior cases have generally required a much higher degree of agreement before finding a punishment cruel and unusual on "evolving standards" grounds. In *Coker, supra,* at 595–596, 97 S.Ct. 2861, we proscribed the death penalty for rape of an adult woman after finding that only one jurisdiction, Georgia, authorized such a punishment. In *Enmund, supra,* at 789, 102 S.Ct. 3368, we invalidated the death penalty for mere participation in a robbery in which an accomplice took a life, a punishment not permitted in 28 of the death penalty States (78%). In *Ford,* 477 U.S., at 408, 106 S.Ct. 2595, we supported the common-law prohibition of execution of the insane with the observation that "[t]his ancestral legacy has not outlived its time," since not a single State authorizes such punishment. In *Solem v. Helm,* 463 U.S. 277, 300, 103 S.Ct. 3001, 77 L.Ed.2d 637 (1983), we invalidated a life sentence without parole under a recidivist statute by which the criminal "was treated more severely than he would have been in any other State." What the Court calls evidence of "consensus" in the present case (a fudged 47%) more closely resembles evidence that we found *inadequate* to establish consensus in earlier cases. *Tison v. Arizona,* 481 U.S. 137, 154, 158, 107 S.Ct. 1676, 95 L.Ed.2d 127 (1987), upheld a state law authorizing capital punishment for major participation in a felony with reckless indifference to life where only 11 of the 37 death penalty States (30%) prohibited such punishment. *Stanford,* 492 U.S., at 372, 109 S.Ct. 2969, upheld a state law permitting execution of defendants who committed a capital crime at age 16 where only 15 of the 36 death penalty States (42%) prohibited death for such offenders.

Moreover, a major factor that the Court entirely disregards is that the legislation of all 18 States it relies on is still in its infancy. The oldest of the statutes is only 14 years old; five were enacted last year; over half were enacted within the past eight years. Few, if any, of the States have had sufficient experience with these laws to know whether they are sensible in the long term. It is "myopic to base sweeping constitutional principles upon the narrow experience of [a few] years." *Coker,* 433 U.S., at 614, 97 S.Ct. 2861 (Burger, C. J., dissenting); see also *Thompson,* 487 U.S., at 854–855, 108 S.Ct. 2687 (O'-Connor, J., concurring in judgment).

The Court attempts to bolster its embarrassingly feeble evidence of "consensus" with the following: "It is not so much the number of these States that is significant, but the *consistency* of the direction of change." *Ante,* at 2249 (emphasis added). But in what *other* direction *could we possibly* see change? Given that 14 years ago *all* the death penalty statutes included the mentally retarded, *any* change (except precipitate undoing of what had just been done) was *bound to be* in the one direction the Court finds significant enough to overcome the lack of real consensus. That is to say, to be accurate the Court's "*consistency*-of-the-direction-of-change" point should be recast into the following unimpressive observation: "No State has yet undone its exemption of the mentally retarded, one for as long as 14 whole years." In any event, reliance upon "trends," even those of much longer duration than a mere 14 years, is a perilous basis for constitutional adjudication, as Justice O'Connor eloquently explained in *Thompson:*

> "In 1846, Michigan became the first State to abolish the death penalty .... In succeeding decades, other American States continued the trend towards abolition .... Later, and particularly after World War II, there ensued a steady and dramatic decline in executions .... In the 1950's and 1960's, more States abolished or radically restricted capital punishment, and executions ceased completely for several years beginning in 1968 ....
>
> "In 1972, when this Court heard arguments on the constitutionality of the death penalty, such statistics might have suggested that the practice had become a relic, implicitly rejected by a new societal consensus.... We now know that any inference of a societal consensus rejecting the death penalty would have been mistaken. But had this Court then declared

> the existence of such a consensus, and outlawed capital punishment, legislatures would very likely not have been able to revive it. The mistaken premise of the decision would have been frozen into constitutional law, making it difficult to refute and even more difficult to reject." 487 U.S., at 854–855, 108 S.Ct. 2687.

Her words demonstrate, of course, not merely the peril of riding a trend, but also the peril of discerning a consensus where there is none.

The Court's thrashing about for evidence of "consensus" includes reliance upon the *margins* by which state legislatures have enacted bans on execution of the retarded. *Ante,* at 2249. Presumably, in applying our Eighth Amendment "evolving-standards-of-decency" jurisprudence, we will henceforth weigh not only how many States have agreed, but how many States have agreed *by how much.* Of course if the percentage of legislators voting for the bill is significant, surely the number of people *represented* by the legislators voting for the bill is also significant: the fact that 49% of the legislators in a State with a population of 60 million voted *against* the bill should be more impressive than the fact that 90% of the legislators in a State with a population of 2 million voted *for* it. (By the way, the population of the death penalty States that exclude the mentally retarded is only 44% of the population of all death penalty States. U.S. Dept. of Commerce, Bureau of Census, Statistical Abstract of the United States 21 (121st ed.2001).) This is quite absurd. What we have looked for in the past to "evolve" the Eighth Amendment is a consensus of the same sort as the consensus that *adopted* the Eighth Amendment: a consensus of the sovereign States that form the Union, not a nose count of Americans for and against.

Even less compelling (if possible) is the Court's argument, *ibid.*, that evidence of "national consensus" is to be found in the infrequency with which retarded persons are executed in States that do not bar their execution. To begin with, what the Court takes as true is in fact quite doubtful. It is not at all clear that execution of the mentally retarded is "uncommon," *ibid.*, as even the sources cited by the Court suggest, see *ante*, at 2249, n. 20 (citing D. Keyes, W. Edwards, & R. Perske, People with Mental Retardation are Dying Legally, 35 *Mental Retardation* (Feb.1997) (updated by Death Penalty Information Center, available at http://www.advocacyone.org/ deathpenalty.html (as visited June 12, 2002) (showing that 12 States executed 35 allegedly mentally retarded offenders during the period 1984–2000)). See also Bonner & Rimer, "Executing the Mentally Retarded Even as Laws Begin to Shift," *N.Y. Times*, Aug. 7, 2000, p. A1 (reporting that 10% of death row inmates are retarded). *If*, however, execution of the mentally retarded *is* "uncommon"; and if it is not a sufficient explanation of this that the retarded constitute a tiny fraction of society (1% to 3%), Brief for American Psychological Association et al. as *Amici Curiae* 7; then surely the explanation is that mental retardation is a constitutionally mandated mitigating factor at sentencing, *Penry*, 492 U.S., at 328, 109 S.Ct. 2934. For that reason, even if there were uniform national sentiment in *favor* of executing the retarded in appropriate cases, one would still expect execution of the mentally retarded to be "uncommon." To adapt to the present case what the Court itself said in *Stanford*, 492 U.S., at 374, 109 S.Ct. 2969: "[I]t is not only possible, but overwhelmingly probable, that the very considerations which induce [today's majority] to believe that death should *never* be imposed on [mentally retarded] offenders ... cause prosecutors and juries to believe that it should *rarely* be imposed."

But the Prize for the Court's Most Feeble Effort to fabricate "national consensus" must go to its appeal (deservedly relegated to a footnote) to the views of assorted professional and religious organizations, members of the so-called "world community," and respondents to opinion polls. *Ante,* at 2249–2250, n. 21. I agree with the Chief Justice, *ante,* at 2254–2256 (dissenting opinion), that the views of professional and religious organizations and the results of opinion polls are irrelevant. Equally irrelevant are the practices of the "world community," whose notions of justice are (thankfully) not always those of our people. "We must never forget that it is a Constitution for the United States of America that we are expounding. ... [W]here there is not first a settled consensus among our own people, the views of other nations, however enlightened the Justices of this Court may think them to be, cannot be imposed upon Americans through the Constitution." *Thompson,* 487 U.S., at 868–869, n. 4, 108 S.Ct. 2687 (Scalia, J., dissenting).

III

Beyond the empty talk of a "national consensus," the Court gives us a brief glimpse of what really underlies today's decision: pretension to a power confined *neither* by the moral sentiments originally enshrined in the Eighth Amendment (its original meaning) *nor even* by the current moral sentiments of the American people. "'[T]he Constitution,' the Court says, 'contemplates that in the end *our own judgment* will be brought to bear on the question of the acceptability of the death penalty under the Eighth Amendment.'" *Ante,* at 2247 (quoting *Coker,* 433 U.S., at 597, 97 S.Ct. 2861) (emphasis added). (The unexpressed reason for this unexpressed "contemplation" of the Constitution is presumably that really good lawyers have moral sentiments superior to those of the common herd, whether in 1791 or today.) The arrogance of this assumption of power takes one's breath away. And it explains, of course, why the Court can be so cavalier about the evidence of consensus. It is just a game, after all. "'[I]n the end,'" *Thompson, supra,* at 823, n. 8 (plurality opinion (quoting *Coker, supra,* at 597 (plurality opinion))), it is the *feelings* and *intuition* of a majority of the Justices that count—"the perceptions of decency, or of penology, or of mercy, entertained ... by a majority of the small and unrepresentative segment of our society that sits on this Court." *Thompson, supra,* at 873, 108 S.Ct. 2687 (Scalia, J., dissenting).

The genuinely operative portion of the opinion, then, is the Court's statement of the reasons why it agrees with the contrived consensus it has found, that the "diminished capacities" of the mentally retarded render the death penalty excessive. *Ante,* at 2250–2252. The Court's analysis rests on two fundamental assumptions: (1) that the Eighth Amendment prohibits excessive punishments, and (2) that sentencing juries or judges are unable to account properly for the "diminished capacities" of the retarded. The first assumption is wrong, as I explained at length in *Harmelin v. Michigan,* 501 U.S. 957, 966–990, 111 S.Ct. 2680, 115 L.Ed.2d 836 (1991) (opinion of Scalia, J.). The Eighth Amendment is addressed to always-and-everywhere "cruel" punishments, such as the rack and the thumbscrew. But where the punishment is in itself permissible, "[t]he Eighth Amendment is not a ratchet, whereby a temporary consensus on leniency for a particular crime fixes a permanent constitutional maximum, disabling the States from giving effect to altered beliefs and responding to changed social conditions." *Id.,* at 990, 111 S.Ct. 2680. The second assumption—inability of judges or juries to take proper account of mental retardation—is not only unsubstantiated, but contradicts the immemorial belief, here and in England, that they play an *indispensable* role in such matters:

> "[I]t is very difficult to define the indivisible line that divides perfect and partial insanity; but it must rest upon circumstances duly to be weighed and considered both by the judge and jury, lest on the one side there be a kind of inhumanity towards the defects of human nature, or on the other side too great an indulgence given to great crimes ...." 1 Hale, *Pleas of the Crown*, at 30.

Proceeding from these faulty assumptions, the Court gives two reasons why the death penalty is an excessive punishment for all mentally retarded offenders. First, the "diminished capacities" of the mentally retarded raise a "serious question" whether their execution contributes to the "social purposes" of the death penalty, viz., retribution and deterrence. *Ante,* at 2250–2251. (The Court conveniently ignores a third "social purpose" of the death penalty—"incapacitation of dangerous criminals and the consequent prevention of crimes that they may otherwise commit in the future," *Gregg v. Georgia,* 428 U.S. 153, 183, n. 28, 96 S.Ct. 2909, 49 L.Ed.2d 859 (1976) (joint opinion of Stewart, Powell, and Stevens, JJ.). But never mind; its discussion of even the other two does not bear analysis.) Retribution is not advanced, the argument goes, because the mentally retarded are *no more culpable* than the average murderer, whom we have already held lacks sufficient culpability to warrant the death penalty, see *Godfrey v. Georgia,* 446 U.S. 420, 433, 100 S.Ct. 1759, 64 L.Ed.2d 398 (1980) (plurality opinion). *Ante,* at 2251. Who says so? Is there an established correlation between mental acuity and the ability to conform one's conduct to the law in such a rudimentary matter as murder? Are the mentally retarded really more disposed (and hence more likely) to commit willfully cruel and serious crime than others?

In my experience, the opposite is true: being childlike generally suggests innocence rather than brutality.

Assuming, however, that there is a direct connection between diminished intelligence and the inability to refrain from murder, what scientific analysis can possibly show that a mildly retarded individual who commits an exquisite torture-killing is "no more culpable" than the "average" murderer in a holdup-gone-wrong or a domestic dispute? Or a moderately retarded individual who commits a series of 20 exquisite torture-killings? Surely culpability, and deservedness of the most severe retribution, depends not merely (if at all) upon the mental capacity of the criminal (above the level where he is able to distinguish right from wrong) but also upon the depravity of the crime—which is precisely why this sort of question has traditionally been thought answerable not by a categorical rule of the sort the Court today imposes upon all trials, but rather by the sentencer's weighing of the circumstances (both degree of retardation and depravity of crime) in the particular case. The fact that juries continue to sentence mentally retarded offenders to death for extreme crimes shows that society's moral outrage sometimes demands execution of retarded offenders. By what principle of law, science, or logic can the Court pronounce that this is wrong? There is none. Once the Court admits (as it does) that mental retardation does not render the offender morally *blameless*, *ante*, at 2250–2251, there is no basis for saying that the death penalty is *never* appropriate retribution, no matter *how* heinous the crime. As long as a mentally retarded offender knows "the difference between right and wrong," *ante*, at 2250, only the sentencer can assess whether his retardation reduces his culpability enough to exempt him from the death penalty for the particular murder in question.

As for the other social purpose of the death penalty that the Court discusses, deterrence: That is not advanced, the

Court tells us, because the mentally retarded are "less likely" than their non-retarded counterparts to "process the information of the possibility of execution as a penalty and ... control their conduct based upon that information." *Ante,* at 2251. Of course this leads to the same conclusion discussed earlier—that the mentally retarded (because they are less deterred) are more likely to kill—which neither I nor the society at large believes. In any event, even the Court does not say that *all* mentally retarded individuals cannot "process the information of the possibility of execution as a penalty and ... control their conduct based upon that information"; it merely asserts that they are "less likely" to be able to do so. But surely the deterrent effect of a penalty is adequately vindicated if it successfully deters many, but not all, of the target class. Virginia's death penalty, for example, does not fail of its deterrent effect simply because *some* criminals are unaware that Virginia *has* the death penalty. In other words, the supposed fact that *some* retarded criminals cannot fully appreciate the death penalty has nothing to do with the deterrence rationale, but is simply an echo of the arguments denying a retribution rationale, discussed and rejected above. I am not sure that a murderer is somehow less blameworthy if (though he knew his act was wrong) he did not fully appreciate that he could die for it; but if so, we should treat a mentally retarded murderer the way we treat an offender who may be "less likely" to respond to the death penalty because he was abused as a child. We do not hold him immune from capital punishment, but require his background to be considered by the sentencer as a mitigating factor. *Eddings v. Oklahoma,* 455 U.S. 104, 113–117, 102 S.Ct. 869, 71 L.Ed.2d 1 (1982).

The Court throws one last factor into its grab bag of reasons why execution of the retarded is "excessive" in all cases: Mentally retarded offenders "face a special risk of wrongful execution" because they are less able "to make a persuasive showing of mitigation," "to give meaningful assistance to their counsel," and to be effective witnesses. *Ante,* at 2252. "Special risk" is pretty flabby language (even flabbier than "less likely")—and I suppose a similar "special risk" could be said to exist for just plain stupid people, inarticulate people, even ugly people. If this unsupported claim has any substance to it (which I doubt), it might support a due process claim in all criminal prosecutions of the mentally retarded; but it is hard to see how it has anything to do with an *Eighth Amendment* claim that execution of the mentally retarded is cruel and unusual. We have never before held it to be cruel and unusual punishment to impose a sentence in violation of some *other* constitutional imperative.

* * *

Today's opinion adds one more to the long list of substantive and procedural requirements impeding imposition of the death penalty imposed under this Court's assumed power to invent a death-is-different jurisprudence. None of those requirements existed when the Eighth Amendment was adopted, and some of them were not even supported by current moral consensus. They include prohibition of the death penalty for "ordinary" murder, *Godfrey,* 446 U.S., at 433, 100 S.Ct. 1759, for rape of an adult woman, *Coker,* 433 U.S., at 592, 97 S.Ct. 2861, and for felony murder absent a showing that the defendant possessed a sufficiently culpable state of mind, *Enmund,* 458 U.S., at 801, 102 S.Ct. 3368; prohibition of the death penalty for any person under the age of 16 at the time of the crime, *Thompson,* 487 U.S., at 838, 108 S.Ct. 2687 (plurality opinion); prohibition of the death penalty as the mandatory punishment for any crime, *Woodson v. North Carolina,* 428 U.S. 280, 305, 96 S.Ct. 2978, 49 L.Ed.2d 944 (1976) (plurality opinion), *Sumner v. Shuman,* 483 U.S. 66, 77–78, 107 S.Ct. 2716, 97

L.Ed.2d 56 (1987); a requirement that the sentencer not be given unguided discretion, *Furman v. Georgia,* 408 U.S. 238, 92 S.Ct. 2726, 33 L.Ed.2d 346 (1972) *(per curiam),* a requirement that the sentencer be empowered to take into account all mitigating circumstances, *Lockett v. Ohio,* 438 U.S. 586, 604, 98 S.Ct. 2954, 57 L.Ed.2d 973 (1978) (plurality opinion), *Eddings v. Oklahoma, supra,* at 110, 102 S.Ct. 869; and a requirement that the accused receive a judicial evaluation of his claim of insanity before the sentence can be executed, *Ford,* 477 U.S., at 410–411, 106 S.Ct. 2595 (plurality opinion). There is something to be said for popular abolition of the death penalty; there is nothing to be said for its incremental abolition by this Court.

This newest invention promises to be more effective than any of the others in turning the process of capital trial into a game. One need only read the definitions of mental retardation adopted by the American Association on Mental Retardation and the American Psychiatric Association (set forth in the Court's opinion, *ante,* at 2245, n. 3) to realize that the symptoms of this condition can readily be feigned. And whereas the capital defendant who feigns insanity risks commitment to a mental institution until he can be cured (and then tried and executed), *Jones v. United States,* 463 U.S. 354, 370, and n. 20, 103 S.Ct. 3043, 77 L.Ed.2d 694 (1983), the capital defendant who feigns mental retardation risks nothing at all. The mere pendency of the present case has brought us petitions by death row inmates claiming for the first time, after multiple habeas petitions, that they are retarded. See, *e.g., Moore v. Texas,* 535 U.S. 1044, 122 S.Ct. 1814, 152 L.Ed.2d 668 (2002) (Scalia, J., dissenting from grant of applications for stay of execution).

Perhaps these practical difficulties will not be experienced by the minority of capital-punishment States that have very recently changed mental retardation from a mitigating factor (to be accepted or rejected by the sentencer) to an absolute immunity. Time will tell—and the brief time those States have had the new disposition in place (an average of 6.8 years) is surely not enough. But if the practical difficulties do not appear, and if the other States share the Court's perceived moral consensus that *all* mental retardation renders the death penalty inappropriate for *all* crimes, then that majority will presumably follow suit. But there is no justification for this Court's pushing them into the experiment—and turning the experiment into a permanent practice—on constitutional pretext. Nothing has changed the accuracy of Matthew Hale's endorsement of the common law's traditional method for taking account of guilt-reducing factors, written over three centuries ago:

> "[Determination of a person's incapacity] is a matter of great difficulty, partly from the easiness of counterfeiting this disability ... and partly from the variety of the degrees of this infirmity, whereof some are sufficient, and some are insufficient to excuse persons in capital offenses. ...
>
> "Yet the law of England hath afforded the best method of trial, that is possible, of this and all other matters of fact, namely, by a jury of twelve men all concurring in the same judgment, by the testimony of witnesses ..., and by the inspection and direction of the judge." 1 *Pleas of the Crown*, at 32–33.

I respectfully dissent.

A lesson of life rather than law
Grutter v. Bollinger,
539 U.S. 306 (2003)

Justice Scalia, with whom Justice Thomas joins, concurring in part and dissenting in part.

I join the opinion of the Chief Justice. As he demonstrates, the University of Michigan Law School's mystical "critical mass" justification for its discrimination by race challenges even the most gullible mind. The admissions statistics show it to be a sham to cover a scheme of racially proportionate admissions.

I also join Parts I through VII of Justice Thomas's opinion. I find particularly unanswerable his central point: that the allegedly "compelling state interest" at issue here is not the incremental "educational benefit" that emanates from the fabled "critical mass" of minority students, but rather Michigan's interest in maintaining a "prestige" law school whose normal admissions standards disproportionately exclude blacks and other minorities. If that is a compelling state interest, everything is.

I add the following: The "educational benefit" that the University of Michigan seeks to achieve by racial discrimination consists, according to the Court, of " 'cross-racial understanding,'" *ante,* at 2339, and " 'better prepar[ation of] students for an increasingly diverse workforce and society,'" *ante,* at 2340, all of which is necessary not only for work, but also for good "citizenship," *ibid.* This is not, of course, an "educational benefit" on which students will be graded on their law school transcript (Works and Plays Well with Others: B+) or tested by the bar examiners (Q: Describe in 500 words or less your cross-racial understanding). For it is a lesson of life rather than law—essentially the same lesson taught to (or rather learned by, for it cannot be "taught" in the usual sense) people three feet shorter and 20 years younger than the full-grown adults at the University of Michigan Law School, in institutions ranging from Boy Scout troops to public-school kindergartens. If properly considered an "educational benefit" at all, it is surely not one that is either uniquely relevant to law school or uniquely "teachable" in a formal educational setting. *And therefore:* If it is appropriate for the University of Michigan Law School to use racial discrimination for the purpose of putting together a "critical mass" that will convey generic lessons in socialization and good citizenship, surely it is no less appropriate—indeed, *particularly* appropriate—for the civil service system of the State of Michigan to do so. There, also, those exposed to "critical masses" of certain races will presumably become better Americans, better Michiganders, better civil servants. And surely private employers cannot be criticized—indeed, should be praised—if they also "teach" good citizenship to their adult employees through a patriotic, all-American system of racial discrimination in hiring. The non-minority individuals who are deprived of a legal education, a civil service job, or any job at all by reason of their skin color will surely understand.

Unlike a clear constitutional holding that racial preferences in state educational institutions are impermissible, or even a clear anticonstitutional holding that racial preferences in state educational institutions are OK, today's *Grutter-Gratz* split double header seems perversely designed to prolong the controversy and the litigation. Some future lawsuits will presumably focus on whether the discriminatory scheme in question contains enough evaluation of the applicant "as an individual," *ante,* at 2343, and sufficiently avoids "separate admissions tracks," *ante,* at 2342, to fall under *Grutter* rather than *Gratz.* Some will focus on whether a university has gone beyond the bounds of a "'good faith effort'" and has so zealously pursued its "critical mass" as to make it an unconstitutional *de facto* quota system, rather than merely "'a permissible goal.'" *Ante,* at 2342 (quoting *Sheet Metal Workers' v. EEOC,* 478 U.S. 421, 495, 106 S.Ct. 3019, 92 L.Ed.2d 344 (1986) (O'Connor, J., concurring in part and dissenting in part)). Other lawsuits may focus on whether, in the particular setting at issue, any educational benefits flow from racial diversity. (That issue was not contested in *Grutter;* and while the opinion accords "a degree of deference to a university's academic decisions," *ante,* at 2339, "deference does not imply abandonment or abdication of judicial review," *Miller-El v. Cockrell,* 537 U.S. 322, 340, 123 S.Ct. 1029, 154 L.Ed.2d 931 (2003).) Still other suits may challenge the bona fides of the institution's expressed commitment to the educational benefits of diversity that immunize the discriminatory scheme in *Grutter.* (Tempting targets, one would suppose, will be those universities that talk the talk of multiculturalism and racial diversity in the courts but walk the walk of tribalism and racial segregation on their campuses—through minority-only student organizations, separate minority housing opportunities, separate minority student centers, even separate minority-only graduation ceremonies.) And still other suits may claim that the institution's racial preferences have gone below or above the mystical *Grutter*-approved "critical mass." Finally, litigation can be expected on behalf of minority groups intentionally short changed in the institution's composition of its generic minority "critical mass." I do not look forward to any of these cases. The Constitution proscribes government discrimination on the basis of race, and state-provided education is no exception.

An exalted court
U.S. v. Windsor,
133 S.Ct. 2675 (2013)

Justice Scalia, with whom Justice Thomas joins, and with whom the Chief Justice joins as to Part I, dissenting.

This case is about power in several respects. It is about the power of our people to govern themselves, and the power of this Court to pronounce the law. Today's opinion aggrandizes the latter, with the predictable consequence of diminishing the former. We have no power to decide this case. And even if we did, we have no power under the Constitution to invalidate this democratically adopted legislation. The Court's errors on both points spring forth from the same diseased root: an exalted conception of the role of this institution in America.

I

A

The Court is eager—*hungry*—to tell everyone its view of the legal question at the heart of this case. Standing in the way is an obstacle, a technicality of little interest to anyone but the people of We the People, who created it as a barrier against judges' intrusion into their lives. They gave judges, in Article III, only the "judicial Power," a power to decide not abstract questions but real, concrete "Cases" and "Controversies." Yet the plaintiff and the Government agree entirely on what should happen in this lawsuit. They agree that the court below got it right; and they agreed in the court below that the court below that one got it right as well. What, then, are we *doing* here?

The answer lies at the heart of the jurisdictional portion of today's opinion, where a single sentence lays bare the majority's vision of our role. The Court says that we have the power to decide this case because if we did not, then our "primary role in determining the constitutionality of a law" (at least one that "has inflicted real injury on a plaintiff") would "become only secondary to the President's." *Ante,* at 2688. But wait, the reader wonders—Windsor won below, and so *cured* her injury, and the President was glad to see it. True, says the majority, but judicial review must march on regardless, lest we "undermine the clear dictate of the separation-of-powers principle that when an Act of Congress is alleged to conflict with the Constitution, it is emphatically the province and duty of the judicial department to say what the law is." *Ibid.* (internal quotation marks and brackets omitted).

That is jaw-dropping. It is an assertion of judicial supremacy over the people's Representatives in Congress and the Executive. It envisions a Supreme Court standing (or rather enthroned) at the apex of government, empowered to decide all constitutional questions, always and everywhere "primary" in its role.

This image of the Court would have been unrecognizable to those who wrote and ratified our national charter. They knew well the dangers of "primary" power, and so created branches of government that would be "perfectly coordinate by the terms of their common commission," none of which branches could "pretend to an exclusive or superior right of settling the boundaries between their respective powers." *The Federalist,* No. 49, p. 314 (C. Rossiter ed. 1961) (J. Madison). The people did this to protect themselves. They did it to guard their right to self-rule against the black-robed supremacy that today's majority finds so attractive. So it was that Madison could confidently state, with no fear of contradiction, that there was nothing of "greater intrinsic value" or "stamped with the authority of more enlightened patrons of liberty" than a government of separate and coordinate powers. *Id.*, No. 47, at 301.

For this reason we are quite forbidden to say what the law is whenever (as today's opinion asserts) "'an Act of Congress is alleged to conflict with the Constitution.'" *Ante,* at 2688. We can do so only when that allegation will determine the outcome of a lawsuit, and is contradicted by the other party. The "judicial Power" is not, as the majority believes, the power "to say what the law is,'" *ibid.*, giving the Supreme Court the "primary role in determining the constitutionality of laws." The majority must have in mind one of the foreign constitutions that pronounces such primacy for its constitutional court and allows that primacy to be exercised in contexts other than a lawsuit. See, *e.g.*, *Basic Law for the Federal Republic of Germany*, Art. 93. The judicial power as Americans have understood it (and their English ancestors before them) is the power to adjudicate, with conclusive effect, disputed government claims (civil or criminal) against private persons, and disputed claims by private persons against the government or other private persons. Sometimes (though not always) the parties before the court disagree not with regard to the facts of their case (or not *only* with regard to the facts) but with regard to the applicable law—in which event (and *only* in which event) it becomes the "'province and duty of the judicial department to say what the law is.'" *Ante,* at 2688.

In other words, declaring the compatibility of state or federal laws with the Constitution is not only not the "primary role" of this Court, it is not a separate, free-standing role *at all.* We perform that role incidentally—by accident, as it were—when that is necessary to resolve the dispute before us. Then, and only then, does it become "'the province and duty of the judicial department to say what the law is.'" That is why, in

1793, we politely declined the Washington Administration's request to "say what the law is" on a particular treaty matter that was not the subject of a concrete legal controversy. 3 *Correspondence and Public Papers of John Jay* 486–489 (H. Johnston ed. 1893). And that is why, as our opinions have said, some questions of law will *never* be presented to this Court, because there will never be anyone with standing to bring a lawsuit. See *Schlesinger v. Reservists Comm. to Stop the War,* 418 U.S. 208, 227, 94 S.Ct. 2925, 41 L.Ed.2d 706 (1974); *United States v. Richardson,* 418 U.S. 166, 179, 94 S.Ct. 2940, 41 L.Ed.2d 678 (1974). As Justice Brandeis put it, we cannot "pass upon the constitutionality of legislation in a friendly, non-adversary, proceeding"; absent a "'real, earnest and vital controversy between individuals,'" we have neither any work to do nor any power to do it. *Ashwander v. TVA,* 297 U.S. 288, 346, 56 S.Ct. 466, 80 L.Ed. 688 (1936) (concurring opinion) (quoting *Chicago & Grand Trunk R. Co. v. Wellman,* 143 U.S. 339, 345, 12 S.Ct. 400, 36 L.Ed. 176 (1892)). Our authority begins and ends with the need to adjudge the rights of an injured party who stands before us seeking redress. *Lujan v. Defenders of Wildlife,* 504 U.S. 555, 560, 112 S.Ct. 2130, 119 L.Ed.2d 351 (1992).

That is completely absent here. Windsor's injury was cured by the judgment in her favor. And while, in ordinary circumstances, the United States is injured by a directive to pay a tax refund, this suit is far from ordinary. Whatever injury the United States has suffered will surely not be redressed by the action that it, as a litigant, asks us to take. The final sentence of the Solicitor General's brief on the merits reads: "For the foregoing reasons, the judgment of the court of appeals *should be affirmed.*" Brief for United States (merits) 54 (emphasis added). That will not cure the Government's injury, but carve it into stone. One could spend many fruitless afternoons ransacking our library for any other petitioner's brief seeking an affirmance of the judgment against it. What the petitioner United States asks us to do in the case before us is exactly what the respondent Windsor asks us to do: not to provide relief from the judgment below but to say that that judgment was correct. And the same was true in the Court of Appeals: Neither party sought to undo the judgment for Windsor, and so that court should have dismissed the appeal (just as we should dismiss) for lack of jurisdiction. Since both parties agreed with the judgment of the District Court for the Southern District of New York, the suit should have ended there. The further proceedings have been a contrivance, having no object in mind except to elevate a District Court judgment that has no precedential effect in other courts, to one that has precedential effect throughout the Second Circuit, and then (in this Court) precedential effect throughout the United States.

We have never before agreed to speak—to "say what the law is"—where there is no controversy before us. In the more than two centuries that this Court has existed as an institution, we have never suggested that we have the power to decide a question when every party agrees with both its nominal opponent *and the court below* on that question's answer. The United States reluctantly conceded that at oral argument. See Tr. of Oral Arg. 19–20.

The closest we have ever come to what the Court blesses today was our opinion in *INS v. Chadha,* 462 U.S. 919, 103 S.Ct. 2764, 77 L.Ed.2d 317 (1983). But in that case, two parties to the litigation disagreed with the position of the United States and with the court below: the House and Senate, which had intervened in the case. Because *Chadha* concerned the validity of a mode of congressional action—the one-house legislative veto—the House and Senate were threatened with destruction of what they claimed to be one of their institutional powers. The Executive choosing not to defend that power, we permitted the House and Senate to intervene. Nothing like that is present here.

To be sure, the Court in *Chadha* said that statutory aggrieved-party status was "not altered by the fact that the Executive may agree with the holding that the statute in question is unconstitutional." *Id.*, at 930–931, 103 S.Ct. 2764. But in a footnote to that statement, the Court acknowledged Article III's separate requirement of a "justiciable case or controversy," and stated that *this* requirement was satisfied "because of the presence of the two Houses of Congress as adverse parties." *Id.*, at 931, n. 6, 103 S.Ct. 2764. Later in its opinion, the *Chadha* Court remarked that the United States' announced intention to enforce the statute also sufficed to permit judicial review, even absent congressional participation. *Id.*, at 939, 103 S.Ct. 2764. That remark is true, as a description of the judicial review conducted in the Court of Appeals, where the Houses of Congress had not intervened. (The case originated in the Court of Appeals, since it sought review of agency action under 8 U.S.C. § 1105a(a) (1976 ed.).) There, absent a judgment setting aside the INS order, Chadha faced deportation. This passage of our opinion seems to be addressing that initial standing in the Court of Appeals, as indicated by its quotation from the lower court's opinion, 462 U.S., at 939–940, 103 S.Ct. 2764. But if it was addressing standing to pursue the appeal, the remark was both the purest dictum (as congressional intervention at that point made the required adverseness "beyond doubt," *id.*, at 939, 103 S.Ct. 2764), and quite incorrect. When a private party has a judicial decree safely in hand to prevent his injury, additional judicial action requires that a party injured by the decree *seek to undo it.* In *Chadha,* the intervening House and Senate fulfilled that requirement. Here no one does.

The majority's discussion of the requirements of Article III bears no resemblance to our jurisprudence. It accuses the *ami-*

cus (appointed to argue against our jurisdiction) of "elid[ing] the distinction between ... the jurisdictional requirements of Article III and the prudential limits on its exercise." *Ante,* at 2685. It then proceeds to call the requirement of adverseness a "prudential" aspect of standing. *Of standing.* That is incomprehensible. A plaintiff (or appellant) can have all the standing in the world—satisfying all three standing requirements of *Lujan* that the majority so carefully quotes, *ante,* at 2686—and yet no Article III controversy may be before the court. Article III requires not just a plaintiff (or appellant) who has standing to complain but *an opposing party* who denies the validity of the complaint. It is not the *amicus* that has done the eliding of distinctions, but the majority, calling the quite separate Article III requirement of adverseness between the parties an element (which it then pronounces a "prudential" element) of standing. The question here is not whether, as the majority puts it, "the United States retains a stake sufficient to support Article III jurisdiction," *ibid.* the question is whether there is any controversy (which requires *contradiction*) between the United States and Ms. Windsor. There is not.

I find it wryly amusing that the majority seeks to dismiss the requirement of party-adverseness as nothing more than a "prudential" aspect of the sole Article III requirement of standing. (Relegating a jurisdictional requirement to "prudential" status is a wondrous device, enabling courts to ignore the requirement whenever they believe it "prudent"—which is to say, a good idea.) Half a century ago, a Court similarly bent upon announcing its view regarding the constitutionality of a federal statute achieved that goal by effecting a remarkably similar *but completely opposite* distortion of the principles limiting our jurisdiction. The Court's notorious opinion in *Flast v. Cohen,* 392 U.S. 83, 98–101, 88 S.Ct. 1942, 20 L.Ed.2d 947 (1968), held that *standing* was merely an element (which it pronounced to be a "prudential" element) of the sole Article III requirement of *adverseness*. We have been living with the chaos created by that power-grabbing decision ever since, see *Hein v. Freedom From Religion Foundation, Inc.*, 551 U.S. 587, 127 S.Ct. 2553, 168 L.Ed.2d 424 (2007), as we will have to live with the chaos created by this one.

The authorities the majority cites fall miles short of supporting the counterintuitive notion that an Article III "controversy" can exist without disagreement between the parties. In *Deposit Guaranty Nat. Bank v. Roper*, 445 U.S. 326, 100 S.Ct. 1166, 63 L.Ed.2d 427 (1980), the District Court had entered judgment in the individual plaintiff's favor based on the defendant bank's offer to pay the full amount claimed. The plaintiff, however, sought to appeal the District Court's denial of class certification under Federal Rule of Civil Procedure 23. There was a continuing dispute between the parties concerning the issue raised on appeal. The same is true of the other case cited by the majority, *Camreta v. Greene*, 563 U.S. ----, 131 S.Ct. 2020, 179 L.Ed.2d 1118 (2011). There the District Court found that the defendant state officers had violated the Fourth Amendment, but rendered judgment in their favor because they were entitled to official immunity, application of the Fourth Amendment to their conduct not having been clear at the time of violation. The officers sought to appeal the holding of Fourth Amendment violation, which would circumscribe their future conduct; the plaintiff continued to insist that a Fourth Amendment violation had occurred. The "prudential" discretion to which both those cases refer was the discretion to *deny* an appeal even when a live controversy exists—not the discretion to *grant* one when it does not. The majority can cite no case in which this Court entertained an appeal in which both parties urged us to affirm the judgment below. And that is because the existence of a controversy is not a "prudential" requirement that we have invented, but an essential element of an Article III case or controversy. The majority's notion that a case between friendly parties can be entertained so long as "adversarial presentation of the issues is assured by the participation of *amici curiae* prepared to defend with vigor" the other side of the issue, *ante,* at 2687, effects a breathtaking revolution in our Article III jurisprudence.

It may be argued that if what we say is true some Presidential determinations that statutes are unconstitutional will not be subject to our review. That is as it should be, when both the President and the plaintiff agree that the statute is unconstitutional. Where the Executive is enforcing an unconstitutional law, suit will of course lie; but if, in that suit, the Executive admits the unconstitutionality of the law, the litigation should end in an order or a consent decree enjoining enforcement. This suit saw the light of day only because the President enforced the Act (and thus gave Windsor standing to sue) even though he believed it unconstitutional. He could have equally chosen (more appropriately, some would say) neither to enforce nor to defend the statute he believed to be unconstitutional, see Presidential Authority to Decline to Execute Unconstitutional Statutes, 18 Op. Off. Legal Counsel 199 (Nov. 2, 1994)—in which event Windsor would not have been injured, the District Court could not have refereed this friendly scrimmage, and the Executive's determination of unconstitutionality would have escaped this Court's desire to blurt out its view of the law. The matter would have been left, as so many matters ought to be left, to a tug of war between the President and the Congress, which has innumerable means (up to and including impeachment) of compelling the President to enforce the laws it has written. Or the President could have evaded presentation of the constitutional issue to this Court simply by declining to appeal the District Court and Court of

Appeals dispositions he agreed with. Be sure of this much: If a President wants to insulate his judgment of unconstitutionality from our review, he can. What the views urged in this dissent produce is not insulation from judicial review but insulation from Executive contrivance.

The majority brandishes the famous sentence from *Marbury v. Madison,* 1 Cranch 137, 177, 2 L.Ed. 60 (1803) that "[i]t is emphatically the province and duty of the judicial department to say what the law is." *Ante,* at 2688 (internal quotation marks omitted). But that sentence neither says nor implies that it is *always* the province and duty of the Court to say what the law is—much less that its responsibility in that regard is a "primary" one. The very next sentence of Chief Justice Marshall's opinion makes the crucial qualification that today's majority ignores: "*Those who apply the rule to particular cases,* must of necessity expound and interpret that rule." 1 Cranch, at 177 (emphasis added). Only when a "particular case" is before us—that is, a controversy that it is our business to resolve under Article III—do we have the province and duty to pronounce the law. For the views of our early Court more precisely addressing the question before us here, the majority ought instead to have consulted the opinion of Chief Justice Taney in *Lord v. Veazie,* 8 How. 251, 12 L.Ed. 1067 (1850):

> "The objection in the case before us is ... that the plaintiff and defendant have the same interest, and that interest adverse and in conflict with the interest of third persons, whose rights would be seriously affected if the question of law was decided in the manner that both of the parties to this suit desire it to be.
>
> "A judgment entered under such circumstances, and for such purposes, is a mere form. The whole proceeding was in contempt of the court, and highly reprehensible.... A judgment in form, thus procured, in the eye of the law is no

judgment of the court. It is a nullity, and no writ of error will lie upon it. This writ is, therefore, dismissed." *Id.*, at 255–256.

There is, in the words of *Marbury*, no "necessity [to] expound and interpret" the law in this case; just a desire to place this Court at the center of the Nation's life. 1 Cranch, at 177, 2 L.Ed. 60.

B

A few words in response to the theory of jurisdiction set forth in Justice Alito's dissent: Though less far reaching in its consequences than the majority's conversion of constitutionally required adverseness into a discretionary element of standing, the theory of that dissent similarly elevates the Court to the "primary" determiner of constitutional questions involving the separation of powers, and, to boot, increases the power of the most dangerous branch: the "legislative department," which by its nature "draw [s] all power into its impetuous vortex." *The Federalist*, No. 48, at 309 (J. Madison). Heretofore in our national history, the President's failure to "take Care that the Laws be faithfully executed," U.S. Const., Art. II, § 3, could only be brought before a judicial tribunal by someone whose concrete interests were harmed by that alleged failure. Justice Alito would create a system in which Congress can hale the Executive before the courts not only to vindicate its own institutional powers to act, but to correct a perceived inadequacy in the execution of its laws. This would lay to rest Tocqueville's praise of our judicial system as one which "intimately bind[s] the case made for the law with the case made for one man," one in which legislation is "no longer exposed to the daily aggression of the parties," and in which "[t]he political question that [the judge] must resolve is linked to the interest" of private litigants. A. de Tocqueville, *Democracy in America* 97 (H. Mansfield & D. Winthrop eds. 2000). That would be replaced by a system in which Congress and the Executive can pop immediately into court, in their institutional capacity, whenever the President refuses to implement a statute he believes to be unconstitutional, and whenever he implements a law in a manner that is not to Congress's liking.

Justice Alito's notion of standing will likewise enormously shrink the area to which "judicial censure, exercised by the courts on legislation, cannot extend," *ibid.* For example, a bare majority of both Houses could bring into court the assertion that the Executive's implementation of welfare programs is too generous—a failure that no other litigant would have standing to complain about. Moreover, as we indicated in *Raines v. Byrd,* 521 U.S. 811, 828, 117 S.Ct. 2312, 138 L.Ed.2d 849 (1997), if Congress can sue the Executive for the erroneous application of the law that "injures" its power to legislate, surely the Executive can sue Congress for its erroneous adoption of an unconstitutional law that "injures" the Executive's power to administer—or perhaps for its protracted failure to act on one of his nominations. The opportunities for dragging the courts into disputes hitherto left for political resolution are endless.

Justice Alito's dissent is correct that *Raines* did not formally decide this issue, but its reasoning does. The opinion spends three pages discussing famous, decades-long disputes between the President and Congress—regarding congressional power to forbid the Presidential removal of executive officers, regarding the legislative veto, regarding congressional appointment of executive officers, and regarding the pocket veto—that would surely have been promptly resolved by a Congress-vs.-the-President lawsuit if the impairment of a branch's powers alone conferred standing to commence litigation. But it does not, and never has; the "enormous power that the judiciary would acquire" from the ability to adjudicate such suits "would have made a mockery of [Hamilton's] quotation of Montesquieu to the effect that 'of the three powers above mentioned ... the JUDICIARY is next to nothing.'" *Barnes v. Kline,* 759 F.2d 21, 58 (C.A.D.C.1985) (Bork, J., dissenting) (quoting *The Federalist* No. 78 (A. Hamilton)).

To be sure, if Congress cannot invoke our authority in the way that Justice Alito proposes, then its only recourse is to confront the President directly. Unimaginable evil this is not. Our system is *designed* for confrontation. That is what "[a]mbition ... counteract[ing] ambition," *The Federalist,* No. 51, at 322 (J. Madison), is all about. If majorities in both Houses of Congress care enough about the matter, they have available innumerable ways to compel executive action without a lawsuit—from refusing to confirm Presidential appointees to the elimination of funding. (Nothing says "enforce the Act" quite like "... or you will have money for little else.") But the condition is crucial; Congress must care enough to act against the President itself, not merely enough to instruct its lawyers to ask *us* to do so. Placing the Constitution's entirely anticipated political arm wrestling into permanent judicial receivership does not do the system a favor. And by the way, if the President loses the lawsuit but does not faithfully implement the Court's decree, just as he did not faithfully implement Congress's statute, what then? Only Congress can bring him to heel by ... what do you think? Yes: a direct confrontation with the President.

II

For the reasons above, I think that this Court has, and the Court of Appeals had, no power to decide this suit. We should vacate the decision below and remand to the Court of Appeals for the Second Circuit, with instructions to dismiss the appeal. Given that the majority has volunteered its view of the merits, however, I proceed to discuss that as well.

A

There are many remarkable things about the majority's merits holding. The first is how rootless and shifting its justifications are. For example, the opinion starts with seven full pages about the traditional power of States to define domestic relations—initially fooling many readers, I am sure, into thinking that this is a federalism opinion. But we are eventually told that "it is unnecessary to decide whether this federal intrusion on state power is a violation of the Constitution," and that "[t]he State's power in defining the marital relation is of central relevance in this case quite apart from principles of federalism" because "the State's decision to give this class of persons the right to marry conferred upon them a dignity and status of immense import." *Ante,* at 2681. But no one questions the power of the States to define marriage (with the concomitant conferral of dignity and status), so what is the point of devoting seven pages to describing how long and well established that power is? Even after the opinion has formally disclaimed reliance upon principles of federalism, mentions of "the usual tradition of recognizing and accepting state definitions of marriage" continue. See, *e.g., ante,* at 2681. What to make of this? The opinion never explains. My guess is that the majority, while reluctant to suggest that defining the meaning of "marriage" in federal statutes is unsupported by any of the Federal Government's enumerated powers, nonetheless needs some rhetorical basis to support its pretense that today's prohibition of laws excluding same-sex marriage is confined to the Federal Government (leaving the second, state-law shoe to be dropped later, maybe next Term). But I am only guessing.

Equally perplexing are the opinion's references to "the Constitution's guarantee of equality." *Ibid.* Near the end of the opinion, we are told that although the "equal protection guarantee of the Fourteenth Amendment makes [the] Fifth Amendment [due process] right all the more specific and all the better understood and preserved"—what can *that* mean?—"the Fifth Amendment itself withdraws from Government the power to degrade or demean in the way this law does." *Ante,* at 2695. The only possible interpretation of this statement is that the Equal Protection Clause, even the Equal Protection Clause as incorporated in the Due Process Clause, is not the basis for today's holding. But the portion of the majority opinion that explains why DOMA is unconstitutional (Part IV) begins by citing *Bolling v. Sharpe,* 347 U.S. 497, 74 S.Ct. 693, 98 L.Ed. 884 (1954), *Department of Agriculture v. Moreno,* 413 U.S. 528, 93 S.Ct. 2821, 37 L.Ed.2d 782 (1973), and *Romer v. Evans,* 517 U.S. 620, 116 S.Ct. 1620, 134 L.Ed.2d 855 (1996)—*all* of which are equal-protection cases. And those three cases are the *only* authorities that the Court cites in Part IV about the Constitution's meaning, except for its citation of *Lawrence v. Texas,* 539 U.S. 558, 123 S.Ct. 2472, 156 L.Ed.2d 508 (2003) (not an equal-protection case) to support its passing assertion that the Constitution protects the "moral and sexual choices" of same-sex couples, *ante,* at 2694.

Moreover, if this is meant to be an equal-protection opinion, it is a confusing one. The opinion does not resolve and indeed does not even mention what had been the central question in this litigation: whether, under the Equal Protection Clause, laws restricting marriage to a man and a woman are reviewed for more than mere rationality. That is the issue that divided the parties and the court below, compare Brief for Respondent Bipartisan Legal Advisory Group of U.S. House of Representatives (merits) 24–28 (no), with Brief for Respondent

Windsor (merits) 17–31 and Brief for United States (merits) 18–36 (yes); and compare 699 F.3d 169, 180–185 (C.A.2 2012) (yes), with *id.*, at 208–211 (Straub, J., dissenting in part and concurring in part) (no). In accord with my previously expressed skepticism about the Court's "tiers of scrutiny" approach, I would review this classification only for its rationality. See *United States v. Virginia*, 518 U.S. 515, 567–570, 116 S.Ct. 2264, 135 L.Ed.2d 735 (1996) (Scalia, J., dissenting). As nearly as I can tell, the Court agrees with that; its opinion does not apply strict scrutiny, and its central propositions are taken from rational-basis cases like *Moreno*. But the Court certainly does not *apply* anything that resembles that deferential framework. See *Heller v. Doe*, 509 U.S. 312, 320, 113 S.Ct. 2637, 125 L.Ed.2d 257 (1993) (a classification "'must be upheld ... if there is any reasonably conceivable state of facts'" that could justify it).

The majority opinion need not get into the strict-vs.-rational-basis scrutiny question, and need not justify its holding under either, because it says that DOMA is unconstitutional as "a deprivation of the liberty of the person protected by the Fifth Amendment of the Constitution," *ante*, at 2695; that it violates "basic due process" principles, *ante*, at 2693; and that it inflicts an "injury and indignity" of a kind that denies "an essential part of the liberty protected by the Fifth Amendment," *ante*, at 2692. The majority never utters the dread words "substantive due process," perhaps sensing the disrepute into which that doctrine has fallen, but that is what those statements mean. Yet the opinion does not argue that same-sex marriage is "deeply rooted in this Nation's history and tradition," *Washington v. Glucksberg*, 521 U.S. 702, 720–721, 117 S.Ct. 2258, 138 L.Ed.2d 772 (1997), a claim that would of course be quite absurd. So would the further suggestion (also necessary, under our substantive-due-process precedents) that a world in which DOMA exists is one bereft of "'ordered liberty.'" *Id.*, at 721, 117 S.Ct. 2258 (quoting *Palko v. Connecticut*, 302 U.S. 319, 325, 58 S.Ct. 149, 82 L.Ed. 288 (1937)).

Some might conclude that this loaf could have used a while longer in the oven. But that would be wrong; it is already overcooked. The most expert care in preparation cannot redeem a bad recipe. The sum of all the Court's nonspecific hand-waving is that this law is invalid (maybe on equal-protection grounds, maybe on substantive-due-process grounds, and perhaps with some amorphous federalism component playing a role) because it is motivated by a "'bare ... desire to harm'" couples in same-sex marriages. *Ante*, at 2693. It is this proposition with which I will therefore engage.

B

As I have observed before, the Constitution does not forbid the government to enforce traditional moral and sexual norms. See *Lawrence v. Texas*, 539 U.S. 558, 599, 123 S.Ct. 2472, 156 L.Ed.2d 508 (2003) (Scalia, J., dissenting). I will not swell the U.S. Reports with restatements of that point. It is enough to say that the Constitution neither requires nor forbids our society to approve of same-sex marriage, much as it neither requires nor forbids us to approve of no-fault divorce, polygamy, or the consumption of alcohol.

However, even setting aside traditional moral disapproval of same-sex marriage (or indeed same-sex sex), there are many perfectly valid—indeed, downright boring—justifying rationales for this legislation. Their existence ought to be the end of this case. For they give the lie to the Court's conclusion that only those with hateful hearts could have voted "aye" on this Act. And more importantly, they serve to make the contents of the legislators' hearts quite irrelevant: "It is a familiar principle of constitutional law that this Court will not strike down an otherwise constitutional statute on the basis of an alleged illicit legislative motive." *United States v. O'Brien,* 391 U.S. 367, 383, 88 S.Ct. 1673, 20 L.Ed.2d 672 (1968). Or at least it *was* a familiar principle. By holding to the contrary, the majority has declared open season on any law that (in the opinion of the law's opponents and any panel of like-minded federal judges) can be characterized as mean-spirited.

The majority concludes that the only motive for this Act was the "bare ... desire to harm a politically unpopular group." *Ante,* at 2693. Bear in mind that the object of this condemnation is not the legislature of some once-Confederate Southern state (familiar objects of the Court's scorn, see, *e.g., Edwards v. Aguillard,* 482 U.S. 578, 107 S.Ct. 2573, 96 L.Ed.2d 510 (1987)), but our respected coordinate branches, the Congress and Presidency of the United States. Laying such a charge against them should require the most extraordinary evidence, and I would have thought that every attempt would be made to indulge a more anodyne explanation for the statute. The majority does the opposite—affirmatively concealing from the reader the arguments that exist in justification. It makes only a passing mention of the "arguments put forward" by the Act's defenders, and does not even trouble to paraphrase or describe them. See *ante,* at 2693. I imagine that this is because it is harder to maintain the illusion of the Act's supporters as unhinged members of a wild-eyed lynch mob when one first describes their views as *they* see them.

To choose just one of these defenders' arguments, DOMA avoids difficult choice-of-law issues that will now arise absent a uniform federal definition of marriage. See, *e.g.,* Baude, "Beyond DOMA: Choice of State Law in Federal Statutes," 64 *Stan. L.Rev.* 1371 (2012). Imagine a pair of women who marry in Albany and then move to Alabama, which does not "recognize as valid any marriage of parties of the same sex." Ala.Code § 30-1-19(e) (2011). When the couple files their next federal tax return, may it be a joint one? Which State's law controls, for federal-law purposes: their State of celebration (which recognizes the marriage) or their State of domicile (which does not)? (Does the answer depend on whether they were just visiting in Albany?) Are these questions to be answered as a matter of federal common law, or perhaps by borrowing a State's choice-of-law rules? If so, *which* State's? And what about States where the status of an out-of-state same-sex marriage is an unsettled question under local law? See *Godfrey v. Spano,* 13 N.Y.3d 358, 892 N.Y.S.2d 272, 920 N.E.2d 328 (2009). DOMA avoided all of this uncertainty by specifying which marriages would be recognized for federal purposes. That is a classic purpose for a definitional provision.

Further, DOMA preserves the intended effects of prior legislation against then-unforeseen changes in circumstance. When Congress provided (for example) that a special estate-tax exemption would exist for spouses, this exemption reached only *opposite-sex* spouses—those being the only sort that were recognized in *any* State at the time of DOMA's passage. When it became clear that changes in state law might one day alter that balance, DOMA's definitional section was enacted to ensure that state-level experimentation did not automatically alter the basic operation of federal law, unless and until Congress made the further judgment to do so on its own. That is not animus—just stabilizing prudence. Congress has hardly demonstrated itself unwilling to make such further, revising judgments upon due deliberation. See, *e.g.*, Don't Ask, Don't Tell Repeal Act of 2010, 124 Stat. 3515.

The Court mentions none of this. Instead, it accuses the Congress that enacted this law and the President who signed it of something much worse than, for example, having acted in excess of enumerated federal powers—or even having drawn distinctions that prove to be irrational. Those legal errors may be made in good faith, errors though they are. But the majority says that the supporters of this Act acted with *malice*—with *the "purpose"* (*ante,* at 2695) "to disparage and to injure" same-sex couples. It says that the motivation for DOMA was to "demean," *ibid.*; to "impose inequality," *ante,* at 2694; to "impose ... a stigma," *ante,* at 2692; to deny people "equal dignity," *ibid.*; to brand gay people as "unworthy," *ante,* at 2694; and to "*humiliat*[*e*]" their children, *ibid.* (emphasis added).

I am sure these accusations are quite untrue. To be sure (as the majority points out), the legislation is called the Defense of Marriage Act. But to defend traditional marriage is not to condemn, demean, or humiliate those who would prefer other arrangements, any more than to defend the Constitution of the United States is to condemn, demean, or humiliate other constitutions. To hurl such accusations so casually demeans *this institution.* In the majority's judgment, any resistance to its holding is beyond the pale of reasoned disagreement. To question its high-handed invalidation of a presumptively valid statute is to act (the majority is sure) with *the purpose* to "disparage," "injure," "degrade," "demean," and "humiliate" our fellow human beings, our fellow citizens, who are homosexual. All that, simply for supporting an Act that did no more than codify an aspect of marriage that had been unquestioned in our society for most of its existence—indeed, had been unquestioned in virtually all societies for virtually all of human history. It is one thing for a society to elect change; it is another for a court of law to impose change by adjudging those who oppose it *hostes humani generis,* enemies of the human race.

* * *

The penultimate sentence of the majority's opinion is a naked declaration that "[t]his opinion and its holding are confined" to those couples "joined in same-sex marriages made lawful by the State." *Ante,* at 2696, 2695. I have heard such "bald, unreasoned disclaimer[s]" before. *Lawrence,* 539 U.S., at 604, 123 S.Ct. 2472. When the Court declared a constitutional right to homosexual sodomy, we were assured that the case had nothing, nothing at all to do with "whether the government must give formal recognition to any relationship that homosexual persons seek to enter." *Id.,* at 578, 123 S.Ct. 2472. Now we are told that DOMA is invalid because it "demeans the couple, whose moral and sexual choices the Constitution protects," *ante,* at 2694—with an accompanying citation of *Lawrence.* It takes real cheek for today's majority to assure us, as it is going out the door, that a constitutional requirement to give formal recognition to same-sex marriage is not at issue here—when what has preceded that assurance is a lecture on how superior the majority's moral judgment in favor of same-sex marriage is to the Congress's hateful moral judgment against it. I promise you this: The only thing that will "confine" the Court's holding is its sense of what it can get away with.

I do not mean to suggest disagreement with the Chief Justice's view, *ante,* pp. 2696–2697 (dissenting opinion), that lower federal courts and state courts can distinguish today's case when the issue before them is state denial of marital status to same-sex couples—or even that this Court could *theoretically* do so. Lord, an opinion with such scatter-shot rationales as this one (federalism noises among them) can be distinguished in many ways. And deserves to be. State and lower federal courts should take the Court at its word and distinguish away.

In my opinion, however, the view that *this* Court will take of state prohibition of same-sex marriage is indicated beyond mistaking by today's opinion. As I have said, the real rationale of today's opinion, whatever disappearing trail of its legalistic argle-bargle one chooses to follow, is that DOMA is motivated by " 'bare ... desire to harm'" couples in same-sex marriages. *Supra,* at 2691. How easy it is, indeed how inevitable, to reach the same conclusion with regard to state laws denying same-sex couples marital status. Consider how easy (inevitable) it is to make the following substitutions in a passage from today's opinion *ante,* at 2694:

> "DOMA's *This state law's* principal effect is to identify a subset of state-sanctioned marriages *constitutionally protected sexual relationships,* see *Lawrence,* and make them unequal. The principal purpose is to impose inequality, not for other reasons like governmental efficiency. Responsibilities, as well as rights, enhance the dignity and integrity of the person. And DOMA *this state law* contrives to deprive some couples married under the laws of their State *enjoying constitutionally protected sexual relationships,* but not other couples, of both rights and responsibilities."

Or try this passage, from *ante,* at 2694:

> "[DOMA] *This state law* tells those couples, and all the world, that their otherwise valid marriages *relationships* are unworthy of federal *state* recognition. This places same-sex couples in an unstable position of being in a second-tier marriage *relationship.* The differentiation demeans the couple, whose moral and sexual choices the Constitution protects, see *Lawrence,*...."

Or this, from *ante,* at 2694—which does not even require alteration, except as to the invented number:

> "And it humiliates tens of thousands of children now being raised by same-sex couples. The law in question makes it even more difficult for the children to understand the integrity and closeness of their own family and its concord with other families in their community and in their daily lives."

Similarly transposable passages—deliberately transposable, I think—abound. In sum, that Court which finds it so horrific that Congress irrationally and hatefully robbed same-sex couples of the "personhood and dignity" which state legislatures conferred upon them, will of a certitude be similarly appalled by state legislatures' irrational and hateful failure to acknowledge that "personhood and dignity" in the first place. *Ante,* at 2696. As far as this Court is concerned, no one should be fooled; it is just a matter of listening and waiting for the other shoe.

By formally declaring anyone opposed to same-sex marriage an enemy of human decency, the majority arms well every challenger to a state law restricting marriage to its traditional definition. Henceforth those challengers will lead with this Court's declaration that there is "no legitimate purpose" served by such a law, and will claim that the traditional definition has "the purpose and effect to disparage and to injure" the "personhood and dignity" of same-sex couples, see *ante,* at 2695, 2696. The majority's limiting assurance will be meaningless in the face of language like that, as the majority well knows. That is why the language is there. The result will be a judicial distortion of our society's debate over marriage—a debate that can seem in need of our clumsy "help" only to a member of this institution.

As to that debate: Few public controversies touch an institution so central to the lives of so many, and few inspire such attendant passion by good people on all sides. Few public controversies will ever demonstrate so vividly the beauty of what our Framers gave us, a gift the Court pawns today to buy its stolen moment in the spotlight: a system of government that permits us to rule *ourselves.* Since DOMA's passage, citizens on all sides of the question have seen victories and they have seen defeats. There have been plebiscites, legislation, persuasion, and loud voices—in other words, democracy. Victories in one place for some, see North Carolina Const., Amdt. 1 (providing that "[m]arriage between one man and one woman is the only domestic legal union that shall be valid or recognized in this State") (approved by a popular vote, 61% to 39% on May 8, 2012), are offset by victories in other places for others, see Maryland Question 6 (establishing "that Maryland's civil marriage laws allow gay and lesbian couples to obtain a civil marriage license") (approved by a popular vote, 52% to 48%, on November 6, 2012). Even in a *single State*, the question has come out differently on different occasions. Compare Maine Question 1 (permitting "the State of Maine to issue marriage licenses to same-sex couples") (approved by a popular vote, 53% to 47%, on November 6, 2012) with Maine Question 1 (rejecting "the new law that lets same-sex couples marry") (approved by a popular vote, 53% to 47%, on November 3, 2009).

In the majority's telling, this story is black-and-white: Hate your neighbor or come along with us. The truth is more complicated. It is hard to admit that one's political opponents are not monsters, especially in a struggle like this one, and the challenge in the end proves more than today's Court can handle. Too bad. A reminder that disagreement over something so fundamental as marriage can still be politically legitimate would have been a fit task for what in earlier times was called the judicial temperament. We might have covered ourselves with honor today, by promising all sides of this debate that it was theirs to settle and that we would respect their resolution. We might have let the People decide.

But that the majority will not do. Some will rejoice in today's decision, and some will despair at it; that is the nature of a controversy that matters so much to so many. But the Court has cheated both sides, robbing the winners of an honest victory, and the losers of the peace that comes from a fair defeat. We owed both of them better. I dissent.

Robbing the people of their most important liberty
Obergefell v. Hodges, 135 S.Ct. 2584 (2015)

Justice Scalia, with whom Justice Thomas joins, dissenting.

I join the Chief Justice's opinion in full. I write separately to call attention to this Court's threat to American democracy.

The substance of today's decree is not of immense personal importance to me. The law can recognize as marriage whatever sexual attachments and living arrangements it wishes, and can accord them favorable civil consequences, from tax treatment to rights of inheritance. Those civil consequences—and the public approval that conferring the name of marriage evidences—can perhaps have adverse social effects, but no more adverse than the effects of many other controversial laws. So it is not of special importance to me what the law says about marriage. It is of overwhelming importance, however, who it is that rules me. Today's decree says that my Ruler, and the Ruler of 320 million Americans coast-to-coast, is a majority of the nine lawyers on the Supreme Court. The opinion in these cases is the furthest extension in fact—and the furthest extension one can even imagine—of the Court's claimed power to create "liberties" that the Constitution and its Amendments neglect to mention. This practice of constitutional revision by an unelected committee of nine, always accompanied (as it is today) by extravagant praise of liberty, robs the People of the most important liberty they asserted in the Declaration of Independence and won in the Revolution of 1776: the freedom to govern themselves.

I

Until the courts put a stop to it, public debate over same-sex marriage displayed American democracy at its best. Individuals on both sides of the issue passionately, but respectfully, attempted to persuade their fellow citizens to accept their views. Americans considered the arguments and put the question to a vote. The electorates of 11 States, either directly or through their representatives, chose to expand the traditional definition of marriage. Many more decided not to. Win or lose, advocates for both sides continued pressing their cases, secure in the knowledge that an electoral loss can be negated by a later electoral win. That is exactly how our system of government is supposed to work.

The Constitution places some constraints on self-rule—constraints adopted *by the People themselves* when they ratified the Constitution and its Amendments. Forbidden are laws "impairing the Obligation of Contracts," denying "Full Faith and Credit" to the "public Acts" of other States, prohibiting the free exercise of religion, abridging the freedom of speech, infringing the right to keep and bear arms, authorizing unreasonable searches and seizures, and so forth. Aside from these limitations, those powers "reserved to the States respectively, or to the people" can be exercised as the States or the People desire. These cases ask us to decide whether the Fourteenth Amendment contains a limitation that requires the States to license and recognize marriages between two people of the same sex. Does it remove *that* issue from the political process?

Of course not. It would be surprising to find a prescription regarding marriage in the Federal Constitution since, as the author of today's opinion reminded us only two years ago (in an opinion joined by the same Justices who join him today):

> "[R]egulation of domestic relations is an area that has long been regarded as a virtually exclusive province of the States."

> "[T]he Federal Government, through our history, has deferred to state-law policy decisions with respect to domestic relations."

But we need not speculate. When the Fourteenth Amendment was ratified in 1868, every State limited marriage to one man and one woman, and no one doubted the constitutionality of doing so. That resolves these cases. When it comes to determining the meaning of a vague constitutional provision—such as "due process of law" or "equal protection of the laws"—it is unquestionable that the People who ratified that provision did not understand it to prohibit a practice that remained both universal and uncontroversial in the years after ratification. We have no basis for striking down a practice that is not expressly prohibited by the Fourteenth Amendment's text, and that bears the endorsement of a long tradition of open, widespread, and unchallenged use dating back to the Amendment's ratification. Since there is no doubt whatever that the People never decided to prohibit the limitation of marriage to opposite-sex couples, the public debate over same-sex marriage must be allowed to continue.

But the Court ends this debate, in an opinion lacking even a thin veneer of law. Buried beneath the mummeries and straining-to-be-memorable passages of the opinion is a candid and startling assertion: No matter *what* it was the People ratified, the Fourteenth Amendment protects those rights that the Judiciary, in its "reasoned judgment," thinks the Fourteenth Amendment ought to protect. That is so because "[t]he generations that wrote and ratified the Bill of Rights and the Fourteenth Amendment did not presume to know the extent of freedom in all of its dimensions...." One would think that sentence would continue: "... and therefore they provided for a means by which the People could amend the Constitution," or perhaps "... and therefore they left the creation of additional liberties, such as the freedom to marry someone of the same sex, to the People, through the never-ending process of legislation." But no. What logically follows, in the majority's judge-empowering estimation, is: "and so they entrusted to future generations a charter protecting the right of all persons to enjoy liberty as we learn its meaning." The "we," needless to say, is the nine of us. "History and tradition guide and discipline [our] inquiry but do not set its outer boundaries." Thus, rather than focusing on *the People's* understanding of "liberty"—at the time of ratification or even today—the majority focuses on four "principles and traditions" that, *in the majority's view,* prohibit States from defining marriage as an institution consisting of one man and one woman.

This is a naked judicial claim to legislative—indeed, *super*-legislative—power; a claim fundamentally at odds with our system of government. Except as limited by a constitutional prohibition agreed to by the People, the States are free to adopt whatever laws they like, even those that offend the esteemed Justices' "reasoned judgment." A system of government that makes the People subordinate to a committee of nine unelected lawyers does not deserve to be called a democracy.

Judges are selected precisely for their skill as lawyers; whether they reflect the policy views of a particular constituency is not (or should not be) relevant. Not surprisingly then, the Federal Judiciary is hardly a cross-section of America. Take, for example, this Court, which consists of only nine men and women, all of them successful lawyers who studied at Harvard or Yale Law School. Four of the nine are natives of New York City. Eight of them grew up in east- and west-coast States. Only one hails from the vast expanse in-between. Not a single Southwesterner or even, to tell the truth, a genuine Westerner (California does not count). Not a single evangelical Christian (a group that comprises about one quarter of Americans), or even a Protestant of any denomination. The strikingly unrepresentative character of the body voting on today's social upheaval would be irrelevant if they were functioning as *judges*, answering the legal question whether the American people had ever ratified a constitutional provision that was understood to proscribe the traditional definition of marriage. But of course the Justices in today's majority are not voting on that basis; *they say they are not*. And to allow the policy question of same-sex marriage to be considered and resolved by a select, patrician, highly unrepresentative panel of nine is to violate a principle even more fundamental than no taxation without representation: no social transformation without representation.

II

But what really astounds is the hubris reflected in today's judicial Putsch. The five Justices who compose today's majority are entirely comfortable concluding that every State violated the Constitution for all of the 135 years between the Fourteenth Amendment's ratification and Massachusetts' permitting of same-sex marriages in 2003. They have discovered in the Fourteenth Amendment a "fundamental right" overlooked by every person alive at the time of ratification, and almost everyone else in the time since. They see what lesser legal minds—minds like Thomas Cooley, John Marshall Harlan, Oliver Wendell Holmes, Jr., Learned Hand, Louis Brandeis, William Howard Taft, Benjamin Cardozo, Hugo Black, Felix Frankfurter, Robert Jackson, and Henry Friendly—could not. They are certain that the People ratified the Fourteenth Amendment to bestow on them the power to remove questions from the democratic process when that is called for by their "reasoned judgment." These Justices *know* that limiting marriage to one man and one woman is contrary to reason; they *know* that an institution as old as government itself, and accepted by every nation in history until 15 years ago, cannot possibly be supported by anything other than ignorance or bigotry. And they are willing to say that any citizen who does not agree with that, who adheres to what was, until 15 years ago, the unanimous judgment of all generations and all societies, stands against the Constitution.

The opinion is couched in a style that is as pretentious as its content is egotistic. It is one thing for separate concurring or dissenting opinions to contain extravagances, even silly extravagances, of thought and expression; it is something else for the official opinion of the Court to do so. Of course the opinion's showy profundities are often profoundly incoherent. "The nature of marriage is that, through its enduring bond, two persons together can find other freedoms, such as expression, intimacy, and spirituality." (Really? Who ever thought that intimacy and spirituality [whatever that means] were freedoms? And if intimacy is, one would think Freedom of Intimacy is abridged rather than expanded by marriage. Ask the nearest hippie. Expression, sure enough, *is* a freedom, but anyone in a long-lasting marriage will attest that that happy state constricts, rather than expands, what one can prudently say.) Rights, we are told, can "rise ... from a better informed understanding of how constitutional imperatives define a liberty that remains urgent in our own era." (Huh? How can a better informed understanding of how constitutional imperatives [whatever that means] define [whatever that means] an urgent liberty [never mind], give birth to a right?) And we are told that, "[i]n any particular case," either the Equal Protection or Due Process Clause "may be thought to capture the essence of [a] right in a more accurate and comprehensive way," than the other, "even as the two Clauses may converge in the identification and definition of the right." (What say? What possible "essence" does substantive due process "capture" in an "accurate and comprehensive way"? It stands for nothing whatever, except those freedoms and entitlements that this Court *really* likes. And the Equal Protection Clause, as employed today, identifies nothing except a difference in treatment that this Court *really* dislikes. Hardly a distillation of essence. If the opinion is correct that the two clauses "converge in the identification and definition of [a] right," that is only because the majority's likes and dislikes are predictably compatible.) I could go on. The world does not expect logic and precision in poetry or inspirational pop-philosophy; it demands them in the law. The stuff contained in today's opinion has to diminish this Court's reputation for clear thinking and sober analysis.

Hubris is sometimes defined as o'erweening pride; and pride, we know, goeth before a fall. The Judiciary is the "least dangerous" of the federal branches because it has "neither Force nor Will, but merely judgment; and must ultimately depend upon the aid of the executive arm" and the States, "even for the efficacy of its judgments." With each decision of ours that takes from the People a question properly left to them—with each decision that is unabashedly based not on law, but on the "reasoned judgment" of a bare majority of this Court—we move one step closer to being reminded of our impotence.

INDEX TO BOOKS CITED BY SCALIA

INDEX